Advances in Spatial Science

Springer
Berlin
Heidelberg
New York
Barcelona
Budapest
Hong Kong
London
Milan
Paris
Santa Clara
Singapore
Tokyo

Titles in the Series

David F. Batten · Charlie Karlsson (Eds.)

Infrastructure and the Complexity of Economic Development

With 40 Figures
and 63 Tables

Professor Dr. David F. Batten
The Temaplan Group
Applied Systems Analysis
for Industry and Government
P.O. Box 3026
Dendy Brighton VIC. 3186
Australia

Professor Dr. Charlie Karlsson
Jönköping University
Jönköping International Business School
P.O. Box 1026
S-55111 Jönköping
Sweden

Die Deutsche Bibliothek - CIP-Einheitsaufnahme

Infrastructure and the complexity of economic development :
with 63 tables / David F. Batten ; Charlie Karlsson (ed.). -
Berlin ; Heidelberg ; New York ; Barcelona ; Budapest ; Hong
Kong ; London ; Milan ; Paris ; Santa Clara ; Singapore ;
Tokyo : Springer, 1996
(Advances in spatial science)
ISBN 3-540-61333-1
NE: Batten, David F. [Hrsg.]

ISBN 3-540-61333-1 Springer-Verlag Berlin Heidelberg New York

SPIN 10516914   42/2202-5 4 3 2 1 0 - Printed on acid-free paper

PREFACE

Few other facets of social and economic life are so poorly understood and yet so indisputably vital for prosperous development as *infrastructure*. Since the early 1980s researchers and policy makers in various OECD nations have started to readdress the issue of infrastructure investments. This renewed interest has been prompted by a variety of concerns. One observation was that such investments were declining from levels which might have been inadequate in the first place. A second observation was that the timing of these cutbacks in infrastructure spending seemed to roughly coincide with lower rates of growth in output or productivity. This raised the intriguing question of whether the latter might be attributable to the former. Could it be that infrastructure investments control an economy's rate of productivity growth? The response in many countries has been to initiate their own research in an attempt to verify or reject this hypothesis.

But the more we learn about the role of infrastructure and its relationships with the rest of the economy, the more complicated it seems to be. Time itself is quite difficult to accommodate given the wide variety of speeds at which different parts of an economy can adjust. Because of this inherent complexity, we tend to break the problem down into "bite-sized chunks", thereby enabling us to isolate the parts of interest to us – such as the impact of infrastructure on productivity. In this way we can ignore the complex interactions between our area of interest and the rest of our world. By saying *ceteris paribus*, we overlook many other key infrastructural impacts like those on the environment and on our overall quality of life. This distorts the true picture.

The selection of papers contained in this volume were presented at an international workshop on "Infrastructure, Economic Growth and Regional Development" held in Jönköping, Sweden during June 1993. All of the authors are leading specialists in the infrastructure field, whose papers represent cutting-edge attempts to grapple with some of the infrastructure issues mentioned above. There was a special reason for holding such a workshop in Jönköping. During the summer of 1990, the Jönköping International Business School (JIBS) Foundation was created with the support of the private and public sectors. Four years later, the Jönköping International Business School was established by an act of Swedish Parliament. In the intervening years, the JIBS Foundation sponsored and organized a series of workshops featuring prominent international scientists in a variety of fields. Their purpose was to stress the intention that the new business school should have a strong research profile – which had been one of the recommendations made by the original proponents of the school (Åke E. Andersson and Charlie Karlsson).

This expansion of higher education and research activities via the new business school was, in itself, a major infrastructure investment in the Jönköping Region. Thus one of the workshop's aims was intertwined with those of the school. A secondary aim was to assess the competitive importance of investments in knowledge-enhancing infrastructure vis-à-vis mobility-enhancing infrastructure. Financial support was provided by the JIBS foundation and the Swedish Transport and Communications Research Board. Held under the auspices of CIB Working Commission W95 (Infrastructure), the workshop was organized by an international committee which included Åke E. Andersson, Börje Johansson, T.R. Lakshmanan and Folke Snickars. Jennifer Wundersitz coordinated the editorial work and Ingrid Lindqvist keyboarded the manuscript. To each of the above, the Editors would like to express their sincere thanks.

<table>
<tr><td>David F. Batten</td><td>Charlie Karlsson</td></tr>
<tr><td>Melbourne, Australia</td><td>Jönköping, Sweden</td></tr>
</table>

CONTENTS

CHAPTER 1

Infrastructure and the Complexity of Economic Development: An Exploratory Introduction

David F. Batten

The Temaplan Group, Melbourne

1.1 THE PROBLEM

1.1.1 Complexity in Economics

In the Preface to his recent book on economic sense and nonsense in this "Age of Diminished Expectations", the MIT economist Paul Krugman wrote:

> "Why is economics such a hard subject?
> Part of the answer has to do with complexity".

The more we learn about the economy, the more complicated it seems to be. Although economics can truthfully claim that it attempts to study human beings engaged in a relatively simple activity (the exchange of goods and services), complications still arise because those same human beings are often assumed to exhibit identical behavioural traits. The kind of rationality normally assumed in economics – perfect, logical, deductive rationality – simply breaks down in many common decision situations. Human agents cannot rely upon other agents to behave in a perfectly rational manner. The truth of the matter is that each economic agent must resort to educated guesswork in a world of subjective beliefs, where there is little room for well-defined premises and perfectly logical choices. In this subjective world, very few problems are simple because many are ill-defined.

Krugman is not alone in his belief that the various oversimplified portraits of human behaviour have retarded progress in economics. Brian Arthur, for example, has argued that in economic decision contexts that are complicated or ill-defined, human beings rely on inductive rather than deductive reasoning. Building on the work of John Holland and other colleagues, Arthur claims that in such situations we induce a variety of mental models or hypotheses available to us at the time, act upon the most credible of these, and later replace these models with newer ones if the original ones cease to work. This kind of reasoning generates an extremely rich psychological world in which each agent's mental models or hypotheses compete for survival against those of others, in an environment formed by other agents' mental models or hypotheses. Such a world is both evolutionary and complex.

The persistent reader can find ample support for the view that the economy is much more complex than customarily portrayed, partly because human beings do not behave rationally and identically. A small but growing band of economists are coming to terms with some of the difficulties, which are even referred to in the works of a few classical economists:

> "The process of social life is a function of so many variables many of which are not amenable to anything like measurement that even mere diagnosis of a given state of things becomes a doubtful matter quite apart from the formidable sources of error that open up as soon as we attempt prognosis." (Schumpeter, 1942)

> "We have suggested that there is no agreement on how economic development proceeds and have implied that this is because the process is not simple. There are many variables involved, and there is a wide range of substitutability among ingredients – land, capital and the quality and quantity of labour, and technology can substitute for one another, above certain minima, although there are at the same time certain complementary relationships among them. The will to economise and organisation are probably the only indispensable ingredients. For the rest, none are necessary and none sufficient." (Kindleberger, 1958)

In this introductory chapter, I shall argue (like Arthur) that in economics we need to pay more attention to inductive reasoning, to path-dependent dynamics, and to the emergent behaviour of complex self-organizing systems (see, e.g. Nicolis and Prigogine, 1977; Haken, 1978; Batten, 1982). More specifically, I shall dwell on a few examples pertaining to transportation infrastructure. Some instances of lock-in and path-dependence associated with certain modes of transportation will be examined and their dynamic learning character revealed. Connections with evolution and complexity will be considered, as a forerunner to a discussion of the articles which follow in the remainder of this book.

1.1.2   The Path-Dependent Character of Infrastructure Systems

The complexity of infrastructure systems arises partly from the interface between a relatively static arena (or backcloth) which supports and constrains a relatively dynamic traffic of activities (see Johnson, 1995). The emergent behaviour of the system depends on the detailed design of the arena and the collective behaviour of the traffic using it. In the case of transportation, the arena has a network structure and so its performance also depends on the connectivity of the network as well as its capacity.

A transportation network forms an arena on which many different decisions are acted out. Although some seem routine (such as the route chosen by different drivers to reach their workplace), each one is based on incomplete information about the choices of other drivers and the state of the system as a whole. Because of the uncertain behaviour of different drivers, we know now that a unique traffic equilibrium is less likely than was first believed by classical transport analysts. Differences in the durability of capital, the speed of information diffusion, and adaptability to changes in the environment jointly determine the time it may take for different transportation systems to reach a new equilibrium or remain out of equilibrium. In the face of multiple candidates, the question of how a particular equilibrium may or may not be selected is of particular importance.

A complete arena of infrastructure changes much more slowly than do the patterns of traffic utilizing it. In order to grapple with the multiple equilibria problem, various processes of change need to be distinguished according to their adjustment speed. Depending on the length of the time period chosen, some processes may be regarded as invariant whereas others may reach their equilibrium rather quickly. The slaving principle implies an ordering of processes in accordance with their adjustment time on a scale from slow to fast (see Haken, 1978). The following Figure illustrates how this principle might help us to distinguish between slow and fast adjustment processes in the context of trade and transportation analysis.

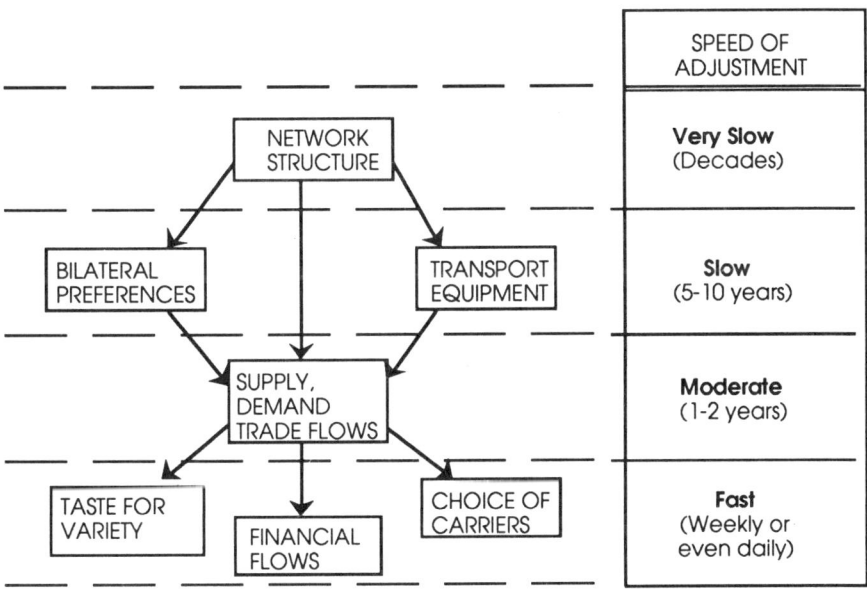

Figure 1.1   Nesting of slow and fast adjustment processes pertaining to trade and transportation

In the face of such differences, it may be relatively easy for a transportation system to "lock-in" to a particular outcome or equilibrium which possesses a perceived economic advantage at the time (see Arthur, 1994b). Examples of technological lock-in are numerous. Two popular ones cited by Arthur and Paul David are the standard keyboard layout (QWERTY) and home tape cassette system (VHS). Neither the QWERTY nor VHS systems are the most efficient solutions technologically, but they established themselves well in advance of better competitors. Their dominance resulted more or less by accident rather than from any demonstrated superiority in the marketplace. Once adopted, they became well and truly "locked in" as standards because of positive feedbacks like user familiarity and the tremendous cost involved to permit changeover to a superior alternative at a later date.

When it comes to transportation and industrial location, lock-in can occur as sequential decisions carve out an advantage which society finds it impossible to escape from at a later date (when the advantages of alternative systems become more apparent). Furthermore, the beneficiaries are not always easy to predict. Take the case of the Erie

Canal. In the early nineteenth century, Philadelphia was a more important port than New York. The opening of the Erie Canal tipped the scales in favour of New York. Although the Erie has been more of a tourist attraction than a serious transportation route for more than a century, New York still dominates the nation's urban hierarchy. We shall never really know whether Philadelphia might have achieved that status if the Erie Canal had never materialized. In cases such as these, path dependence really matters.

To complicate matters further, the perceived advantages of one system over another may change over time. Take the case of road and rail transportation. Each mode was self-reinforcing when introduced. The more heavily it was used, the more funds became available for investment in capital improvements which attracted further users. Once they were regarded as substitutes, however, road transportation began to dominate; gradually replacing rail for personal and freight transportation (see Figure 1.2). Yet it is also clear that trains cause far less environmental damage than do road vehicles. Because road users only bear a small fraction of the full costs of their mode of transportation, an enormous cross-subsidy would be needed to bring the rail system level with the privileged advantages currently enjoyed by the road system.

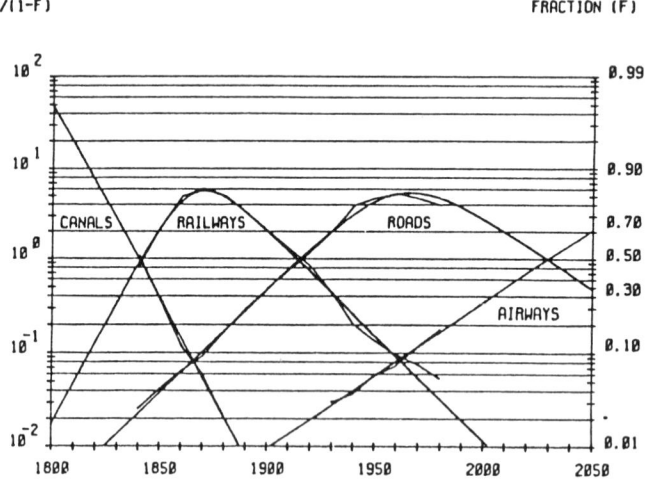

Figure 1.2   Substitution of transport infrastructures in the U.S.A., shares in length
(Source: Nakicenovic, 1989)

The importance of transportation network changes as chance events affecting the location of households and industry is rather obvious once it is pointed out. Nevertheless, the role of path dependence and historical accidents has not been widely explored in the field of transportation economics. Neither is lock-in regarded as a significant factor in economic development, despite the fact that it is perpetuated by the relatively slow ability of infrastructure to adapt to rapidly changing demands among the various users.

Because the nature of lock-in and path dependence are discussed more fully by *Jonathan Gifford* in Chapter 10, I shall not dwell at length on them here. Gifford points to the shortcomings of the famous French "star" system of rail tracks emanating from Paris. Originally designed to complement the well-developed canal system by concentrating on passengers moving to and from the nation's capital, the resulting star network turns out to be very inefficient for moving freight. Yet the cost of investing in a more efficient network is so high that the old one still remains today. We can all think of infrastructure systems which have passed their "use-by" date but which remain in place despite their obsolescence and obvious inefficiency. Their widespread proliferation suggests that it is time to readdress some of our criteria for infrastructure planning and management.

1.1.3 Managing Traffic at the Edge of Chaos

Partly because of our unwillingness to update outmoded forms of infrastructure, many metropolitan areas continue to suffer from a transportation demand which largely exceeds capacity. Amidst growing concerns about environmental quality, there seems to be little desire on the part of governments to renew or extend capacity to meet this demand. Thus efficient management of the existing systems has become a high priority. Common management strategies include fast mass transit systems, route guidance information systems, car pooling, congestion pricing and elaborate parking fees.

Because man-made transportation systems are highly complex, they are actually very difficult to manage efficiently. Certain traffic management measures may produce counter-intuitive results simply because of their own complicated dynamics. For example, the addition of a new street to a particular road network can lead to a *reduced* overall capacity and make all travellers worse off (see Cohen and Kelly, 1990). Such unexpected outcomes are usually attributed to conflicts between the collective travel plans that permit maximal throughput (the System Optimum) and the individual traveller's optimal plans (the User or Nash Equilibrium). In reality, their cause often lies in the self-organizing nature of traffic behaviour on networks.

Transportation dynamics is the aggregated result of thousands, or in some cases, millions of individual trip-making decisions by quite diverse groups – producers, consumers, holidaymakers, etc. As we mentioned earlier, many of these decisions may seem routine. The problem is that every decision is based on incomplete information about the state of the transportation system as a whole. How does each traveller reason in such an ill-defined situation?

According to modern psychology, humans are much better at pattern recognition than they are at deductive logic. In situations which are complicated or ill-defined, we tend to search for recognizable patterns and then try to simplify the problem by using these patterns to build temporary mental models or hypotheses to work with (see Arthur, 1994a). We can see this pattern recognition at work among drivers on a road network. For example, most drivers base their route choice decisions on expected traffic densities on the pertinent links, which are in turn based on their recollection of densities in the recent past. Drivers use these recollections, together with advice from other sources, to build up a picture of expected flow patterns. Having formed their own hypotheses, they then make traffic decisions based on these mental maps – even to the extent of analysing the possible implications of alternative route choices. Sometimes they are obliged to revise their current hypotheses, or possibly find new ones, if the traffic behaviour does not conform to their current expectations.

This whole sequence – pattern recognition, hypothesis formation, deduction using the currently-held hypothesis, and replacement of hypothesis if needed – enables us to grapple with the uncertainty of traffic behaviour. As drivers, we need to construct plausible but simple models that help us to cope with a poorly defined situation. Some drivers may even hold several hypotheses in mind simultaneously. These more experimental drivers "learn" over time which of their hypotheses work. Some learn faster than others. Older drivers often cling to a particular belief because it has worked well in the past, and must accumulate a record of failure before discarding it. The result is a heterogeneous population of drivers, harbouring a diverse collection of hypotheses and precipitating a slow turnover of hypotheses acted upon.

Consider the following traffic problem. Based on computer experiments conducted by Arthur (1994a) and Nagel and Rasmussen (1994), it shows how the predictability of travel time can decrease suddenly even when advanced flow control systems try to improve the traffic flow. Henceforth I shall refer to it as the ANR (Arthur-Nagel-Rasmussen) problem.

N drivers decide independently each morning whether to drive to work by way of a single lane freeway (i.e. a closed loop of length L). We define a subsegment of length l (less than L) and measure, for each vehicle, the travel time t_l between entry and exit of this subsegment. The flow capacity (maximum number of vehicles per hour) through this subsegment is f_{max} and each driver deems the route to be reasonable and worth repeating the next day if the route is not too congested – more specifically, if the travel time through the subsegment is no more than t_{max}. Full technical particulars of this freeway traffic model may be found in Nagel and Schreckenberg (1992).

In this situation, there is no way of knowing how many vehicles will be there in advance. Thus a driver chooses this route only if he expects his travel time to be no more than t_{max}, but chooses another route if the expected travel time is more than t_{max}. There is no collusion or prior communication among drivers and the only information available is the travel time experienced in past days (or weeks or months). The reader may recognize this as belonging to a wider family of commons or coordination problems (with limited coordination) such as the Bar Problem or noontime lunchroom crowding. Of primary interest is the dynamics of individual travel time, from day to day and from vehicle to vehicle.

Brian Arthur has recognized two interesting features of this class of problem. First, a deductive solution would be possible if there was an obvious model that all drivers could use to forecast traffic density and travel time. But this is not possible here. Given the varying travel times experienced in the recent past, a wide variety of expectational models are both likely and reasonable. Since each driver cannot know which model other drivers might choose, no single driver can choose his model in a well-defined way. Nobody can resort to a deductively rational solution. Because his problem is ill-defined, each and every driver is plunged into a world of induction.

Second, any commonality of expectations will be broken up. If all drivers believe that only a *few* will choose this route, then *all* will choose it – thus invalidating that belief. Likewise if all drivers believe that *most* will choose it, *nobody* will choose it, invalidating that belief.

To understand how predictions might be attempted in this inductive world, I shall give the ANR problem some concreteness. Let the subsegment length (l) be 1km, the space occupied by one car be 7.5m and the maximum possible speed through the subsegment (v_{max}) be 120 km/hr. If it is uncongested, each driver can travel through it very quickly ($t_{min} = 30$ secs). Assume that every driver considering that route can form one or several predictors (hypotheses), in the form of functions that map the past d days travel times through the subsegment into the next day's. For example, recent travel times for Driver A might be:

.... 42 85 34 160 48 125 46 360 81 59 74

Some of the particular hypotheses or predictors might be:
I predict tomorrow's travel time to be
- the same as yesterday's (74)
- the same as last Monday's (125)
- the same as three days ago (81)
- an average of the last five days (124)
- an average of the last four Mondays (98)
- any number between 30 and 600

Drivers keep track of their own set of predictors, and base their daily route decisions on the currently most accurate predictor in their set (the *active* predictor). Once decisions are taken, each driver notes that day's travel time and then updates the accuracies of his monitored predictors. Like in Arthur's Bar Problem, the set of active hypotheses determines the travel times experienced, but the travel time history also determines the set of active hypotheses. These active hypotheses form an *ecology* which also evolves over time.

There is one important difference between the Bar Problem and the AMR traffic problem. In the former, the predicted outcome (bar attendance) is the same for all agents. Thus Arthur's computer experiments showed that mean attendance converges always to a fixed percentage (60%). The set of predictors self-organize into an equilibrium pattern which is "almost organic in nature.........something like a forest whose contours do not change but whose individual trees do" (Arthur, 1994a).

Even the contours of the emergent "ecology" can change in the AMR traffic problem, because the predicted outcome (travel time) can differ significantly for each driver. From the Nagel-Rasmussen experiments, we know that the simulated traffic subsegment reaches capacity (maximum flow) $f_{max} = 0.318$ at a density of $D^* = D(f_{max}) = 0.086$ for a long single-lane freeway. Keeping this in mind, it is revealing to examine individual travel time and its variation among vehicles using the same subsegment. The results are shown as a function of density in the Figure 1.3.

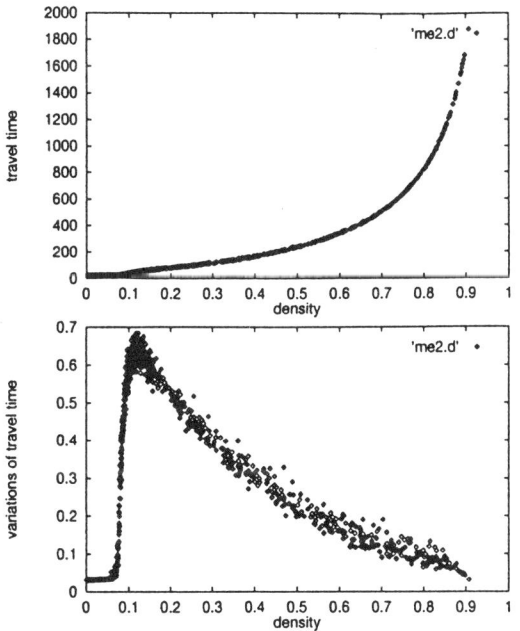

Figure 1.3   Variations of travel time as a function of density
(Source: Nagel and Rasmussen, 1994)

Both the average travel time and its variation among the vehicle population are approximately constant up to a density of about 0.09. Once the travel time starts to rise as a function of density, the fluctuations from vehicle-to-vehicle go up very steeply and reach a maximum near $D = 0.11$. This emergent phenomenon is quite striking. It shows that, when passing from slightly below to slightly above capacity, the traffic moves from a regime where the travel time is predictable to within an accuracy of about 3% to a regime where the error climbs to 65% or more (Nagel and Rasmussen, 1994).

The interesting conclusion is that the predictability of travel time on a traffic network can decrease sharply if the system is pushed towards a regime of maximum flow. Traffic as a whole can be driven closer to this critical condition with the aid of advanced traffic management systems. Once traffic is near this critical regime, further control measures will have unpredictable consequences. Although such phase transitions may not be truly critical, their unpredictable outcomes are further exacerbated by the different learning rates of drivers.

1.2   THE BOOK'S ORIENTATION

1.2.1   Infrastructure and Productivity

Transportation is only one type of infrastructure. Relationships between output, productivity and other classes of infrastructure have been the focus of plenty of recent research (for a review, see Rietveld 1989). Yet the insights gained have been divergent and ambiguous. For example, economists have devised production function models to test whether particular types of infrastructure affect, or even improve, the productivity of conventional factors such as labour and capital. An immediate difficulty is that we do not know the extent to which infrastructure is physically embodied in the productivity of specific inputs as against whether its disembodied effects accrue more generally to the overall productivity of firms.

In their chapter on infrastructure and manufacturing productivity, *Edward Bergman and Daoshan Sun* focus on this problem by considering locally-accessible and regionally-accessible infrastructure components as co-production factors in North Carolina County's manufacturing sector. A Cobb-Douglas production function is used to estimate the contributions of conventional factors (manufacturing capital and labour) and each of thirteen different infrastructure components (measured in service units). The productive effects of each of these components are complex because their relationships can be competitive, complementary or both. For example, as Bergman and Sun point out, the highway system in a region not only adds capacity to the region's transportation system, but also affects the functioning of other parts of the system (e.g. airports).

Some of the conclusions reached at the end of this chapter serve to emphasize the complexity of the relationships involved. Even within the same type of region (county), seemingly similar forms of infrastructure can have opposite effects. Not all forms of infrastructure accomplish the goals or benefits assumed and some actually subtract from their intended objective. As was noted earlier, the addition of a new street to an existing road network can sometimes inadvertently lead to a *reduced* overall capacity. Although some unexpected effects may be a natural outcome of a region's stage of economic development, many counterintuitive outcomes stem from our ignorance about the complicated dynamic relationships between changes to the network itself and those occurring within the traffic using the network.

In Chapter 3, *Remy Prud'homme* makes use of regionally-estimated production functions to assess the contribution of infrastructure to the French economy during a modest period of development (1981-1988). He finds that the marginal productivity of infrastructure appears to be similar to (but slightly lower than) that of private capital in France today. Like Koichi Mera (1973), Prud'homme argues that his results may underestimate the rate of return on public capital because (1) the quality of data is uncertain, (2) the spillover effects of infrastructure in neighbouring regions are excluded, and (3) public investments are not undertaken solely to increase output. These results confirm that we know very little about the rates of return on infrastructure in the very long run.

Although evaluations of the costs and benefits to users of investments in transportation projects have been attempted on many occasions, quantitative evidence proving that such investments are the sources of economic growth, development or productivity gains, or that they improve welfare or competitiveness, is difficult to find. In the USA, the Federal Highway Administration (FHWA) has begun to address the question "How do changes in highway investment translate to private productivity at the national level?" Their three approaches (macroeconometrics, microeconomic industry analysis and highway system assessment) are discussed by *Susan Binder and Theresa Smith* in Chapter 4. They dwell on the distributional effects of infrastructure investment, which are particularly important because gains for one region may correspond to losses for other regions (see Batten, 1990). Their review further confirms that our knowledge of the relationship between investment in public capital and economic growth is inadequate.

Infrastructure has been referred to as the "engine of economic growth". Until recently, however, macroeconomics has paid scant attention to the impacts of publically provided infrastructure on the growth of private sector output and productivity. In Chapter 5, *Jacco Hakfoort* examines the impact of infrastructure at the macrolevel by way of a survey of theoretical and empirical literature in the field of economic growth. After summarizing recent advances in the new endogenous growth theory, he mentions some well-known drawbacks of the Cobb-Douglas production function approach and then summarizes some examples of the cost function approach. Finally Hakfoort points to the need for relaxation of the many oversimplifying assumptions inherent in economic analysis.

Far from being a pure public good, some infrastructure can be both rival and excludable. Quite often it is not provided optimally and it is in any case extremely difficult to estimate the benefits accruing to final consumers through its public provision. Furthermore, its spillover effects are poorly understood. While *Hakfoort* optimistically views these difficulties as challenging new research areas, they also add to the lengthening list of complications. There is a strong possibility that no convincing analytical devices can be devised to reveal the true significance of such a complex arena.

1.2.2 Infrastructure Policy: Pricing and Ownership Issues

Attempts have also been made to combine the best features of several modelling traditions. In modelling infrastructure as a local public good, *Andrew Haughwout* combines both the production (function) and compensating variation approaches. In the latter approach, sometimes known as the capitalization model, long run local prices are deemed to reflect the value of non-traded local attributes. Haughwout's spatial equilibrium model has the same structure as the "open city, absentee landlord" model described in Fujita (1989). Wages and land prices must adjust to ensure an equilibrium, whereupon firms and households react to these by conditioning their demands for land, capital and labour. Since the model is recursive, the wage and property price equations can be estimated consistently. The results show that infrastructure's effects on property markets are substantial, and that partial equilibrium approaches for studying the impact of local fiscal policy on urban economies may provide misleadingly low and biased estimates of the effects that local prices have on the demand for labour.

In Chapter 7, *Juliet Musso and John Quigley* consider the extent to which California's highly fragmented fiscal structure serves the needs of its regionally diverse economy. More precisely, they examine whether the state's public sector might be a *fiscal federalism*, i.e. one with both centralized and decentralized levels of decision-making in which choices made at each level concerning the provision of public goods such as infrastructure are determined largely by the demands for these services by local economic agents and residents. Their findings show that the equity implications of major changes to the tax base can be quite ambiguous. The fact that the mix of public services provided directly by state, federal or local agencies, often changes unexpectedly in response to political whims further emphasizes the complexity of the infrastructure issue.

Contemplated changes in the provision of infrastructure by many governments leads us to ask the question "Which policy leads to higher efficiency in infrastructure provision?" Although privatization is the most popular option being actively explored by many federal and regional governments, viable alternatives also exist. In her chapter, *Frannie Humplick* looks at the option of introducing multiplicity in the production of these services – by fostering competition in and for service production and devolving responsibilities to regional, state or local authorities. The results of her empirical studies suggest that multiplicity is important, if not more important than private ownership, and that reducing the degree of vertical integration is likely to improve performance just as much as transfers of ownership. Also important is the nature of the institutional environment in which these services are introduced.

Numerous studies have attempted to find unambiguous links between infrastructure provision and economic development. Regrettably the results of these studies have not been conclusive. Causation is difficult to establish, partly because it may be cumulative and recursive. *Kenneth Button* takes a critical look at some of these studies in the context of transportation infrastructure. At both the macro and the microlevels, he finds that the evidence is ambiguous at best. Button questions the "public good" character of transportation infrastructure, as well as other common but partial economic arguments for it. In calling for a more comprehensive and consistent approach to the economic analysis of infrastructure, he alludes to the decreasing cost pricing problem as the key issue and cites both market and government failures in the pricing area.

1.2.3   The Complexity of Economic Development

In the concluding part of this volume, the reader will find an assortment of chapters which address quite diverse aspects of the infrastructure problem. Topics discussed emphasize the importance of (a) the dynamic nature of the urban environment, (b) increasing returns and path dependence, (c) varying timescales of adjustment among production factors, (d) short term versus long term effects, (e) the role of innovative capacity and the production milieu, (f) qualitative versus quantitative analyses, and (g) estimating the social costs to the environment. The result is a kaleidoscope of ideas confirming that the relationship between infrastructure and economic development is an exceedingly complex one.

Jonathan Gifford questions whether the effects of urban infrastructure investment decisions can be anticipated and evaluated systematically because of the complexity, adaptiveness and dynamic nature of the urban environment. The criteria adopted for most of these decisions are based on scientific and technical rationality. They often presume order and equilibrium. Because of the diversity and complexity of infrastructure systems, Gifford demonstrates that the presence of increasing returns may undermine the validity of scientific rationality and give rise to multiple equilibria, inefficiencies, lock-in and path dependence. This is a thought-provoking introduction to the challenges posed by complexity and the need for more flexible planning solutions.

In Chapter 11, *Börje Johansson and Rune Wigren* present a series of Swedish studies examining how the production milieu influences the performance of manufacturing and service industries as well as the entire regional economy. They argue that some production factors and regionally-located resources adjust on slower timescales than are generally assumed in conventional economic theory. Moreover, they demonstrate that the notion of a production milieu may be a more fundamental one than that of technology alone; partly because it encompasses specific resources and agglomeration economies which may accrue persistently to certain kinds of regions, and are therefore vital to our understanding of the relative success of some regions and failure of others. It is the consequences (or use) of the infrastructure, rather than its size or value, which constitute the regional milieu. In short, the Johanssson-Wigren analysis provides a more convincing foundation on which to build an analysis of economic and locational dynamics.

In anticipation of the plight of the developing nations, *Christine Kessides* (Chapter 12) presents a basic review of the linkages between infrastructure and economic development and looks at the necessary conditions for economic benefits from infrastructure to accrue. She lists possible impacts on a broad front, points to the needed complementarity between infrastructure and other resources, advocates user charges and concludes that the degree of reliability and quality of services is of the utmost importance.

Frank Bruinsma, Gerard Pepping and Piet Rietveld analyse trip-related economic impacts of the opening of a major infrastructure project in the Netherlands – the Amsterdam Orbital Motorway. The impacts include changes in route choice, accessibility and journey time gains, and a reinforcement of the existing zonal distribution of office prices in place beforehand. One of the problems which their study obviates is the need to distinguish between the short and long term benefits. Tradeoffs between short-term and long-term gains (to potentially different populations) are gradually drawing more attention as we try to cope with the dynamics of transportation systems and the need to recognize different intergenerational objectives.

In Chapter 13, *Luis Suarez-Villa* looks at the relationship between invention and infrastructural investment by an analysis of infrastructural and patent age cycles. Distinguishing clearly between invention and innovation (application of inventions), he measures *innovative capacity* as the stock of all inventive knowledge available as patents for innovative purposes. It was impossible to detect a positive association between infrastructure spending and changes in innovative capacity, even though patent and infrastructure age cycles were found to have similar trajectories. This result further highlights the complexities and uncertainties involved.

In the final contribution to this volume, *Emile Quinet* addresses the difficult but important question of how to value infrastructural impacts on the environment. He reviews valuation methods and concludes that there are many difficulties to be overcome – e.g. in measuring a person's "willingness-to-pay" for a cleaner environment or "willingness-to-accept" compensation for a dirtier one. After summarizing recent studies concerning the environmental effects of transport, he concludes that the very large dispersion of results suggests that qualitative, rather than quantitative, considerations should be given more attention. There is clearly an urgent need to consider the social costs to the environment when deciding upon infrastructure investments and their pricing.

1.3 FINAL REMARKS

A disturbingly shallow degree of consensus can be gleaned from the contents of this volume. The uncontested part of that consensus says that a durable and efficient system of infrastructure *seems* to be a good thing for an economy. Historically, investments in infrastructure have been thought to confer two-fold benefits on a region or nation: firstly, by improving the potential productivity of the population and, secondly, by attracting modern industries because of the population's greater potential. Various methods of economic analysis have been devised to estimate these impacts. As we saw in Part A of this volume, the production function models developed for this purpose are incapable of providing unambiguous results. They fail to identify the precise relationships because of too many oversimplifying assumptions prompted by too few obervables. Thus there is an urgent need to search beneath the traditional aggregate and beyond the usual deductive view of economic systems in order to unravel the underlying complexities.

Consideration of lower-level complexities breeds little consensus among the authors herein. The findings in Part C serve only to emphasize the multifarious facets of economic development and the high degree of uncertainty associated with all of them. Space and time pose daunting problems. Paradoxes seem to abound. For example, the approximation of deterministic, predictable traffic patterns seems less and less correct the more one approaches a highly efficient traffic system. The fact that high performance often has the downside of high variability may not just be true in transportation systems. Chances are that it is also true of many economic systems.

The reader who nurtures a healthy skepticism towards science and mathematical modelling will not be surprised by these findings. After all, Gödel has shown us that a truly complex system is more complex than any formalization in which the entailment is purely syntactic (Rosen, 1991). Thus there are qualities pertaining to any complex system which will remain unencoded by any attempt to quantify them in a formal model. In the case of an economy, for example, we should never forget that human agents have a semantic dimension which is tied to their own environment and cultural background. Local values, customs and knowledge create the semantics which adds complexity to any simpler syntactic representation.

There is evidence that the duality between the quantitative and the qualitative may boil down to a relative question of simplicity versus complexity. The natural tendency for social and economic evolution is from the simple towards the complex, from the few towards the many, and from a lower level to a higher one. It may be argued that a system as complex as a post-industrial economy defies formalization. Part of the difficulty stems from the fact that complexity is more subjective than objective. Furthermore, many of the qualitative impacts of infrastructural investments are dynamic in character. In these cases, the emergent behaviour only becomes apparent with the help of detailed microsimulations.

Economic development cannot be treated as purely objective until our formalism takes full and proper account of the society and environment in which that economy operates. The degree to which any economic model reflects reality depends entirely on how the logical structure of the model and the logical structure of real world observables match up. And it is precisely this relationship that the philosopher Ludvig Wittgenstein claimed we cannot express in language – in this case, the language of mathematics (see, e.g. Casti, 1994).

Small wonder that precious little economic formalism has moved seriously in this direction. Progress along this tortuous path must reject simplifying assumptions and ad hoc aggregations. A higher level simplicity is much easier to think about than some chain of complexities that causes it (see Cohen and Stewart, 1994). The correct representation of a higher-level simplicity must emerge only as an explicit consequence of an accurate representation of its lower-level complexities. As a first step towards a meaningful economic formalism, we might do well to look more closely at the inductive and path dependent aspects of human behaviour. But much more than this needs to be done. The reader might like to contemplate whether the complete task is simply too formidable.

REFERENCES

Arthur, B, 1994b, *Increasing Returns and Path Dependence in the Economy*, The University of Michigan Press, Ann Arbor.

Arthur, B., 1994a, "Inductive Behaviour and Bounded Rationality", *American Economic Review*, 84:406-411.

Batten, D.F., 1982, "On the Dynamics of Industrial Evolution", *Regional Science and Urban Economics*, 12:449-462.

Batten, D.F., 1990, "Infrastructure as a Network System: Mera Revisited", in Anselin, L. and M. Madden, (eds.), *New Directions in Regional Analysis*, Belhaven Press, London and New York, 76-89.

Casti, J., 1994, *Complexification*, Abacus, London.

Cohen, J. and F. Kelly, 1990, "A Paradox of Congestion in a Queuing Network", *Journal of Applied Probability,* 27:730-734.

Cohen, J. and I. Stewart, 1994, *The Collapse of Chaos: Discovering Simplicity in a Complex World*, Penguin Books, New York.

Fujita, M., 1989, *Urban Economic Theory: Land Use and City Size*, Cambridge University Press, New York.

Haken, H., 1978, *Synergetics: An Introduction*, Springer-Verlag, Berlin.

Johnson, J., 1995, "The Multidimensional Networks of Complex Systems", in Batten, D.F., J.L. Casti, and R. Thord (eds.), *Networks in Action*, Springer Verlag, Berlin.

Kindleberger, C.P., 1958, *Economic Development*, McGraw-Hill, New York.

Krugman, P., 1994, *Peddling Prosperity: Economic Sense and Nonsense in the Age of Diminished Expectations*, W.W. Norton, New York and London.

Mera, K., 1973, "Regional Production Functions and Social Overhead Capital: An Analysis of the Japanese Case", *Regional and Urban Economics,* 3:157-186.

Nagel, K. and S. Rasmussen, 1994, "Traffic at the Edge of Chaos", Sante Fe Institute Working Paper No.94-06-032.

Nagel, K. and M. Schreckenberg, 1992, "A Cellular Automaton Model for Freeway Traffic", *Journal of Physics I France*, 2, 2221.

Nakicenovic, N., 1989, "Expanding Territories: Transport Systems Past and Future", in Batten, D.F. and R. Thord (eds.), *Transportation for the Future*, Springer, Berlin.

Nicolis, G. and I. Prigogine, 1977, *Self-Organization in Nonequilibrium Systems*, Wiley, New York.

Rietveld, P., 1989, "Infrastructure and Regional Development: a Survey of Multiregional Economic Models", *The Annals of Regional Science*, 23:3-22.

Rosen, R., 1991, *Life Itself: A Comprehensive Inquiry into the Nature, Origin and Fabrication of Life*, Columbia University Press, New York.

Schumpeter, J.A., 1942, *Capitalism, Socialism and Democracy*, Harper and Row, New York.

PART A: INFRASTRUCTURE AND PRODUCTIVITY

CHAPTER 2

Infrastructure and Manufacturing Productivity:
Regional Accessibility and Development Level Effects

Edward M. Bergman   Daoshan Sun
University of North Carolina   University of North Carolina

2.1   INTRODUCTION

Infrastructure – and its consequences for regional development – has been treated in business, urban economics, regional science, geography and engineering literatures. Depending upon the tradition favored by the analyst, one might frame rather different questions. Duffy-Deno and Eberts (1991), for example, claim "The importance of public capital for regional growth stems from its effect on production and location decisions of private industry". Accordingly, infrastructure might be studied to detect whether its early availability stimulates substantial accumulations of private capital investment. Assuming first that infrastructure is fixed capital – subsidized or wholly provided by the state – this could be approached as some variant of the *industrial location question*. Roads, bridges, railways, water supply, basic utilities (gas, electricity), assembled land and public services, and traditional public works are the staple infrastructure elements considered in such studies.

Accumulated stocks of public and private capital in regions may indeed result from some version of this infrastructure-driven industrial location process. Or capital formations and infrastructure may represent nothing more than random stocks and vintages of private capital and infrastructure that happened to survive wars, depressions and industrial (or political) revolutions. In either case, analysts might still wish to inquire about the contemporary role specific types of infrastructure play in the *marginal investment decisions* made by firms and industries. What are the qualities of particular types of existing infrastructure that make their marginal investment decision attractive to such firms?

Questions such as these take us beyond industrial location frameworks to consider how modern production decisions are made. If one accepts that production regimes are in rapid flux and being reformed with more flexible and entrepreneurial capacities; if corporate structures and interindustry relations are being reshaped into smaller, more diverse and closely networked units; and if human capital and technological innovation continue to drive this process, we need perspectives beyond those available from location theory in any of its known variants. At the very least, we are led to investigate a wider range of infrastructure and to do so from different perspectives.

2.2   INFRASTRUCTURE AND REGIONAL ADVANTAGE

An expanded range of relevant infrastructure might include telecommunications, air transportation, point or diffusion sources of technological advance, producer service centers, industrial networks and production complexes, and numerous measures of skilled human capital. Some of these are the technological extensions of existing transportation and communications infrastructure that have been referred to by Hansen (1965) and others as "Economic Overhead Capital". A few bear strong resemblance to agglomeration and localization economies (centers, networks, complexes), while Hansen's "Social Overhead Capital" denotes forms of infrastructure which might be directly embodied in the labor force as human capital or represented in the region by social institutions that improve the quality and productivity of human capital. Still others identify what is called milieu, sometimes also termed "business or entrepreneurial climate"; more recent studies stress what might be called "Civic Overhead Capital", a form of infrastructure that can be derived from the research of Robert Putnam (1992) who convincingly demonstrates the economically beneficial civic advantages certain (Italian) regions hold over others. In this study, we will focus our attention on infrastructure comprised of economic and social overhead capital.

As Hansen and others also point out, certain infrastructure exerts beneficial effects only when a region's stage of development allows infrastructure to meet both necessary *and sufficient* development conditions. In poorly developed regions, some forms of infrastructure may satisfy neither necessary nor sufficient conditions and its provision may stimulate nothing over the long term in the absence of more fundamental infrastructure. But there is precious little evidence concerning which types of infrastructure do have effects or what these effects are in developed countries. Citing a study of Mexican regions by Looney and Frederiksen (1981), Eberts (1990) observes "..economic overhead capital has a significant effect on gross domestic product *for intermediate regions* but not for lagging regions..". If true, this argues for a research design that permits one to detect systematic infrastructure differences in regions at different development levels.

At the other far end of this spectrum, highly developed regions encounter severe capacity limitations and congestion of infrastructure such that further provision essentially satisfies only unmet, pent-up demand but offers no efficiency gains; added infrastructure primarily serves to hold existing private capital in the region, thereby maintaining stock levels that would have otherwise been depleted as depreciation or technological obsolescence took their toll. Eberts summarizes the pertinent findings of Costa et al. (1987): "They find that the larger the stock of public capital relative to private capital within a state, and the larger the stock of public capital per capita, the smaller the impact of public capital stock on manufacturing production". Decreasing private returns to infrastructure or diseconomies of urban and regional scale may arise at rather early development stages for manufacturing, even with large increases in infrastructure.

Finally, transportation (and perhaps also telecommunications) infrastructure offers greater interregional accessibility that may trigger comparative advantages of healthier core areas to exploit infrastructure in ways that work to the detriment of poorly developed neighboring peripheral areas. If a peripheral area lacks sufficient conditions to benefit from infrastructure improvements that increase accessibility, their provision may improve access but accelerate the "backwash effects" à la Hirschman and Myrdl in the process, thereby permanently penalizing the very regions intended as beneficiaries (Bergman and Maier, 1991). As described later, this possibility is taken into account by the combined use of potential variables and regional interaction terms.

A research design issue arises as the definition of infrastructure expands to include many possible factors that may increase the productivity and economic efficiency of private capital. The problem worsens as additional considerations such as the level of development or accessibility-based backwash is introduced. One is led to adopt ad hoc research designs that best fit the full range of infrastructure, type of region or conveniently available data sources. Such ad hoc designs are then so idiosyncratic that they do not permit useful generalization or they become uninterpretable since their findings are borne of promiscuous theoretical parentage. To reduce this possibility, we join, and extend somewhat, the work of many other researchers from different fields who apply regional production functions to investigate the effects of infrastructure.

2.3 TESTING INFRASTRUCTURE CONTRIBUTIONS TO REGIONAL PRODUCTIVITY

The Cobb-Douglas production function is the most frequently used form in empirically based research of infrastructure. For example, Mera (1973) estimates the effects of public capital in three different sectors: primary, secondary, and tertiary, with certain public capital considered ex ante as related to particular sectors. Alternatively, the translog function is a more general formulation, but in application it may yield statistical estimates for its many necessary parameters that are more difficult to interpret (Costa et al, 1987); this is particularly the case when additional infrastructure variables are introduced or when the function is applied to the noisy spatial data that are used to estimate regional production functions. The choice of functional form should depend on its appropriateness in relation to the questions of concern, and also quite often, on the limitations imposed by data and other analytical features of the research design.

Production function models permit one to account for the partial contribution to output made by the paid, internally supplied factors of production, *and* to attribute some of the residual productivity to externally sourced infrastructure and other inputs. These models are sufficiently flexible to allow testing whether the independent presence of specific, measurable forms of infrastructure improve productivity. But since this relationship has been shown to differ by industry sector in the work of Johansson (1993) and Mera (1973) as well as in studies summarized by Rietveld (1989), it is considered important to control for the mix of sectors when estimating regional production functions.

On the other hand, such models should permit one to test whether a particular type of infrastructure interacts with and qualitatively improves the productivity of conventional factors (e.g., labor and capital). This is roughly equivalent to the conceptual differences illustrated by "embodied and disembodied" technological progress; the question is whether infrastructure is physically embodied in the productivity of specific inputs or whether its disembodied effects accrue generally to the overall productivity of firms. It is quite conceivable that some types of infrastructure could function as both embodied and disembodied contributors to productivity.

Firms often deliberately reorganize production processes in ways that build upon regional infrastructure, a possibility anticipated by Williamson's seminal work on transaction cost minimization (1975, 1979). This view is examined in several essays (Bergman, Maier and Todtling, 1991), and introduced as elements in an infrastructure-based network (via Coase, 1947) by Johansson and Karlsson (1991). While Johansson and Karlsson argue "...the intraregional infrastructure is an arena for the formation and maintenance of economic, as well as supportive networks", Williamson speaks of "asset specific investments" taken by firms. One recent primer (USDOT, 1992) summarizes a proposed method of estimating the restructuring effects on choice of production technology, e.g., firms might adopt JIT inventory control or other adjustments made possible by improved transportation infrastructure. Or revised production technologies could build upon embedded inputs and efficiencies made available through telecommunicated network agreements with its suppliers and customers. Internal investments are made more productive because the inputs supplied contractually embody agreed-upon qualities that boost each firm's productivity (see Bergman and Ke, forthcoming, for empirical estimates of asset specific investments made by the computer and electronics industry). The infrastructure analog may deserve additional attention, particularly in cases where private and public investments are made simultaneously through informal or other agreements (witness rapid growth of public-private partnerships), although an equivalent logic applies even in the absence of contractual co-investment.

It is also possible to represent forms of infrastructure that permit various degrees of interregional accessibility. Biehl (1993) advances the useful distinction between "point infrastructure" whose access is essentially limited to local populations and "network infrastructure" whose benefits are shared across larger regions. On the latter point, Rietveld (1989, p. 259) notes "A certain region may not have its own university or airport but still benefit from a university or airport nearby. This may be solved by using the concept of *accessibility* of certain types of infrastructure in the production function".

Even when nominally accessible (as measured by potentials or other distance sensitive-adjustments), infrastructure may be further price rationed by direct cost or user fees, and its use by one may exclude use by others. For example, some types of infrastructure are regionally accessible, non-rivalrous, and require no user fee (e.g., public transportation facilities or university libraries and published research). Others may be fully accessible but require fees or payments that exclude others (regional stocks of human capital or supplies of producer services), and still others are limited to users within regions, by site or network geography, and require fees for exclusive use (gas, water, electrical, and other physically networked, metered utilities).[1] Knowing the effects and mechanisms by which a certain type infrastructure contributes to productivity equips policymakers with the information necessary to apply or withdraw fees in some cases, or to widen coverage of spatially fixed infrastructure.

2.4   INFRASTRUCTURE MODEL FOR NORTH CAROLINA COUNTIES

This chapter adopts a research approach that considers a wide range of infrastructure components as co-production factors in a county's total manufacturing sector. Those components are further postulated as affecting production in a multiplicative manner. The benefits resulting from one type of infrastructure facility, airports, for example, are determined by the quantities and quality of the whole system of transportation and communication. Therefore, the highway system in a region not only adds capacity to the region's transportation system, it also determines the functioning of other parts of the whole system, including airports. For this reason, a Cobb-Douglas type production function that incorporates all infrastructure components is preferable.

Given this function, we divide its left and right sides by labor input and take logarithms to express labor productivity as:

(1) $\log(Y/L) = \beta_0 + (\beta_1 + \beta_2 - 1)\log L + \beta_2\log(K/L) + \sum\alpha_i\log X_i$

where *Y, L, K* are output, labor input, and capital input, respectively. X_i is the *i*th infrastructure component. The α's and β's are elasticities with respect to corresponding factors.

This model is used for statistically estimating the contributions of internal factors (manufacturing capital and labor) and each of several infrastructure components.[2]

---

[1]   For a similar approach to identifying infrastructure based on accessibility, see Johansson (1993).

[2]   Some researchers argue that OLS estimation of production functions involves simultaneous equations bias in parameters of production factors due to dual directional causation (Hoch, 1958). This possibility is a less important consequence for this model, since our interests are limited to examining the presence and direction of ex post technical relations between labor productivity and

Parameters are interpreted as the percentage change in labor productivity from a one percent change in an infrastructure variable, except for dummy variables that measure the percentage change in the presence of dichotomous conditions.

The model presented here has been developed for the counties in North Carolina, a state that has relied heavily upon general infrastructure investments to stimulate economic activity. Since it remains a relatively poor state, levels of infrastructure service range from well served, infrastructure-rich places to places with only the barest necessities met.[3] We will focus our attention on manufacturing activity in the mid-1980s, a period that begins at the bottom and ends near the peak of NC's business cycle, during which private (and public) factor and infrastructure utilization was lowest and highest, respectively. The model permits in-depth data from the 1982 and 1987 Economic Census to be combined with County Business Patterns and national level capital stock data to estimate important manufacturing variables (see Appendices for final model variables and data sources). Infrastructure data, intercounty accessibility, and other variables useful to this model have been collected for the mid-1980s by Bergman and Maier (1992) in preparing their simulation model studies. Combining 1982 and 1987 data permits the use of a pooled, cross-sectional model with twice the observations, thereby also revealing recession vs. boom effects on regional productivity.

The model described above tests for effects on regional productivity, expressed here as value-added per manufacturing employee. The ratio for 1987 should exceed the 1982 ratio for each county. This can be amply demonstrated by Figure 2.1, in which value-added per employee is rank ordered according to 1987 values (crosses), all but a handful of which exceed the 1982 (boxed) values. The 1987 values are higher overall, reflecting the +50% jump in nominal productivity (see descriptive statistics, Appendix 1).

The gap in measured productivity between the years is due, in part, to real productivity increases over the five year period, which will be explained by infrastructure and other input variables, as well as other effects. The jagged 1982 line surely reveals the uneven spatial incidence of various infrastructure effects on productivity.[4] But since productivity is also maximized when the most efficient factors are employed, some of the difference may reflect the 1987 business cycle peak vs. the 1982 trough (controlled with a dummy variable for 1982 observations). Its jagged profile may also indirectly reflect sporadic arrivals of new – or departures of old – sectors whose individual productivity contributions can profoundly affect the average measured county productivity between 1982 and 1987, particularly in small counties whose base is heavily affected by changes in a few firms.[5]

---

infrastructure. Were one directly concerned with causal relations, e.g., estimating unbiased inputs proportioned correctly to produce a certain output, simultaneous equation bias would become an important issue.

[3] We build upon considerable familiarity with the State and previous research (Bergman and Maier, 1991 & 1992; Sun, 1992) in designing the model and interpreting these results. The results apply directly to recent and projected policies, particularly those that surround many new business incentive and infrastructure proposals. These include a $9.2 billion funded highway plan, a proposed air-cargo airport, a newly announced state-of-the-art electronic highway initiative (ATM/fiber cable/SONET capacity) to link every county in the state, and several recent initiatives to improve NC's social infrastructure (child care, a health plan, education at all levels). The State's 100 counties provide a reasonably large cross-section of uniformly sized units that span a coast-piedmont-mountain range; the counties are of widely varying size and urban percentage, and they differ markedly in development level and industrial mix (from a Research Triangle Park to impoverished, post-agricultural communities in coastal and mountain counties).

[4] Johansson and Karlsson (1991) adopt a quasi-dynamic model that assumes such differences are due to differential adjustment speeds and lags by resident firms to the infrastructure advantages in the region.

[5] Investment in county manufacturing that reflects such arrivals and departures will be analyzed in a related paper.

The infrastructure variables proposed for testing in this model include both economic and social(*) overhead capital infrastructure. These are further divided into types of infrastructure accessible only to firms (or workers) located within counties – and network-based infrastructure that is regionally accessible to anyone in counties – that host such facilities and within others willing to spend the time on and cost of transportation. Regionally accessible infrastructure variables are calculated for all counties using empirically observed distance decay functions and traditional potential formulations.[6] It is necessary to adjust additional control variables for spatial and temporal differences as well as energy cost and industry composition differences in the observations.

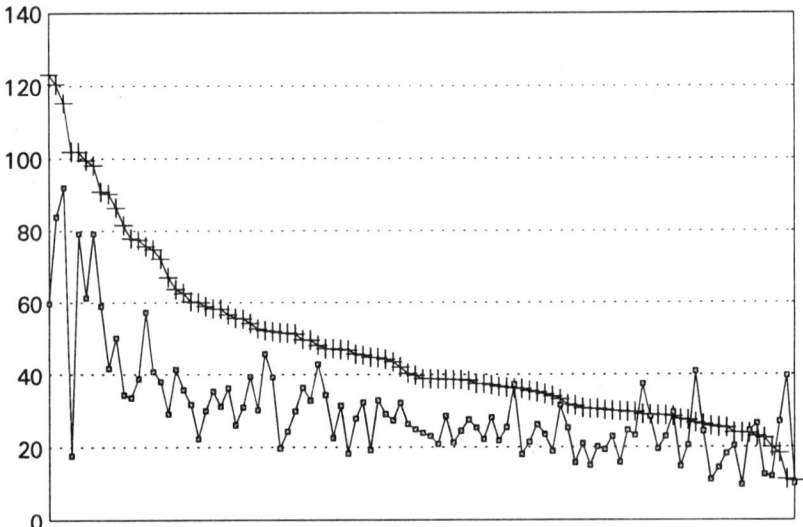

Figure 2.1 Productivity growth 1982-1987

Locally Accessible Infrastructure
1. Degree of development of the county's internal road service
2. Degree of availability of public water & treatment
3. Availability of natural gas service
4. Availability of digitally switched telephone system
5. Degree of availability of child care(*)

Regionally Accessible Infrastructure
1. Degree of access to U.S. Interstate Highway System(s)
2. Availability of daily rail service
3. Degree of access to daily scheduled airline service
4. Degree of access to university research facilities
5. Degree of access to college facilities
6. Stock of college level human capital @ region's population(*)
7. Stock of high school level human capital(*)
8. Stocks of community college level human capital(*) (by type of program)

---

6 Rather than separate neighboring county and home county effects to create two variables (as applied earlier by Bergman and Maier), this model follows the traditional method of summing all effects into a single variable for each county, which provides the unit of analysis.

Control Variables
1. Recession year (1982) dummy
2. County development level dummy (highest/lowest thirds)
3. Unit costs of electrical service
4. Manufacturing mix (percent of employment in resource, capital, labor or technology-intensive sectors)

Infrastructure in this model is measured in real facility or service units.[7] Testing several types of infrastructure in regression equations could, as Eberts (1990) observes, present collinearity problems, but real unit-scaling of "lumpy" infrastructure may actually be less likely to produce collinearity than individual dollar-denominated value estimates. Real unit measurement also permits the emphasis to remain on *assessing the nature and relative size of contributions made by alternative infrastructure options* (see also Johansson, 1993). Estimating monetary-valued infrastructure elasticities is less important for this chapter than gaining evidence of what appears to work and the mechanisms through which infrastructure affects productivity, even though one forfeits the comparative assessment of cost-benefit relationships.[8]

2.5   MODEL RESULTS

When using counties as quasi-firms (actually counties represent mini-aggregates of manufacturing firms and their production relations), controls are necessary to adjust for the overall effects on county productivity due to urbanization and agglomeration economies. The standard intercept is therefore augmented with two dummy variables that apply to counties with the highest and lowest levels of urbanization. Moreover, data from these 100 counties were collected in two years, 1982 and 1987. These also require dummy controls, since they measure the trough and peak of the most recent recession.

Overall, Table 2.1 shows that manufacturing in the most urbanized counties does indeed show higher average productivity, precisely as one might expect. Moreover, firms everywhere appear to have lower average productivity in 1982 (-1.41%) than five years later in 1987. Taken together, the county intercepts and controls shown in the top layer permit one to consider the evidence drawn from 200 total observations of the contribution that capital and labor factors make to labor productivity. Manufacturing productivity in all counties is higher with greater capital intensification, as follows: for every 1% increase in capital per worker, output per worker is 0.34% higher. For every 1% increase in labor employed, labor productivity quite logically diminishes (by -0.085%) in every county.

Although the control variable and internal factor parameters happen to be of equal size in all counties, Table 2.1 actually summarizes the *net* effect of a given variable on manufacturing value-added per employee *plus* interaction-term equivalents calculated for different types of counties. This modeling procedure detects whether estimated parameters yield the best overall fit when infrastructure effects are allowed to differ by level of county development.[9] For example, a 1% increase in the availability of child care shows no effect on the average county's labor productivity, but its availability in the most developed counties boosts productivity there by about 0.093% (0.093= 0.00+ [0.093].

---

[7] See Biehl (1993) for a service-based index of infrastructure that permits aggregation of individually estimated service levels. Biehl's standardized service index for each form of infrastructure is constructed similarly to this study's use of potential formulations applied to dichotomous variables: the initial values observed are then spatially standardized by use of distance decay functions.

[8] For summaries of such estimates, see Munnell (1992) and Hakfoort (1996).

[9] Infrastructure variables are interpreted in Table 2.1 if estimated coefficients are significant at the .10 level or better. Quite clearly, not all infrastructure variables measured and tested here have effects on manufacturing productivity.

(See Figure 2.2 for illustration). The net effects of infrastructure in particular types of counties by level of development will be discussed here. (The raw effects derived directly from regression estimates are supplied in Appendix 2.)

The second layer of Table 2.1 includes infrastructure elements[10] that are available only to firms located in each county. From the above example, availability of child care slots permits higher labor productivity, but only in the most urbanized counties. This may indicate that child care provided by state-approved centers in urbanized areas permits its families – actually, their manufacturing workers – to become somewhat more productive (0.093% per 1% increase in child care slots) than families who rely upon these or other arrangements (perhaps extended families or friends) in less urbanized counties. This form of social overhead capital may return added benefits to families everywhere if it can be made available and at reasonable cost.

Table 2.1 Effects of infrastructure variables on productivity

Variables	Effects in average/ other areas	Effects in developed areas	Effects in less developed areas
Intercept	1.400	2.556	1.400
capital/labor	0.337	0.337	0.337
MFG employment	-0.085 #	-0.085 #	0.085 #
SITE-SPECIFIC/LOCALIZED INFRASTRUCTURE			
Local road system	0	-0.229	0
Gaspipe	0.146	0.146	0.146
Child care slots	0	0.093	0
REGIONAL/NETWORK INFRASTRUCTURE			
Air service	0	0	0.123
Rail access (daily)	0	0	-0.116
Interstate system	0.209	-0.014	-0.232
Universities	-0.102	0.094	-0.015 #
Technical CC-FTE	0	0	0.080 #
Occupational CC-FTE	0	0	-0.197
INDUSTRY MIX AND OTHER CONTROL VARIABLES			
Electricity rate	0.492	0.492	0.492
Resource %	3.153	3.153	1.350
Technology %	1.740	1.740	1.740
Capital %	0	0.761	0
Labor %	-0.730	-0.730	1.410
Dummy 1982	-1.410	0	0
Note: Numbers should be interpreted as the percentage of contribution to productivity.			

On the other hand, natural gas service permits overall manufacturing productivity improvements in all counties where it is available. Natural gas as a direct production input or comparatively inexpensive energy source appears to improve manufacturing productivity equally everywhere it is available. The other form of economic overhead capital available locally, the level of service in local road systems, is wholly unrelated to

---

[10] Two other county-specific, networked infrastructure elements were tested, but neither showed significant effects on productivity. These include: water and sewer capacity and digitally switched telephone systems.

manufacturing productivity in all but the most urbanized counties where it appears to exact a penalty (-0.229% per service level) on local firms. The ordinal variable used to measure the service level of local road networks does not permit it to be standardized by cardinal measures of demand or density.[11] Therefore, "high" levels of service actually measure local road systems that have been designed and built to permit dense residential traffic, local shopping, and other service travel. As such, high measured levels may provide no extra service of value to urban manufacturers; this index may, in fact, signal heavy residential usage, urban congestion and decreasing returns to manufacturing. In short, local road levels of service may provide a good proxy for the manufacturing "diseconomies" of urban location.

Layer three consists of several forms of infrastructure that are available within the immediate region, i.e., infrastructure that is not restricted to specific users by network architecture or residence in the particular county where it is located. For example, interstate highway access is afforded by highway interchanges located within a county; a county with interchanges on one interstate system is coded with "1" or "2" if it happens to be served by a second distinct highway system. But nearby county manufacturers lacking internal interchanges are not coded "0" since they may also enjoy access to that network simply by overcoming frictions of distance. These "frictions" discount the value of such access to counties where interstate access is available; frictions are estimated by use of distance decay functions and incorporated in potential variables.[12]

Interstate highway access confers productivity benefits (0.209% for each 1% increase of interstate highway access) for manufacturers, but only in counties that are neither wholly urban nor rural (Figure 2.2). This implies that the benefits of urban adjacency and related services available in these counties allow inexpensive manufacturing sites and labor to be assembled productively when also served by interstate highway access. On the other hand, there is a negligible productivity penalty on manufacturers located within the most urbanized areas that are served by interstate highways (the overall interstate gain of +0.209 is slightly overcome by the urban -0.223% penalty). Rural manufacturers that lack complementary infrastructure and services appear seriously handicapped by their interstate access: rural manufacturing productivity is penalized by -0.232% per 1% increase of interstate highway access. Highway access increases the mobility of workers in those areas. Highly qualified workers are more easily able to commute (or move) to capture better wages in the most productive areas, thereby leaving the less productive behind. The predicted pattern of infrastructure advantage for intermediate regions, posed earlier by Hansen (1965) and Eberts (1990), is reflected in these effects; but the relative rural diasadvantages also reveal the backwash effects of highways observed by Bergman and Maier (1991).

Other forms of transportation infrastructure only show productivity effects on manufacturers in the least developed counties. Strong effects on employment growth and development in metropolitan areas are generally expected from the availability of air service, although these effects are probably mutually causal during periods when unregulated air service levels follow, rather than lead, regional growth.[13] No visible effects of air service on manufacturing productivity are apparent for either urban or nearby counties. These results are consistent with certain earlier findings that reveal

---

[11] Stuart et al. (1989) compiled an ordinal, four-level index of internal accessibility for North Carolina's counties using "...eight variables [that] described system size and urbaness [sic], system condition and quality, and traffic and system density."

[12] For a discussion of how such functions are converted to variables useful in regression models, see Bergman and Maier, 1991.

[13] Further empirical tests by the authors using cross-section data for North Carolina in 1979 and 1984 show no contemporary effects of air service on the growth of privately generated payrolls, although earlier period growth of such payrolls does significantly affect the growth of subsequent period airline service.

strong effects on total growth from air service for the 1300 counties of the southern states of the U.S.A., but no airline service effects of any kind upon manufacturing growth in these same counties (Rosenfeld et al., 1989).

productivity elasticity

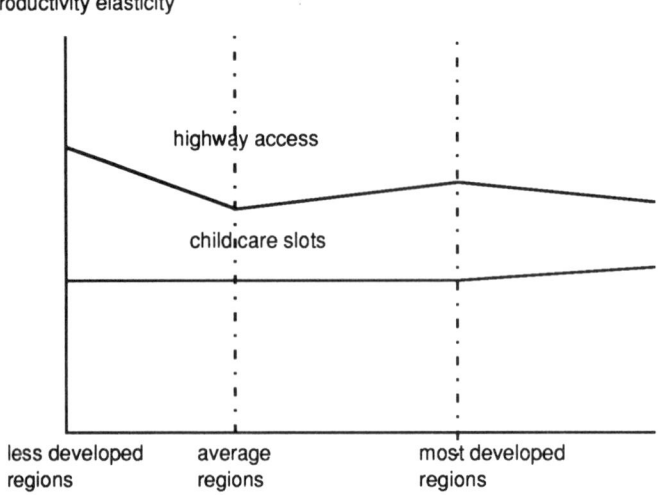

Figure 2.2 Effects differ in different areas

Relative access to nearby scheduled air service helps promote labor productivity (0.123% productivity bonus per 1% increase in access to scheduled air service) in rural manufacturing, while similar access to rail service *penalizes* productivity -0.116% per 1% increase in access to daily rail service. Taken together, these may signal shifts away from weight-intensive production toward value- or information-intensive production in rural manufacturing. However, the long lags in adjusting rail service levels to actual need – as compared with very rapid shifts in deregulated airline service – may also identify rural counties whose earlier industrial structure dissipated more rapidly than the rail service it previously required. This contrast illustrates the unavoidable difficulty of measuring and interpreting the economic significance of fixed infrastructure based on differing vintages and technologies.

Universities that grant PhD degrees can be considered as a source of technological diffusion, either directly through their commercial research and technology development resources or indirectly through their supply of skilled scientists and engineers and their sponsorship of development initiatives, such as research and technology parks. Whatever the mechanisms, it is usually assumed that early product cycle manufacturing, due to its attendant requirements for advanced skills and technology, is more likely to locate in metropolitan areas, near research universities (variable coding convention similar to interstate highways, above), or both to capture these advantages.[14] The industrial structure of other regions that are less dependent upon universities has received little attention, perhaps because such regions are thought to be unaffected. Our results are generally consistent with overall expectations: for every 1% increase in access to universities, manufacturing productivity in *urban* counties increases by 0.094% This urban advantage stands in strong contrast to penalties of -0.015% and -0.102% for rural and other less urban counties, respectively. It indicates that urban manufacturers success-

---

[14] For a thorough discussion of these and related points, see Luger and Goldstein (1991).

fully incorporate university-based advantages into their production, while manufacturers in other counties cannot capitalize on university access – perhaps due to absence of essential producer services – and actually suffer productivity losses. The productivity penalties in more peripheral counties may result from losses of skilled workers and engineers who are drawn from nearby firms to their most urban competitors who can incorporate and reward their skills more effectively.

Two forms of social overhead capital have significant effects on rural manufacturing productivity, although each has opposite effects for different but interesting reasons. In both cases, they are measured as accumulated stocks of local workers who have been trained during the previous seven years in specific programs run by one of North Carolina's 58 Community Colleges. The Community College system offers several different programs of study for recreational purposes, to complete high school equivalency degrees, to prepare for college transfer, and to acquire work-related skills. Not surprisingly, the only significant effects on productivity were associated with work-related training programs, and only in rural counties. For students who enrolled in the 1 or 2 year *technical curricula*, each additional 1% of stock improved rural manufacturing productivity by 0.08%. Considering that technical occupations can be pursued for many non-manufacturing sectors, it is remarkable that accumulated stocks of technical skill were systematically incorporated into manufacturing productivity.

Contrast this advantage with *occupational extension* programs offered by the same Community Colleges. These programs are frequently made available as a business incentive to newly recruited firms that relocate or expand their production. Firms do so on the condition that the state offers "no-cost" training of ready-to-employ workers by using the recruited firm's proprietary techniques, methods and practices. The accumulated stock of workers trained in these programs exact a -0.197% average productivity penalty for each 1% increase in size. This may appear counter-intuitive, but there are logical factors to consider that support the finding. First, these extension programs operate for as few as 30 days and many for no more than 90 days, thereby offering little of long-run use to manufacturers in the absence of continuous skill upgrading. Second, what is taught in this short time is highly specific to particular firms and may not be sufficiently generic to transfer as job skills when workers move between firms. And rural restructuring of manufacturing was intense during this period, causing many workers to lose work permanently or to find work in entirely different firms and industries (Bergman, 1989; Rosenfeld et al. 1989). Third, the firms that dominate rural manufacturing and more frequently claim this incentive are disproportionately labor-intensive. Results from Table 2.1 illustrate the considerable state-wide reductions in productivity associated with labor-intensive firms. Taken together, it is entirely logical that an otherwise useful "training program" that helps generate new jobs and work opportunities for local workers could present a tradeoff by assembling a workforce for low value-added, labor intensive firms. Such firms are, by definition, characterized by low productivity, but their less productive workers do benefit from employment and are clearly better off in the short term.

Additional control variables adjust for industry mix differences among the counties and for important electrical energy cost differentials faced by firms that force them to adopt energy-saving production processes, all of which exert important background effects on observed labor productivity.[15] Consistent with the findings of World Bank and other studies, labor productivity was greater by 0.492% in every county where each 1%

---

[15] As can be seen from the segmented modelling results in Table 2.2, the inclusion of these controls in model 5 had modest effects on the relatively stable infrastructure variables. Larger effects occurred with the capital/labor ratio (all counties from 0.78 to 0.34; urban counties from 0.56 to 0), the recession dummy (4.21 to 1.73), and the intercepts (all counties from -.429 to 0; urban counties from 3.15 to 0.54). When the county-type intercepts were first added in model 2, the original labor factor coefficient dropped from 0.11 to insignificance; it later became negatively, and more logically, significant (-0.07) in model 5 as additional controls were added.

of higher electrical costs stimulated the adoption of newer or more efficient production techniques. On the matter of industry mix, the controls worked as expected such that 1% of additional:
1. technology-intensive manufacturing boosts average productivity 1.74% everywhere;
2. resource-intensive manufacturing boosts average productivity 1.35 % in rural counties and 3.15% in all other counties;
3. capital-intensive manufacturing boosts average productivity 0.76% in the most urban counties alone;
4. labor-intensive manufacturing penalizes average productivity -0.73% in every non-rural county, but boosts it by 1.41% in rural counties.

The controls do appear to provide useful adjustments when estimating regional production functions for county aggregates of manufacturing firms. Moreover, the coefficients reflect reasonable industry mix and energy cost effects that are consistent with other findings.

2.6   CONCLUSIONS

Taken together, the results permit several overall conclusions; some concern technical insights about the empirical estimation of regional production functions, others assess the benefits of local vs. regional infrastructure to manufacturers operating in counties at different development levels, while still other conclusions permit a better understanding of the unexpected backwash and tradeoff effects of infrastructure. First, the model demonstrates that reasonable production relations can be simulated and effects of infrastructure estimated by using aggregate manufacturing and infrastructure data from counties, but only if adequate control variables are used to account for lack of uniformity among these units of observation. Table 2.2 demonstrates the risks of using an underspecified regional production function and illustrates the markedly different conclusions one could reach in the absence of fuller specification and suitable controls.

   The open question of how productivity depends upon the development level of industrialized economies in which manufacturing firms are located, and infrastructure is available, can be answered. First, even after infrastructure and other factors are accounted for, overall average labor productivity is higher in the most highly urbanized counties, thereby extending further support for the well-established role of agglomeration economies. Beyond this overall productivity effect, various types of infrastructure have markedly distinct effects in counties at different development levels. Some form of economic infrastructure capital (EOC) is important for all types of counties, but the productivity effects of social overhead capital (SOC) arise only in certain types of counties (child care only in urban counties; community college graduates only in rural counties). As a general pattern, *only those manufacturers in the heavily urbanized counties are affected by every local, site-confined infrastructure*, while *only manufacturers in the most rural counties are affected by every regionally accessible infrastructure*. Productivity effects that deviate from this general pattern are limited to the cases of natural gas service (local) and interstate highways and universities (regional).

   Locally accessible infrastructure is, perhaps, better able to exert influence on manufacturing productivity in the presence of other urban conditions such as unmeasured public services, additional urbanization and agglomeration effects or congestion pricing (e.g., internal roads). On the other hand, regionally accessible infrastructure is relatively invariant and of roughly equal value to manufacturers in all non-rural counties and therefore shows no systematic effect. But since rural areas are far more *unevenly* served by regionally accessible infrastructure, the variance of its effects are more readily measured by the estimation procedures used here. The complexity of how and where infrastructure of many different kinds stimulates productivity reveals more than typical

Table 2.2 Comparison of model specifications

VARIABLES	DVP LEVELS	MODEL 1	MODEL 2	MODEL 3	MODEL 4	MODEL 5
Intercept	A	1.04 ***	0.27	0.18	0.32	1.40 **
	H		2.36 **	2.10 **	3.15 **	1.15
	L		0.11	-0.32	-0.97	-0.54
K/L ratio	A	0.70 ***	0.95 ***	0.91 ***	0.78 ***	0.34 *
	H		-0.64 ***	-0.66 ***	-0.56 **	-0.16
	L		-0.09	-0.09	-0.01	-0.19
Labor input	A	0.11 ***	-0.001	-0.03	-0.02	-0.08 #
	H		0.08	0.03	0.06	0.03
	L		0.09	0.02	0.07	0.04
Dummy 1982	A	-0.36 ***	-0.30 ***	-0.23 *	-0.40 ***	-0.41 ***
	H		-0.12	-0.03	0.02	0
	L		-0.02	0.09	0.40*	0
Local road system	A			-0.07	0.04	0
	H			-0.16	-0.23	-0.23 ***
	L			0.19	0.30	-0.16
Gaspipe	A			0.08	0.19 *	0.15 **
	H			0.03	-0.20	0
	L			-0.001	-0.04	0
Child care	A			0.05	0.06	0
	H			0.09	0.04	0.09 **
	L			0.07	-0.01	0
Air transportation	A				-0.16 *	0
	H				0.19 *	0
	L				0.22 ***	0.12 ***
Interstate highway	A				0.20 **	0.21 ***
	H				-0.28 **	-0.22 **
	L				-0.44	-0.44 *
Daily rail access	A				0.10	0
	H				-0.01	0
	L				-0.24 **	-0.12 ***
University access	A				-0.09 *	-0.10 ***
	H				0.17 ***	0.19 ***
	L				-0.15	-0.12 #
Technical community college FTE	A				-0.01	0
	H				-0.004	0
	L				0.15	0.08#
Occupational community college FTE	A				-0.03	0
	H				-0.01	0
	L				-0.12	-0.20**
% resource intensive industry	A					3.15 ***
	H					-1.80 *
	L					0
% technology intensive industry	A					1.74 ***
	H					0
	L					0
% of capital intensive industry	A					0
	H					0.76**
	L					0
% of labor intensive industry	A					-0.73 ***
	H					0
	L					2.14***
Electricity rate	A					0.53 ***
	H					0
	L					0

Notes to Table 2.2: Model (1): Inputs & business cycle variables only, R^2=.45; (2): development levels controlled, R^2=.51; (3) Adding localized infrastructure variables, R^2=.56; (4): Adding regional infrastructure variable, R^2=65; (5): Adding industry mix and utility rate, R^2=.77. Development (DVP) levels: A = Average, H = High, L = Low.

conclusions about justifiable volumes of additional public investment in "general" infrastructure.

But more can also be concluded about the consequences of infrastructure effects that reduce rather than stimulate manufacturing productivity in certain regions. As we have seen in the cases of interstate highways and research universities, the productivity of rural manufacturing exposed to these common forms of infrastructure is reduced, perhaps as a form of "backwash" described at length in other works (Bergman and Maier, 1991). This finding is a logical outcome of Hansen's (1965) general point that links development levels with infrastructure effects, but goes further to show unintended consequences of the "spatial reach" some infrastructure exerts to reduce productivity in certain neighboring locales. At minimum, provision of infrastructure should be undertaken with its spatial consequences firmly in mind. Even within the same type county, seemingly similar forms of infrastructure can have opposite effects. As the community college evidence demonstrates, programs established to yield important benefits can produce outcomes that conflict with the attainment of other benefits. This simple illustration demonstrates the risks of summing monetary values (or service level indices) for a variety of infrastructure programs on the assumption of simple additivity: not all forms of infrastructure accomplish the goals assumed and some actually subtract from the intended objective.

APPENDIX 1 Descriptive statistics of variables

VARIABLES (*: plus potential)	Minimum	Maximum	Mean	Std. Dev
VA/labor, 1982	9.6875	373.5031	33.8877	37.4730
VA/labor, 1987	10.8000	331.4286	50.4793	37.0444
K/labor, 1982	10.73	451.72	43.22	45.80
K/labor, 1987	8.93	149.26	40.22	16.42
MFG employment, 1982	20	56,800	7,965	10.5015
MFG employment, 1987	20	56,900	8,441	11.0585
Air service (*), 1981	0	70.5113	2.9635	8.2808
Air service (*), 1985	0	159.7704	5.5326	18.1434
Rail access (*), 1981	0.0705	1.2682	0.9574	0.4358
Rail access (*), 1985	0.0697	1.2678	0.9470	0.4476
Local road system, 1985	1	4	2.3100	0.9816
Interstate system, 1985	1	6	2.1900	1.6496
Gas service, 1986	0	1	0.56	0.4989
Electricity rate, 1989	1.21	2.7500	2.4645	0.5157
Universities (*), 1987	0.0036	1.0722	0.0899	0.2624
Technical CC-FTE (*), 1982	0.3669	19879	587	2057
Technical CC-FTE (*), 1987	144	48756	2581	3677
Occupational CC-FTE (*), 1982	7	17199	2344	2375
Occupational CC-FTE (*), 1987	314	48756	5479	5804
Child care slots, 1985	0	2966	207	394
Child care slots, 1990	0	7482	548	924
Capital, 1982	2.54	2870.05	311.76	463.17
Capital, 1987	1.39	3896.94	365.22	601.12
Value added, 1982	0.4464	4035.7000	286.5051	519.3844
Value added, 1987	1.0000	5469.7000	476.4102	782.7274
Resource %, 1984	0	0.4879	0.0668	0.0678
Capital %, 1984	0	0.4986	0.1098	0.1069
Technology %, 1984	0	0.2027	0.0405	0.0480
Labor %, 1984	0	0.4815	0.1427	0.1131
Recession dummy, 1982	0	1	0.5	0.5

APPENDIX 2 Statistical results of parameter estimation

VARIABLES	Effects in average/ other areas		Difference for developed areas		Difference for less developed areas	
Intercept	1.400	(2.06) **	1.155	(1.52) #	-0.539	(0.59)
Capital/labor	0.337	(1.84) *	-0.156	(0.79)	0.187	(0.89)
MFG employment	-0.085	(1.28) #	0.030	(0.40)	0.041	(0.52)
SITE-SPECIFIC/LOCALIZED INFRASTRUCTURE						
Local road system	0		-0.229	(2.50)***	0.164	(1.14)
Gaspipe	0.146	(2.39) **	0		0	
Child care slots	0		0.093	(2.32)**	0	
REGIONAL/NETWORK INFRASTRUCTURE						
Air service	0		0		0.123	(4.12) ***
Rail access (daily)	0		0		-0.116	(2.51) ***
Interstate system	0.209	(2.58) ***	-0.223	(2.23) **	-0.441	(1.97) **
Universities	-0.102	(2.70) ***	0.196	(4.37) ***	-0.139	(1.63) #
Technical CC-FTE	0		0		0.080	(1.40) #
Occupational CC-FTE	0		0		-0.197	(2.05) **
INDUSTRY MIX AND OTHER CONTROL VARIABLES						
Electricity rate	0.492	(4.32) ***	0		0	
Resource %	3.153	(7.35) ***	0		-1.803	(1.91) *
Technology %	1.740	(3.39) ***	0		0	
Capital %	0		0.761	(2.17) **	0	
Labor %	-0.730	(2.58) ***	0		2.140	(4.62) ***
Dummy 1982	-0.410	(7.65) ***	0		0	

N=200, R-square=0.7664, Adj. R-square=0.7249
Numbers in parentheses are absolute values of *t*-statistics.
*** significant at 0.01 level,
** significant at 0.05 level,
* significant at 0.10 level,
\# close to 0.10 level (accepting null hypothesis likely involves Type-II error)
Parameters should be interpreted as percentage of contribution to productivity.

APPENDIX 3 Variable constructs and data sources

VARIABLES	MEASUREMENT	DATA SOURCE
Labor productivity, 1982, 1987	Value added per manufacturing employee in 1987 prices. Value added and employment data are from the same source.	Census of Manufactures, 1982, 1987, U.S. Department of Commerce, Bureau of Census
Capital, 1982, 1987	Capital stock of manufacturing industry. County values are obtained in the following way: Ratios of capital stock to personal income generated in 20 2-digit manufacturing industries are calculated at the national level. These ratios are then multiplied by county level personal income generated in the 20 sectors. Those sectors' capital stock is summed as county manufacturing capital. More detailed sector decomposition would improve the accuracy of calibration, but missing information on the county level made it impossible. Sensitivity tests using estimates and known levels of capital values subject to N.C. taxes in 60 of 100 counties confirm the overall reliability of this method.	*Fixed Reproducible Tangible Wealth in the United States*, U.S. Department of Commerce, Bureau of Economic Analysis
Air service, 1980, 1985	Number of commercial operations plus potentials, for calculation of potentials, see Bergman and Maier, 1992.	*National Plan of Integrated Airport Systems (NPIAS)*.
Rail access, 1981, 1985	Dummy variable for rail service (or potentials).	See Bergman and Maier, 1992
Local road system	Rank order of local road accessibility.	Bergman and Maier, 1992
Interstate System	Rank order of interstate highway accessibility.	Bergman and Maier, 1992
Telecomm, 1981, 1986	Dummy variable for availability of digital dialing services.	Bergman and Maier, 1992
Gaspipe, 1986	Dummy variable for availability of gas service.	Bergman and Maier, 1992
Electricity rate, 1989	Use adjusted index of base rates.	Bergman and Maier, 1992
University	Dummy variable for presence of university granting Ph.D degrees, plus potentials.	Bergman and Maier, 1992
College years	Total years of college education of population 25 years or older	U.S. Department of Commerce, Bureau of Census, *Census of population,* 1980, and Bergman and Maier, 1992
Technical CC-FTE	Enrollment in community college technical training program, full time equivalent	Bergman and Maier, 1992
Occupational CC-FTE	Enrollment in community college occupational extension program, full time equivalent	Bergman and Maier, 1992
High school years	Total years of high school education of the population, 25 years or older, without higher education	U.S. Department of Commerce, Bureau of Census, *Census of population*, 1980
Child care slots, 1985, 1990	Daycare slots approved for purchase17	Dept. of Human Resources Services, North Carolina

Resource %, 1984	Percent of resource intensive industry employment of all employees in a county	Bergman and Maier, 1992
Technology %, 1984	Percent of technology intensive industry employment of all employees in a county	Bergman and Maier, 1992
Capital %, 1984	Percent of capital intensive industry employment of all employees in a county	Bergman and Maier, 1992
Labor %, 1984	Percent of labor intensive industry employment of all employees in a county	Bergman and Maier, 1992

REFERENCES

Bergman, E., 1989, Industrial Transition Paths, Final Report to U.S. Economic Development Administration, U.N.C. Institute for Economic Development, Chapel Hill.

Bergman, E. and G. Maier, 1991, "Spread and Backwash in the Spatial Diffusion of Development", in E. Bergman, G. Maier and F. Toedtling (eds.), *Regions Reconsidered,* Cassel Books, London.

Bergman, E. and G. Maier, 1992, Economic Development in North Carolina Counties, Storyboard (IBM) electronic report prepared by UNC Institute for Economic Development for the N.C. Rural Economic Development Center, Raleigh.

Bergman, E., G. Maier and F. Toedtling (eds.), 1991, *Regions Reconsidered*, Cassell Books, London.

Bergman, E. and S. Ke, forthcoming, "Supplier Certification and Asset-Specific Investment in Computer and Electronic Sectors", U.N.C. Institute for Economic Development, Chapel Hill.

Biehl, D., 1995, "The Role of Infrastructure in Regional Development", in R.W. Vickerman (ed.), *Infrastructure and Regional Development*, Pion, London.

Coase, R. H., 1937, "The Nature of the Firm", *Economica*, 4:386-405.

Costa, J., R. Ellson and R. Martin, 1987, "Public Capital, Regional Output, and Development: Some Empirical Evidence", *Journal of Regional Science*, Vol. 27, 3:419-436.

Duffy-Deno, K. and R. Eberts, 1991, "Public Infrastructure and Regional Economic Development: A Simultaneous Equations Approach", *Journal of Urban Economics*, 30:329-343.

Eberts, R., 1990, "Public Infrastructure and Regional Economic Development", *Economic Review,* 26:15-27

Hakfoort, J., 1996, "Public Capital, Private Sector Productivity and Economic Growth: A Macroeconomic Perspective", Ch. 5, this volume.

Hansen, N., 1965, "Unbalanced Growth and Regional Development", *Western Economic Journal*, 4:3-14.

Hoch, I. 1958, "Simultaneous Equations Bias in the Context of the Cobb-Douglas Production Function", *Econometrica*, 26:566-578.

Johansson, B, 1993, "Infrastructure, Accessibility, and Economic Development", *International Journal of Transportation Economics*, Vol. XX, 2:131-156.

Johansson, B. and C. Karlsson, 1991, "Technology Development and Regional Infrastructure", draft presented at the 38th NARSA-meeting in New Orleans.

Looney R. and P. Frederiksen, 1981, "The Regional Impact of Infrastructure in Mexico", *Regional Studies*, Vol. 15, 4:285-296.

Luger, M. I. and H. A. Goldstein, 1991, *Technology in the Garden: Research Parks and Regional Economic Development*, UNC Press, Chapel Hill.

Mera, K., 1973, "Regional Production Functions and Social Overhead Capital: An Analysis of the Japanese Case", *Regional and Urban Economics*, Vol. 3, 2:157-186.

Moomaw, R. and M. Williams, 1991, "Total Factor Productivity Growth in Manufacturing: Further Evidence from the States", *Journal of Regional Science*, 31:17-34.

Morrison, C. J., 1993, *A Microeconomic Approach to the Measurement of Economic Performance*, Springer-Verlag, New York.

Munnell, A., 1992, "Policy Watch: Infrastructure Investment and Economic Growth", *Journal of Economic Perspectives*, Vol. 6, 4:189-198.

Putnam, R., 1992, *Making Democracy Work: Civic Traditions in Modern Italy*, Princeton University Press, Princeton.

Rietveld, P., 1989, "Infrastructure and Regional Development", *The Annals of Regional Science*, 23:255-274.

Rosenfeld, S. A., E. M. Bergman and S. Rubin, 1989, "Making Connections: After the Factories Revisited", Research Triangle Park: Southern Growth Policies Board.

Stuart, A. W., D. T. Hartgen, W. A. Walcott and J. W. Clay, 1989, "Classification of North Carolina Counties", Transportation Publication Report No. 15, UNC-Charlotte, NC.

Sun, D., 1992, "A Production Function Approach to Regional Economic Development", paper presented in Southern Regional Science Association Annual Conference.

Williams, M. and R. Moomaw, 1989, "Capital and Labor Efficiencies: A Regional Analysis", *Urban Studies*, 26:573-585.

Williamson, O., 1975, *Markets and Hierarchies: Analysis and Anti-Trust Implications: A Study in the Economics of Internal Organization*, Free Press, New York.

Williamson, O., 1979, "Transaction-Cost Economics: The Governance and Contractual Relations", *Journal of Law and Economics*, 22:233-261.

CHAPTER 3

Assessing the Role of Infrastructure in France by Means of Regionally Estimated Production Functions

Rémy Prud'homme
Université de Paris XII

3.1 INTRODUCTION

A number of studies have attempted to utilize production functions to estimate the contribution of infrastructure to economic development. They postulate a relationship of the following type:

$$Y = f(L, K, J)$$

in which Y stands for output, for the entire economy or for a specific sector, for a given year; L for labor; K for the stock of private capital at the beginning of the year; and J for the stock of public capital, i.e., for infrastructure, also at the beginning of the year.

These studies, which are reviewed in Quinet (1992), Bell and McGuire (1992) and Munnell (1992), can be divided into two groups. A first group consists of studies that have tried to estimate the contribution of J (and of the other factors of production) on the basis of time series for a given economy. They include the well-known studies of Aschauer (1989) and Munnell (1990a). A second group consists of studies that utilize data pertaining to different regions or countries to estimate the parameters of the production function. They include the pioneering work of Mera (1973), and more recently studies by Biehl (1986), Costa et al. (1987) and Munnell (1990b).

No such studies have been conducted for the case of France. Navarre and Prud'homme (1984) did attempt to relate indicators of infrastructure endowment by region to indicators of economic performance by region, but the lack of data on the stock of private capital by region prevented them from utilizing production functions. This chapter is a modest attempt to fill this gap.

For administrative purposes, France is divided into 22 regions. Two are excluded from the present analysis: Corsica, which is too small (about 150,000 inhabitants) and for which data is notoriously unreliable; and the Ile de France (Paris) region, which is too specific and might introduce undesired economies of scale effects in the analysis. We are therefore left with 20 regions quite different in terms of population (from about 700,000 inh. to 5 million inh.) and area, but also in terms of output, labor force, and capital endowment. The analysis is conducted for 1988. It is also conducted for the 1981-88 period. During this period, economic development in France was modest. It was accompanied by increases in the stock of private capital and in the stock of infrastructure, but not by an increase in the labor force, which remained virtually at the same level during these years.

3.2   THE MODELS

The models utilized to establish a causal relationship between infrastructure and economic output are illustrated by Figure 3.1.

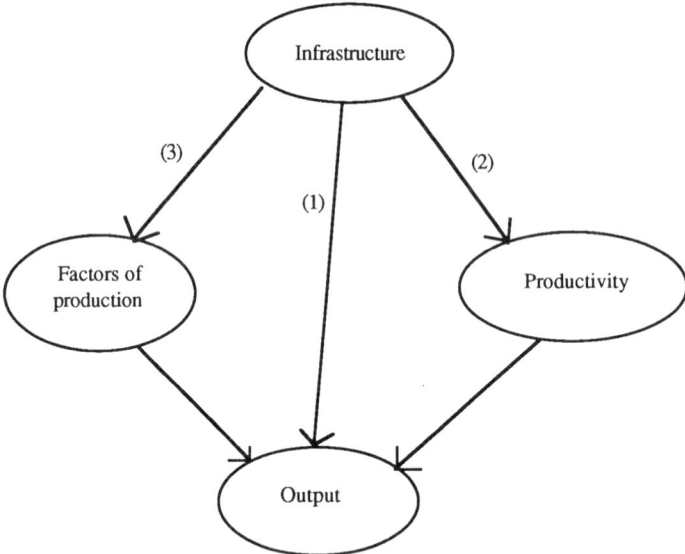

Figure 3.1 Causal relationships

One can postulate that the stock of infrastructure (J) of a region – together with the stock of private capital (K) and the labor force (L) of the region – is a determinant of the output (Y) of the region:

$$Y = f(L, K, J).$$

It can also be argued that what is likely to play a role is the quantity and quality of public services, which are functions of the stock of infrastructure (J), but also of the labor force employed in the public sector (F, for functionaries). The previous relationship can therefore be enriched, and becomes:

$$Y = f(L, K, J, F).$$

It can also be observed that infrastructure serves at the same time people/enterprises *and* *space* (S). Consider two regions that are identical in terms of population, private capital, labor force and stock of infrastructure, but very different in terms of size, with region A several times larger than region B. It is intuitively obvious that region A will be less well "serviced" than region B – except in the unlikely case in which all of the people and activities of region A are located in one corner of region A that is the size of region B. In general, therefore, the contribution of infrastructure to output will be greater in region B than in region A. There are several ways of taking this spatial effect into consideration. One, suggested and utilized in Biehl (1986), introduced a distinction between "point infrastructures" (such as schools), which could be related to population, and "network infrastructures" (such as roads), which should be related to area. Another, which will be utilized here, tries to relate output per capita (Y/P) to the standard production factors per capita (L/P, K/P), to infrastructure per capita (J/P) and also to infrastructure per square km (J/S), per stock of capital (J/K) or per worker (J/L), or to infrastructure per a combination of space and a relevant variable X (J/(aX+bS)). X can be the population P, but also the labor force L or the stock of capital K:

$$Y/P = f\ (L/P,\ K/P,\ J/P\ \text{or}\ J/S\ \text{or}\ J/K\ \text{or}\ J/L)$$
$$Y/P = f\ (L/P,\ K/P,\ J/(aX+bS)).$$

Such relationships can be useful to assess and measure the contribution of infrastructure to economic development. But they do not contribute much to explaining this potential contribution. A good infrastructure endowment can contribute to economic development in two ways. First, it can increase the productivity of the standard factors of production. Second, it can attract these relatively mobile factors of production. Two different sets of models can be developed to capture these two distinct effects.

First, we can try and relate labor (or capital) productivity to the stock of infrastructure per unit of labor (or capital), and/or to the stock of infrastructure per area, or to the stock of infrastructure per a combination of area and a relevant variable X (such as labor or capital):

$$Y/L\ = f\ (K/L,\ J/L,\ J/S)$$
$$Y/L\ = f\ (K/L,\ J/(aX+bS))$$
$$Y/K\ = f\ (L/K,\ J/K,\ J/S)$$
$$Y/K\ = f\ (L/K,\ K/(aX+bS)).$$

To assess the relationship between infrastructure and the mobility of factors, we can try to relate relative increases in the stock of private capital ($\Delta K/K81$ or $\Delta K/P81$) and in the labor force ($\Delta L/L81$ or $\Delta L/P81$) during a given period to the stock of infrastructure at the beginning of the period relative to population, or to capital, or to area, or to a combination of these variables (J81/P81 or J81/K81 or J81/(aX+bS)) or to the relative increase in the stock of infrastructure ($\Delta J/J81$) during the same period, and to other factors such as the productivity of capital (Y81/K81) or of labor (Y81/L81) at the beginning of the period:

$$\Delta K/K81\ = f\ (J81/P81\ \text{or}\ J81/(aX+bS),\ \Delta J/P81,\ Y81/K81)$$
$$\Delta L/L81\ = f\ (J81/P81,\ \Delta J/P81,\ Y81/L81).$$

It might be desirable to "consolidate" the two relationships into a reduced form model. This, however is made very difficult by the fact that they do not refer to similar time frames. The productivity equation refers to 1988. The factors mobility equation refers to 1981 and to what happened in the 1981-88 period. In addition, as will be seen, only one of the two relationships appears to be significant.

A possible weakness of regionally-estimated production functions is that interregional differences in input prices could distort findings. It is interesting to note that, in the case of France, particularly when the Paris region is excluded from the analysis, such differences in labor or in capital costs are likely to be small – much smaller than in the USA.

3.3   DATA

Such models are simple and straightforward. If they are not more often implemented, it is because the data required to implement them is not readily available, and has to be developed.

In the case of France, there are no problems with regional output figures, which are easily available and reasonably reliable. The concept of regional output utilized here excludes agriculture and non-profit activities. The exclusion of agriculture and of non-profit activities can be justified by the argument that infrastructure endowment does not impact upon agricultural or non-profit sector output the way it does upon industrial and service output. But this exclusion is explained by the fact that data on the stock of private capital by region can only be obtained for the industrial and service sectors, not for agriculture nor for non-profit activities.

Neither are there problems with data on the labor force by region. It goes without saying that data on the labor force utilized refer to the labor force outside agriculture and non-profit sectors.

Difficulties begin with data on the stock of private capital (in the non agricultural and non not-for profit sectors) by region. The figures are estimated for *France as a whole* by INSEE, the Statistical Office, and are reliable. In addition, there is a local tax (called *taxe professionelle*) which is a business tax assessed on the wages paid and on the stock of capital utilized by each establishment. Tax assessment is conducted for local governments by the Ministry of Finance in a uniform fashion throughout the country. We obtained (from the Ministry of Finance) unpublished data on the capital share of the tax base *by region*, and utilized this data to allocate the nationally estimated stock of capital. Agricultural enterprises and non-profit organizations are excluded from the tax. This is why we could not figure out the capital stock of these enterprises, and decided to exclude them from the entire analysis. The assessed value of the capital of enterprises (for *taxe professionelle* purposes) may not be a very good estimator of the effective value of this capital. But there are no reasons to think that it could introduce a bias in the interregional distribution of the stock of capital, which is what matters for our purpose. Our data for K is therefore likely to be reasonably accurate.

Data on public infrastructure is more difficult to produce. We utilized published data on yearly public investments by region for the period 1971-1989, for both central government investments in the various regions, and sub-national governments investments. These figures were deflated for price increases, then depreciated at various rates, and added. We verified that utilizing a 1%, 2% or 5% rate of depreciation did not matter much, and kept the figures obtained with a 2% rate. The figures thus obtained were used to allocate regionally a total amount of infrastructure stock, which has been estimated for France as a whole by INSEE.

There is one weakness in this procedure. It assumes that the stock of infrastructure that existed in 1971 in each region is proportional to the cumulated investments in each region. There are reasons to doubt this assumption. More investment must have been made in the regions that grew faster. As a result we overestimate the 1971 stock of capital in these regions, and therefore the 1988 stock. The magnitude of this bias is difficult to assess, but may not be immense. First, at least in terms of population, the relative importance of the various French regions did not change much over the period considered. Then, the 1971 stock of public capital must, to a certain (and theoretically difficult to determine) extent, be depreciated: even at a low 2% rate, it is reduced by nearly 40% 18 years later. And it is known that many elements of the stock of infrastructure are relatively new in France. In the case of bridges, for instance, it has been shown (Llanos, 1992) that more bridges (in terms of square meters) have been built in this period than existed in 1971. However, our proxy for the stock of infrastructure can also be taken for what it is: cumulated public investments over the 1971-88 period.

Production and productivity will then be said to be explained by the stock of private capital and recent (1981-88) infrastructures.

As indicated in Section 3.2 above, the stock of infrastructure J was related not only to the population, private capital, labor force and the surface of each region, but also to a combination of surface and other variables X, i.e. to a*X+b*S. How were a and b selected? Several combinations were utilized. In one, a was taken equal to 1 and b such that:

$$b*\Sigma S = \Sigma X$$

which yielded P + 100*S for the combination of surface and population, L + 40*S for the combination of surface and labor force, and K + 6.2*S for the combination of surface and capital. Another explanatory variable was also created with P + 200*S. Regression analysis was also utilized, with a and b the calculated coefficients of the following equations:

$$J = a*X + b*S + c,$$

which yielded 25*P + 93*S, 86*L + 92*S, and 0.31*K + 505*S.

Table 3.1 indicates the distribution of some of the variables utilized and gives the orders of magnitude of the relevant variables. It shows, for instance, that the stock of infrastructure represents about half the stock of private capital, on average, and that the capital-output ratio is (always on average) close to 1.5 if only private capital is considered and to 2.1 if both private and public capital are considered. It also shows that the variance of the variables used is reasonably large, although the variance of the most interesting variable, labor productivity, is the smallest.

Table 3.1 Distribution of relevant variables, 1988

	Min	Max	Mean	Standard err.	Dispersion
Y (Output, in M Francs)	23,459	242,534	84,104	50,965	0.585
K (Capital, in M Francs)	28,747	395,584	126,803	81,107	0.639
J (Infrastructure, in M Francs)	22,481	138,460	55,999	29,582	0.528
L (Labor force, '000)	181	1917	596	328	0.551
F (Civil servants, '000)	65	402	177	89	0.5
P (Population, '000)	727	5275	226	1140	0.504
S (Area, in Km2)	8,280	45,348	36,164	10,710	0.409
Y/P (Output per capita)	32.282	46.981	37.769	4.568	0.121
K/P (Capital per capita)	38.204	81.778	54.799	11.988	0.218
J/P (Infras. per capita)	20.667	33.916	24.850	3	0.121
L/P (Activity rate)	0.221	0.308	0.262	0.021	0.08
Y/L (Labor productivity)	129	162	144	8.749	0.06
K/L (Capital per worker)	150	284	207	34	0.162
J/L (Infras. per worker)	74.6	133.1	95.4	14.9	0.156
Y/K (Capital productivity)	0.565	0.864	0.705	0.089	0.126
J/K (Infras. per unit of capital)	0.292	0.782	0.478	0.137	0.286
J/(P+100S)	7.760	17.801	11.304	2.788	0.246
J/(L+40S)	21.768	63.845	33.956	10.299	0.303
J/(K+6.2S)	0.124	0.308	0.191	0.046	0.24

3.4   FINDINGS

The models sketched above have been estimated by means of regression analysis. Both logarithmic and linear forms have been used; but only the results of logarithmic forms are reported here. Table 3.2 tries to relate (non merchant, non agricultural) output to production factors, including infrastructure. Table 3.3 does the same thing for per capita output.

Table 3.2 Output and infrastructure, 1988

| | Explanatory variables | | | | | |
	L	K	J	F	Interval	R2
Dependent variable						
Y	0.804	0.228	0.011	-	-2.12	0.995
	(5.882)	(3.098)	(0.131)		(-5.263)	
Y	0.770	0.237	-0.006	0.043	-1.86	0.995
	(4.554)	(2.974)	(-0.066)	(0.359)	(-1.96)	

Note: the figures in parentheses are the t statistics; coefficients (and t statistics) in bold type are significant at the 1% level.

Table 3.2 shows no influence whatsoever of infrastructure on output. Introducing the number of civil servants in the regression does not add anything. For this reason, F was ignored in the rest of the analysis.

Table 3.3 Output per capita and infrastructure, 1988

| | Explanatory variables | | | | | | | | |
	L/P	K/P	J/P	J/S	J/(P+100S)	J/(L+40S)	J/(K+6.2*S)	Interval	R2
Dependent variable									
Y/P	0.716	0.256	-0.012					3.663	0.863
	(3.615)	(3.06)	(-0.109)					(4.849)	
Y/P	0.822	0.119		**0.044**				3.905	0.890
	(4.367)	(2.622)		**(1.966)**				(7.584)	
Y/P	0.796	0.214			**0.087**			3.031	0.891
	(4.296)	(2.939)			**(2.015)**			(5.349)	
Y/P	0.839	0.207				**0.075**		3.669	0.891
	(4.449)	(2.803)				**(2.029)**		(7.488)	
Y/P	0.811	0.246					**0.086**	3.880	0.892
	(4.372)	(3.363)					**(2.055)**	(7.676)	

Note: the figures in parentheses are the t statistics; coefficients (and t statistics) in bold type are significant at the 1% level.

Table 3.3 is more encouraging, and yields an interesting finding. Infrastructure per capita (as could be implied from Table 3.1) is not a determinant of output per capita. But infrastructure per square km is, at a 3% threshold. So is infrastructure related to a combination of space and population, space and labor or space and capital? The results obtained with the values of a and b calculated by regression analysis are not reported here because they are not significant.

The elasticity of output to infrastructure appears to be about 0.08. Taking into account the absolute values of the stock of capital and of the output, this means that an addition of 100 F. to the stock of infrastructure leads to an increase of about 12 F. in terms of output. Similarly, an elasticity of output to private capital of about 0.21 means that an addition of 100 F. to the stock of private capital leads to an increase of about 14 F. in terms of output. The marginal productivity of infrastructure would therefore appear to be comparable to, or slightly lower than, that of private capital in today's France.

These figures, which can be interpreted as rates of return on investment, are plausible. 14% is a reasonable rate of return for private investment, very much in line with what is known on the subject. 12% for public investment is reassuring. In France, public investments by the central government are not supposed to be undertaken when they exhibit a projected rate of return lower than 10%. But it could be feared that projections do not always materialize, or that some projects with lower rates of return are undertaken for political reasons, or that local government investments are not subjected to this rigorous test. Indeed, many reports and publications have shown, for limited cases, that public money has been occasionally wasted. Our findings suggest that such cases cannot and should not be generalized. They appear to be the exception rather than the rule. The average rate of return of infrastructure is about as high as that of private investment. Even if infrastructure were financed at the expense of private capital – a very strong and unlikely assumption – public investment would not reduce output in France today.

It can even be argued that the 12% rate on public investment is in fact probably higher than the 14% rate on private investment, for three reasons. One is that the great uncertainty about the quality of our data on infrastructure by region tends to lower the estimated coefficients for infrastructure in the regression equations, and therefore the calculated rate of return. A second reason is that our analysis ignores the spillover effects. It only captures the impacts of the stock of infrastructure in region i on the output of region i, thus neglecting the impacts on other, particularly adjacent, regions. Many US studies have shown that the smaller the units of analysis, the lower the elacticities calculated. A third reason is quite obvious: public investments are not solely undertaken to increase output, they also aim at improving safety, at protecting the environment, or at rendering unpriced services to households. As is well known, the social rate of return is higher than the economic rate of return, and is the relevant rate to be considered in appraising public investments. For all these reasons, 12% is an underestimation and should be translated into higher figures: 15% or 16% appear to be conservative estimates.

Table 3.4 relates labor productivity and capital productivity to infrastructure. It confirms some of the findings of Tables 3.2 and 3.3. Infrastructure per capita explains neither labor nor capital productivity. What matters is infrastructure per square km, which is significant at a 3% threshold in the case of labor productivity, and, even more clearly, infrastructure per a combination of area and population, area and capital, or area and labor. The most significants results are obtained for labor productivity. The elasticity of labor productivity relative to infrastructure is again around 0.08.

There remains the question of whether infrastructure attracts production factors. Table 3.5 attempts to provide an answer.

This answer happens to be negative. The only explanatory variable that appears to be significant is the productivity of capital at the beginning of the period: investments locate preferentially where Y/K81 is highest. Infrastructure in 1981, however, whether related to the initial stock of private capital or to combinations of population and space or of capital and space, is never significant. Nor is the relative increase in the stock of infrastructure. This finding must be taken with great caution. First, the data used are fragile. Estimates of the stock of infrastructure in 1981, in particular, are not very reliable. As explained earlier, estimates of the stock of infrastructure are based on the sum of yearly public investments since 1971; this might be acceptable to figure out the accumulated stock in 1988; but it is probably less acceptable to figure out the accumulated stock in 1981. Second, the models used are probably too simplistic to fully explain the regional location of investments in the 1981-88 period. This admittedly weak finding would have (if it were confirmed) one interesting implication. It would mean that the relationship between infrastructure and output is due to the relationship between infrastructure and productivity, not to the relationship between infrastructure and factor location. This is very much in line with some of the previous findings, namely that the relationship between infrastructure and productivity is stronger than the relationship between infrastructure and output.

Table 3.4 Productivity and infrastructure, 1988

				Explanatory variables						
Dependent variable	K/L	L/K	J/K	J/P	J/S	J/(P+100S)	J/(L+40S)	J/(K+6.2*S)	Interval	R2
Capital productivity										
Y/K		0.599		-0.048					0.929	0.756
		(6.774)		(-0.372)					(-0.748)	
Y/K		0.674			0.046				-2.148	0.788
		(7.682)			(1.632)				(-4.467)	
Y/K		0.626				0.076			-2.165	0.779
		(7.59)				(1.369)			(-3.341)	
Y/K		0.781					**0.073**		-1.849	0.907
		(12.638)					**(2.06)**		(-10.102)	
Y/K		0.740						**0.084**	-1.386	0.907
		(12.765)						**(2.069)**	(-12.213)	
Labor productivity										
Y/L	0.242		-0.013						8.905	0.491
	(1.633)		(-0.153)						(5.08)	
Y/L	0.259			-0.011					8.814	0.491
	(3.648)			(-0.106)					(5.495)	
Y/L	0.204				**0.044**				8.749	0.589
	(3.128)				**(2.026)**				(12.26)	
Y/L	0.215					**0.087**			8.426	0.593
	(3.464)					**(2.077)**			(11.731)	
Y/L	0.219						**0.073**		3.548	0.593
	(3.537)						**(2.06)**		(11.48)	
Y/L	0.26							**0.084**	3.723	0.594
	(4.494)							**(2.069)**	(11.724)	

Note: the figures in parentheses are the t statistics; coefficients (and t statistics) in bold type are significant at the 1% level. The fact that some coefficients and t-values are identical for different dependent variables was double-checked and does not result from a typing error.

Table 3.5 Factor mobility and infrastructure, 1981-88

	L/P81	Y/K81	J/K81	ΔJ/J81	J81/(K81+5.6*S)	ΔJ/(K81+5.6*S)	Interval	R2
					Explanatory variables			
Dependent variable:								
ΔK/K81	0.448	4.39	-0.505				-0.525	0.415
	(0.183)	(2.415)	(-0.556)				(-0.144)	
ΔK/K81	1.643		1.464	.916			2.62	0.203
	(0.401)		(1.273)	(0.744)			(0.346)	
ΔK/K81		4.31	-0.567	0.031			-1.139	0.414
		(2.292)	(-0.65)	(0.04)			(-0.908)	
ΔK/K81	1.241	3.948			-0.271		0.296	0.408
	(0.548)	(2.598)			(-0.364)		(-0.536)	
ΔK/K81		3.368		0.175	-0.137		-1.002	0.398
		(2.949)		(0.237)	(-0.182)		(-0.536)	
ΔK/K81		3.368			-0.312	0.175	-1.002	0.398
		(2.949)			(0.337)	(0.237)	(-0.536)	

Note: the figures in parentheses are the t statistics; coefficients (and t statistics) in bold type are significant at the 1% level.

3.5   CONCLUSIONS

This first attempt to assess the economic contribution of infrastructure in France by means of regionally estimated production functions has led to some useful results. First, infrastructure endowment has been shown to contribute to labor productivity. Second, this contribution is best shown when infrastructure is related to a combination of area and people or area and labor or area and capital. Third, the elasticity of productivity relative to infrastructure appears to be about 0.08. This is to be compared with an elasticity of productivity relative to private capital of about 0.25. It translates into a rate of return of infrastructure of about 12%, and a rate of return of private capital of about 14%. Fourth, when one takes into account spillover effects and externalities, the rate of return of infrastructure increases by an unknown amount, but to a level most probably as high or higher than that of private capital. Fifth, the infrastructure endowment at the beginning of the 1981-88 period, and/or the increase in infrastructure during this period, do/does not seem to explain the increase in private capital during the same period. This means (if this finding is strong, which is not really the case) that the impact of infrastructure on output is obtained via an increase in productivity rather than an increase in capital. In other words, it suggests that infrastructure creates growth rather than merely displacing it.

This piece remains preliminary and tentative. More work should, could, and will be done, in a number of directions. The sectoral composition of economic activity in regions could or should be introduced, to ensure that the impact attributed to infrastructure is not in fact caused by industry mix. One could also attempt to capture spillover effects by incorporating the infrastructure endowment of neighboring regions, properly "dis-counted" with some accessibility index. The coefficients a and b utilized to produce combinations of surface and other variables as explanatory variables are exogenous and ad hoc: an attempt could be made to endogenize them. Better data on the stock of infrastructure could be produced; it is not impossible (although it is difficult) to obtain data on the physical stock of roads, schools, harbours, etc., by region, and to aggregate the various elements by means of cost figures; public works data have also been available by region since the mid 1970s, and can be treated to produce estimates of accumulated infrastructure investments. A different concept of output, namely industrial output, can be utilized. One can speculate that it is industrial output, rather than total output, which is influenced by infrastructure; the difficulty here is to obtain estimates of the stock of private capital in industry by region, which are not readily available. Then, "infrastructure" can be disaggregated into several categories (transportation, education, etc.) that can be utilized as explanatory variables.

ACKNOWLEDGEMENT

The author wishes to thank Bernard Fritsch, a graduate student at the University of Paris XII, for data collection and processing. This revised version of my paper presented at the Jönköping Workshop benefited from comments by workshop participants and anonymous referees.

APPENDIX: LIST OF VARIABLES

F   = Number of civil servants, in 1988
J   = Infrastructure, or stock of public capital in 1988
J81 = Infrastructure, or stock of public capital in 1981
ΔJ = Increase in the stock of infrastructure between 1981 and 1988
K   = Stock of private capital, excluding agriculture and non profit activities, in 1988
K81 = Stock of private capital, excluding agriculture and non profit activities, in 1981
ΔK = Increase in the stock of private capital between 1981 and 1988
L   = Labor force excluding agriculture and non profit activities, in 1988
L81 = Labor force, excluding agriculture and non profit activities, in 1981
P   = Population in 1988
S   = Surface (in km2)
X   = Variable to which infrastructure can be related, such as population, labor force, capital
Y   = Output, excluding agriculture and non profit activities, in 1988
Y81 = Output, excluding agriculture and non profit activities, in 1981

REFERENCES

Aschauer, D., 1989, "Is Public Expenditure Productive?", *Journal of Monetary Economics*, 23:177-200.
Aschauer, D.,1990, "Highway Capacity and Economic Growth", Federal Reserve Bank, Chicago.
Bell, M. and T. McGuire, 1992, Macroeconomic Analysis of the Linkages Between Transportation Investments and Economic Performance: An Interim Report, mimeo, The Johns Hopkins University Institute for Policy Studies and the University of Illinois Institute of Government and Public Affairs.
Biehl, D., 1986, "Equipements collectifs, développement économique, croissance et plein emploi", in Terny, G. and R. Prud'homme, *Le Financement des équipements publics de demain*, Economica, Paris, pp. 83-107.
Costa, J., R. Ellson and R. Martin, 1987, "Public Capital Regional Output and Development: Some Empirical Evidence", *Journal of Regional Science*, 27:419-437.
Llanos, J., 1992, *La Maintenance des ponts routiers: Approche économique*, Presses de l'Ecole Nationale des Ponts et Chaussées, Paris.

Mera, K., 1973, "Regional Production Functions and Social Overhead Capital", *Regional and Urban Economics,* 3:157-186.

Munnell, A., 1990a, "Why has Productivity Growth Declined? Productivity and Public Investment", *New England Economic Review,* January/February, pp. 3-22.

Munnell, A. with assistance of L. Cook, 1990b, "How Does Public Infrastructure Affect Regional Economic Performance?", in A. Munnel (ed.), *Is There a Shortfall in Public Capital Investment?*, Federal Reserve Bank of Boston.

Munnell, A., 1992, "Infrastructure Investment and Economic Growth", *The Journal of Economic Perspectives*, 6:4-21.

Navarre, F. and R. Prud'homme, 1984, "Le rôle des infrastructures dans le développement régional", *Revue d'Economie Régionale et Urbaine*, 1:5-22.

Quinet, E., 1992, *Infrastructures de Transport et Croissance*, Economica, Paris.

CHAPTER 4

The Linkage Between Transportation Infrastructure Investment and Productivity: A U.S. Federal Research Perspective

Susan J. Binder

U.S. Department of Transportation

Theresa M. Smith

U.S. Department of Transportation

4.1 INTRODUCTION

Recent studies suggest that diminished investment in the quality and quantity of public infrastructure induced the decline in U.S. output growth rates and output per hour (productivity) growth rates. Over the years, during various downturns in the economy, many explanations have been offered for such slowdowns. However, even the best known economists conclude that the sources remain a mystery. While research on this linkage began some years ago, recent national level studies directed attention to the productive effects of public capital and highway infrastructure. In 1989, in light of the post-Interstate era and an increasingly constrained financial environment, the Federal Highway Administration (FHWA) began to reexamine this hypothesis and its implications for national investment through a research agenda on the interrelationship between transportation infrastructure investment and productivity. In this research the FHWA hopes to act as an intelligent consumer of the research findings, while at the same time acting as a program manager, serving to stimulate rigorous research on the issue.

In the U.S. the importance of transportation facilities to the economy's efficiency and to the economic well-being of society is generally accepted, but many of the intuitive relationships are not analytically established. This generally recognized link with economic development continues to justify significant public expenditures in transportation systems at the local, State, and federal levels. Although evaluations of the user costs and benefits of investments in transportation projects are possible, it is difficult to quantitatively link such investments to national or regional growth, to economic development, to industry or national productivity, to growth in economic welfare, or to the Nation's *competitiveness* in the international market.

This chapter details the methodologies and anticipated research products for the research agenda sponsored by the Office of Policy Development at FHWA. Since this research agenda is coordinated with several other entities (such as the Transportation Research Board), some collateral research will also be presented. Discussion will include objectives and results of the projects recently completed and currently underway in this research agenda. Where possible, the data variables, functional form, estimation technique, statistical significance, and sensitivity to replication will be presented.

4.2   FEDERAL HIGHWAY ADMINISTRATION RESEARCH AGENDA AND RESULTS

The FHWA research effort will develop a better understanding of the linkage between investment in highways and bridges and the Nation's capacity to sustain economic performance and growth. This effort will clarify, as quantitatively as possible, both the short- and the long-term influences of highway infrastructure investment and service on the economy, to make more informed decisionmaking possible, and respond to the productivity slowdown. That is, to address the question "How do changes in highway investment translate to private productivity at the national level?"

This research agenda, discussed in more detail in the FHWA publication *High Priority Research Areas for the Office of the Associate Administrator for Policy*, utilizes three approaches concurrently: *macroeconometrics, microeconomic industry analysis, and highway system assessment*. The first approach entitled *macroeconometric analysis*, investigates national and State-level linkages using econometric methodologies such as the production function. The second perspective, *microeconomic industry analysis* explores the connection between individual industries and transportation infrastructure from the perspective of firms. A third dimension, *highway system assessment*, examines the value of infrastructure through service network or system characteristics. Figure 4.1 presents the methodologies incorporated in these perspectives. These approaches are only a starting point for a thorough analysis. The FHWA research agenda currently focuses only on domestic systems and their economic linkages.

Research on transportation infrastructure investment and economic productivity linkages is being pursued at numerous levels: national, regional, State-level, metropolitan area, project specific results, industry level, and system level. As displayed in Figure 4.1, the methods implemented include: production, cost and profit functions, sources of growth models, the needs approach, the constant proportion analysis, and sectoral use coefficients. Other methods include logistics analysis, surveys, case studies, risk analysis, performance analysis, cost effectiveness analysis, multivariate analysis, correlation analysis, simultaneous equations and input output analysis. Measures of productivity and economic growth which have been investigated include: output per capita, output per labor hour, output per unit of capital, total factor productivity, labor productivity, gross state product, State employment, and manufacturing output.

It is helpful to identify the objectives of infrastructure investment first, since infrastructure investment may have a variety of objectives. Lewis (1993) differentiates areas of economic activity where "the influence of infrastructure investment is verifiable" into distributional and growth categories. Infrastructure investment may cause *distributional* effects on: (1) the structure of employment; (2) personal income; (3) regional output and income; and (4) sectoral output and income. Likewise, infrastructure investment can yield *growth* in (1) economic output; (2) productivity; (3) employment; and (4) economic welfare. Infrastructure's effectiveness in promoting change in each of these areas varies tremendously.

Unfortunately, current investment objectives do not consider all of the potential impacts of infrastructure investment. A 1990 survey of U.S. projects (Hickling, 1991) reported that 87 percent of infrastructure investment appraisals identified distributional objectives as their main purpose. Lewis (1993) questions the effectiveness of infrastructure investment as a distributional tool as opposed to a growth tool. Indeed, Eberts (1992) acknowledges that "the growth of individual regions may not necessarily lead to national growth, if one region's gain is another region's loss".

In practice, the U.S. transportation objective has focused on mobility and an intuitive sense of the benefits to connectivity rather than specific distributional or economic growth objectives. Since countries demand different types of projects depending on their particular objectives, researchers investigating this issue might first identify a country's current objectives as compared to potential objectives. Early research by Hansen (1965) shows that the effect of infrastructure investment can vary depending on the current stage of the economy (i.e. Is a country or region's development: congested, intermediate, or lagging?) Eberts (1992) confirms that other issues to identify would be the current economic conditions and the type of infrastructure already in place. A final step in the research arena would be to focus on ways for public policy makers to accomplish the desired objectives (i.e. Remember who your ultimate constituents are!)

I. **ASSESS MACROECONOMIC IMPACTS**
    (Macroeconometrics Approach)

    Methods:
    – Time-series and cross sectional analysis
    – Production, cost, and profit function analyses
    – Input-output analysis to estimate modal efficiency
    – Incorporation of State density and size into regional analyses

    Research Product:
    Analysis of credibility of relationships between macro level productivity and transportation.

II. **IDENTIFY INDUSTRY IMPACT MECHANISMS**
    (Microeconomic Industry Analysis Approach)

    Methods:
    – Cross-sectional analysis of industry sectors
    – Logistical and econometric approaches
    – Identification of effects of highway service on industry mix

    Research Product:
    Quantification of productivity and efficiency impacts of transportation and the highway system on industry.

III. **INTERPRET HIGHWAY SYSTEM LINKAGES**
    (Highway System Assessment Approach)

    Methods:
    – Calculation of composite measures of highway system performance
    – Analysis of effects of intermodalism and congestion on productivity
    – Incorporation of network attributes of public capital into systems analysis
    – Comparison of highway maintenance and operational impacts to those of
      construction

    Research Product:
    Estimation of the contribution of the highway network with its performance and operational characteristics on productivity.

Figure 4.1   Concurrent methodological approaches to the study of the interrelationship between highway investment and economic productivity

4.2.1 The Macroeconometric Approach

Initially, projects in the *macroeconometric approach* reflected the structure and logic of the arguments associated with the works of economists such as Aschauer, Jorgensen, and Munnell. These works addressed the impacts of transportation *investment* or *capital stock* on economy-wide output growth. Early efforts sponsored by the FHWA have attempted to extend and assess the existing national level productivity studies to understand whether we are underinvesting in the U.S. highway system. Later projects implementing this approach will move toward state or regional econometric analyses and may include input-output analyses at the national level. Extensions will test the hypothesis that transportation infrastructure investment is more productive than prospective private capital investments.

(i)   Highways and Macroeconomic Productivity: Phase I and II

FHWA emphasis on the relationship between highway infrastructure investment and economic productivity began in fiscal year (FY) 1990 when FHWA sponsored several brief, exploratory papers and an in-house roundtable discussion to supplement ongoing staff assessments of the subject. Later in FY 1990, FHWA supported a limited set of case studies to identify practical examples of how transportation relates to industrial productivity gains and how these gains may be thwarted by inadequate highway transportation service. In January 1992, the FHWA-sponsored study, "Highways and Macroeconomic Productivity" was completed. This project critically evaluated the hypotheses and conclusions of frequently cited macroeconometric analysis concerning the relative magnitude of effects of public and private capital investment on economic growth. This study provided us with an objective view of the relative technical merit of these approaches, the quality of their implementation, and means to improve the quality of results.

Phase I of this effort by Nienhaus pursued replication and sensitivity testing of Aschauer's (1989) and Munnell's (1990a, 1990b) production function results using national aggregate time series data with output per hour as output; and the following data as inputs: public capital stock, capital utilization, and labor productivity. Aschauer and Munnell's results are frequently criticized because of the unbelievably large size of the coefficients; many suggest that the results may arise from simple correlation or reverse causation. Although this Phase I effort duplicated key equation results of the Aschauer and Munnell studies, slight changes to the data were made and mixing of the data sets led to extremely sensitive results.

Although Nienhaus did not use first differences to compensate for the possibility of similar trends, Tatom (1991) used this technique and finds a much smaller magnitude for the effect of public capital on the productivity variable. Nienhaus tested the robustness of Munnell's (1990b) State-level analysis with the addition of State, year, and regional dummy variables. He found that State dummy variables led to an insignificant public capital coefficient; dummy year variables had little effect; and in the case with regional dummy variables the coefficient of public capital was still significant, but much smaller. When separate regressions for regions were estimated, all coefficients were significant. Nienhaus concluded like Hulten (1991) that the results of Aschauer's and Munnell's national level analyses might indeed be due to accidental correlation or time trends. For more detail on this research refer to *Assessing the Relationship Between Transportation Infrastructure and Productivity* (FHWA,1992) or FHWA report *Highways and Macroeconomic Productivity: Phase I* (Nienhaus, 1991).

In phase II of this effort, McGuire investigated State-level relationships using pooled cross-section, time series data on gross state product as output; and the following inputs: private capital stock for structures and equipment; public capital stock, including educational buildings and highway capital as separate categories; and labor, either nonagricultural or total labor. State-level public capital stock was not available so national data was distributed to the State-level. Results indicated a positive and statistically significant role for public capital in determining output using a Cobb-Douglas production function with: no control for State effects; control for State fixed effects; control for State random effects, and; translog with no control for State effects. When McGuire tested highways separately from public capital, highways had the strongest effect of the public capital components included. McGuire (1992) found coefficient's on public capital ranging from 0.034 to 0.053 and from 0.121 to 0.127 for highway capital.

McGuire also concluded that the results of regional sources of growth models which indicate no role for public capital or highway infrastructure investments may not be contrary to State and national level results because no tests of significance are possible for this methodology. Regional models may indeed be confirming a small but positive role for public capital. Unfortunately, while regional analysis may capture inherent variation across localities, it may miss external benefits outside the region. Table 4.1 shows the range in elasticities found in a sample of the literature.

Using first differences or the Cobb-Douglas functional form on regional subsets of the data resulted in a statistically insignificant coefficient on public capital and highways. Cost functions were also tested. However, the data was found to be too limited to comfortably pursue this methodology. Overall, McGuire concluded that public capital has a small but positively significant impact on productivity. For more detail on this research refer to FHWA publications: *Assessing the Relationship Between Transportation Infrastructure and Productivity* (FHWA, 1992) or *Highways and Macroeconomic Productivity: Phase II* (McGuire, 1992).

In a recent extension of this research, Garcia-Milà et al.(1993) used the above data set to further explore a variety of specifications. This paper used first differences based on the Bhargava, Franzini, and Narendranthan test; chose State fixed effects over no State effects or State random effects based on Hausman, Taylor, and Chow tests; rejected measurement error and endogeneity based on the Griliches and Hausman test and the Hausman endogeneity test. Cobb-Douglas functional form was used for ease of comparability with earlier studies. Although there are problems with the data and lengthy time series are not available, production and cost functions were tested. In the preferred specification, first differences with State fixed effects, the public capital variables were not significant, however, the State fixed effects and private input variables were significant. The authors conclude that "while growth in public capital does not contribute to growth in output (GSP), the different output growth rates of the States cannot be accounted for only by differences in the States' input growth rates".

(ii)   Update and Improve Transportation Capital Stock

Initial stages of the National Cooperative Highway Research Program (NCHRP) project 2-17(3), "Update and Improve Transportation Capital Stock Measures" concluded that a full updating of the measures of net transportation capital stock similar to those prepared in 1974 for the U.S. Department of Transportation was not feasible or ideal. Rather, this project built a database of transportation infrastructure investment and transportation capital stock for selected modes. Two industry-specific, State-level private capital stock series were generated using U.S. Bureau of Economic Analysis national figures on employment and output as allocators. Additional State-level data utilized U.S. Bureau of the Census investment data for six types of infrastructure, including four transportation categories: highways, mass transit, airports, and waterways. Assembly of similar data for other countries would provide a sensitivity comparison.

Table 4.1 Infrastructure's impact on productivity selected estimated elasticities

This table shows the variation in the researchers estimates. The coefficients, which in most cases are also elasticities (if the equation estimated used logged variables), show the strength of the estimated effect, that is, for a 1 percent change in the infrastructure variable the elasticity indicates the percentage change that can be expected in the productivity variable. The productivity variable is typically some measure of output which serves as a proxy for productivity.

Researcher	Coef-ficient	Level of analysis	Infrastructure variable	Productivity variable
Aschauer (1989)	0.39	National	public capital	national output
Aschauer (1989)	0.24	National	core public capital	national output
Munnell (1990a)	0.33	National	public capital	national output
Lynde & Richmond (1991)	0.20	National	public capital	national output
Hulten & Schwab (1991)	0.03	National	public capital	national output
Munnell (1990b)	0.15	State	public capital	gross state product
Munnell (1990b)	0.06	State	highway capital	gross state product
Costa, Ellson & Martin (1987)	0.20	State	public capital	output
Garcia-Milà & McGuire (forthcoming)	0.04	State	highway capital	gross state product
Moomaw & Williams (1991)	0.25	State	highway density	total factor productivity
Deno (1988)	0.31	Metro area	highway capital	manufacturing output
Duffy-Deno & Eberts (1989)	0.08	Metro area	public capital	personal income
Eberts (1986)	0.03	Metro area	core public capital	manufacturing value added

Numerous empirical techniques were pursued to investigate the linkages between transportation investment and productivity. One effort studying demand for transportation services at the State-level offered preliminary evidence that investment flows are not necessarily good proxies for level of services, thereby supporting the need to further develop measures reflecting the level and quality of transportation service. Another analysis compared various estimates of public capital. An extension tested different public capital measures and their impacts; surprisingly, the results were very similar. The authors concluded that inaccurate estimates of public capital were not responsible for estimates showing a weak positive relationship from public capital to output.

Explorations with a neoclassical growth function did not show a strong role for public capital or transportation in output or productivity growth. State-level industry specific production functions found the linkage between highway investment and gross state product varied by industry analyzed. Many of the results of these empirical tests are preliminary and further research is necessary to verify the strength of these results. However, results do indicate that improvements in the data as well as further research by industry, at the State and local level would be beneficial. The final report will include a literature review, data description and documentation, research reports, and limitations, refinements and possible extensions.

(iii)   Primer on Transportation, Productivity and Economic Development

This NCHRP 2-17(1) effort, directed by the American Association of State Highway and Transportation Officials (AASHTO) and administered by the Transportation Research Board of the National Research Council resulted in the publication of Report 342, the *Primer on Transportation, Productivity and Economic Development* in September 1991. This research successfully identified, described, and evaluated available methodologies for analyzing relationships between transportation and the economy. This effort emphasizes the importance of cost-benefit analysis and rate of return calculations. However, cost-benefit analysis is difficult to apply at the aggregate national level and frequently several aspects of a project are neglected. This information could be applied effectively and efficiently by other countries.

4.2.2 Microeconomic Industry Analysis Approach

While the macroeconometric approach is important to establish the national magnitude of the impacts, a companion approach, *microeconomic industry analysis,* holds great promise to identify the mechanisms through which highway *investment* is converted into increased private sector productivity at the microeconomic or industry level. The projects within this approach implement both logistics and econometric analyses at the industry level.

(i)   Industry Studies of the Relationship Between Highway Transportation and Productivity

Industry case studies are underway to identify firm-specific relationships between transportation, specifically highways, and productivity in a selected first set of industries, including: paper mills, pharmaceuticals, motor vehicles, the citrus industry, the medical supply field, and grocery stores. Logistics costs, as well as service characteristics such as reliability, flexibility, and just-in-time service are being incorporated. The "indirect impacts" of industrial gains in productivity and the resulting gains in economic development, rather than savings in direct transportation costs or the effect on transportation industries themselves are being explored. By identifying benefits not usually quantified, such as: transit time reduction; reliability of arrival time; inventory reductions; decreased product damage rates; and decreased freight costs, these efforts hope to better understand the linkages between highway infrastructure investment and economic performance. Preliminary results from survey interviews confirm that company officials believe transportation services play a major role in their companies' productivity. In effect, infrastructure is viewed as "An enabling agent for significant improvements in logistics performance, particularly since deregulation" of transportation. A final report incorporating FHWA review and potential economy-wide applications of the six industries analyzed in this project is expected by the Fall of 1993.

(ii)   **Measuring the Relationship Between Freight Transportation Services and Industry Productivity**

This project, directed by NCHRP, runs parallel to the FHWA-sponsored industry analysis. The contractor, Hickling, Corp. is exploring six industries and plans to survey a sample of firms from each industry selected, collecting data to estimate elasticities of cost and total public benefits from proposed transportation infrastructure improvements. Some of the industries selected for analysis include: retail food; autoparts; telecommunications; and surgical and medical supplies. Following the survey, expert panel sessions will assess the degree of risk and uncertainty involved in the estimation parameters. A Monte Carlo simulation will define confidence intervals for estimated benefits. The industry analysis will address industries' "willingness to pay" for infrastructure services and whether travel time and reliability improvements might complement logistics costs. This research may serve as an important guide in the future because, as Hickling noted in a recent progress report, "The nature of available freight services will determine much of the structure of private sector capital. Freight services will determine the degree to which firms centralize or disperse operations, the location and numbers of plants and warehouses, the degree of to which firms may specialize and serve larger markets, and the consequent location of entire populations".

4.2.3 Highway System Assessment Approach

The third approach, *highway system assessment*, will focus directly on the efficiency and productivity of the *services* provided through the use of highway facilities rather than either their asset value or investment expenditures for highways over time. This approach will study the value of the highway system through its unique nature and its enhancement of highway system connectivity as seen in: (1) network aspects, (2) public utility aspects, (3) pervasiveness, (4) extensiveness, and (5) maturity. This approach will take advantage of FHWA's existing databases describing highway capital expenditures, highway facilities, and highway system performance. Impacts of changing industrial transportation demand and its impacts on the highway system will also be considered. A national approach will capture spillover benefits of the network.

(i)   Performance Based Measures of the Transportation Productivity Linkage

This exploratory effort currently underway at Oak Ridge National Laboratory (ORNL) focuses on the importance of highway density and network connectivity, both inter- and intra-State, to economic growth. Using data on highway performance and conditions from FHWA's Highway Performance Monitoring System (HPMS) as published by FHWA in both *Highway Statistics* and periodic reports to the United States Congress by the Secretary of Transportation in *The Status of the Nation's Highways and Bridges: Conditions and Performance*, measures for operating characteristics, physical conditions, and safety, have been assessed in relation to economic vitality. Highway congestion measures studied include volume service flow ratio and average annual daily traffic per lane, which indicate mobility and accessibility. While physical highway conditions refer to pavement conditions, roadway alignment, lane widths, and bridge conditions, this analysis investigated physical conditions as described in the present serviceability rating (PSR). Safety characteristics were incorporated through a measure of highway fatalities.

Early results of the cross-section time-series correlations for the 48 contiguous States in the U.S. over two time periods, 1985-88 and 1980-88 complement the macro-econometric findings of production and cost functions, showing positive correlations between highway infrastructure measures and the level and growth rate of gross state product (i.e. income) per labor force member. The ORNL (1993) study shows a positive correlation between income growth and intensity of usage (measured by the volume-to-capacity ratio and the ratio of vehicle-miles traveled per lane mile of local highway). Pavement quality (PSR) has a positive relationship with income growth. Vehicle-miles per labor force member is positively correlated with the level of income but negatively correlated with the growth rate of income. Without controlling for other factors, the ORNL study cannot separate out simultaneity effects. Fatal traffic accidents, per labor force member and per vehicle mile traveled (VMT) are positively correlated with the level of income, but both show a negative relationship to income growth. Overall, the correlations between the measures of highway performance and economic productivity are significant and satisfactorily strong.

These findings support the belief that highway performance measures and infrastructure figures belong in the investigation of a productivity linkage discussion. Indeed, this project points out intervening variables between highway stock and transportation service. It is anticipated that this research will point to specific variables which would be useful proxies for transportation investment or asset value. The second phase of this analysis is proceeding with modeling interactions using simultaneous equations.

(ii)   Resources versus Results: Comparative Performance of State Highway Systems

Although not sponsored by FHWA, a related State-level study by Hartgen and Krauss (1992) for 1984 to 1990 focused on a comparison of the level of highway performance as a result of U.S. expenditures. In order to do this, highway performance operating characteristics, physical conditions, and safety as well as highway revenues and expenditures for each State were studied. The States were then graded on performance for 13 different measures by comparing each State's progress to national trends.

The study concluded that the U.S. highway system is in good shape and has been improving over the last decade. The overall performance of the U.S. highway system on all measures except congestion improved. Limitations of this study include: lack of lagged variables, no treatment of effects of neighboring States, no adjustment for variations in labor costs across the country, and no analysis of need, such as changes in population or auto registrations.

4.3   REFLECTIONS

Eberts (1986) asks, "Have increased international competition and the restructuring of American industry altered the types of public works needed to support future economic growth?" Several structural transformations are underway throughout the world: changes in production processes; changes in the structure of the industrial sector; shifts in the location of various economic activities; the increasing importance of the service sector in the economy (McDowell and Bell, 1991). In the area of transport, there is a shift away from heavier outputs and inputs to lighter higher value products. Christy (1993) asks if the physical infrastructure needed in a knowledge based society is the same as that in an industrialized society. Will telecommunications capabilities supplant the necessity of face-to-face meetings Eberts (1992). Structurally the changes in the European Community must also be considered. While physical obstacles remain, institutional barriers are being progressively lowered by the EC. Bayliss (1993) notes that over the last 100 years transport has been developed sometimes in a systematic and planned fashion and sometimes not. Christy (1993) asserts that as the global economy becomes a reality, "national security will increasingly be defined in economic terms rather than military terms". The alterations to European regulations, industries, and markets will change the method of analysis as well as affect the data necessary to investigate these relationships.

Other issues which will have more prominence in the future transportation outlook include: (1) new patterns of demand for transport; (2) a shift toward intermodalism; (3) responsiveness to customer needs; (4) performance measures and accountability; and (5) efficiency and cost effectiveness.

The FHWA research initiative, macroeconometric perspective is now moving away from production and cost function analyses towards other methodologies at the national level, such as input-output analysis. The FHWA microeconomic industry analysis approach continues to examine and develop a variety of methodologies at the industry level. More comprehensive industry level information and improved measures of the service industry would accelerate this investigative analysis of infrastructure's impact on industry. Even if the stimulative effect of infrastructure is as great as some studies have concluded, these studies are based on historical relationships and provide little guidance regarding the types of infrastructure investment that would bring about the greatest returns to specific regions in the future (Eberts, 1992).

Cost-benefit analysis proves an ideal method of assessing which project to pursue, but applications at a national level remain inadequate. Lewis has recommended that the U.S. federal government require an "Economic Appraisal Process" similar to the Environmental Impact Statement as part of the Transportation Improvement Plan (the major planning document for securing U.S. federal assistance) established by the Intermodal Surface Transportation Efficiency Act of 1991.

At the system level, the FHWA highway system assessment approach has focused on performance and quality measures as a way to investigate the relationship between system effectiveness of highway infrastructure and economic performance. Some in the U.S have suggested that FHWA hold States responsible for more efficient usage of their infrastructure dollars. Meanwhile others recognize the difficulty in comparing States or countries with dissimilar transport geography, investment policies, and economic conditions. Yet, performance and quality measures of the infrastructure system are lacking for most countries and need to be pursued. Are there other countries who have the ability to produce performance measures? How might we standardize these across countries? How might we avoid ranking countries by their individual performance ratings?

4.4   CONCLUSIONS

This essay has presented FHWA research and collateral efforts consistent with the FHWA priority initiative, "Interrelationships Between Transportation Infrastructure Investment and Productivity". Projects within this agenda are unique, pursuing several levels of analysis and divergent methodologies to achieve a full complement of answers to questions such as:
*   How does the quality and performance of highway infrastructure promote employment, income, output or economic productivity?
*   Are industries or countries effected differently by transportation infrastructure?

We hope to use the information learned through this research initiative to enhance the productivity and efficiency of the highway system and to respond to structural changes in the economy. None of the studies reviewed in this chapter are detailed enough or designed to support an aggressive public policy action based only on the research. Our knowledge of the relationship between public capital investment and economic growth is insufficient to argue that expanding investment in infrastructure will ensure economic growth. As Eberts (1992) notes, "While it does not appear that public infrastructure investment will provide quick remedies to current budget problems by instantly stimulating growth, most researchers agree that an infrastructure system that is allocated efficiently and is well maintained is necessary to support future economic growth". Further study of the relationship between infrastructure investment and productivity growth is needed to develop strategic infrastructure investment policies that will provide policy guidance at the programmatic level and for alternative policy option tradeoffs in order to maximize the contribution to economic vitality.

ACKNOWLEDGEMENTS

The contents of this report reflect the views of the authors who are responsible for the facts and accuracy of the data presented herein. The contents do not necessarily reflect the official policy of the United States Department of Transportation. The United States Government does not endorse the products or manufacturers. Trademarks or manufacturers' names appear herein only because they are considered essential to the objective of this document. This report does not constitute a standard, specification, or regulation.

REFERENCES

Aschauer, D.A., 1989, "Is Public Expenditure Productive?", *Journal of Monetary Economics*, 23:177-200.

"Assessing the Relationship Between Transportation Infrastructure and Productivity", 1992, Searching for Solutions: A Policy Discussion Series, U.S. Department of Transportation, FHWA-PL-92-022.

Bayliss, D., 1993, "Multi-Modal Review of Transport Infrastructure Trends in Europe", presented at the 72ND Annual Transportation Research Board Meetings, Washington, D.C.

Christy, L., 1993, "Sort out Government and Industry Roles", *Governing Magazine,* January:50-51.

da Silva Costa, J., R.W. Ellson and R.C. Martin, 1987, "Public Capital, Regional Output and Development: Some Empirical Evidence", *Journal of Regional Science*, 27:419-437.

Deno, K.T., 1988, "The Effect of Public Capital on U.S. Manufacturing Activity: 1970 to 1978", *Southern Economic Journal,* 55:400-411.

Duffy-Deno, K.T. and R.W. Eberts, 1991, "Public Infrastructure and Regional Economic Development: A Simultaneous Equations Approach", *Journal of Urban Economics*, 30:329-343.

Eberts, R.W., 1986, "An Assessment of the Linkage Between Public Infrastructure and Economic Development", Final Report, National Council on Public Works Improvement, Washington, D.C.

Eberts, R.W., 1992, "Public Infrastructure and Regional Economic Development", presented at the Federal Highway Conference on Highway-Related Transportation Industry Productivity Measures, Washington, D.C.

Garcia-Milà, T. and T.J. McGuire, forthcoming, "The Contribution of Publicly Provided Inputs to States' Economies", *Regional Science and Urban Economics*.

Garcia-Milà, T., T. McGuire and R. Porter, 1993, "The Effect of Public Capital in State-Level Production Functions Reconsidered", Working Paper, University of Illinois at Chicago.

Hansen, N.M., 1965, "Unbalanced Growth and Regional Development", *Western Economic Journal*, 4:3-14.

Hartgen, D. and R. Krauss, 1992, "Resources versus Results: Comparative Performance of State Highway Systems, 1984-1990", University of North Carolina at Charlotte.

High Priority Research Areas for the Office of the Associate Administrator for Policy, 1992, Federal Highway Administration, U.S. Department of Transportation.

Hulten C.R., 1991, "Public Capital Formation and the Growth of Regional Manufacturing Industries. Part 1", *National Tax Journal*, 44:121-134.

Hulten, C.R. and R.M. Schwab, 1991, "Public Capital Formation and the Growth of Regional Manufacturing Industries. Part 1", *National Tax Journal*, 44:121-134.

Lewis, D., 1993, "Objectives and Decision Criteria for Infrastructure Investment: A Summary of Research Findings of Project 2-17 of the NCHRP, NRC", Sponsored by AASHTO and conducted by TRB.

Lynde, C. and J. Richmond, 1991, "Public Capital and Total Factor Productivity", Working Paper, University of Massachusetts, Boston.

McDowell, B.D. and M.E. Bell, 1991, "The Value of Infrastructure to America", Background paper, U.S. Corps of Engineers, Washington, D.C.

McGuire, T. 1992, "Highways and Macroeconomic Productivity: Phase II", Prepared for the Federal Highway Administration, U.S. Department of Transportation.

Moomaw, R. and M. Williams, 1991, "Total Factor Productivity in Manufacturing: Further Evidence from the States", *Journal of Regional Science*, 31:17-34.

Munnell, A., 1990a, "Why Has Productivity Growth Declined? Productivity and Public Investment", *New England Economic Review*, January/February:3-22.

Munnell, A. with assistance of L. Cook, 1990b, "How Does Public Infrastructure Affect Regional Economic Performance?", in A. Munnell (ed.), *Is There a Shortfall in Public Capital Investment?*, Federal Reserve Bank, Boston.

Nienhaus, M., 1991, "Highways and Macroeconomic Productivity: Phase I", Prepared for the Federal Highway Administration, U.S. Department of Transportation.

Primer on Transportation, Productivity, and Economic Development, 1991, Report 342, Hickling Corporation, Prepared for the Transportation Research Board.

Tatom, J.A., 1991, "Public Capital and Private Sector Performance", *St. Louis Federal Reserve Bank Review*, Vol. 73, 3:3-15.

CHAPTER 5

Public Capital, Private Sector Productivity and Economic Growth: A Macroeconomic Perspective

Jacco Hakfoort

University of Amsterdam and Tinbergen Institute

5.1 INTRODUCTION

Infrastructure and the effects of changes in its stock and composition on the economy have been the object of study in a large variety of contexts (Rietveld, 1989).

At the micro-level, governments aided by economists have evaluated costs and benefits of specific projects, increasingly taking non-monetary side-effects of the construction and operation of new infrastructure into account. A large number of good textbooks on cost-benefit analysis have become available since World War II and many governments practice what these text books preach.

At the regional level, there is overwhelming evidence on the scale of the backward linkages of infrastructure investments for various regions and countries. New techniques have been developed to estimate forward linkages. The concept of accessibility has regained interest among transport economists and regional scientists. New multi-regional models have been developed to explain factor mobility and regional trade.

In this chapter, the impact of infrastructure on the *macro-level* is examined by providing a survey of the theoretical and empirical literature in the field of economic growth. This research should in my view be considered as complementary to the studies at a more disaggregated level rather than as a substitute. There are two reasons for a separate survey of this topic.

The first reason is that, until recently, macroeconomics – with a very few exceptions – did not have anything to say about the impact of infrastructure on the growth path of the economy. The interest it has gained recently is an outflow of a revived interest in the origins of growth.

This raises the question – the second reason for this survey – what relates the results found at the macro-level to the results at the regional level? What can one learn from the results of regressions with highly aggregated variables on the left and right hand sides of the equation for policy purposes?

This chapter is organised as follows. Section 5.2 gives a short overview of the 'new' or endogenous growth theory. In Section 5.3 one way of testing this theory at a more aggregated level, the production function approach, is presented and an overview of the empirical results up to date is given.

The production function approach has its limitations. A number of studies have therefore chosen to test their hypothesis either in the form of a profit function (Section 5.4) or in the form of a cost function (Section 5.5), making use of the duality principle.

Section 5.6 provides a research agenda and Section 5.7 gives concluding remarks.

5.2 'NEW' OR ENDOGENOUS GROWTH THEORY

Recent developments in growth theory have shed new light on the determinants of long-term growth by endogenizing technical change. A general feature of the models employed is that there are constant or even increasing returns to scale to the factors that can be accumulated. To reconcile increasing returns to scale at the firm level with the assumption of perfect competition, a part of the literature assumes that these increasing returns are external to a firm (e.g. van der Ploeg and Tang, 1992).[1]

Among the external factors that have been put forward as the "engine of economic growth", one of the most prominent is publicly provided material and immaterial infra-structure (see Barro, 1990; and Barro and Sala-i-Martin, 1992). To incorporate this variable in the theory, the production function of the representative producer is extended to include productive government services that can raise the productivity of private capital. The implications of this theory are obvious: there is an important role for the government in promoting growth prospects through an optimal provision of infra-structure.

The idea that there is a relation between investment in infrastructure on the one hand and productivity and growth on the other, is intuitively appealing (Ford and Poret, 1991). Investments in transport infrastructure are likely to lead to shorter, faster and better connections; investments in health care and education will lead to higher productivity – at least in the long run – and so on.

It is therefore remarkable that macroeconomics has – until recently – paid little attention to the effects of publicly provided infrastructure on private sector output and productivity growth,[2] both in theory and in applications (Berndt and Hansson, 1991). This is even more surprising in the light of the extensive literature that exists on this link in both the fields of regional and urban economics and in the field of development economics.[3]

A further indication of the potential importance of the public capital stock in indus-trialized economies is its relative size. Munnell (1990a), for example, finds that in 1987 the public capital stock in the United States was about 46% of the value of the private capital stock. Similarly, Berndt and Hansson (1991) report that for Sweden the public infrastructure capital stock in 1988 was about 43% of the private sector stock. Munnell (1992) estimates the stock of public capital in 1991 to be nearly half of the private capital stock.

With the benefit of hindsight, one can discern a number of reasons for the recent theoretical and empirical examination of the effects of public capital on the private sector of the economy.

---

[1] The other possibility to allow for increasing returns at the firm level is, of course, to relax the assumption of perfect competition.

[2] Notable exceptions are Arrow and Kurz (1970), Grossman and Lucas (1974), Ogura and Yohe (1977), von Furstenberg (1978) and Eisner (1980).

[3] In the older literature, the theory of *economic growth* was dedicated to industrialized countries, while the theory of *economic development* addressed the growth potential of developing countries, constituting separate disciplines in economic research. One of the positive aspects of the new growth theory is that it tries to find a universal explanation for economic growth for both types of countries and the convergence between these countries.

The coincidence between the widely observed decline in productivity growth in a large number of industrialized countries since the early 1970s and the simultaneous slowdown in public capital formation in these countries raises the question whether there is a cause-effect relation between the two variables. If public capital makes a positive contribution to productivity and output – as argued by the theory – it is at least possible that underinvestment in public capital is one of the underlying causes of the observed productivity slump.

The increased research efforts are also due to the commitments the EC countries have made with respect to their monetary and budgetary policies in the path towards integration. One of the few discretionary tools left to increase the international competitiveness of a country is believed to be a shift of their government spending from consumption to investment, particularly in infrastructure. The argument that an adequate level of infrastructure might increase productivity and international competitiveness and may therefore create jobs was one of the underlying reasons for the promises of more spending on infrastructure in the 1992 Clinton-Gore election campaign for the U.S. presidency.

Seitz (1992) has mentioned yet another reason for research. He points to the need for information to support and direct the efficient allocation of public investment expenditures for the construction of the former Eastern Europe.

5.3   THE PRODUCTION FUNCTION APPROACH

The specification used in some of the earlier papers in the literature is the production function (in most cases assumed to be of the Cobb-Douglas type) that relates the output or value-added of an economy or industry, Y to the quantities of labor input L, private capital input K and public (infrastructure) capital G:

$$Y = F(L,K,G).$$

The function F describes the technological possibilities available to the economy or industry. By making the additional assumptions that factor markets are characterized by perfect competition, and that the public capital stock is a pure public good in the sense of Samuelson (1954) which can be approximated as an unpaid factor, we have brought some economic theory into the exercise. The usual questions about the returns to scale over all three factors and the influence of the public capital stock on factor demands are interesting when interpreting the empirical results.

Table 5.1 gives an overview of some studies that have adopted a production function to estimate the impact of public capital on economic growth. The level of aggregation of data is divided into N (national), R (regional) and M (metropolitan).

Most studies that estimate the contribution of public capital to growth use time series, and impose the Cobb-Douglas form in logarithmic form. However, there are a few exceptions.

With regard to the specification, Toen-Gout and Jongeling (1993) impose the Cobb-Douglas form but use first differences of logs instead of logs. Costa et al. (1987), Eberts (1990) and Merriman (1990) impose the translog production function, which is a more flexible specification than the Cobb-Douglas function. Finally, Mera (1973) and Costa et al. (1987) use cross-section state data instead of time series.

Table 5.1   Overview of production function estimates with public capital as an input by country, time period and level of aggregation of the data

Study	Country	Time period	Data
Mera (1973)	Japan	1954-1963	R
Ratner (1983)	United States	1949-1973	N
Costa et al. (1987)	United States	1972 (CS)	R
Aschauer (1989)	United States	1949-1985	N
Duffy-Deno & Eberts (1991)	United States		M
Eberts (1990)	United States		M
Merriman (1990)	United States	1972 (CS)	R
	Japan	1954-1963	R
Munnell (1990a)	United States	1949-1987	N
Munnell (1990b)	United States	1949-1987	R
Ford & Poret (1991)	United States	1957-1988	N
	Japan	1969-1988	N
	Germany	1961-1987	N
	France	1971-1987	N
	United Kingdom	1973-1987	N
	Canada	1963-1988	N
	Belgium	1967-1988	N
	Finland	1967-1988	N
	Norway	1975-1986	N
	Australia	1967-1987	N
Holtz-Eakin (1991)	United States	1969-1986	R
Berndt & Hansson (1991)	Sweden	1964-1988	N
Toen-Gout & Jongeling (1993)	Netherlands	1960-1989	N

Table 5.2 gives the reported estimates for the output elasticity of public capital in the studies mentioned above.

As can be judged from the survey given in Tables 5.1 and 5.2, the estimates for the income elasticity of public capital range from negative to more than unity. A particularly disturbing aspect is not only that this range is so wide, but also that there are contradicting studies for the same country. It is therefore not surprising that this approach to testing for the impact of public capital has come under attack.

The use of the Cobb-Douglas production function to test for the impact of public capital on productivity and growth can be criticized on at least three grounds.

Table 5.2   Overview of point estimates for the output elasticity of public capital in studies using the production function approach

Study	Reported output	Elasticity of public capital
Ratner (1983)	United States	0.06
Costa et al. (1987)	United States	0.20
Aschauer (1989)	United States	0.39
Duffy-Deno & Eberts (1991)	United States	0.08
Eberts (1990)	United States	0.03
Munnell (1990a)	United States	0.34
Munnell (1990b)	United States	0.15
Ford & Poret (1991)	United States	0.29-0.34
	Japan	0.15-0.39
	Germany	0.53-0.68
	France	-0.34-0.70
	United Kingdom	-0.18-0.29
	Canada	0.63-0.77
	Belgium	0.54-0.57
	Finland	0.27-0.89
	Norway	-0.19-0.80
	Australia	0.34-0.70
Holtz-Eakin (1991)	United States	0.20
Berndt & Hansson (1991)	Sweden	0.69-1.60
Toen-Gout & Jongeling (1993)	Netherlands	0.48

The restrictions of the functional form are apparent from the fact that the substitution-elasticities between the various inputs are constant and equal to unity. This implies that any additional investment raises *by assumption* the average and marginal productivity of the other inputs. The possibility that public and private capital stock are complementary is not allowed for in this setting. The use made of the Cobb-Douglas function in these studies also implies that all inputs are truely variable; a more appropriate assumption would be that some factors are fixed in the short run (private and public capital are quasi-fixed) while the other inputs are variable in the short run (raw materials, energy, employment). A more flexible form of the production function like the translog form used by Eberts (1986) and Costa et al. (1987) allows for such extensions.

Another problem with this approach is that it is unclear which direction the causality between infrastructure and output runs; in other words, there is a question of what is endogenous and exogenous. The use of OLS (Ordinary Least Squares) in general leads to inconsistent and biased estimators when there is a simultaneous equation bias. The inclusion of the capacity utilization measure is likely to increase this problem, since – almost by definition – this measure is related to the fluctuations in output.

A third flaw of the Cobb-Douglas approach is that optimality of the public capital stock is reached when the marginal product of public capital is unity, again by assumption.

5.4   THE PROFIT FUNCTION APPROACH

A number of studies have used the profit function instead of the production function as the starting point of analysis (the underlying assumptions are of course linked through duality theory, see Section 5.5). The question of importance is then: how great is the contribution of public capital services to the rate of profit?

Deno (1988) uses a translog profit function to estimate this contribution for 36 states in the period 1970-1978. The output elasticity of total public capital was estimated to be 0.69 (0.61 in growing areas, and 0.73 in declining areas). Of the components of total capital, highway and sewer capital had the highest output elasticity, and water capital the lowest. An intriguing finding by Deno is that the use of a flexible form instead of the Cobb Douglas function increases the estimate of the output elasticity of public capital 17 times. A further result is that the relationship between the private inputs (private capital and labor) and public capital is found to be complementary.

Lynde and Richmond (1992) find for the non-financial corporate business sector for the period 1958-1988 in the United States that a 1% increase in the mean value of the public capital stock would raise the mean real profit rate by 1.2%. (In a related study, Aschauer (1988) found 2.5% for this elasticity). Lynde and Richmond cannot reject the constant returns to scale assumption, adding to the growing list of evidence that the constant returns to scale assumption *at the aggregate level* over all three inputs is a reasonable assumption to make.

5.5   COST FUNCTION APPROACH

Yet another line of research uses the duality between production and cost functions and applies the research on generalized cost functions. The role public capital plays is expressed by the shadow price of public capital in the cost function; i.e. the effect an additional unit of public capital has on overall cost.

The duality principle (Varian 1992, Chapter 6) states that both lines of research should, given certain assumptions, contain essentially the same information: "any concept defined in terms of the properties of the production function has a "dual" definition in terms of the properties of the cost function and vice versa".

Most studies assume that:
– firms do not pay for public capital (public capital is "manna from heaven");
– public capital consists of "pure" public goods;[4]
– there is only causality from public capital to private sector productivity and factor demand, and not the other way around.[5]

The production function describing the technology of the individual firm or industry is, as before, of the form:

$$y = A(t)f(L,K,G)$$

---

[4] That is, public capital is non-rival and non-excludable. In real life, of course, public capital is an impure public good (e.g. congestion).

[5] There is considerable discussion whether this assumption is appropriate for industrialized countries. The argument is that governments in these countries invest in infrastructure to remove bottlenecks rather than to create or initiate economic development or growth.

where y denotes output, $A(t)$ is a factor representing technical progress and the function f is assumed to be homogeneous of degree 1 in L, K, and G. The public capital stock can be seen as a production externality.

Markets are competitive, and total private costs are $p_L L + p_K K$ where p_L is the wage rate and p_K denotes the user cost of capital.

The cost-minimization problem facing the firm can then be written as:

$$C(p_L, p_K, y, G, t) = \min_{L,K} p_L L + p_K K$$

$$\text{s.t. } A(t)f(L, K, G) = y.$$

Solving the constraint for K, and L gives the conditional demand functions for L and K:

$$L^* = g_L(A(t)^{-1}p_L, A(t)^{-1}p_K, A(t)^{-1}y, G)$$

and solving for the cost function:

$$K^* = g_K(A(t)^{-1}p_L, A(t)^{-1}p_K, A(t)^{-1}y, G)$$
$$C^* = C(p_L, p_k, y, G, t) = p_L L^* + p_K K^* = A(t)H(A(t)^{-1}p_L, A(t)^{-1}p_K, At^{-1}y, G).$$

If we apply the envelope theorem, or to be more specific Shephard's lemma (Varian, 1992, Chapter 5), we find that the following equalities hold:

$$L^* = \frac{\partial C}{\partial p_L}$$

$$K^* = \frac{\partial C}{\partial p_K}$$

$$\lambda^* = \frac{\partial C}{\partial y}$$

$$-\lambda^* A(t)f_G = \frac{\partial C}{\partial G}$$

where λ^* is a Lagrange multiplier and f_G is the partial derivative of f with respect to G.

The last equation gives an expression for the shadow price of public capital. It denotes the change in private production costs in the firm or industry if the public capital stock G is expanded by one additional unit.

To decompose the cost changes with respect to an increase in G into adjustment effects on private labor and capital, we can write, by using the relevant conditional factor demand functions:

$$-\lambda^* A(t)f_G = p_K\left(\frac{\partial K^*}{\partial G}\right) + p_L\left(\frac{\partial L^*}{\partial G}\right).$$

If an increase in the public capital stock leads to a change in costs this effect can be decomposed into cost changes or adjustment costs on labor and cost changes or adjustment costs of capital.

An increase in public capital is always cost saving – has a negative shadow price – if labor and private capital are both substitutes of public capital. If one of the factors is, however, complementary to the public input the effect is undetermined. It is positive (there are cost savings) if the substitutive effects outweigh the complementary effect.

The effect of public investment expenditures is essentially dependent on whether private and public factors are complementary or substitutable.

A number of empirical studies have appeared that used this method to test for the impact of public capital on private sector output and growth: Berndt and Hansson (1991); Seitz (1992); Morrison and Schwartz (1992); Nadiri and Mamuenas (1991); Shah (1992); Lynde and Richmond (1992).

Berndt and Hansson (1991) estimate a normalized generalized Leontief cost function with public capital as a component using Swedish data for the period 1960-1988. Their results indicate that the constant returns to scale over all factors assumption is rejected, as are the restrictions implied by constant returns to scale over private inputs only. The authors obtain a definition of the optimal level of public provision of infrastructure by assuming that optimality is reached when social marginal benefits are equal to social marginal costs. In 1988 there was an excess amount of public infrastructure in Sweden of about 10%, though this excess amount had been falling in the 1980s.

Seitz (1992) estimates the flexible cost function for 31 German industries over the period 1970-1989. His panel-estimation indicates that the estimated shadow price of capital (for the core infrastructure) is 0.00364; that is, an increase of 1 DM spending on infrastructure reduces the private cost of the 31 industries by 0.00364 DM.

Morrison and Schwartz (1992) have estimated a flexible cost function for a panel of 48 U.S. states for the period 1971-1987. They also report that the direct cost impact of infrastructure investment is quite extensive, although not as great as that found by other researchers. The shadow shares of public capital range between 15 and 20% in the Northern and Eastern states and between 20 and 30% in the Western and Southern states.

A study by Nadiri and Mamuenas (1991) also suggests that there are important productive effects from public capital.

5.6   A RESEARCH AGENDA

The results discussed in Sections 5.3, 5.4 and 5.5 can be summarized as follows. Almost all empirical research points to a positive contribution of publicly provided infrastructure to private sector output and growth. Most studies that use the cost function approach or a flexible production approach find that private and public capital are complementary rather than substitutable. This we do know. But there are important questions still unresolved that might change the results dramatically when taken into account.

(a)   Infrastructure as an Impure Public Good

The first is: what happens to the results if we relax the assumption that infrastructure is a pure public good? The privatization of British rail and the private ownership and exploitation of toll roads in France present clear evidence that infrastructure might be rival and excludable, just like any private good.

Another point of interest in this respect is that the studies presented above indicate in general that there are constant returns to scale over all factors *at the aggregate level.* There can only be increasing returns to scale at the micro-level – as the theory predicts – in this case if public capital is subject to congestion.

In their theoretical growth model, Barro and Sala-i-Martin (1992) distinguish two cases: publicly-provided private goods and publicly provided goods that are subject to congestion (impure public goods). In the latter case, the production function facing the individual producer is assumed to be:

$$y = Ak \ (G/K)^{\alpha}.$$

Given the assumption of identical producers, aggregate production exhibits constant returns to scale. The G/K ratio is an index of congestion. Aschauer (1988) and Lynde and Richmond (1992) report that for the United States this ratio has been falling during the last two decades, indicating an increased level of congestion. The important point is that by maximizing profits, the individual producer takes the G/K ratio as given. In the absence of a user fee, this leads to a suboptimal growth path (see Section 5.6.c).

Only one empirical contribution pays attention to the possibility of congestion. Shah (1992) does this by defining the quality of public infrastructure:

$$G_E = G \ (I)^{\theta}$$

where G is public infrastructure and I is an index of use. The value of θ is estimated; a value of 0 means that G is a public good and a value of 1 would suggest that it is a private good. In his study of the Mexican industry, Shah finds a value of 1.000812 for θ with a t-value of 51.6 and therefore highly significant. This indicates that, in the case of Mexico, public infrastructure can be viewed as a private good or a highly-congested public good.

Since congestion also seems relevant for industrialized countries, extending the analysis to incorporate the rivalry and excludability aspects seems only natural. This might provide a powerful explanation of why results from studies of states differ from national results, as noted by Holtz-Eakin (1991).

(b)   Optimality of Provision of Infrastructure Capital

If infrastructure is publicly provided, how can we be sure that it is provided optimally? Or, if this is not the case, can we measure how much the deviations from the optimal level are? This is also a question of great public and political interest.

Berndt and Hansson (1991) provide a measure of optimality. Under the assumption that infrastructure is a pure public good, total marginal benefits of public capital are the sum of all shadow values over all private sector firms, plus the sum of all marginal benefits over all final consumers. In the absence of congestion, the total marginal benefit could be the largest benefit accruing to any one or set of consumers, rather than the sum over all consumers. Marginal benefits must then equal marginal cost, where the latter is the one-period social price of public infrastructure capital.

In their empirical section, Berndt and Hansson use the calculated shadow prices of the public infrastructure capital that reduce the cost of the private business sector as a measure of the marginal benefits. Marginal costs are measured as the ex ante rental prices of private capital. The authors note that (p. 24-25):

"To the extent that the benefits computed in this way are understated (since any benefits to final consumers are not incorporated), *ceteris paribus,* the ratio of (the optimal public capital stock) to (the actual public capital stock) is also understated. Moreover, since the optimal private capital stock rises with decreases in the one-period rental price of capital P, *ceteris paribus,* to the extent that corporate taxes are not incorporated into the measure of (the one period rental price of private capital), the ratio of (the optimal private capital stock) to (the actual private stock) is overstated. Hence, there is some reason to believe that both of these ratios are understated. However, if the bias can plausibly be argued to be relatively constant over time, the time trend in these ratios can still provide useful information."

This raises some important questions: can we estimate the benefits received by final consumers through public provision of infrastructure? Growth models as in Barro (1990) and Barro and Sala-i-Martin (1992) typically assume that the economy consists of household-producers. Extending the models to allow for consumers and producers as separate entities might provide new insights in the role infrastructure plays in the process of economic growth. After all, infrastructure is used (and congested) by both producers and consumers.

Note that the congestion argument made above also has its effect on the definition of optimality made by Berndt and Hansson (1991). In fact, if there is congestion, the results presented may be quite misleading.

(c)   The Financing of Infrastructure

The models presented above typically assume (with the exception of the theoretical models) that infrastructure is an unpaid factor. This is not a very realistic assumption: infrastructure is paid through a variety of taxes, licence fees, levies and user charges. The neglect of this channel implicates that the models overestimate the effects of infrastructure investment (see also Winston, 1991).

The implications of the use of income taxes vs. lump sum taxation, and the implications of distortionary taxation in a second-best world *are*, however, explored in the theoretical models. Barro and Sala-i-Martin (1992) find that if infrastructure is a private good and the technology is Cobb-Douglas with private and public capital as inputs, lump sum taxation (like a consumption tax) is to be preferred from a social welfare point of view since it equalizes private and social returns to investment and thereby reaches a Pareto optimal situation. The same holds true if infrastructure can be considered a pure public good.

If, however, infrastructure can be considered to be an impure public good then taxes on output or income are to be preferred in the simple growth model presented by Barro and Sala-i-Martin (1992) because they internalize the excessive use of the infrastructure.

The model does not consider government borrowing on the capital market. In most of the literature it is assumed that Ricardian equivalence holds, and that the two ways of financing have the same (if any) effects on the real economy. Van der Ploeg and Tang (1992) argue that this is a very strong assumption, since it implies that private consumption is unaffected when the government finances a temporary tax-cut with short-term borrowing and a long-run increase in taxation. Ricardian debt neutrality may therefore fail for a whole range of reasons. According to van der Ploeg and Tang, it is more likely that debt creation does lead to a lower rate of economic growth as compared with taxation.

Unless government funds are "earmarked", however, it is difficult to apply this knowledge in an empirical setting. However, the theoretical argument for user charges for infrastructure as often encountered in the transport economics literature, still remains valid in the context of growth theory.

(d)   International Spillovers of Infrastructure Supply

Another neglected point in the research presented in this chapter is the possibility of international spillovers of infrastructure investment. Transport networks are an obvious example. There has been almost no research in the context of growth theory that I know of. As is the case with the international spillovers of environmental pollution and the like, this may prove an highly exciting new area of research.

5.7   CONCLUDING REMARKS

This chapter has aimed at providing an overview of what we know and what we do not
know about the macroeconomic link between public provision of infrastructure and the
private sector.

The empirical results generally indicate that infrastructure has a positive and significant
impact on output, profits and costs. Studies using a flexible functional form tend to find
that private capital and public capital are complementary factors of production.

Infrastructure research has developed very rapidly in the last few years. Working on
refinements like the relaxation of the pure public good assumption, the extension of the
optimality criterion to the benefits received by consumers, the relaxation of the "unpaid
factor" model and extensions to international spillovers of infrastructure supply seem to
be very promising areas of research.

REFERENCES

Arrow, K.J. and M. Kurz, 1970, "Public Investment, the Rate of Return, and Optimal
  Fiscal Policy", *Resources For The Future*, John Hopkins Press, Baltimore/London.
Aschauer, D.A., 1988, "Government Spending and the 'Falling Rate of Profit'",
  Economic Perspectives, 12:11-17.
Aschauer, D.A., 1989, "Is Public Expenditure Productive?", *Journal of Monetary Eco-
  nomics*, 23:177-200.
Barro, R.J., 1990, "Government Spending in a Simple Model of Endogenous Growth",
  Journal of Political Economy, 98:103-125.
Barro, R.J. and X. Sala-i-Martin, 1992, "Public Finance in Models of Economic
  Growth", *Review of Economic Studies*, 59:645-661.
Berndt, E.R. and B. Hansson, 1991, "Measuring the Contribution of Public Infrastruc-
  ture Capital in Sweden", NBER Working Paper No. 3842.
Conrad, K. and H. Seitz, 1992, "The Economic Benefits of Public Infrastructure: The
  Case of Germany", Discussion Paper No. 469-92, IVW, University of Mannheim.
Costa, J. da Silva, R.W. Ellson and R.G. Martin, 1987, "Public Capital, Regional Out-
  put and Development: Some Empirical Evidence", *Journal of Regional Science,*
  27:419-437.
Deno, K.T., 1988, "The Effect of Public Capital on US Manufacturing Activity: 1970 to
  1978", *Southern Economic Journal*, Vol. 55, 2:400-411.
Duffy-Deno, K.T. and R.W. Eberts, 1991, "Public Infrastructure and Regional
  Economic Development: A Simultaneous Equation Approach", *Journal of Urban
  Economics*, Vol. 30, 3:329-343.
Eberts, R.W., 1986, "Estimating the Contribution of Urban Public Infrastructure to
  Regional Economic Growth", Working Paper No. 8610, Federal Reserve Bank of
  Cleveland.
Eberts, R.W., 1990, "Public Infrastructure and Regional Economic Development",
  Federal Reserve Bank of Cleveland Economic Review (Quarter 1, 1990), pp. 15-27.
Eisner, R., 1980, "Total Income, Total Investment and Growth", *American Economic
  Review*, Vol. 70, 2:225-231.
Ford, R. and P. Poret, 1991, "Infrastructure and Private Sector Productivity", Economic
  and Statistic Department Working Papers No. 91, OECD, Paris.
Grossman, H. and R. Lucas, 1974, "The Macroeconomic Effects of Productive Public
  Expenditures", *The Manchester School of Economic and Social Studies* XLII:162-
  170.
Holtz-Eakin, D., 1991, "Public Sector Capital and the Productivity Puzzle", NBER
  Working Paper 4144.

Lynde, C. and J. Richmond, 1992, "The Role of Public Capital in Production", *Review of Economics and Statistics*, 74:37-44.

Mera, K., 1973, "Regional Production Functions and the Social Overhead Capital: An Analyzis of the Japanese Case", *Regional and Urban Economics*, Vol. 3, 2:157-185.

Merriman, D., 1990, Public Capital and Regional Output", *Regional Science and Urban Economics*, 20:437-458.

Morrison, O.J. and A.E. Schwartz, 1992, State Infrastructure and Productive Performance", NBER Working Paper No. 3981.

Munnell, A.H., 1990a, "Why Has Productivity Declined? Productivity and Public Investment", *New England Economic Review*, January/February 1990, Federal Reserve Bank of Boston, 3-22.

Munnell, A.H. with the assistance of L.M. Cook, 1990b, "How Does Public Infrastructure Affect Regional Economic Performance?", *New England Economic Review*, September/October 1990, Federal Reserve Bank of Boston, 11-32.

Munnell, A.H., 1992, "Infrastructure Investment and Economic Growth", *Journal of Economic Perspectives*, Vol. 6, 4:189-198.

Nadiri, M.I. and T.P. Mamuenas, 1991, "The Effects of Public Infrastructure and R & D Capital on the Cost Structure and Performance of US Manufacturing Industries", NBER Working Paper No. 3887.

Ogura, S and G. Yohe, 1977, "The Complementarity of Public and Private Capital and the Optimal Rate of Return to Government Investment", *Quarterly Journal of Economics*, 91:651-662.

Ploeg, F. van der and P.J.G. Tang, 1992, "The Macroeconomics of Growth: An International Perspective", *Oxford Review of Economic Policy*, Vol. 8, 4:15-28.

Ratner, J.B., 1983, "Government Capital and the Production Function for US Private Output", *Economics Letters*, 13:213-217.

Rietveld, P., 1989, "Infrastructure and Regional Development", *The Annals of Regional Science*, 23:255-274.

Samuelson, P.A., 1954, "The Pure Theory of Public Expenditures", *Review of Economics and Statistics*, 36:387-389.

Seitz, H., 1992, "Public Capital and the Demand for Private Inputs", ZEW Discussion Paper No. 92-08, Mannheim.

Shah, A., 1992, "Dynamics of Public Infrastructure, Industrial Productivity and Profitability", *Review of Economics and Statistics*, 74:28-36.

Toen-Gout, M.W. and M.M. Jongeling, 1993, "Investeringen in infrastructuur en economische groei", *ESB* 12-5-1993, 424-427.

Varian, H.R., 1992, "*Microeconomic Analysis*", Third edition, W.W. Norton & Company.

von Furstenberg, G.M., 1980, "*The Government and Capital Formation*", Ballinger Publishing Company, Cambridge, Mass,

Winston, C.M., 1991, "Efficient Transportation Infrastructure Policy", *Journal of Economic Perspectives*, pp. 113 - 127.

PART B: INFRASTRUCTURE POLICY: PRICING AND OWNERSHIP ISSUES

CHAPTER 6

Infrastructure, Wages and Land Prices

Andrew F. Haughwout
Princeton University

6.1   INTRODUCTION

The importance of infrastructure investment and its contribution to welfare has been the subject of considerable recent debate in both policy and academic circles. In this study, I propose a somewhat different treatment of infrastructure than has previously been adopted. Specifically, I model infrastructure investment as a *local* public good, and discuss how to measure its costs and benefits in this context. Section 6.2 of this study provides a synthesis of two models which have traditionally been used to examine the effects of local attributes, including fiscal attributes and infrastructure, on local economies. Recent research on the impact of fiscal policy has roughly been concentrated in two areas: studies which calculate "willingness to pay" for local attributes by estimating implicit price models, and studies which attempt to calculate the direct effect of infrastructure stocks and other public policy instruments on aggregate variables like employment and output. Section 6.3 shows that these two approaches should not be considered exclusively of each other and provides a simple general equilibrium framework which incorporates elements of each.

Any attempt to determine whether a nation's infrastructure stocks are sufficient to service the needs of a growing economy and population must begin with a clear notion of how to measure the benefits of public investment. Section 6.3 provides a simple means of calculating the full range of local benefits that infrastructure provides, from changes in land values to employment.

Section 6.4 empirically estimates the parameters of the theoretical model developed in Section 6.3. I utilize 1974-1986 microdata from the *Annual Housing Survey* and fiscal data from Census' *City Finances* series to examine the role that infrastructure plays in determining local land values, wages, and employment. The dataset contains over 11,000 individual observations, with fiscal information for 28 cities for this 13 year period. (Included cities and the method used to estimate their infrastructure stocks are described in the Appendices.) The use of microdata allows the estimation of not only the level, but also the distribution, of infrastructure benefits. The regression results clearly indicate the strengths of the microdata, general equilibrium formulation. In particular, I find that the primary beneficiaries of local public investment are those who own land in the jurisdiction. The capitalization of infrastructure's long run benefits into local land values provides landowners with a powerful incentive to favor its maintenance and expansion. Thus, landowners provide a natural constituency favoring local public investment. The empirical results also reveal that infrastructure plays an important role in job creation.

These two effects, on land prices and on employment, provide the basis for calculating the efficiency of local public capital stocks.

6.2   PREVIOUS RESEARCH

The literature on household and firm reactions to local public policy is rich and varied. Studies range from the survey-based work pioneered by Schmenner (1982), through the regional production function estimates typified by the papers in Munnell (1990), to the compensating variation framework employed by Brueckner (1979, 1982, 1983), Gyourko and Tracy (1989a, 1989b, 1991), and Voith (1991). In this section, I briefly review some of these studies, paying particular attention to the interpretation of the empirical results and pointing out the limitations in the literature to this point.

6.2.1 The Production Approach

The production approach can be broken down into two subcategories: studies which directly estimate production functions at either the regional or urban level, and those that attempt to estimate the direct role played by local fiscal policies, including tax and expenditure policy, in business and employment location decisions.

In the former subcategory are many papers in the tradition of Mera (1973), Eberts (1990), and Munnell (1990). In general, the approach may be summarized as follows: Aggregate measures of infrastructure, private capital, employment, and occasionally land, are treated as inputs to an aggregate production function. The dependent variable is usually the logarithm of aggregate value added or gross regional or urban product. The resulting coefficient on infrastructure is interpreted as the elasticity (in the standard log-log formulation) of output with respect to public goods.

The second subcategory, which is succinctly reviewed and utilized in Herzog and Schlottmann (1991), typically estimates a function in which employment or business start-ups is the dependent variable, and regressors include local variables such as the wage rate, land price, tax rates, expenditure levels, and, occasionally, the use of fiscal incentives like firm-specific tax incentives or industrial development bonds. Coefficients on the tax and expenditure variables are interpreted as the impacts of policy instruments on employment and/or business location.

6.2.2 The Compensating Variation Approach

Compensating variation or capitalization studies have traditionally analyzed the effect that variations in urban amenities have on local land and labor markets. This line of research, pioneered by Roback (1982), has been applied to local economies which include a public sector by Brueckner (1979, 1982, 1983), Voith (1991), and Gyourko and Tracy (1989a, 1989b, 1991). The fundamental assumption that is common to all these studies is that, in long run equilibrium, utility and profits cannot be altered by relocation. If this assumption holds, then long run local prices must reflect the value of non-traded local attributes such as amenities and fiscal policy. In order to estimate the value of local fiscal policy, regressions of the form

$$W = f(R,H,A,G)$$
$$R = g(W,V,A,G)$$

are estimated, where W is the wage, R is the land price, H is a vector of worker characteristics, V is a vector of house characteristics, and A and G are vectors of local amenities and fiscal policy variables, respectively. The simultaneous nature of the system is accounted for by the use of a multi-equation method like two-stage least squares. The coefficients on fiscal policy variables are combined and interpreted as values for fiscal attributes. In a similar model which excludes the labor market, Brueckner analyzes the efficiency of local public good provision. His results show that property value is maximized at the efficient level of public expenditure. Two recent papers (Gyourko and Tracy 1989b, 1991) have shown that the labor market **does** reflect variations in local policy. Brueckner's model is most appropriate for the analysis of a **given** urban area which acts as a single labor market, i.e. a single wage pertains. Gyourko and Tracy's model is applicable to a system of cities, where commuting from one to another is impossible, and both land and labor prices may vary over space.

In this chapter, I present a model which incorporates both the production and compensating variation approaches. In the next section I outline the general structure of the model, and examine its comparative static properties. I also compare and contrast the model presented here with those discussed above. This discussion reveals biases inherent in the production approaches, as well as the limitations of the capitalization model.

6.3   MODEL

6.3.1 Economy

Consider an economy made up of many discrete political jurisdictions whose boundaries are fixed. All land is owned by landlords absent from the economy, and all jurisdictions are spatially separated such that it is impossible to commute across jurisdictional lines. Households and firms must choose where to locate, given the fiscal policy, amenities, wages, and land prices which characterize each jurisdiction. The model has the same structure as the "open city, absentee landlord" model described in Fujita (1989).[1]

6.3.2 Households

Households are assumed to be freely mobile, utility-maximizing agents which inelastically supply a single unit of homogeneous labor.[2] Each household maximizes its utility subject to the constraint that its expenditure on a numeraire all-purpose consumption good, taxes, and land equals its wage income. Although non-wage income is assumed to be zero for simplicity, relaxing this assumption has no effect on the model's substantive results. The free mobility assumption is tempered by the constraint that commuting is impossible: each household must live and work in the same jurisdiction. Thus each jurisdiction may be treated as a distinct labor market.[3] The household's problem may then be formulated as follows

---

[1]   Although this is a paper about the effects of fiscal policy, I assume that fiscal variables are exogenous, that is, I include no model of local government behavior. When derivatives with respect to levels of public spending are examined, the reader is invited to imagine an exogenous increase or decrease in aid from other levels of government. I believe I have taken the simplest possible approach to make the point. For analyses of the determinants of public capital spending, see Holtz-Eakin and Rosen (1993), and Haughwout (1993).

[2]   The free mobility assumption implies that households can compare the utility levels available at different locations and move to that area which offers them the highest level of well-being. Free mobility across jurisdictions is, of course, simply a useful abstraction. What matters is that local prices are set by a marginal potential mover, a much more attractive expression of the same notion.

[3]   In reality, labor markets are more accurately defined as PMSAs. The Philadelphia PMSA, for example, contains over three hundred separate Minor Civil Divisions, each with some control over its fiscal policy. However, tractability considerations, combined with the observation that central city

$$\max_{Q,L} U(Q,L,G,A) \quad \text{subject to} \quad (1-t_y)W = Q+(1+t_p)RL \tag{1}$$

where Q is consumption of the numeraire composite good; L is the household's consumption of land; G is the available level of local public goods; A is the level of local amenities[4]; t_y is the local income (wage) tax rate; W is the local wage; t_p is the local *ad valorem* property tax rate; and R is the local (annualized) price per unit of land. I assume that the utility function is increasing in all arguments but at a diminishing rate.[5] This assumption implies nonsatiation, i.e. that utility is strictly increasing in income W.

Defining the gross of tax land price as $R^g = (1+t_p)R$, the solution of the household's problem yields demand functions for the composite good

$$Q^d = Q^d(W,R^g,t_y,G,A) \tag{2}$$

and land

$$L_h^d = L_h^d(W,R^g,t_y,G,A). \tag{3}$$

Substitution of these demand functions into the household's utility function yields the indirect utility function

$$V(W,R^g,t_y,G,A). \tag{4}$$

The free mobility assumption implies that, in long run equilibrium, no household can increase its utility by moving. This condition in turn means that utility must equalize over space. Thus, at equilibrium

$$V(W,R^g,t_y,G,A) = V_0 \tag{5}$$

where V_0 is the equilibrium level of utility available in the nation as a whole. From the point of view of any one locality, V_0 is exogenous; that is each locality is a utility-taker. However, it is important to note that for the system of cities as a whole, the equilibrium utility level is endogenous.

The importance of the equilibrium condition expressed by (5) is that it implicitly states that, for any given set of fiscal policies (and amenities), local wages and land prices must adjust to ensure that the equilibrium level of utility obtains in all jurisdictions. In order to express this condition analytically, we invert the indirect utility function (5) and solve for wage income[6], which yields

---

labor market conditions often differ substantially from those in the suburbs, provide some justification for the adoption of this assumption.

[4] By amenities I have in mind such non-produced, publicly available goods as beaches, warm winters, and the like. For firms (see below), these amenities might include natural deep-water ports, proximity to export product markets, etc. I do not notationally distinguish amenities valued by firms from those valued by households to indicate the possibility of overlap; e.g. a coastal location may be valuable to both firms and households.

[5] While urban disamenities, for example pollution, may affect utility, the assumption is perfectly general insofar as we treat the **lack** of disamenities as amenities. Thus "clean air" may well be an element of the vector A.

[6] The ability to invert the utility function with respect to W depends on the assumption that utility is strictly increasing in income. This condition is guaranteed by the local nonsatiation assumption introduced above.

$$W_h^d = E(R^g, t_y, G, A, V_0). \tag{6}$$

Equation (6) can be considered a "wage demand" function: given each locality's fiscal policy, amenities, and land prices, in order to obtain the equilibrium level of utility V_0 the household must receive a wage of W_h^d. Note, however, that this is precisely the definition of the household's expenditure function (Varian, 1984, p.122). W_h^d represents the minimal amount of income necessary to achieve utility V_0 given local conditions R, t_y, t_p, G, and A.[7] This fact will prove quite useful later in the analysis.

Comparative statics of the expenditure function are straightforward. Wages are increasing in those variables which households consider "bad", i.e. R^g and t_y, and decreasing in those it considers good, G and A. Otherwise utility would deviate from V_0. If the equilibrium level of utility itself changes, then wages must change in the same direction, *ceteris paribus*. Thus $\partial W_h^d / \partial V_0 > 0$. Curve HH in Figure 6.1 shows the relationship between wages and land prices that the equal-utility formulation requires. Changes in local fiscal policy, such as a reduction in local wage tax rates accomplished through improved technical efficiency in production of the local public good, will shift this curve, in this case downward and to the right. The "larger" public good allows households to accept lower wages and higher land prices while they continue to enjoy utility V_0.

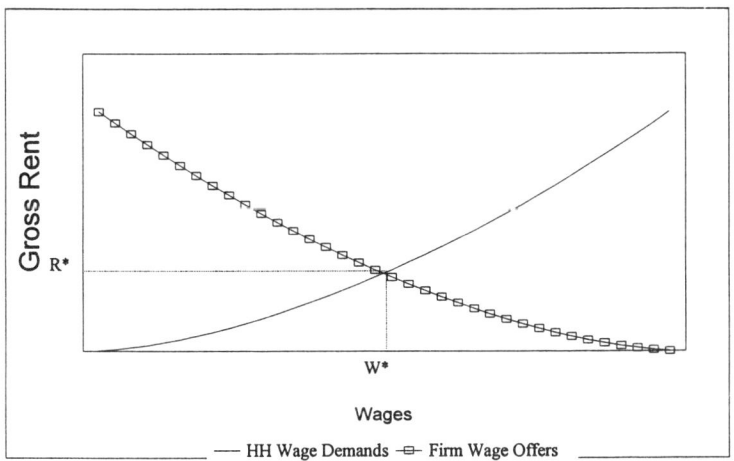

Figure 6.1 Equilibrium wages and land prices

6.3.3 Firms

Firms are profit maximizing enterprises which, like households, are freely mobile over space. For simplicity, production is assumed to be constant returns to scale, and both input and output markets are perfectly competitive. The constant returns assumption allows us to write the firm's problem as

$$\min_{N,K,L} C = WN + rK + R^gL \text{ subject to } X(N,K,L,G,A) = 1 \tag{7}$$

---

7   The Varian formulation is based strictly on prices and utility. Here, I include other local conditions, namely fiscal policy and amenities, as arguments in the expenditure function. Because these factors are external to the individual decision process, the analogy is exact.

where N is the amount of labor employed by the firm; r is the rental rate of private capital, assumed to be determined nationally; K is the firm's private capital stock; and $X(\cdot)$ is the firm's production function, by means of which it produces the composite output good X.

The firm selects that mix of inputs which minimizes its cost per unit of output. Note the absence of the income tax rate t_y from the firm's problem. This reflects the assumption that households are nominally responsible for paying income taxes. This does not necessarily mean, however, that the burden of income taxes will fall entirely on households. If the demand for labor by city firms is relatively inelastic, then households may be able to shift some of the burden of the tax onto their employers.

In a procedure analogous to the method used to analyze the household, we can obtain the firm's demands for labor,

$$N_f^d = N_f^d(W,R^g,r,G,A) \tag{8}$$

capital,

$$K_f^e = K_f^e(W,R^g,r,G,A) \tag{9}$$

and land

$$L_f^d = L_f^d(W,R^g,r,G,A) \tag{10}$$

per unit output. Substituting these demands into the firm's cost identity, we obtain the minimum cost function per unit output, which depends only on those variables which are exogenous to the firm

$$C(W,R^g,r,G,A). \tag{11}$$

Again, in a fashion analogous to the household problem, we utilize the long run spatial equilibrium condition. In a perfectly competitive, free-mobility environment, the equilibrium rate of economic profit must be zero everywhere. Thus, the minimum cost per unit of output must equal its sale price

$$C(W,R^g,r,G,A) = P_x. \tag{12}$$

Solving this condition for the wage yields what I will call the firm's "wage bid" function[8]

$$W_f^b = W_f^b(R^g,r,G,A,P_x). \tag{13}$$

Wage bids by firms must be decreasing in other components of cost, i.e. R^g and r, and increasing in the productivity-enhancing factors G and A. As the price of the output good X rises, the firm makes excess profits until entry bids up market wages. Thus $\partial W_f^b/\partial P_x > 0$. Curve FF in Figure 6.1 shows the equilibrium relationship between W_f^b and R^g.

6.3.4 Urban Equilibrium

In order to qualitatively describe the aggregate characteristics of an urban equilibrium, we will need to simultaneously solve the following seven equations, which result directly from the above discussion:

---

[8] Again, this inversion requires that costs be strictly increasing in wages. This condition will hold as long as firms are not at a "corner solution" with respect to labor, i.e. that they employ some labor. I assume that labor is a requirement of production.

$$W^* = E(R^*, t_y, G, A, V_0) \tag{14}$$

$$P_x = C(W^*, R^*, r, G, A) \tag{15}$$

$$N^* = N_f^d(W^*, R^*, r, G, A) * X^* \tag{16}$$

$$L_h^* = L_h^d(W^*, R^*, t_p, G, A) * N^* \tag{17}$$

$$K^* = K_f^d(W^*, R^*, r, G, A) * X^* \tag{18}$$

$$L_f^* = L_f^d(W^*, R^*, r, G, A) * X^* \tag{19}$$

$$L_h^* + L_f^* = L_0. \tag{20}$$

Here, variables with asterisks indicate equilibrium values (R^* represents the equilibrium value of R^g), while L_0 represents the (fixed) land area of the jurisdiction.

Equations (14) and (15) enforce the spatial equilibrium conditions that utility and profits must equalize over space. Equation (16) gives the equilibrium population of the city as the product of the per unit output labor demanded by firms and the equilibrium urban output, while (17) gives the total land area consumed by households. Equations (18) and (19) determine the equilibrium private capital stock and land use by firms, respectively, while (20) enforces the constraint that total land consumption must equal land area.[9]

In reality, the system is not fully simultaneous. The first two equations, which are the compensating variation model, determine the equilibrium levels of wages and gross of tax land prices, while the next five use these local prices to solve for urban aggregates. In this context, wages and land prices must adjust to ensure equilibrium. Once equilibrium wages and land prices have been determined, firms and households condition their demands for land, capital, and labor upon these prices. The fact that local wages and land prices are independent of population and output may initially appear counter-intuitive. However, in the absence of congestion, *prices* must adjust to ensure equilibrium. Firms and households decide what price levels are warranted by the amenity and fiscal policy "packages" offered by each locality, then locate accordingly.

6.3.5 Comparative Statics of the Equilibrium Prices W^* and R^*

The general functional form in which the model has been presented obviously precludes explicit solution of (14)-(20). Yet we can gain some insight into the relationships between public goods and urban attributes by exploring the comparative statics of the system. To facilitate this examination, I will make use of two important principles of microeconomic duality theory:

a) *First partial derivatives of the household expenditure function with respect to prices represent compensated demand functions.*

b) *First partial derivatives of the firm's cost function with respect to input prices represent conditional input demand functions.*

These two facts will greatly simplify the discussion to come, so they merit some justification. Formal proofs of the propositions are given by Varian (1984, pp.54-55, 122-123), so I will argue only that they are appropriate in the present context. To do so, I

---

[9] I ignore the possibility of vacant land and assume that the local public sector does not compete with households and firms in the land market. This assumption makes the model most appropriate for the analysis of improvements in an existing stock of infrastructure, the situation prevailing in most of the cities considered in the empirical section.

need simply to demonstrate that the household demand functions are compensated demands and that the firm input demands are conditional on the level of output. As to the first, the equal-utility assumption ensures that *all* demand functions in this model are of the compensated variety. Prices adjust via (14) and (15) to ensure that the utility level obtainable in all jurisdictions is the same. Thus compensated demands evaluated at the equilibrium prices are equivalent to Marshallian demands. As for firms, the derivation of the cost function (11) assumed a given level of output, namely one unit. Thus the conditional demands are per unit of output. Therefore, both the compensated consumption demand and the conditional factor demand functions are easily interpretable in the current context.

a) Effect of Fiscal Policy on Equilibrium Local Prices

These principles from microeconomic theory will simplify our examination of the comparative statics of the system (14)-(20). Let us turn first to the responses of equilibrium local prices W^* and R^* to changes in fiscal policy. From the properties of the household expenditure function, partial differentiation of equation (14) yields

$$\partial E(\cdot)/\partial R^* = L_h^d .$$

The properties of the cost function (15) allow us to write

$$\partial C(\cdot)/\partial R^* = L_f^d$$
$$\partial C(\cdot)/\partial r = K_f^d$$
$$\partial C(\cdot)/\partial W^* = N_f^d .$$

Recalling that V_0 and P_x are determined nationally, total differentiation of (14) and (15) yields

$$dW^* = L_h^d \, dR^* + \partial E/\partial t_y \, dt_y + \partial E/\partial G \, dG + \partial E/\partial A \, dA \tag{14'}$$

$$dP_x = 0 = L_f^d \, dR^* + K_f^d \, dr + \partial C/\partial G \, dG + \partial C/\partial A \, dA + N_f^d \, dW^*. \tag{15'}$$

We are particularly interested in the effects of fiscal policy, so let us examine[10]

$$\frac{dR^*}{dG} = \frac{-1}{L_f^d}\left[\left(1 - \frac{N_f^d L_h^d}{L_f^d + N_f^d L_h^d}\right)\partial C/\partial G + \frac{N_f^d L_h^d}{L_f^d + N_f^d L_h^d}\,\partial E/\partial G\right] \tag{21}$$

and

$$\frac{dW^*}{dG} = \frac{L_f^d}{L_f^d + N_f^d L_h^d}\left[\left(-L_h^d/L_f^d\right)\partial C/\partial G + \partial E/\partial G\right]. \tag{22}$$

Noting that the term $\dfrac{N_f^d L_h^d}{L_f^d + N_f^d L_h^d} < 1$ if firms consume land, the total effect of a "larger"

---

[10] Because space is limited, I do not discuss the comparative static effects of changes in the tax variables t_y and t_p. However, they exhibit characteristics converse to those for the public good G.

level of public good is unambiguously positive on land prices unless one sector is actually repelled by increased public good availability.[11] Assuming that public goods are of benefit to both firms and households, both $\partial C/\partial G$ and $\partial E/\partial G$ are negative. Note, however, that even if one of the sectors assigns no positive or negative value to marginal changes in G, (21) is still positive.

The effect shown in (22) is more complicated. Because households and firms are linked through the labor market, the comparative static effects on wages are ambiguous. Increased public good provision allows households to lower wage demands, but encourages firms to raise wage offers. In general, it is impossible to predict *a priori* the sign of (22). It will be positive if

$$\left(1/L_h^d\right)\partial E/\partial G \;>\; \left(1/L_f^d\right)\partial C/\partial G$$

or, roughly speaking, if firms value the additional public good more than households do.

b) Effects of Fiscal Policy on the Urban Aggregates

Let us now examine the comparative static properties of the remaining endogenous variables in the model. Differentiating (16)-(20), we obtain

$$\frac{dN^*}{dG} = X * \left(\partial N_f^d / \partial R * \frac{dR^*}{dG} + \partial N_f^d / \partial W * \frac{dW^*}{dG} + \partial N_f^d / \partial G \right) + N_f^d \frac{dX^*}{dG} \tag{23}$$

$$\frac{dL_h^*}{dG} = N * \left(\partial L_h^d / \partial R * \frac{dR^*}{dG} + \partial L_h^d / \partial W * \frac{dW^*}{dG} + \partial L_h^d / \partial G \right) + L_h^d \frac{dN^*}{dG} \tag{24}$$

$$\frac{dL_f^*}{dG} = X * \left(\partial L_f^d / \partial R * \frac{dR^*}{dG} + \partial L_f^d / \partial W * \frac{dW^*}{dG} + \partial L_f^d / \partial G \right) + L_f^d \frac{dX^*}{dG} \tag{25}$$

$$\frac{dK_f^*}{dG} = X * \left(\partial K_f^d / \partial R * \frac{dR^*}{dG} + \partial K_f^d / \partial W * \frac{dW^*}{dG} + \partial K_f^d / \partial G \right) + K_f^d \frac{dX^*}{dG} \tag{26}$$

$$\frac{dL_0}{dG} = 0 = \frac{dL_h^*}{dG} + \frac{dL_f^*}{dG} \tag{27}$$

The simultaneity of the model, combined with the presence of the wage and land price derivatives, makes the comparative statics given by (23)-(27) rather complex. Each of the aggregates depends on at least one of the others, with W^* and R^* providing much of the driving force in the model. Even a cursory examination of (23)-(27) reveals that inferences based on simple production and employment location regressions must be drawn with care. It is to these techniques and their limitations that I now turn.

---

[11] If the public sector activity dG is a new clean air regulation, firms will be repelled, while households will be attracted. We would expect wages to fall, while the effect on land prices would be indeterminate.

6.3.6 Implications for Partial Equilibrium Approaches

a) Production and Location Studies

Equations (23)-(27) reveal the necessity of a careful interpretation of the results of urban production functions.

Consider the model

$$ln\ X^* = \beta_0 + \beta_1\ ln\ G + \beta_2\ ln\ N^* + \beta_3\ ln\ K^* + \beta_4\ ln\ L_f^* \qquad (28)$$

which is representative of the form of a broad class of models estimated in the urban and regional production function literature.[12] As noted above, the coefficient β_1 is usually interpreted as the contribution of public goods to private productivity. But (23)-(27) reveal that the impact of public goods is much more complex, due to the interactions of firms and households through local land and labor markets. In general, the elasticity of output with respect to public goods is **not** directly recoverable from β_1. Only in the case in which public goods have no effect on local wages and land prices will the estimates retrieved from (28) be reliable approximations of the impact of infrastructure levels on private output. Yet there is by now considerable empirical evidence that fiscal policy differentials do affect local prices (See, for example, Gyourko and Tracy 1989a, 1989b, 1991), and thus all urban aggregates that depend on those prices – N^*, K^*, L_f^*, L_h^*, and X^* – will vary with fiscal policy. The endogeneity of employment, for example, implies that β_1 only captures part of the impact of infrastructure levels on private production. Note also that even if households have no value for the public good G, the increased wage and/or land price offers by firms that increasing G causes will have indirect impacts on households through the land and labor markets. If increased availability of public goods increases firm wage offers, for example, then employment may increase even if households have no direct value for the "larger" public good. The failure of the production approach to consider the fact that land and labor are traded in local markets makes the results of such studies very difficult to interpret.

The employment and business location analyses reviewed in the recent Herzog and Schlottmann volume (1991) fall victim to a similar pitfall. If wages depend in part on fiscal policy then the coefficient α_1 in the model

$$N = \alpha_0 + \alpha_1\ G + \alpha_2\ W^* + \alpha_3\ R^* \dots \qquad (29)$$

will provide only part of the impact of fiscal policy on employment. The rest will be found spread among α_2, α_3, and the coefficients on any other endogenous variables treated as exogenous. Similarly, the model

$$M = \Gamma_0 + \Gamma_1\ G + \Gamma_2\ W^* + \Gamma_3\ R^* \dots \qquad (30)$$

where M is a measure of the number of firms or start-ups, is subject to the same difficulty.

If the second order effects described by the above model are small, all this may simply be a tempest in a teapot, a technical point which has little bearing on the usefulness of estimates retrieved from equations like (28)-(30). Recent evidence in Gyourko and Tracy (1989) shows that variation in local fiscal policy is almost as important as worker

---

[12] See, for example, Eberts (1990). This paper is significantly more sophisticated than the simple production approach model in that Eberts explicitly models the role of public capital in attracting private inputs. But his analysis fails to consider the important effects that infrastructure may have on local prices.

characteristics in determining local wage levels. This fact, coupled with microeconomic theory's prediction that wage levels significantly affect employment, implies that the second order effects described above may be large indeed, perhaps even surpassing the direct effects in magnitude. The ambiguity in the theoretical signs of the second order effects suggests that only careful empirical tests of the propositions presented above can resolve the question of the importance of local price adjustment in the response of firms and households to fiscal initiatives.

b) Compensating Variations Approach

The model outlined above is very much in the spirit of the compensating variations approach, inasmuch as it assumes that the rates of profit and utility must be equal over space. It shares a shortcoming with compensating variation models, in that it assumes that the system is always in a long run equilibrium. The fact that migration of people and capital takes time may invalidate this assumption. Yet the present model goes further by examining the implications of the local price adjustment mechanism for such important urban characteristics as population, employment, land use and private capital stock. In general, the compensating variation framework is silent on some of the most important questions in urban economics: the level and growth of urban aggregates.

6.4   DATA AND EMPIRICAL IMPLEMENTATION

In order to examine the predictions of the theoretical model, this section presents empirical estimates of three of the seven equations. These equations represent the heart of the model because they provide the basis for measuring the welfare effects of changes in infrastructure provision.

Note that this formula captures all the benefits that the public sector provides to firms and households. The other equations in the theoretical model presented in Section 6.2 have no direct welfare interpretation. Since this is a crucial point, let us consider each equation in turn. Equations (1.24) and (1.26) give the change in land consumption by households and firms that is induced by changes in fiscal policy. But once the value of this land is accounted for, as it is in the first term in equation (3.1), local residents and landowners are indifferent to the division of its area between sectors. Equation (1.25) and (1.27) express the response of private capital stocks and output to fiscal decisions. Yet in zero-profit long run equilibrium, returns to capital and profits, like the utility of those who do not own land, must be uniform. Again, there is no welfare implication.[13]

Since the model is recursive, the wage and property price equations can be estimated consistently. The other five equations, however, are fully simultaneous, and thus the estimates of the impact of output on employment must be interpreted with care.

6.4.1   Data Requirements

General equilibrium estimates of the role of fiscal policy in local economies require data on housing characteristics and value, salary and worker characteristics, city amenities like climate, and fiscal policy. We also require data on the level of urban aggregates in each

---

[13]   One possible exception is the taxation of capital. If the property tax applies to private capital as well as to land, then taxpayers may be better off if local stocks increase. I argue that such third order effects are likely to be small relative to the first and second order effects I emphasise. At any rate, data on central city private capital stocks are unavailable, precluding their inclusion in the empirical analysis.

city at each point in time. In particular, since the focus of this work is on the role of infrastructure in the growth of urban aggregates, it is important to have careful measures of the stock of local public capital available in each city at each period of time.

6.4.2 Data Sources

Table 6.1 provides variable names, definitions, sources, and descriptive statistics. Data on individual housing and worker characteristics are taken from the American Housing Survey (AHS), formerly called the Annual Housing Survey, for the years 1974-1985. The AHS provides two separate datasets: the first is the so-called "National" file, in which the housing in over sixty separate Metropolitan Statistical Areas (MSAs) are sampled each year (every two years after 1982). The second AHS dataset is the "MSA" file, which annually provides larger samples for approximately twenty of the sixty MSAs that make up the national file. The results presented here are based on the national sample, and thus the dataset is a traditional panel, with each house represented in each of the years 1975-1983. Unfortunately, the panel "breaks" in 1985, when a new sample was drawn. Thus the houses in the 1985 sample are different units from those present in the other years. I was able to obtain data on 34 cities for which I have fiscal information.

Data on local amenities are from the County and City Data Book for 1983, and are collected at the MSA level. It seems reasonable to assume that variables like percentage of possible sunshine, mean January temperature, and the like do not vary substantially over time or within the MSA.

Fiscal data are from City Government Finances for the period 1905 to 1986. For property taxes and capital outlays, I require only data for the year in question. However, a special methodology was required for the calculation of local infrastructure stocks. (See Appendix 1 for details.)

Table 6.1 Variable definitions and descriptive statistics

Variable		Definition	Mean	S.D.	Source
	ln R	Log house and land value	10.66	0.71	AHS
	ln W	Log wage and salary earnings	9.58	0.72	AHS
	ln N	Log employed labor force	13.20	0.78	CBP
H:	MALE	Dummy = 1 if householder is male	0.83	0.37	AHS
	WHITENH	Dummy= 1 if non-Hispanic white	0.77	0.42	AHS
	EXP	labor force experience (years)	22.70	12.60	AHS
	EXPSQ	Labor force experience squared	673.00	601.20	AHS
	EDUC	Highest grade completed by householder	13.20	2.90	AHS
C:	BEDRMS	Number of bedrooms in house	2.98	0.81	AHS
	BATHS	Number of bathrooms in house	2.07	1.53	AHS
	NEW	Dummy = 1 if house built since 1970	0.02	0.14	AHS
	CENTAIR	Dummy = 1 if central air conditioning	0.28	0.45	AHS
A:	MJANTEMP	Mean January temperature	36.56	13.29	CCDB
	MPRECIP	Mean annual precipitation	31.40	121.00	CCDB
G:	LPCTTP	Log tax payments per dollar house value	-4.11	1.41	AHS
	LPTAXPC	Log property tax revenue per capita	4.64	0.73	CF
	LOTHREV	Log other revenue per capita	5.15	0.63	CF
	LSTKPA	Log infrastructure density ($000/square mile)	15.92	0.81	CF
	LNONWELF	Log non-welfare expenditures ($)	1.59	126.58	CF
S:		Log PMSA retail sales	15.22	0.87	SMM

Sources: AHS = Annual Housing Survey, CF = City Government Finances, CCBD = County and City Data Book, CBP = County Business Patterns, SMM = Sales and Marketing Management

6.4.3 Econometric Specification

The theory suggests that disentanglement of the effects of fiscal policy on local economies requires the simultaneous estimation of land and labor prices, as well as the "urban aggregates". Because data on output and private capital stock by city are unavailable, and because the welfare effects of local fiscal policy are completely described by these equations, only three of the model's five equations are estimated. They are

(1) $R = R(C, A, G, W, Z)$
(2) $W = W(H, A, G, R, Z)$
(3) $N = N(W, R, A, G, E, S, Z)$

Here, R is house price, C is a vector of house characteristics, A is a vector of local climatological amenities, G is a vector of local fiscal policy variables, W is wage of the householder, Z is a vector of local control variables, H is a vector of householder traits, N is total number of jobs in the city economy, E is a vector of national business cycle controls, and S is total retail sales in the region. This last variable is designed to act as a proxy for X, the level of output or firms, presented in the theory.

An important question arises as to the proper specification of the infrastructure variable. If infrastructure is a pure local public good, then its services are equally available to all residents (both households and firms) of a given jurisdiction. Then the absolute level of infrastructure in place is the proper regressor. If, on the other hand, infrastructure is a quasi-private good, then its per capita level is the important factor. A final possibility is that the physical **density** of infrastructure matters most. This implies that a physically large city like Houston requires a larger capital stock than a small city like Boston if it is to provide the same level of service. This measure has the most intuitive appeal, as the public good qualities of infrastructure stocks imply that per capita stocks are not particularly meaningful. Since much of local infrastructure provision consists of roadways and sewer systems, the amount of physical space that the stock must serve is critical.

For the purposes of estimation, the equations are generally specified as

(1') $\ln R = a_0 + a_1 \ln W + a_2 C + a_3 A + a_4 G + a_5 Z + u$
(2') $\ln W = b_0 + b_1 \ln R + b_2 H + b_3 A + b_4 G + b_5 Z + v$
(3') $\ln N = c_0 + c_1 \ln W + c_2 \ln R + c_3 S + c_4 A + c_5 G + c_6 E + c_7 Z + w$

where ln indicates a natural logarithm. The functional form selected is based on the presumption, suggested in previous literature, that wages and house prices are lognormally distributed, as well as to control for the possibility of heteroscedasticity in the land price and wage equations.

The simultaneity of the system requires an estimator which accounts for the fact that endogenous regressors are correlated with the error terms u, v, and w. In order to correct for the possibility of endogenous variable bias, I use the three-stage least squares estimation procedure. While two-stage least squares accounts for simultaneity among regressors, the third stage controls for the possibility that the error terms are correlated across equations. This last situation will arise if unmeasured factors "shock" the error terms of the various equations in a systematically correlated fashion.

Columns (a)-(c) of Table 6.2 show the results of the three-stage least squares estimation procedure. As noted above, the results in the table are for the "density" specification: infrastructure stocks are measured in value of stock per square mile of city area.

6.4.4 Estimation and Results I: Housing Price and Wage Equations

a) Housing and Human Capital

The housing characteristics perform as expected in equation (1') [column (a)]. An extra bedroom or bathroom increases house value by 6.1 and 2.0 percent, respectively, while the presence of central air conditioning adds about 11 percent. Perhaps surprisingly, new housing is somewhat less valuable, as houses built since 1970 are worth an average of about 7.2 percent less after controlling for their characteristics. A large portion of the houses in the sample were built in the "old" period, and I have no controls for renovation and rehabilitation. The newer homes in the sample may have smaller rooms and are likely to be located farther from the CBD. Overall, the basic housing characteristics imply that the housing data are reasonably reliable, and that the model is performing as anticipated.

Results for personal characteristics in the wage equation [column (b)] are, likewise, consistent with research on human capital models of earnings. An additional year of labor force experience[14] adds about 1.2 percent to earnings. The negative coefficient on the square of this term implies that this effect diminishes over an individual's lifetime. An additional year of education is more valuable than workforce experience, adding about 3.4 percent to earnings. Males earn an average of 33 percent more than similarly qualified females, while non-Hispanic whites earn 9.8 percent more than their black and Hispanic counterparts. As was the case for the land price equation, the overall wage regression results are consistent with previous work and provide confirmation that the data are reasonably accurate.

b) Climatological Amenities and Fiscal Policy

The climatological amenities also perform as expected. The results in column (a) imply that warm winters and sunny days are attractive amenities for a jurisdiction to offer. The wage equation results in (b) indicate that households are the sector driving the results: wage demands are higher in areas with high precipitation and lower in areas with warm winters. We would expect urban firms to be relatively indifferent to precipitation (except in cases where lack of rain is so dramatic as to affect the price of water), although we might expect them to be attracted to the relatively lower utility bills that warm winters engender. Overall, however, the household sector's affinity for warm, dry environs is strong enough to cause them to demand, and receive, compensation in the labor market for enduring their absence.

The results for the fiscal variables provide strong support for the basic theory. Before proceeding to describe the results, however, a note is warranted. Because the local public sector is subject to a balanced budget constraint, its spending and revenues are usually very close to identical. Thus, the inclusion of all spending and revenue categories on the right hand side of a regression equation introduces near-perfect collinearity among the fiscal measures considered. This presents a major problem for the researcher interested in estimating the impact of all types of spending and revenue raising efforts, as the coefficients will be estimated inefficiently and their standard errors will be biased. As Helms (1985) and Mofidi and Stone (1990) point out, however, the omission of one (either spending or revenue) category will in general eliminate the multicollinearity problem, thus allowing the efficient estimation of the fiscal parameters. In the results presented here, I have followed the Helms-Mofidi and Stone approach and eliminated welfare payments from the equation. This adjustment, however, requires that the coefficients in the regression be interpreted with care: since the included categories are regarded as fixed, each parameter shows the estimated effect of a small change in the

---

14   Defined as Age-education-6.

category in question **assuming that the omitted category will change accordingly**. Thus, in column (b), the coefficient on the property tax rate is interpretable as the change in land value that would ensue if property tax rates were increased and the money raised were spent on welfare payments. Likewise, the coefficient on NONWELF shows the value of non-welfare relative to welfare spending.

With these caveats in mind, let us turn to the results for the fiscal variables. The results in Table 6.2 provide consistent evidence of fiscal capitalization into both house prices and wages. A one percent rise in property taxes rates (e.g. from 1.0% to 1.01%) is estimated to reduce land value by about .08% and increase wage demands by .05%. Recall from the theory that fiscal "bads" like taxes are expected to reduce land (housing) prices, but their effect on the labor market is indeterminate: they will reduce wages if they are incident mainly on firms, while wages will increase if households must pay the taxes. We thus conclude that households expect to bear most of the brunt of higher property taxes, and part of they compensation the demand is received through the labor market. The results for other sources of local revenue are strikingly dissimilar: a one percent rise in other revenues per city resident increases land values by 0.02% and reduces wages by 0.017%. Households appear to be attracted to non-property tax financing of local welfare spending.

Table 6.2 Three-stage least square parameter estimates

| Dependent variable | Equation | | | |
	(a) lnR	(b) lnW	(c) lnN	(PA) lnN
Parameter estimate Standard error				
Intercept	3.2765 a 0.2546	1.6886 a 0.3092	2.7072 a 0.1081	2.7934 a 0.1035
lnW	0.5860 a 0.0166	– – –	-0.0869 a 0.0064	-0.0058 a 0.0027
lnR	– – –	0.7328 a 0.0255	0.1074 a 0.0069	0.0067 a 0.0020
H: MALE	– – –	0.3279 a 0.0151	– – –	– – –
WHJTENH	– – –	0.0979 a 0.0125	– – –	– – –
EXP	– – –	0.0117 a 0.0013	– – –	– – –
EXPSQ	– – –	-0.0002 a 0.000	– – –	– – –
EDUC	– – –	0.0339 a 0.0025	– – –	– – –
C: BEDRMS	0.0607 a 0.0052	– – –	– – –	– – –
BATHS	0.0202 a 0.0027	– – –	– – –	– – –
NEW	-0.0717 a 0.0277	– – –	– – –	– – –

Table 6.2 cont.

Dependent variable	Equation			
	(a) lnR	(b) lnW	(c) lnN	(PA) lnN
Parameter estimate Standard error				— — —
CENTAIR	0.1120 a 0.0102	— — —	— — —	
A: MJANTEMP	0.0078 a 0.0005	-0.0061 a 0.0007	-0.0005 a 0.0002	0.0004 b 0.0002
MPRECIP	-0.0113 a 0.0005	0.0084 a 0.0006	0.0004 a 0.0002	-0.0008 a 0.0001
G: LPCTTP	-0.0817 a 0.0040	0.0519 a 0.0052	— — —	— — —
LOTHREV	0.0230 0.0156	-0.0169 0.0182	0.1591 a 0.0051	0.1616 a 0.0050
LPTAXPC	— — —	— — —	0.1211 a 0.0036	0.1204 a 0.0036
LSTKPA	0.0345 a 0.0110	-0.0139 0.0126	0.0994 a 0.0051	0.1010 a 0.0050
LNONWELF	0.0332 0.0218	-0.0321 0.0253	-0.2536 a 0.0078	-0.2480 a 0.0076
Z: LCPOP	0.0411 b 0.0183	-0.0191 0.0213	0.3396 a 0.0096	0.3267 a 0.0092
TIME	0.0376 a 0.0024	0.0115 a 0.0005	-0.0112 a 0.0010	-0.0099 a 0.0009
LSALES	— — —	— — —	0.2518 a 0.0088	0.2717 a 0.0083
AREA	— — —	— — —	0.0002 a 0.0000	0.0002 a 0.0000
UNEMP	— — —	— — —	0.0105 a 0.0012	0.0098 a 0.0012
INTRATE	— — —	— — —	-0.0005 0.0009	0.0018 b 0.0009
Adjusted R squared*	0.481	0.316	0.962	0.965
Mean square error*	0.307	0.414	0.023	0.022

a: Significantly different from zero at > 99% confidence level
b: Significantly different from zero at 95-99% confidence level
*: Calculated from second stage of procedure

The split between welfare and non-welfare spending appears to be of little consequence to firms or households at the margin. A one percent increase in per capita non-welfare spending at the expense of welfare spending has no significant effect on either land values or wages. Homeowners during this period appeared to prefer that spending by cities be reduced, and that the money recovered be used for property tax relief. The passage of Propositions 13 and 2 1/2 and the ascendancy of the smaller government philosophy of the Reagan administration during the period would appear to support this hypothesis.

The results for public capital stocks are also consistent with the theory. Recall that the variable LSTKPA is the logarithm of physical infrastructure per unit of city area, reflecting the "density" of public capital available. The results show that the elasticity of land values with respect to public capital density is about .04. Interestingly, this value is very similar in magnitude to findings of the elasticity of private sector **output** with respect to infrastructure stocks (See Eberts, 1990 and Munnell, 1990). The similarity may arise from the fact that households and firms compete in the land market and that the output effects of infrastructure are reflected in their bids for land. The consistency of this finding with earlier work provides further support for the model outlined in Section 6.2.

In the wage equation, the coefficient estimate on the density of public capital is insignificant. In accordance with the theoretical model, this finding implies that the benefits of public capital are spread relatively evenly among households and firms. Again, the general equilibrium approach allows relaxation of the "production approach" assumption that public capital is strictly an input into production. These results show, as we would expect a priori, that the household sector shares in the benefits of infrastructure spending through reduced roadway congestion, better and more reliable sewerage systems, and the like. By implicitly assuming that only firms benefit directly from public capital spending, the production approach ignores an important set of potential beneficiaries: households.

c) Control Variables

In order to control for unexplained national trends, the variable TIME, a linear time trend, is included in the equations. As expected, the coefficient implies that both wages and land prices are increasing slightly over the period, above the increases explained by the other explanatory variables in the models. City population is included to account for unexplained city-size effects, including agglomeration economies in consumption or production. After controlling for the fiscal and climatic environments, large cities tend to have higher land prices than small. Households and firms apparently benefit from the agglomeration economies that large cities provide, such as a wide variety of shopping, entertainment, and other amenities.

Finally, notice that the lnW and lnR variables are each significantly positive in the other equation. The coefficient estimates are directly interpretable as elasticities. The Roback (1982) model predicts that in economies composed of both households and firms wages and property prices are simultaneously determined, a prediction strongly supported here.

6.4.5 Estimation and Results II: Jobs

Since the model is recursive, the wage and land price equations can be estimated separately and consistently. Using this information, we may estimate an equation for N, city employment. Employment depends, of course, on the level of firm activity in a city, which itself is an endogenous variable. Here, I proxy for firm activity by using S, the dollar value of retail sales in the PMSA. Note that to the extent that S is endogenous, its coefficient estimate will be inconsistent. We must thus speak cautiously about its value. Examining the estimates in Table 6.2, we find that, as expected, the elasticity of labor demand with respect to wages is significantly negative. The point estimate is -.086. As discussed more fully below, the general equilibrium results in columns (a)-(c) provide substantially larger and more precise estimates of the wage elasticity of labor demand than does the aggregate production approach presented in column (PA).

The significantly positive coefficient on value implies that land and labor are weak substitutes in production. A one percent increase in the price of land increases the demand for labor by about 0.1%. This does not mean that in the face of higher land prices firms close a factory and hire more workers. Rather, it means that those cities which are characterized by high land values and low wages will attract industries which are relatively labor intensive. Such a city might be characterized by relatively high percentages of service firms, labor-intensive manufacturing, and other low land-intensity industries.

The elasticity of labor demand with respect to regional sales is estimated at approximately .45, a figure which will be asymptotically biased if S is endogenous, as the theory suggests it is. Nonetheless, the sign is positive, as expected.

Finally, let us turn to the fiscal variables. The revenue variables perform somewhat unexpectedly. Property tax collections[15] and other revenues per capita appear to attract employment, a result which is at odds with intuition. Previous research on the impact of local fiscal policy on business location decisions has been plagued by similarly surprising results (Newman and Sullivan 1988). Likewise, nonwelfare spending, like the revenue variables, appears to be undesirable for job creation. Recall that local welfare spending is the omitted category of the local government budget. Taken together, the results suggest that firms' demands for labor are significantly increased by local welfare spending. Because the wages measured in this study are those of homeowners only, I have not controlled for renters' wages. It may be the case that renters in cities with high levels of welfare spending are willing to work at relatively low wages, thereby inducing firms to employ more labor in those cities.

Infrastructure density exhibits a strong positive effect on job creation, with an estimated elasticity of .099. Note that since output has been controlled for, albeit by the proxy S, this result indicates strong complementarity between public capital and labor. Policy makers who wish to maximize employment would do well to develop and maintain their infrastructure stocks.[16]

6.4.6 Comparison with Partial Equilibrium Approach

The simultaneous equations method described above is uncharacteristic of current research on the impact of local fiscal policy on local economies. As described in Section 6.3, partial equilibrium approaches dominate the literature. For the purposes of comparison, I estimated equation (3') alone, and present the results in column (PA) of Table 6.2. It is easy to see that the estimates are quite different. The coefficients on the endogenous variables W and R are the most affected, as econometric theory would predict. The partial equilibrium model dramatically underestimates the (negative) elasticity of labor demand with respect to wages by a factor of 15. This is due to the failure of that approach to properly disentangle the effects of fiscal policy: the simultaneity of wages and land prices means that the effects of fiscal policy are spread throughout the estimated parameters of the model. But the general equilibrium model presented above reveals that fiscal policy has important impacts on land prices in particular, and through secondary effects described in Section 6.3, on wages. In addition, it allows us to determine who benefits from public capital services. The effects are complex. The positive and strongly

---

[15] Here, since labor demand is an aggregate phenomenon, an aggregate measure of property taxes, total collections per capita, is the appropriate regressor.

[16] As with the other empirical estimates, changes in specification, including weighting to further control for heteroscedasticity, do not change the qualitative results presented here.

significant effect of infrastructure on land values demonstrates that its services are of benefit on balance, while its insignificant coefficient in the wage equation reveals that both sectors benefit in roughly comparable fashion. Finally, the high positive elasticity of labor demand with respect to infrastructure shows that firms view it as significantly complementary to their labor forces.

6.5 CONCLUSIONS

The simultaneous equations method described above allows for a more precise determination of the impact of fiscal policy on urban economies. The important predictions of the theory outlined in Section 6.2 are largely verified. The large differences in the estimates obtained from partial and more general equilibrium models strongly support the notion that previous work in this area presents only a part of the story. The results show that infrastructure's effects on property markets are substantial, and that partial equilibrium estimates of aggregate demand equations provide misleadingly low and biased estimates of the effects that local prices have on labor demand. The simultaneous equations method clearly allows a more thorough examination of fiscal policy's role in local economies. In particular, the estimated infrastructure stock effect on land values implies that complete analysis of the economic effects of infrastructure provision must include consideration of spatial equilibrium and the land market.

APPENDIX 1: CALCULATION OF INFRASTRUCTURE STOCKS

This Appendix describes the method employed in construction of the public capital stock estimates used in this study. The stock estimates were constructed using the perpetual inventory technique, which has formed the basis of the most widely-cited estimates of national public capital stocks (see BEA 1987, Boskin et al. 1987). The technique requires the accumulation and depreciation of real investment outlays in each year, and provides estimates of the stock in place for each cross-sectional unit in each year.

The national totals provided by Boskin and BEA are extremely useful. However, the need to overcome the econometric difficulties inherent in the analysis of aggregate national time series require the measurement of the public capital stocks owned by each city in each year. Earlier efforts at the construction of such a panel have been hampered by data limitations. Holtz-Eakin (1994) and Munnell (1990) estimate capital stocks held by each cross sectional unit in each year by allocating the BEA national totals. Holtz-Eakin bases this allocation on each state's share of total national investment in 1960, while Munnell bases hers on estimated growth of stocks for the period 1958-1988. While Munnell allocates the national BEA totals to states and localities for each year, Holtz-Eakin uses his estimated 1960 stocks as a benchmark, and applies the perpetual inventory technique to investment data for 1960-1988. Both analysts thus apportion national data to states and localities based on relatively recent behavior in their investment spending. This benchmarking procedure may thus introduce errors into the estimates, as investments made in 1960 (Holtz-Eakin) or 1958-1988 (Munnell) may not accurately reflect the historical pattern of capital accumulation by individual state and local governments. Eberts (1990) uses a method similar to that employed here to construct capital stock estimates for 1958-1981.

The application of the perpetual inventory technique to our investment data results in the following equation for total public capital:

$$G_t - \left(1-\delta^e\right)G_{t-1}^e + I_t^e + \left(1-\delta^c\right)G_{t-1}^c + I_t^c + \left(1-\delta^I\right)G_{t-1}^I + I_t^I \tag{A.1}$$

where e, c, and l refer to equipment, construction, and land and existing structures, respectively, G is real stock and I is the real flow of investment spending. Jurisdictional subscripts have been omitted.

Estimations of infrastructure levels require information on flows of capital spending over time, depreciation rates, and costs. For the series employed in the current study, physical capital expenditure data were taken from *City Finances* for the years 1905-1990. Lack of prior data forces us to assume that no infrastructure in place in 1905 survives to the present. For most years, spending is available for each of three categories: equipment, construction, and land and existing structures. In those years where only total investment outlays are available, I apportioned the total to categories using historical averages for each city. In the more unusual case of missing total investment outlay data, I used simple averages of the surrounding years' data. Depreciation assumptions are adapted from Boskin et al. (1987) and are:

Equipment: 8 percent per year;

Construction and existing structures: 2 percent per year; and

Land: 0 percent per year.

National equipment price indices, obtained from BEA's Implicit Price Deflator for Producers' Durable Equipment, were used to deflate the equipment outlays. Data from Engineering News Record's Construction Cost Indices (Annual) were used to construct individual construction cost indices for each cross-sectional unit. This deflator was used to convert the construction and structures data to real terms. The variable used in the analysis, LNSTKPA, is the logarithm of total infrastructure stock divided by the land area of the jurisdiction in question. A limitation of these data is that they do not allow for the breakdown of infrastructure stocks by function: construction of roads, for example, cannot be distinguished from construction of public buildings. Nonetheless, the total infrastructure stocks employed in this study are, I believe, more reliable than the majority of those currently in use.

APPENDIX 2: CITIES ANALYZED

ATLANTA	LOS ANGELES
BALTIMORE	MILWAUKEE
BOSTON	MINNEAPOLIS
CHICAGO	NEW ORLEANS
CINCINATTI	NEW YORK
CLEVELAND	OKLAHMA CTY
COLUMBUS	PHILADELPHIA
DALLAS	PHOENIX
DENVER	PITTSBURGH
DETROIT	ST. LOUIS
HT. WORTH	SAN DIEGO
HOUSTON	SAN FRANCISCO
INDIANAPOLIS	SEATTLE
KANSAS CITY	TOLEDO

ACKNOWLEDGEMENTS

An earlier draft of this paper was presented at the 1992 Regional Science Association International meeting in Chicago, Illinois. The author gratefully acknowledges helpful comments from participants in that session and from an anonymous referee.

REFERENCES

US Bureau of Economic Analysis (BEA), 1987, Fixed Reproducible Tangible Wealth in the United States, 1925-1985, Washington D.C.

Boskin, M., M. Robinson and A. Huber, 1987, "New Estimates of State and Local Government Tangible Capital", NBER Working Paper No. 2131.

Brueckner, J., 1979, "Property Values, Local Public Expenditure and Economic Efficiency", *Journal of Public Economics*, 11:223-245.

Brueckner, J., 1982, "A Test for Allocative Efficiency in the Local Public Sector", *Journal of Public Economics*, 19:311-331.

Brueckner, J., 1983, "Property Value Maximization and Public Sector Efficiency", *Journal of Urban Economics*, 14:1-15.

Eberts, R., 1990, "Cross-Sectional Analysis of Public Infrastructure and Regional Productivity Growth", Federal Reserve Bank of Cleveland Working Paper 9004.

Fujita, M., 1989, *Urban Economic Theory: Land Use and City Size*, Cambridge University Press, New York.

Gyourko, J. and J. Tracy, 1989a, "Local Public Sector Rent Seeking and its Impact on Local Land Values", *Regional Science and Urban Economics*, 19:493-516.

Gyourko, J. and J. Tracy, 1989b, "The Importance of Local Fiscal Conditions in Analyzing Local Labor Markets", *Journal of Political Economy*, 97:1208-1231.

Gyourko, J. and J. Tracy, 1991, "The Structure of Local Public Finance and the Quality of Life", *Journal of Political Economy*, 99:774-806.

Haughwout, A., 1993, "Infrastructure in American Cities: A Theoretical and Empirical Examination", Ph.D. dissertation, University of Pennsylvania.

Helms, L., 1985, "The Effect of State and Local Taxes on Economic Growth: A Time Series-Cross Section Approach", *Review of Economics and Statistics*, 67:574-582.

Herzog, H. and A. Schlottmann, 1991, Industrial Location and Public Policy, University of Tennessee Press, Knoxville.

Holtz-Eakin, D., 1994, "Public Sector Capital and the Productivity Puzzle", *Review of Economics and Statistics*, 76:12-21.

Holtz-Eakin, D. and H. Rosen, 1993, "Municipal Construction Spending: An Empirical Examination", *Economics and Politics*, November.

Mera, K., 1973, "Regional Production Functions and Social Overhead Capital: An Analysis of the Japanese Case", *Regional Science and Urban Economics*, 3:157-185.

Mofidi, A. and J. Stone, 1990, "Do State and Local Taxes Affect Economic Growth?" *Review of Economics and Statistics*, 72:686-691.

Munnell, A., ed., 1990, "Is There a Shortfall in Public Capital Investment?", (Proceedings of a Federal Reserve Bank of Boston Conference held in June 1990).

Newman, R. and D. Sullivan, 1988, "Econometric Analysis of Business Tax Impacts on Industrial Location: What Do We Know and How Do We Know It?", *Journal of Urban Economics*, 23: 215-234.

Roback, J., 1982, "Wages, Rents, and the Quality of Life", *Journal of Political Economy*, 90:1257-1278.

Schmenner, R., 1982, *Making Business Location Decisions*, Prentice Hall, Englewood Cliffs, N.J.

Varian, H., 1984, *Microeconomic Analysis*, W.W. Norton, New York.

Voith, R., 1991, "Capitalization of Local and Regional Attributes into Wages and Rents: Differences across Residential, Commercial, and Mixed Use Communities", *Journal of Regional Science*, 31:127-145.

CHAPTER 7

Intergovernmental Fiscal Relations in California:
A Critical Evaluation

Juliet A. Musso
University of Southern California

John M. Quigley
University of California, Berkeley

7.1   INTRODUCTION

This chapter provides an overview and evaluation of state and local finance in California. This evaluation may be timely, since national and state policy makers have again raised the issue of intergovernmental fiscal reform. Initiatives at the national level include the "New Federalism" of the Nixon and Reagan administrations, as well as more recent proposals by the Clinton administration and the Republican opposition to devolve the welfare function to state governments. The National Council of State Legislators has recommended that state governments reexamine the assignment of fiscal powers between state and local government. At the same time, policy makers in many other nations have expressed interest in governance reform, and particularly in decentralization of fiscal functions.

In this chapter, we assess the efficiency and effectiveness of California's fiscal structure. The theory of fiscal federalism, and related public choice theories, provide criteria for evaluating intergovernmental fiscal arrangements. California's internal structure is not federal in a *political* sense; local governments derive their powers from the state, and consequently do not enjoy any area of exclusive sovereign power. Moreover, as part of the U.S. national federation, California's state and local governments are strongly affected by intergovernmental grants and regulation from the central government. However, California *may* satisfy Oates's (1972, p.25) economic definition of a *fiscal* federalism: "A public sector with both centralized and decentralized levels of decision-making in which choices made at each level concerning the provision of public services are determined largely by the demands for these services of the residents of (and perhaps others who carry on activities in) the respective jurisdiction."

From an economic perspective, the primary importance of fiscal decentralization is as a means of matching public good service levels to local preferences. In this chapter, we consider the extent to which California's highly fragmented fiscal structure serves the varying needs of its regionally diverse economy. The chapter proceeds as follows. The first section provides a brief overview of California, highlighting recent demographic and economic trends, and describing the governance structure and political landscape. It also identifies key normative criteria for evaluating the state's fiscal system. The second section describes the state's fiscal constitution, including own-source revenues, intergovernmental grants, and intergovernmental regulation. The third section illustrates changing revenue patterns of general purpose governments – the state, counties and cities. Finally, Section 7.4 presents analytic findings.

7.1.1 An Overview of California

California is the third largest of the United States, with an area of more than 150,000 square miles and 1,200 miles of coastline. The state is distinguished by strikingly varied geography, a rapidly growing, ethnically mixed population and a relatively strong, diverse economy. California also harbors strong regional variations in terms of industrial base, ethnic composition, and political culture.

Demographic and economic trends. California is the most populous of the fifty states, with almost 30 million residents, or about 12 percent of the U.S. total. It has grown rapidly – 32 percent between 1980 and 1990 – and while population recently has slowed somewhat, it nonetheless will outpace the national average during the next decade.

Immigration has played an important role in the state's growth. As Table 7.1 indicates, between 1980 and 1993, approximately one-half of the new California residents were recent migrants, and almost 40 percent were foreign immigrants. As a result of these trends, an increasing share of California's total population is of Asian or Hispanic ancestry. The shift in California's ethnic makeup is expected to continue, particularly given that net domestic migration is expected to be negative. By the year 2000, ethnic minorities will account for one-half of California's population.

Table 7.1 Components of Annual Population Change (thousands per year)

	Actual 1980-1993	Projected 1993-2005
Natural Increase	317.1	325.0
Total Migration	304.0	238.2
Foreign	242.1	275.0
Domestic	61.9	-36.8
Annual Population Growth	621.1	563.2

Source: Center for the Continuing Study of the California Economy, 1992. California Economic Growth, Palo Alto, California.

California has the largest economy of the fifty states, ranking first in nonagricultural and manufacturing employment, value added by manufacturing, gross state product (GSP), and total personal income. California's economy is a diverse mix of industries, including manufacturing, transportation and communications, domestic and foreign trade, and financial and other services. California's mild climate, balanced industry mix, access to foreign markets, and attractive environment are conducive to economic growth. However, California businesses also must cope with increasing infrastructure needs, environmental contamination, high housing costs, and the need to educate a culturally diverse, multi-lingual student population. While California's strong economic growth is expected to continue, future economic performance depends, to some extent, on California's success in coping with these challenges.

Governance. The general structure of governance within California parallels that of the U.S. federal system. The state government comprises three branches: the bicameral legislature; the executive, presided over by the Governor; and the judiciary. The legislature has the power to enact laws which are administered by the executive. The judicial branch is responsible for settling civil and criminal disputes, and interpreting statutes and the state Constitution. Although the state provides some services directly, its Constitution delegates many of the powers and functions of government to local units. In 1992, California had over 6,700 local governments, including 57 counties, one combined City-County (San Francisco), 466 cities, 1,200 school districts, and 4,995 other special districts. The constitutional functions and powers of local government are largely a product of history and political expedience:

- The state Constitution defines counties to be "legal subdivisions of the State," and requires that they administer a variety of programs, including public health and public assistance programs, trial courts, tax collection, jails and elections. They also provide municipal type services, such as road maintenance and police protection, to county residents who do not live within city limits.

- Incorporated cities have considerable power over land use within their limits, and provide sanitation services, police, and fire protection. Cities also provide such services as community development, transportation, public utilities, culture and recreation. Cities are not, however, administrative arms of the state, and do not have the same close programmatic and fiscal links to state agencies that counties do.

- The powers of special districts are considerably more restricted than those of cities or counties. Districts cannot control land use and are limited to collecting a portion of the property tax, special assessments, and fees. Some special districts provide a single type of service, such as fire protection or mosquito abatement. Others are multipurpose, such as county service areas, which provide a mix of services to the residents of unincorporated areas. Some 1,200 special districts provide schools and education, including elementary, secondary, and community college districts.

With reference to Musgrave's characterization of the branches of the public economy, the state and counties share responsibility for distributive functions, while all the various agencies have some responsibility for the allocative function. Primary and secondary educational services are primarily provided by school and community college districts, with substantial state financial assistance and regulation.

The political landscape. Several important political and constitutional factors shape governance in California. First, the California Constitution grants the electorate extraordinary powers of initiative, referendum and recall. Under these provisions of the Constitution, the electorate may directly propose and vote on statutes and Constitutional amendments, may approve or reject statutes enacted by their representatives, and may vote to recall elected officials. In recent years California voters have confronted increasing numbers of initiative measures; for example, the 1990 state election had a total of 17 measures on the state ballot alone.

In the late seventies and eighties, the initiative process become a vehicle for a populist "tax revolt" which fundamentally changed public finance and intergovernmental fiscal relations in California. In 1978, the passage of Proposition 13 severely restricted the imposition of property taxes by cities and counties, and required approval of most new taxes by a two-thirds popular vote. It also required a two-thirds vote of the Legislature on any revenue or appropriation measure. Two years later, the voters approved another proposition which imposed limits on state and local appropriations and required the state to reimburse local governments for the costs of any new or increased program requirements imposed by the Legislature.

California's initiative process continues to be a primary vehicle for enacting fiscal measures and other policy initiatives. For example, the voters recently approved Proposition 98, which earmarked approximately 40 percent of the state budget for education. Proposition 99 imposed a 25 cent per package tax on cigarettes, the proceeds of which have been allocated for health, education, and recreation. The passage of

Proposition 187 in 1994 restricted the access of undocumented residents to state social services and education.[1]

7.1.2 Evaluative Criteria

Evaluating the fiscal constitution of a multiple level government requires that one consider both the assignment of functional responsibilities and the system of financing services. The fiscal structure should (1) accommodate regional variation in preferences; (2) facilitate preference revelation among service consumers; (3) rely as far as possible on pricing mechanisms which reflect scarcity; (4) address intergovernmental externalities; (5) prevent bureaucratic rent seeking behavior by promoting intergovernmental competition; and (6) rely on relatively progressive and elastic revenue sources.

Assignment of functional responsibilities. The classic normative theory describing the assignment of functional responsibilities is the fiscal federalism model described by Oates (1974). This model argues that the *stabilization* and *redistributive* functions of government should be relatively centralized, in order to avoid the deadweight losses that result from local government competition and residential and business mobility. In contrast, the decentralization theorem argues that the *allocative* function should generally be the responsibility of *lower-level* governments, so that municipal public service levels will better reflect resident preferences. The assignment of functions between governments should consider the geographical incidence of benefits and costs, and balance the welfare losses from political compromise against the welfare gains from exploiting economies of scale in production. The assignment should attempt to reduce costs of collective decision making, and avoid the congestion or free-rider problems that may result from residential mobility.

A system of local governance in which there are many fiscally autonomous local service providers also allows residential exit to promote efficiency in public service provision. Public economists suggest that a mechanism for inducing efficient local service provision is the potential migration of residents, as initially proposed by Tiebout (1956). If residents are relatively mobile and there are sufficient numbers of local service providers, citizens can reveal their preferences for public goods through their choice of communities. Moreover, public choice theorists argue that resident migration improves residential "voice" and limits self-serving behavior by local bureaucrats because it requires local governments to act, in effect, as competitors.[2]

Financing services. Several considerations are important in designing a system to finance services, including the elasticity of the revenue source, its progressivity, and its effects on resource allocation, both in terms of public and private goods.[3] To promote efficiency in public resource allocation, a system of local taxation should explicitly link benefits and costs. If government services have private good characteristics, such as excludability and congestibility, user fees that reflect marginal costs can improve efficiency. User charges force citizens to reveal information about the demand for services; they also induce resource-saving behavior among consumers. However, services that are more public in character, such as law enforcement or social services, are not appropriate for marginal cost pricing.

In the Tiebout model mentioned above, reliance on a head tax, in conjunction with costless mobility, sufficient numbers of local service providers, and several other assumptions, allows the tax to serve as a "price" for service, and local service provision to emulate a competitive market. Actual governance systems hardly meet the conditions necessary for Pareto optimal public good provision. Despite this lack of correspondence,

---

[1] The constitutionality of Proposition 187 is under court challenge.

[2] Hirschman (1970).

[3] Prud'homme (1987).

several policy implications are clear. For example, the financing system should embody a benefit principle wherein local residents who desire a higher level of services pay higher taxes to finance them. Policy makers must consider the effect of taxation on private resource allocation and residential choices. Use of a property tax, for example, can lead to fiscal zoning or else to residential cycling, as wealthy individuals seek to avoid the redistributive effects of taxation.

As Prud'homme (1987) points out, most local financing sources are relatively income inelastic, regressive and have segregative effects. Moreover, problems of imperfect correspondence frequently arise in a decentralized system of government. One way to address these problems is with intergovernmental grants. The two major justifications for interjurisdictional grants are:

- *Spillovers.* If individual jurisdictions respond primarily to local resident preferences, they will tend to undervalue those benefits from public services that accrue to residents of other jurisdictions. One way to address this problem is to provide an open-ended matching grant whose rate equals the marginal value of the spillover relative to total benefits.

- *Horizontal equity.* A problem with a federal system is that wealthier communities can meet revenue requirements with lower relative tax rates, leading to inequitable tax burdens. Such disparities can induce individuals to migrate into wealthy communities, leading to distortions in the allocation of resources.[4] From this perspective, unconditional grants may equalize effective purchasing power between rich and poor communities. Central tax sources–such as the income tax–have the added advantages of greater elasticity and progressivity.

These arguments for the use of intergovernmental grants assume that a governmental entity can be treated as analogous to an individual consumer. Because in theory a lump-sum grant has a pure income effect, it should have the same effect on expenditures as a similar reduction in federal taxes, or any other exogenous increase in constituent incomes.[5] In contrast, matching grants effectively change the price of local services. As a result, the public good becomes less expensive relative to private goods, and the community will choose to spend more on public goods.

A large body of empirical literature, however, throws doubt on the validity of this rational choice model of intergovernmental grant effects. For example, a lump sum grant should increase spending by approximately $0.05 to $0.10 for each dollar of spending, consistent with estimated income effects.[6] Yet the estimated effects on spending in grant programs have generally ranged between $0.25 to $1.00 per $1.00 of grant funds.[7] The difficulty in predicting the effect of intergovernmental grants to some extent diminishes their value as tools for influencing the behavior of lower level government. At the least, it suggests that representatives of the central government cannot expect to "micro-manage" lower level governments through spending policy.

Given this, it may be preferable to allow Coasian type bargaining between local entities to facilitate joint action to address many intergovernmental externalities (Oates, 1974). Any desire to promote vertical income redistribution should be achieved through grants to *individuals*, rather than *governments*, while horizontal inequities should be addressed through non-categorical block grants or revenue sharing programs that promote local autonomy over spending policy. The use of matching grants to address externalities should be minimized unless there is reason to believe that transaction costs,

---

4   Oates (1972), p. 88.
5   Bradford and Oates (1971).
6   Gramlich (1977).
7   Arthur Okun termed this phenomenon the "flypaper effect" because money "sticks where it hits" (Courant et al., 1979). A number of theories have been advanced to explain this phenomenon; see Quigley and Smolensky (1993) for a recent review of this literature.

problems in assigning properly rights, or strategic behavior will result in serious inefficiencies from spillover effects.

7.2   CALIFORNIA'S "FISCAL CONSTITUTION"

State and local governments in California are financed by a progressive income tax, a property tax, a retail sales tax, charges for current services, and intergovernmental grants. Taxing powers and, consequently, the relative reliance on these sources varies considerably across levels of government in California.

7.2.1 Major Own Source Revenues

The state Constitution gives the state government the exclusive right to tax corporate franchises, banks and public utilities, but prohibits the state from assessing local property for taxation, and from imposing any tax for local purposes. The Constitution allows cities to impose any tax not specifically *prohibited* by the state Constitution or by statute. In contrast, counties are only *permitted* to enact those taxes for which they are given specific statutory authority.[8] As a consequence, cities have more diverse tax structures than do most counties.[9] All local governments have the power to tax real property under general law, although the provisions of Proposition 13 severely limit these powers.

The income tax. The State personal income tax is relatively progressive, with basic tax rates ranging from 0 percent to 11 percent, with exclusions for income from social insurance and unemployment benefits, in-state moving expenses and California Lottery winnings.[10] The tax is indexed annually by the California consumer price index. The state also imposes a tax on corporate net income at a marginal tax rate of 9.3 percent. International corporations are required to pay corporate income tax on net income earned in California.

The retail sales tax. California has a state sales tax rate of 4.75 percent, and a uniform local sales tax rate of 1.25 percent.[11] The tax applies to goods, excluding food; most services are also excluded from the tax. Eighty percent of the gross revenue is distributed among cities and counties based on the location of sales. The remaining 20 percent is distributed by formula to counties to fund transportation programs. In addition, counties are permitted to levy an additional 0.5 percent tax under certain circumstances.[12] The state administers both the state and local portion of this tax. Because local governments have very limited power to increase the tax rate or to modify the tax base, the local sales tax is actually closer to a state revenue sharing program than a local revenue source.

The local property tax. Until 1978, the property tax was the primary funding source for most local governments. Each local government imposed an *ad valorem* rate on real property within its jurisdiction; tax rates imposed by various local governments were added to determine the total effective tax rate on each property. Just prior to the passage

---

8   The taxing powers of single purpose agencies such as special districts and school districts are even more restricted.

9   The combined City and County of San Francisco is a unique exception.

10   California conforms to the federal definition of Adjusted Gross Income as the base for personal income taxation. There is a $58 personal exemption (for each dependent) and a $2,169 standard deduction.

11   California also enacted a one-year increase in the sales tax (0.25 percent) to fund earthquake relief in 1991, and in 1993, extended a temporary one-half cent sales tax increase to fund county services.

12   Counties may impose an additional rate of up to 0.5 percent for transit purposes. In addition, counties with populations less than 350,000 may impose up to a 0.5 percent rate for general purposes. The two taxes combined cannot exceed 0.5 percent.

of Proposition 13, the average combined property tax exceeded two percent of assessed value. During the 1970s, sharp increases in housing prices and aggressive local reassessment practices resulted in rapid increases in the property tax liabilities of homeowners. This growth, along with a large state budget surplus, led to the passage of Proposition 13 in June 1978. Passage of this measure ended the use of property taxes as a flexible financing source.

Proposition 13 limited the total combined property tax rate to one percent of assessed value, and limited growth in the assessed value of property to two percent per year, with reassessment at full market value upon sale. The revenues generated by the property tax are distributed among local agencies within each county based on the proportion of countywide property tax revenues each agency received in the prior year.[13] Because this basic formula has been in effect since 1979, the amount of property tax revenue received by an entity is strongly influenced by the property tax policy the agency pursued in 1978.[14]

In sum, California's "fiscal constitution" reserves the income tax to the state government, and the property tax to local governments. The property tax, however, has become effectively a fixed revenue source – local governments cannot increase the tax rate, and the allocation factors are controlled at the state level.[15] The state government allocates the local share of the uniform sales tax to cities and counties based on point of sale, so that local agencies can only control sales tax revenues indirectly, through development decisions. Because local governments have extremely limited control over the local sales tax and property tax, these revenue sources function more like statewide general revenue sharing programs. Finally, while local governments have the authority to impose various other local taxes, their ability to do so is severely constrained by the super-majority vote requirements of Proposition 13.

7.2.2 Intergovernmental Grants

Public services are provided in California through an interactive system involving the federal, state and local governments. A few programs are funded and administered directly by state or federal agencies. For example, the Supplemental Security Income Program, which provides cash grants to aged, blind and disabled persons, is fully funded by the federal government and is federally administered through field offices.[16] Other programs are primarily provided and financed locally, such as household waste disposal, water supply, street lighting, and police. A great many programs, however, involve more than one level of government. The federal and state governments use two basic mechanisms to shape lower-level government action: intergovernmental grants and regulation.

Overview. Intergovernmental policy in California has been shaped by two major forces. First, changing intergovernmental policies at the federal level have affected both the state and local governments. During the 1960s and early 1970s, the federal government dramatically increased grant activity for social services. Between 1960 and 1978, federal intergovernmental grants more than quadrupled in constant dollars,

---

[13] The single major exception to this rule involves community redevelopment agencies. These agencies, which are basically arms of the cities, receive all of the incremental tax revenue generated each year within their redevelopment project areas.

[14] Extreme examples are cities which had imposed no property tax prior to Proposition 13. To this day, these so-called no-property-tax cities do not receive a property tax allocation.

[15] There is one exception. Proposition 46, enacted in 1986, allows property taxes to be increased to finance local bonds for capital projects with two thirds voter approval.

[16] Even this program involves lower-level governments. The state has elected to supplement the SSI grant through the State Supplemental Program (SSP), and pays the full costs of this supplement.

growing from 1.4 percent to 3.6 percent of GNP.[17] Federal grants-in-aid peaked in 1978, and began to decline moderately in the late years of the Carter administration. President Reagan's aggressive policy of federal disengagement contributed to a diminished federal role throughout the 1980s. Real federal grants dropped by 16.7 percent between 1980 and 1982, and then grew slowly throughout the decade of the eighties. In 1990, federal grants-in-aid represented 2.5 percent of GNP.

Second, a number of measures enacted by state voters through the initiative process have shaped intergovernmental affairs in California. The taxation limits enacted in Proposition 13 sharply limited local taxing authority, requiring greater state intervention in local finance to maintain service provision. Several subsequent initiative measures have influenced intergovernmental policy, including Proposition 4, which requires the state to reimburse local governments for the costs of new programs, and Proposition 98, which established a minimum state funding level for the local public schools. In the remainder of this section we assess intergovernmental relations within California, and discuss how this system changed during the late seventies and eighties.

Table 7.2 indicates the major intergovernmental grant programs in place in 1992. These grants fall into three major groupings: (1) comparatively unrestricted revenue sharing and block grants: (2) categorical grants for health and social services; and (3) the public school finance system.

Five major revenue sharing programs provide general financial assistance to local governments. By far the most significant of these is the sales and use tax program, which is treated as a local revenue source in most data sources and is discussed above. The state highway users program remits a portion of fuel excise tax revenues to cities and counties. These revenues are earmarked for road construction and maintenance. State vehicle license fees form a major general purpose revenue source for cities and counties. The state Constitution prohibits the state from imposing restrictions or regulations on the use of these funds by local governments. In addition, the federal government provides cities and counties with block grants for urban development.

A number of state and federal programs provide funding for health and public assistance programs:

- The Aid to Families with Dependent Children (AFDC) provides cash grants to impoverished families. The state sets eligibility and service levels for AFDC within allowable levels established by the federal government. The program is administered by the counties, and the costs of the grants and program administration are shared by counties, the state, and the federal government.

- The Medi-Cal program pays the costs of medical treatment for AFDC recipients and other eligible individuals (for example, impoverished pregnant women and individuals under age 21). County welfare offices determine eligibility for Medi-Cal, and the state Department of Health administers payments and other aspects of the program. The state establishes program requirements subject to federal regulation. The program is financed in equal measure by state and federal funds.

- County medical services. The state requires counties to provide medical services to needy individuals who do not qualify for Medi-Cal. Until recently, these services were funded partly by the county, and partly through a system of state categorical grants. The county established program requirements subject to state regulation. In 1991, the state replaced the categorical grants with a general revenue sharing system and repealed many of the regulations governing administration of this program.

---

17   Federal grants-in-aid include grants for payments to individuals as well as lower level governments.

Table 7.2 Major intergovernmental grant programs in California (1992 budget year)

Grant	Donor	Recipient	Type	Basis of Distribution
Sales Tax	State	Cities and counties	General revenue sharing, part of it restricted for transportation uses.	Location of sale
Motor vehicle fuel taxes	State	Cities and counties	Categorical revenue sharing for roads	Various: number of registered vehicles, population, miles of road, assessed value of property
Vehicle license fees	State	Cities and counties	General and categorical revenue sharing	Various, including population, sales tax receipts
Homeowners' exemption reimbursement	State	Counties	General purpose block grant	Reimbursement of local revenue losses from state property tax exemption for homeowners
Trial Court Funding	State	Counties	Categorical block grant	Payment per judgeship
Aid to Families with Dependent Children	State and federal	Counties	Open-ended matching grant	State program requirements, federal regulation, funding 50% federal, 47.5% state, 2.5% county
AFDC administration	State and federal	Counties	Open-ended matching grants	Federal 50%, state 25%, county 25%, based on eligible costs
Health and social service revenues [1]	State	Counties	Earmarked revenue sharing	Allocated to counties for public health and mental health responsibilities shifted to counties in 1992
Medi-Cal (Medicaid) grants	Federal	State	Open-ended categorical matching grant	50% state-federal match for required services
General school apportionments	State	School districts	General matching grant	State-established revenue "floor" per student; state pays difference between revenue floor and local revenues
Special education	State and federal	School districts	Various categorical programs	Varies with state-approved school plans
Other educational assistance	State and federal	School districts	Various categorical block and matching grants	Over 60 grants providing funding and technical assistance for various activities
State mandate reimbursement	State	Cities, counties, school districts, special districts	General block grant	Reimburses costs associated with qualifying state requirements

[1] The 1991 county-state health program realignment repealed block and matching grants, repealed many program requirements, and established a revenue sharing source for funding indigent health programs.

Sources: State of California, Legislative Analyst's Office, February 1991. "The county-state partnership," in The 1991-92 Budget: Perspectives and Issues.

The third set of intergovernmental grants is the state system for public school finance. The single largest intergovernmental grants program in California, the general school apportionment, amounted to almost $10.4 B in 1992. The state also provides categorical grants for special education and desegregation activities, and administers over sixty additional programs providing categorical grants and technical assistance for specific activities.

The changing role of grants-in-aid. This section presents more detail on the level and types of intergovernmental payments to California cities and counties. First, we analyze intergovernmental finance in California in the aggregate and characterize the degree of centralization of state finance and expenditures. Next we indicate the composition of state and federal grants to lower-level governments. Third, we discuss the grants received by general purpose local governments.

Figure 7.1 illustrates the total level of state and federal grants distributed in California from 1975 through 1991, the most recent year for which data are available.[18] Federal payments to California governments mirror the national trend noted above; they peak in 1977, decline further in 1980 and 1981, and remain fairly stable thereafter. Turning to state aid, we clearly see the response to Proposition 13: state aid to local governments increased 24 percent between 1977 and 1978. This is followed by a trough in state aid in the early 1980s, which reflects the fact that the state passes a substantial portion of federal aid to local governments. In the mid-eighties, state intergovernmental payments began a steady climb, exceeding $34 B by 1990.

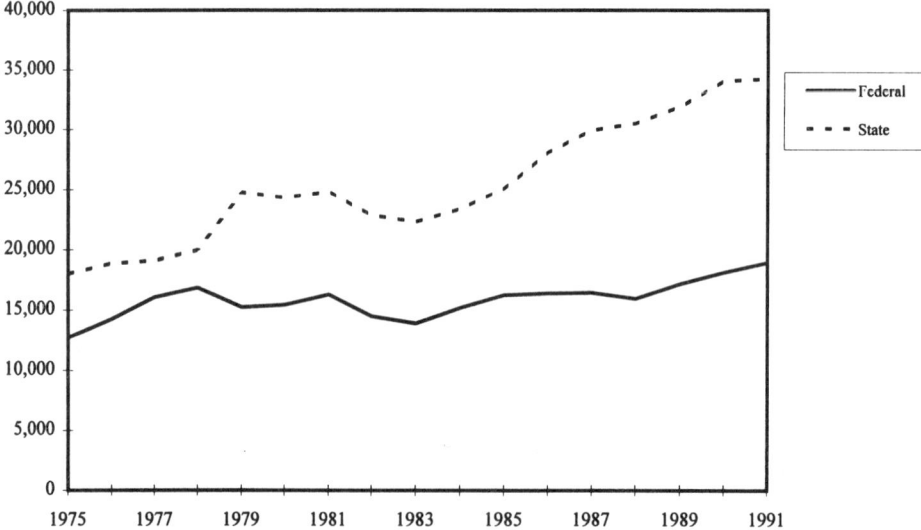

Figure 7.1   Federal and state grants to California Local Government (millions of 1990 dollars)

Source: United States Department of Commerce, Bureau of the Census. Various years. Government Finances: (Year).

---

[18]   Note that state payments to local governments include federal aid that is given to the state and then redirected to localities. For example, federal AFDC grants are reported as federal-to-local grants, and also as state-to-local grants. Consequently, it is not possible to calculate the total amount of intergovernmental aid. Also note that state intergovernmental aid does not include sales tax revenues, which are treated as a local revenue source. For these and following tables, the data reflect 1990 constant dollars.

Table 7.3 indicates that funding in California is relatively decentralized, while spending is fairly centralized. The first three columns show the portion of total state and local expenditures in California financed by the federal, state and local governments.[19] Between 1975 and 1991, the portion of state and local expenditures financed with federal funds declined slightly, reflecting the federal policy shift away from grants-in-aid. The portion of expenditures financed by the state increased from 39 percent in 1975 to 49 percent in 1988, but then declined slightly, to 47 percent in 1991. This shift reflects the financial arrangements adopted in response to Proposition 13, most notably the state assumption of public school financing.

The last two columns show the state and local shares of spending in California. Although the state government has assumed a somewhat larger share of expenditures over the years, spending in the state nonetheless is relatively decentralized. Local governments in California were responsible for a larger share of expenditures than the national average in 1988.[20] At the same time, local governments assume a somewhat smaller share of financing than the national average. Thus, California is characterized by a unique combination of relatively centralized financing and decentralized spending for public services.[21]

Table 7.3   Level of funding and spending by state and local governments (millions of 1990 dollars)

	Funding level			Spending level			
	Federal	State	Local	State	Local	Total	Percent Change
1975	19%	39%	42%	29%	71%	$68,326	
1976	20	39	42	30	70	72,811	7%
1977	20	39	40	33	67	78,579	8
1978	20	41	39	34	66	84,253	7
1979	21	48	32	30	70	73,224	-13
1980	21	49	31	32	68	75,256	3
1981	22	47	32	30	70	75,579	0
1982	19	46	34	32	68	74,449	-1
1983	19	46	35	31	69	73,696	-1
1984	19	47	35	33	67	81,222	10
1985	20	48	32	34	66	82,150	1
1986	18	49	32	34	66	88,778	8
1987	17	49	34	33	67	96,551	9
1988	16	49	35	33	67	100,545	4
1989	17	48	35	32	68	102,233	2
1990	16	48	36	32	68	110,724	8
1991	17%	47%	37%	32%	68%	$114,600	4%

Source: United States Department of Commerce, Bureau of the Census. Various years. Government Finances: (Year).

---

[19] These data do not include direct federal expenditures in California. Thus they exclude federal expenditures at military bases and research laboratories, as well as the expenditures of federal field offices.

[20] At 68 percent, the local share of expenditures in California was the highest in the nation.

[21] Only two other states, Nevada and Wisconsin, combined a greater-than-average local share of expenditure with a lower-than-average local financing share.

The general trend toward diminished federal intergovernmental aid masks a federal shift in priorities in favor of the state over the local level in California. Federal grants to the state (in Figure 7.2) reveal a period of moderate decline in the late seventies and early eighties, followed by gentle growth throughout the remainder of the decade. This growth is primarily due to increasing federal payments for entitlement programs administered by the state, most notably the AFDC and Medi-Cal programs. In contrast, direct federal payments to cities and counties peaked in 1977 and declined steadily throughout the following years.

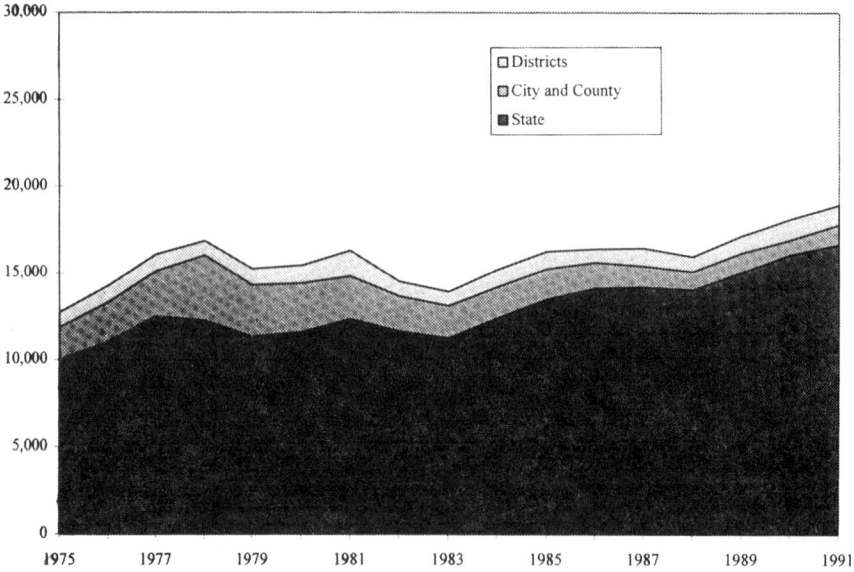

Figure 7.2 Federal grants to California Local Government (millions of 1990 dollars)
Source: United States Department of Commerce, Bureau of the Census, Various years, Government Finances: (Year).

Table 7.4 summarizes the functional composition of federal grant payments to the state and local governments from 1978 to 1991. This table shows relative stability over time in the composition of federal transfers to these entities. Over the years, welfare programs have generally accounted for about one-half of the federal grants allocated to the state. In contrast, a very small share of the direct federal funding provided to local governments is for welfare and education. Direct aid to local governments consists of a variety of categorical grants not separately identified within standard data sources.

Figure 7.3 documents state payments to cities and counties from 1975 to 1991. Again, state grants include federal pass-through dollars. The state response to Proposition 13 is evident in the sharp increases in funding to counties in 1979. County receipts increased throughout the 1980s. In contrast, state grants to cities declined slightly during this fifteen-year period.

Table 7.4   Federal grants to California by level of recipient and type of funding (in percent)

	Federal Grants to the State			Federal Grants to Localities		
Year	Welfare	Education	Other	Welfare	Education	Other
1978	45%	18%	37%	0%	9%	91%
1979	47	13	40	0	10	90
1980	45	20	35	0	11	89
1981	49	19	32	0	8	92
1982	53	18	29	0	7	93
1983	53	17	30	1	9	90
1984	48	19	34	1	7	93
1985	46	17	37	0	6	94
1986	45	18	37	0	8	92
1987	48	17	35	0	8	92
1988	47	17	36	0	11	89
1989	46	17	37	0	13	87
1990	47	17	36	0	17	83
1991	50%	18%	32%	0%	9%	90%

Source: United States Department of Commerce, Bureau of the Census. Various years. Government Finances: (Year).

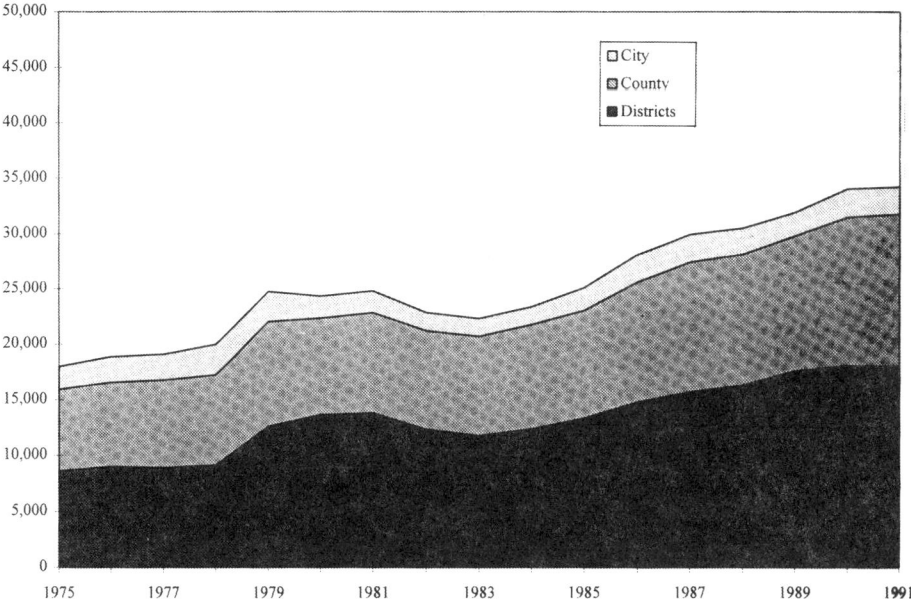

Figure 7.3   State grants to local governments by level of recipient (millions of 1990 dollars)
Source: United States Department of Commerce, Bureau of the Census. Various years. Government Finances: (Year).

Table 7.5 presents the functional composition of state grants to lower-level governments. The share of state grants going to welfare programs remained stable throughout the 1980s, as did the share allocated to higher education. In 1992, however, the share of grants allocated for welfare *increased* sharply to 35 percent, while the share of payments going to education declined to 48 percent. This trend is in part attributable to higher welfare reimbursements as a result of the state recession, as well as state reimbursements for increased costs associated with federal Medicaid (Medi-Cal) mandates. Throughout the 1980s the share of general assistance provided to lower level governments continued to decline, largely due to the phasing out of federal general revenue sharing money to cities and counties. Although the federal government financed general revenue sharing, a large portion of the grants was allocated by the state government.

Table 7.5   Functional composition of state grants to lower governments in California (millions of 1990 dollars)

Year	Education	Welfare	Highways	Corrections	General	Other	Total
1975	52%	25%	5%	0%	13%	4%	$18,250
1976	48	28	5	0	14	4	18,627
1977	46	31	4	0	12	6	19,626
1978	45	31	4	0	14	5	20,082
1979	51	26	3	0	15	4	25,367
1980	56	26	3	1	10	5	25,123
1981	52	28	3	0	11	5	25,767
1982	51	30	3	1	9	6	23,781
1983	52	29	4	1	9	6	23,222
1984	55	28	4	0	6	7	23,859
1985	53	27	3	1	7	9	26,623
1986	54	26	4	1	7	8	29,089
1987	55	26	3	1	7	7	31,535
1988	56	26	3	1	8	8	32,614
1989	57	25	3	1	7	8	35,034
1990	53	27	3	1	7	10	35,174
1991	51	29	3	1	7	10	34,502
1992	48%	35%	3%	1%	6%	7%	$36,200

Source: United States Department of Commerce, Bureau of the Census, Various years. Government Finances: (Year).

One of the shortcomings of the U.S. Census Bureau data discussed above is that federal pass-through funding is included in the figures reported for state grants. Consequently, it is not possible to determine the relative weight of state and federal payments within the local government grant structure. In the next section, we analyze financial data reported by California cities and counties. These data are not directly comparable to the series discussed above.[22] However, grants-in-aid are reported based on the origin of the grant, so that it is possible to separate federal and state grants to local entities.

---

[22]   One reason is that they do not include all state and federal grants to California governments; for example, they exclude payments to special districts. Another is that the financial transactions data are reported by all cities, counties and school districts, whereas the Census Bureau data are based on a sample of governments in California.

Figures 7.4 and 7.5 illustrate state and federal grants to counties for welfare, health and other purposes. State payments for welfare programs increased steadily throughout the seventies and eighties. State payments for health programs also increased steadily throughout the eighties. During this period the State assumed responsibility for Medicaid, but subsequently restricted eligibility standards for medically indigent adults. The financial assistance provided to counties in response to Proposition 13 shows up as a sharp peak in "other state grants" received in 1978. In the years following Proposition 13, other state aid declined slightly, then began to climb steadily. The growth in this grant category in the late eighties is primarily attributable to state payments for correctional facilities, trial court funding, and aid to distressed counties.

Federal funding for county welfare programs fluctuated somewhat in the late seventies and early eighties. In the late eighties, however, federal welfare grants grew moderately. Other federal payments to the counties peaked in 1978, consistent with trends discussed above, and then declined steadily throughout the eighties. Federal aid to counties for health programs remained at a low but stable level throughout the period, reflecting the limited federal involvement in local health programs.[23]

California cities received a small and declining share of state and federal grants during the 1970s and 1980s. This relative fiscal independence relates to the strong history of municipal home rule in California. Cities have a much more diverse and independent revenue authority than do counties. Moreover, although they derive their corporate powers from the state, cities do not generally serve as agents in providing state-required services. Consequently, California cities are fairly autonomous – fiscally and politically - relative to county governments.

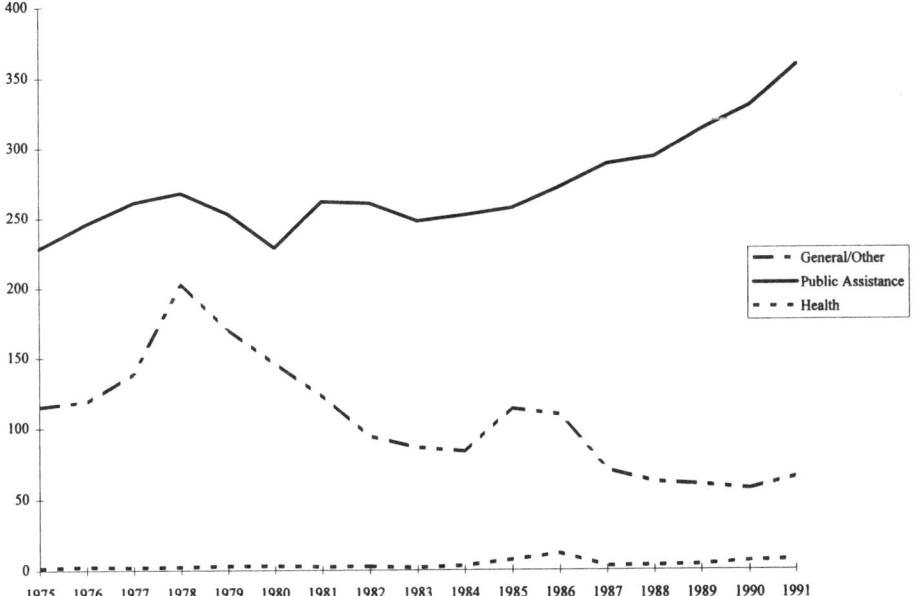

Figure 7.4 Federal grants to counties by function (millions of 1990 dollars)
Sources: State of California, Office of State Controller. Various years. Annual Report of Financial Transactions Concerning Cities of California and Annual Report of Financial Transactions Concerning Counties of California.

---

23 Federal involvement in the health function is limited primarily to its participation in the Medi-Cal program.

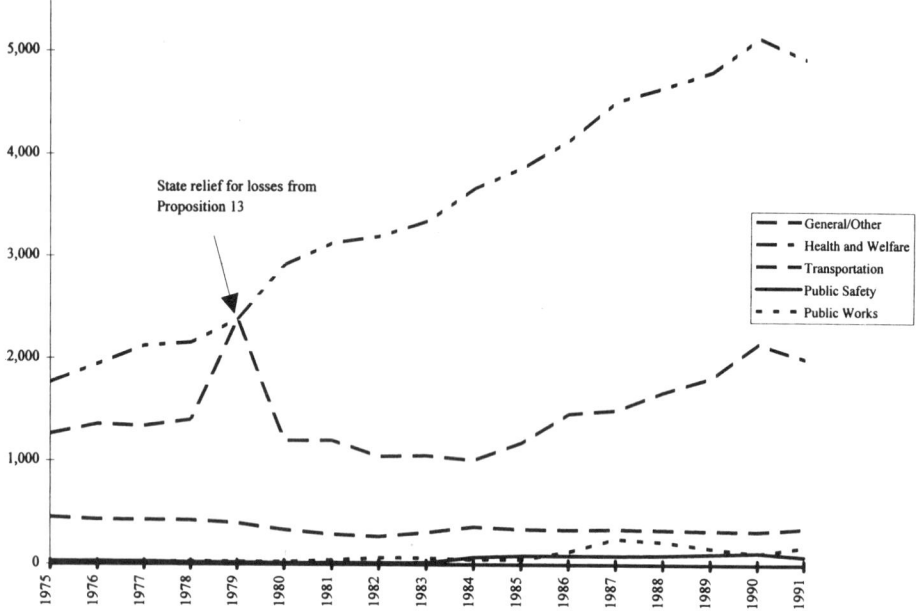

Figure 7.5 State grants to counties by function (millions of 1990 dollars)
Sources: State of California, Office of State Controller. Various years. Annual Report of
Financial Transactions Concerning Cities of California and Annual Report of Financial
Transactions Concerning Counties of California.

7.2.3 Revenue Patterns

State and local tax burdens do not appear to be extraordinarily large in California, relative
to other states in the nation. For example, although California ranks as a high-revenue
state on a per capita basis, its collections are not particularly high relative to personal
income. In 1988 California ranked tenth out of fifty states in terms of state and local
revenue per capita, but only thirtieth in tax collections as a fraction of personal income.
California state and local governments are slightly *less* reliant on aid from the federal
government than are other states. Federal aid is 15.5 percent of California's total revenue,
compared to 16.2 percent nationally, and California ranks 19th in terms of federal aid per
capita. California state and local governments are also slightly *less* reliant on property and
income taxes, and somewhat more reliant on sales, corporate taxes, and fees for services.
In the remainder of this section, we examine in more detail revenue trends for
California's state government, as well as cities, counties and school districts.

State revenue. Table 7.6 summarizes the sources of state revenue from 1975 to 1991,
the most recent year for which data are available. During this period, there was a gradual
decline in the fraction of funding from federal grants and the sales and use tax, while
reliance on the income tax increased. The percentage of total revenues from public
employee retirement contributions and earnings also increased during this period. Other
revenue sources remained relatively constant. Total state revenues more than doubled in
real terms during the 16 year period, but there were declines in real revenues during
several of the years.

Table 7.6   Sources of revenue for state government in California (millions of 1990 dollars)

Year	Total	Income Taxes	Property Taxes	Sales Taxes	Other Taxes	Federal Transfers	Service Charges	Other[1]
1975	$43,259	20%	–	26%	5%	22%	4%	23%
1976	48,053	19	–	24	5	22	4	26
1977	52,715	20	–	23	5	22	4	25
1978	55,355	23	–	23	5	20	4	24
1979	50,396	24	–	19	6	21	5	25
1980	56,975	25	–	24	5	20	4	23
1981	56,747	24	–	23	5	21	4	22
1982	57,069	24	–	23	5	20	5	23
1983	56,818	23	–	23	5	20	5	24
1984	62,987	25	–	22	4	20	5	25
1985	69,424	25	–	21	4	19	5	26
1986	74,751	24	–	20	4	19	5	28
1987	79,620	26	–	20	5	18	5	27
1988	79,783	24	–	20	5	17	5	28
1989	85,248	26	–	20	5	18	5	27
1990	88,704	25	–	19	5	18	5	28
1991	$87,239	23%	–	21%	5%	19%	5%	25%

Source: United States Department of Commerce. Bureau of the Census. Various Years. State Government Finances in (Year). Series GF/91-3. U.S. Government Printing Office, Washington, D.C.

[1] Other category includes pension contributions.

County revenue. The impact of Proposition 13 is quite clear in Table 7.7, which summarizes county revenue sources. Between 1978 and 1979 the contribution of property taxes to county revenues fell by more than half, from 32 percent to 15 percent. The declining importance of property tax revenues was accompanied by an increase in the proportion of state funding, which showed slow but steady growth throughout the eighties. County reliance on current service charges and enterprise funding also increased substantially following Proposition 13, and grew moderately in subsequently years. In contrast, county reliance on federal revenue declined following a peak in 1978. Between 1975 and 1991, real revenues grew by 75 percent, although the counties experienced declines in real revenues in the late 1970s due to Proposition 13.

City revenue. Table 7.8, which displays city revenue by source, also shows that cities dramatically reduced their reliance on property tax revenues following Proposition 13. This decline did not appear to lead to major changes in relative reliance on any single revenue source. Rather, all revenue sources increased proportionately, with the largest increase occurring in current service charges and enterprise revenues. Overall, the passage of Proposition 13 had a much smaller impact on the composition of city revenue than that of counties, due to the wider array of financing sources available to city policy makers. From 1974 to 1989, city revenues adjusted for inflation almost doubled, although the cities also experienced a few years of declining resources.

Table 7.7   Sources of revenue for county government in California (millions of 1990 dollars)

Year	Total	Income Taxes	Property Taxes	Sales Taxes	Other Taxes	Federal Transfers	State Transfers	Service Charges	Other[1]
1975	$13,941	–	34%	2%	1%	22%	24%	12%	6%
1976	14,856	–	34	2	–	22	24	12	5
1977	15,411	–	34	2	1	23	24	12	4
1978	16,310	–	32	2	1	25	23	12	4
1979	15,206	–	15	2	1	25	32	19	6
1980	14,736	–	18	3	1	23	29	20	7
1981	15,432	–	18	2	1	23	29	20	7
1982	15,515	–	19	2	1	22	30	20	7
1983	16,141	–	20	2	1	20	30	22	7
1984	17,067	–	20	2	1	19	30	22	7
1985	18,035	–	20	2	1	18	29	23	7
1986	19,740	–	20	2	1	17	30	23	7
1987	20,957	–	20	1	1	16	30	23	8
1988	21,285	–	21	1	1	16	31	24	6
1989	22,801	–	20	1	1	16	30	24	7
1990	23,435	–	21	1	1	16	32	20	9
1991	$24,414	–	21%	1%	1%	17%	31%	20%	8%

Source: State of California, Office of State Controller. Various Years. Financial Transactions of Counties in California: (Year). Sacramento, California.
1 Includes pension contributions.

Table 7.8   Sources of revenue for city governments in California (millions of 1990 dollars)

Year	Total	Income Taxes	Property Taxes	Sales Taxes	Other Taxes	Transfers[1]	Service Charges	Other[2]
1975	$10,529	–	17%	13%	7%	20%	35%	8%
1976	11,676	–	16	12	7	22	36	7
1977	12,130	–	16	12	8	22	35	7
1978	13,393	–	15	12	7	25	34	7
1979	12,971	–	7	13	8	26	37	9
1980	13,127	–	9	14	9	21	39	9
1981	13,535	–	9	13	9	19	41	9
1982	12,867	–	9	14	11	17	42	7
1983	12,835	–	10	13	12	15	42	8
1984	14,358	–	9	13	13	14	41	10
1985	15,687	–	9	13	13	15	40	10
1986	16,975	–	9	12	13	15	39	12
1987	16,793	–	10	13	14	13	41	10
1988	18,263	–	10	12	14	12	40	13
1989	19,041	–	10	12	14	11	41	12
1990	20,086	–	10	12	14	10	41	13
1991	$20,521	–	10%	11%	14%	11%	40%	14%

Source: State of California, Office of State Controller. Various Years. Financial Transactions of Cities in California: (Year). Sacramento, California.
1 Includes both state and federal transfers. 2 Includes pension contributions.

7.2.4 Summary

The revenue data exhibit a number of consistent trends. The first is the declining importance of federal aid to all entities in the years following 1978. This is consistent with the national trend; federal intergovernmental expenditures peaked in 1978 and declined steadily in following years.[24] The largest single grant eliminated was general revenue sharing, which was phased out in the mid-eighties. Some other examples of declining federal grant programs include community services block grants, urban renewal, and training and employment services grants. Within education, the cuts in federal aid were concentrated in bilingual education and compensatory education grants.

The second obvious trend is the decline of property tax revenues to local entities as a result of Proposition 13. The combination of declining federal aid and the demise of the property tax had differing effects on the revenue composition of the various local agencies, depending largely on the functional role and fiscal powers accorded to the agency. In the case of schools, the state basically supplemented lost property tax revenues with state funding. Counties received greater state support, but also dramatically increased their reliance on current service charges. Cities, with a tradition of home rule and substantial taxing powers, responded by spreading the burden of financial support across all revenue sources.

7.3   LOCAL POWER AND DISCRETION

There are two major constraints on the autonomy of local lawmakers: regulations imposed by higher level governments, and the constitutional restrictions that have been imposed as a result of grass roots action through the initiative process.

7.3.1 Top-down Restrictions: Intergovernmental Regulation

Both the state and local governments in California are subject to a wide variety of regulatory orders from higher-level governments. Some of these are statutes or executive orders, others are the outcomes of judicial action. Unfortunately, there is no comprehensive catalog of intergovernmental regulations, much less any data indicating their fiscal or economic effects. Thus we can only provide a cursory sketch of the impact of regulations within California.

A typology of mandates. Throughout much of its history, the relationship of the U.S. federal government with the states – and by extension, their localities – has been shaped by the competing doctrines of national supremacy and dual sovereignty, or state powers. During the past few decades, indeed during most of the twentieth century, the forces toward centralization have been strengthened, and there has been a general movement toward greater federal fiscal and regulatory involvement in state policy.

One of the major means of federal intervention is the power of the purse. A variety of regulations guide the use of federal grants-in-aid. The federally funded entitlement programs discussed above come accompanied by literally volumes of regulations regarding eligibility and payment levels. Even the Community Development Block Grant program, conceived to be a means of streamlining federal urban aid, embodies 32 separate conditions of use.[25] Moreover, the federal government has often used its spending powers indirectly to coerce state compliance, or enacted direct orders or partial regulatory preemptions. A typology of mandates includes:[26]

---

[24] Quigley and Smolensky (1991).
[25] Advisory Commission on Intergovernmental Relations (1984).
[26] Conlan (1991).

- *Broad requirements,* which apply across a variety of grant programs. For example, the Civil Rights Act of 1964 bars racial and other types of discrimination in federally assisted programs;

- *Cross-over sanctions,* which specify that a failure to comply with one federal requirement will result in a loss of funds from a related or marginally related grant program. An example was a recent requirement that states raise the legal drinking age to 21 or lose a portion of federal highway funding.

- *Direct orders,* in which the federal government directly requires or bars action by a local government. Federal direct orders are relatively rare; one example is the Equal Employment Opportunity Act of 1972, which bars job discrimination by state and local governments.

- *Partial preemptions,* under which the federal government imposes a regulatory standard, but allows states to exceed the standard at their option. An example is the Clean Air Act, which establishes minimum air quality and emissions standards.

Federal requirements. Since 1960 the federal officials have increased reliance on intergovernmental regulatory mechanisms. Ironically, as illustrated in Figure 7.6, heavy reliance on intergovernmental regulation was evident even during the 1980s, a decade during which political opinion generally supported deregulation.[27] New requirements enacted during the 1980s are summarized in Table 7.9.

Although the costs of these requirements within California are unknown, they are likely to be high. For example, federally mandated extended coverage under the Medicaid program is estimated to have costed the states $2.56 billion in 1992.[28] The Safe Drinking Water Act Amendments of 1986 are estimated to increase public water system costs by $2 - $3 billion per year nationally, while compliance with the Asbestos Hazard Emergency Response Act is expected to cost American public schools $3 billion over thirty years. The Americans with Disabilities Act and the Clean Air Act also impose high costs on state and local governments.

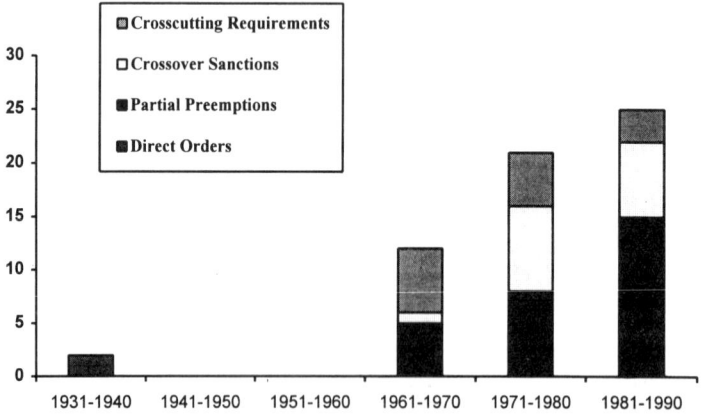

Figure 7.6 Federal intergovernmental regulatory statutes enacted by decade, 1931-1990
Source: Taken from Conlan, T.J. 1991. "And the Beat Goes on: Intergovernmental Mandates and Preemption in an Era of Deregulation," Publius: The Journal of Federalism 21:43 - 57.

---

27 Conlan (1991).
28 Conlan (1991), p.47.

Table 7.9 Major new statutes and statutory amendments regulating state and local governments, 1981-1990

Measure	Public Law	Type
Surface Transportation Assistance Act of 1982	97-424	Crossover
Voting Rights Act Amendments of 1982	97-205	Direct Order
Social Security Amendments of 1983	98-21	Direct Order
Child Abuse Amendments of 1984	98-457	Crossover
Hazardous and Solid Waste Amendments of 1984	98-616	Partial Preemption
Highway Safety Amendments of 1984	98-363	Crossover
Voting Accessibility for the Elderly and Handicapped (1984)	98-435	Direct Order
Age Discrimination in Employment Act Amendments of 1986	99-592	Direct Order
Asbestos Hazard Emergency Response Act of 1986	99-519	Direct Order
Commercial Motor Vehicle Safety Act of 1986	99-570	Crossover
Consolidated Omnibus Budget Reconciliation Act (1986)	99-272	Direct Order
Education of the Handicapped Act Amendments of 1986	99-457	Crossover
Emergency Planning and Community Right-to-Know (1986)	99-499	Partial Preemption
Handicapped Children's Protection Act of 1986	99-372	Crossover
Safe Drinking Water Act Amendments of 1986	99-339	Partial Preemption, Direct Order
Civil Rights Restoration Act of 1987	100-259	Crosscutting
Water Quality Act of 1987	100-4	Preemption, Direct Order, Crosscutting
Drug-Free Workplace Act of 1988	100-690	Crosscutting
Fair Housing Act Amendments of 1988	100-430	Direct Order
Lead Contamination Control Act of 1988	100-572	Direct Order
Ocean Dumping Ban Act	100-688	Direct Order
Americans with Disabilities Act	101-327	Crosscutting, Direct Order
Clean Air Act Amendments of 1990	101-549	Partial Preemption
Education of the Handicapped Act Amendments of 1990	101-476	Crossover

Source: Taken from Conlan, T.J., 1991. "And the Beat Goes on: Intergovernmental Mandates and Preemption in an Era of Deregulation," Publius: The Journal of Federalism 21:43 - 57.

State requirements. The political and legal constraints on state regulation of local governments differ from those governing federal intergovernmental relations. Because local governments derive their powers from the state, there are relatively few legal restrictions on state regulation of local governments. The major political constraint on state intergovernmental regulations is Proposition 4, which requires the state government to reimburse local governments for the costs of many new programs or increased service levels imposed by state law. The state currently spends several hundred million dollars annually as reimbursements for state mandates.

There is even less information available about state intergovernmental regulation than federal regulation. A 1979 study of state and federal mandates found that one city in California was subject to over 700 federal restrictions and almost 1200 state requirements.[29] It is not clear, however, how many of these federal or state requirements have substantial effects. Nor did the study attempt to quantify the fiscal or economic costs of the state or federal requirements.

In sum, there is no comprehensive body of information available about the scope or fiscal impacts of state or federal regulations in California. Clearly, intergovernmental regulation is an important mechanism for controlling the actions of lower-level

[29] Lovell et al. (1979).

governments. Most intergovernmental grants are substantially restricted in their use, and may also be used by higher level governments to achieve unrelated or marginally related goals. Moreover, both the federal and the state government rely on more coercive regulations, such as direct orders and regulatory preemption. Direct orders are more commonly used, however, by the state than the federal government. This is because local governments have no sovereign powers.

7.3.2 Bottom-up Restrictions: The Citizen Initiative Process

In addition to the restrictions imposed on state and local lawmakers by higher level governments, in the last two decades citizens have enacted through the initiative process a number of measures that affect the power of elected officials to tax and spend. These measures are listed in Table 7.10. Although most of the measures have the effect of restricting taxes or expenditures, two measures actually increase revenues, the state lottery and the excise tax on cigarettes.

Of these measures, the most important undoubtedly are Proposition 13, the appropriations limit, income tax indexing, and the spending guarantee for public schools. Income tax indexing and the education spending guarantee, in conjunction with the existence of many entitlement programs with statutory cost-of-living adjustments, have made it increasingly difficult for state lawmakers to assert control over the state budget. In recent years, state officials have confronted a seemingly intractable budget gap.

In 1991, the California Legislature faced a massive $14.3 billion budget deficit due to declining state revenues and increased social welfare expenditures. The Legislature enacted a temporary one-half cent sales tax increase, shifted some program responsibilities to counties, gave counties increased discretion with regard to other programs, and replaced the system of state block grants with a revenue sharing system. This realignment did not, however, resolve the budgetary problem, and the Legislature faced budget shortfalls again in the following two years.

In 1993, the Legislature handled another multi-billion dollar budget shortfall by shifting $2.6 billion in property tax revenues from counties and cities to the public schools, and reducing state general fund support for education by a commensurate amount. In return, the Legislature relieved counties of some statutory responsibilities, and extended the temporary one-half cent sales tax imposed in 1991, earmarking the revenues for public safety programs. Cities lost almost $300 million as a result of the property tax shift, while counties lost $2 billion in property tax revenues, an amount which was partially offset by increased sales tax revenues.

At the local level, tax limitations also constrain political choices. As discussed above, Proposition 13 removes local policy discretion over the ad valorem property tax, and makes it considerably more difficult for local governments to increase other taxes. Local government officials have been able to obtain voter approval of tax increases, usually sales taxes, for transportation, jails, public safety, and school operations.[30] They have had much less success, however, in obtaining voter approval of general purpose tax increases.

The appropriations limit, enacted as Proposition 4 in 1979, has had somewhat less influence on state and local budgets than Proposition 13, primarily because tax restrictions and economic factors kept state and local budgets well below the limit for most of the last decade. During the early 1980s, a mild recession in California kept state and local revenues down, while rapid population growth and high national inflation rates amplified the amount state and local governments were authorized to spend. During the middle of the decade, state expenditures began to approach the limit, and in 1987, a revenue windfall related to federal tax reform caused the state to exceed the limit by $1.1

---

30 Some of these sales tax increases have been challenged in court as violating Proposition 13.

billion. After considerable partisan wrangling and an attempt by the Superintendent of Schools to divert the revenue windfall to education programs, the state mailed rebate checks to the taxpayers in time for Christmas. In recent years the appropriations limit has not been binding, because an ongoing recession (and a series of fiscally conservative governors) kept state revenues relatively low.

Table 7.10 State initiative measures related to taxing and spending

Year	Description of Measure
1978	*Proposition 13*. Property tax rate limited to 1 percent; no new ad valorem property taxes; growth in property assessment limited to 2 percent per year with reassessment to market value on sale; 2/3 voter approval for increase local taxes; 2/3 vote required by state legislators to increase state taxes.
1979	*Proposition 4*. State, local appropriations limited to 1978 spending, adjusted annually for population growth and inflation. Voter approval required to exceed or modify appropriations limit. State reimbursement of local mandates.
1982	*Propositions 5 and 6*. Abolition of state gift and inheritance taxes.
1982	*Proposition 7*. Indexing of state income tax for inflation.
1984	*Propositions 23 and 31*. No increase in property assessment for tax purposes on improvements made for seismic safety and fire prevention.
1984	*Proposition 37*. State lottery; 34 percent of revenues earmarked for education.
1986	*Proposition 46*. With 2/3 local voter approval, increased property tax to finance bonds.
1986	*Proposition 47*. Constitutional guarantee of allocation of motor vehicle license fee revenues to cities and counties.
1986	*Propositions 48 and 50*. No increased property assessment on properties transferred between family members, or on restorations and replacements due to a disaster.
1986	*Proposition 60*. Elderly homeowners purchasing a less expensive home may transfer current property tax assessment to new home.
1986	*Proposition 62*. Two-thirds governing board approval and majority voter approval required for any measure to increase general purpose local taxes.
1988	*Proposition 98*. Minimum state funding level for public schools equal to the proportion of the general fund spent on education in 1988, or about 40 percent of general fund revenues.
1988	*Proposition 99*. Twenty-five cent per pack excise tax on cigarettes; earmarked for education, medical services; research into tobacco related illnesses.
1990	*Proposition 140*. Term limits for state lawmakers; reduced operating budget for legislature.
1992	*Proposition 162*. Restricts use of public employee and teacher retirement funds.
1992	*Proposition 163*. Repeal state sales tax on snacks and bottled water.
1994	*Proposition 187*. Restrict access of illegal immigrants to state and local services.

Source: California Journal. Various years.

It is more difficult to assess the impact of the appropriations limit on local expenditure policy. In the case of counties, the appropriations limit does not appear to be binding. An analysis of the most recent reported county financial transactions data reveals that total county expenditures were only 67 percent of the summed appropriations limits in 1992. All of the largest counties had comfortable spending margins, and only two small counties, Monterey and Napa, had expenditure levels within 10 percent of the limit. During most of the decade, county spending has been constrained not by the appropriations limit, but by slow growth in revenue sources, most of which are relatively inelastic, and over which local officials have little direct control.

A similar analysis for city expenditures reveals that total city spending in the state was 65 percent of the summed city appropriations limits in 1991, the latest year for which data are available. This overall trend masks a great deal of variance, however. Thirty-five of the state's 466 cities are at or close to their appropriations limits, suggesting that the limits might be restraining expenditures in some cases. Two cities reported spending slightly in excess of the limit; whether these cities received voter approval to exceed the limit or simply have not been challenged is not clear. In any event, all of the cities with spending close to the limit are quite small, indicating that the appropriations limit may not have hindered big city spending policies.

Between 1980 and 1987, local voters faced 189 different measures to create or modify spending limits for cities, counties or special districts. Only twice did they reject these measures.[31] Some of these were measures allowing an agency to exceed the appropriations limit, as was the case for Santa Barbara County during the mid-eighties. However, many of these measures established appropriations limits for newly created cities or special districts, or modified limits upon territorial annexation. Consequently it is difficult to determine the extent to which appropriations limits directly constrained local government expenditures, or the willingness of local residents to relax the limits when they did.

7.4   EVALUATION AND CONCLUSIONS

Historically, as is true elsewhere in the United States, local governments in California were financed primarily by property taxes, and the state government was financed by income and sales taxes. The income tax in California had a more progressive rate structure than in most states and a large fraction of state sales tax revenue was remitted to local governments by state law. A large portion of local welfare expenditures were financed by state grants while primary and secondary education was largely financed by local property tax revenue.

Proposition 13, passed by voter initiative in 1978, disturbed this equilibrium. Local property taxes were rolled back to one percent of assessed value throughout the state and local assessments of market value were replaced by an arbitrary but uniform statewide assessment rule. As indicated in this chapter, the immediate effect of this reform was to reduce substantially the scope for autonomous economic behavior by local government. Denied a substantial portion of their historic tax bases, local governments greatly increased their reliance on user charges and fees. The shortfall in local revenues was also ameliorated by increased grants and intergovernmental transfers from the state to local governments.

The equity implications of these complex changes are somewhat ambiguous. On the one hand, these changes have increased reliance on the progressive state income tax to finance the expenditures of all governments within the state. On the other hand, the large one-time reduction in property tax rates surely benefited upper income taxpayers. Given the skewed pattern of wealth holding by income class, the net result of these changes was

---

[31] R. Schmidt (1987).

probably an improvement in the economic circumstances of the wealthier individuals who resided in California in 1978. Greater reliance on user charges and sales taxes also increased the overall regressivity of these changes. Importantly, in the changed fiscal climate resulting from the "tax revolt," it is far more difficult to finance local services which might benefit lower income households.

From an efficiency viewpoint, there are clear gains to increased reliance on user-charge financing. However, the effect of eliminating property tax rate differences among jurisdictions was to reduce the efficiency with which public resources are allocated. Removal of property tax differences eliminated a major reason for Tiebout sorting, in which consumers who demanded higher levels of public service could move to high-tax, high-service localities. The reduction in spending possibilities for local government surely reduces the choices available to the population, and hence the efficiency of resource allocation.

These shortcomings are exacerbated by increasing reliance on the sales tax to finance local services, particularly because the state allocates sales tax revenues to localities based on point of sale. This shared revenue structure creates incentives for localities to compete for retail development, and allows municipalities which contain lucrative establishments (e.g., car dealerships or shopping malls) to export the costs of local services to regionally based customers, many of whom probably do not benefit from such services. This ability to export the cost of services further erodes the link between service costs and benefits.

Another trend that violates the benefit principle is the increased reliance of state and federal policy makers on a variety of intergovernmental mandates. In California, Proposition 4 limits the ability of state legislators to impose mandates on local governments without reimbursing their costs. However, there are a large number of exceptions to Proposition 4 (one of which allows the state to pass on the costs of federal mandates).

A major problem with these regulations and mandates is that they may fail to acknowledge variation in resident preferences or fiscal capacity. Another is that decision makers at the higher level of government do not directly incur the "costs" – political or financial – of the activities they require of local governments. Insufficient fiscal discipline in the legislative process, and strong incentives for political credit claiming, may lead legislators to enact mandates whose costs exceed social benefits.

The special position of primary and secondary education makes the changes in finance and in the allocation of responsibilities more difficult to evaluate. Proposition 13 increased state financial responsibility for primary and secondary schooling in California. In this respect, the changes are consistent with long term secular changes in the US.[32] Increased state responsibilities also reduced the variation in educational spending across school districts and eliminated property-tax barriers to access. If one believes that the externalities of primary and secondary education are sizable, then it follows that these changes increased welfare and economic efficiency. Further, if one believes that a more equal distribution of educational spending is more equitable, then these changes in intergovernmental relations were also equity enhancing.

Overall, the trends in fiscal relations analyzed in this chapter point to a substantial increase in the role of the state at the expense of local government in the financing of government services and in the regulation of economic decision making. The locus of economic decision making and control of service delivery is increasingly at the state level. This centralization is ironic since a major objective of the proponents of the tax limitations of the 1970s and 1980s was a reduction in the importance of government. Finally, the implication of these trends may be to reduce the extent of fiscal federalism in California. In considering Oates's definition of fiscal federalism, quoted in the introduction, it seems

---

32 According to Poterba (1994), in 1929-30 the local share of primary and secondary spending in the US was 82.7 percent. In 1947-48 it had declined to 57.9 percent, and by 1990-91 it had fallen to 46.5 percent.

less and less true that public service financing and allocation decisions "are determined largely by the demands for the services of the residents" or others who directly benefit from local government.

REFERENCES

Advisory Commission on Intergovernmental Relations, 1991, *Significant Features of Fiscal Federalism,* Washington, D.C.

Advisory Commission on Intergovernmental Relations, 1984, *Regulatory Federalism: Policy, Process, Impact and Reform,* Washington, D.C.

Bergstrom, T.C. and R.P. Goodman, 1973, "Private Demands for Public Goods," *American Economic Review,* 63:280-296.

Bewley, R., 1981, "A Critique of Tiebout's Theory of Local Public Expenditures," *Econometrica,* Vol. 49, 3:713-740.

Bish, R., 1971, *The Public Economy of Metropolitan Areas,* Rand McNally/Markham, Chicago.

Bradford, D. and W.E. Oates, 1971, "Towards a Predictive Theory of Intergovernmental Grants," *American Economic Review,* Vol. 61, 2:440-448.

Brueckner, J.K., 1979, "Property Values, Local Public Expenditures and Economic Efficiency," *Journal of Public Economics,* 11:399-423.

Brueckner, J.K., 1982, "A Test for Allocative Efficiency in the Local Public Sector," *Journal of Public Economics,* 19:311-331.

Buchanan, J. M., 1965, "An Economic Theory of Clubs," *Economica,* 33:1-14.

California Journal, Various years.

Center for the Continuing Study of the California Economy, 1989, *California Population Statistics,* Palo Alto, California.

Coase, R., 1960, "The Problem of Social Costs," *Journal of Law and Economics,* 3:1-44.

Conlan, T. J., 1991, "And the Beat Goes on: Intergovernmental Mandates and Preemption in an Era of Deregulation," *Publius: The Journal of Federalism,* 21:43-57.

Courant, P.N., E.M. Gramlich, and D.L. Rubinfeld, 1980, "Why Voters Support Tax Limitation Amendments: The Michigan Case," *National Tax Journal,* 33:1-20.

Courant, P.N., E.M. Gramlich, and D.L. Rubinfeld, 1979, "The Stimulative Effects of Intergovernmental Grants: Or Why Money Sticks Where it Hits," in P. Mieszkowski and W. Oakland, eds., *Fiscal Federalism and Grants-in-Aid,* The Urban Institute, Washington.

Dilorenzo, T. J., 1981, "The Expenditure Effects of Restricting Competition in Local Public Service Industries: The Case of Special Districts," *Public Choice,* 37:569-578.

Ellickson, B., 1977, "The Politics and Economics of Decentralization," *Journal of Urban Economics,* 4:135-149.

Filimon, R., T. Romer and H. Rosenthal, 1980, "Asymmetric Information Control: The Bases of Monopoly Power in Public Spending," *Journal of Public Economics,* 17:51-70.

Fisher, R.C., 1982, "Income and Grant Effects on Local Expenditure: The Flypaper Effect and other Difficulties," *Journal of Urban Economics,* Vol. 12, 3:324-345.

Gayk, W.F., 1991, "The Taxpayers' Revolt," in Kling, R., S. Olin and M. Poster, eds., *Postsuburban California: The Transformation of Orange County Since World War II,* University of California Press, Berkeley and Los Angeles.

Gramlich, E.M., 1977, "Intergovernmental Grants: A Review of the Empirical Literature," in Oates, W.E., ed., *The Political Economy of Fiscal Federalism,* D.C. Heath, Lexington, Ma.

Gramlich, E.M. and D.S. Laren, 1984, "Migration and Income Redistribution Responsibilities," *The Journal of Human Resources,* 29:489-511.

Gramlich, E.M., D.L. Rubinfeld and D.A. Swift, 1981, "Why Voters Turn Out for Tax Limitation Votes," *National Tax Journal*, 34:115-124.

Hamilton, B.W., 1976, "Capitalization of Intrajurisdictional Differences in Local Tax Prices," *American Economic Review*, 66:743-753.

Hamilton, B.W., 1975, "Zoning and Property Taxation in a System of Local Governments," *Urban Studies*, 12:205-211.

Hardin, G., 1968, "The Tragedy of the Commons," *Science*, 162:1243-1248.

Henderson, J.V., 1985, "The Tiebout Hypothesis: Bring Back the Entrepreneurs," *Journal of Political Economy*, 93:248-264.

Hirschman, A.O., 1970, *Exit, Voice and Loyalty*, Harvard University Press, Cambridge.

Hochman, H.M. and G.E. Peterson, eds., 1974, *Redistribution Through Public Choice*, Columbia University Press, New York and London.

Hoyt, W.H., 1990, "Local Government Inefficiency and the Tiebout Hypothesis: Does Competition among Municipalities Limit Local Government Inefficiency?," *Southern Economic Journal*, Vol. 57, 2:481-496.

Inman, R.P., 1978, "Testing Political Economy's 'as if' Proposition: Is the Median Income Voter Really Decisive?," *Public Choice*, 33:45-65.

Inman, R.P. and D.L. Rubinfeld, 1989, Federalism in an Imperfect World: An Economic Perspective, unpublished paper.

Lovell, C.H., R. Kneisel, M. Neiman, A. Rose and C. Tobin, 1979, *Federal and State Mandating on Local Governments: An Exploration of Issues and Impacts*, University of California, Riverside.

Lowery, D and W.E. Lyons, 1989, "The Impact of Jurisdictional Boundaries: An Individual-level Test of the Tiebout Model," *Journal of Politics*, 51:1.

McGuire, M., 1974, "Group Segregation and Optimal Jurisdictions," *Journal of Political Economy*, 82:112-132.

Musgrave, R., 1959, *The Theory of Public Finance; A Study in Public Economy*, McGraw-Hill, New York.

Musgrave, R. and A.T. Peacock, eds., 1964, *Classics in the Theory of Public Finance*, St. Martins Press, New York.

National Conference of State Legislatures, 1987, *Recommendations of the Task Force on State-Local Relations*.

Nelson, 1987, "Searching for Leviathan," *American Economic Review*, Vol. 7, 1:198-204.

Niskanen, W.A. Jr., 1971, *Bureaucracy and Representative Government*, Aldine-Atherton, Chicago.

Oates, W.E., 1969, "The Effects of Property Taxes and Local Spending on Property Values," *Journal of Political Economy*, 77:957-971.

Oates, W.E., 1972, *Fiscal Federalism*, Harcourt Brace Jovanovich, New York.

Oates, W.E. 1985, "Searching for Leviathan," *American Economic Review*, Vol. 75, 4:748-757.

Oates, W.E., 1989, "Searching for Leviathan, a Reply and Some Further Reflections," *American Economic Review*, Vol. 79, 3:578-583.

Oates, W.E., ed., 1977, *The Political Economy of Fiscal Federalism*, D.C. Heath, Lexington, Ma.

Okun, A.M., 1975, *Equity and Efficiency: The Big Tradeoff*, The Brookings Institute, Washington D.C.

Ostrom, V., 1973, "Can Federalism make a Difference?," *Publius*, 3:198-237.

Ostrom, V., R. Bish and R. Warren, 1961, "The Organization of Government in Metropolitan Areas: A Theoretical Inquiry," *American Political Science Review*, 55:831-42.

CHAPTER 8

Does Multiplicity Matter more than Ownership in the Efficiency of Infrastructure Services?

Frannie Humplick

The World Bank, Washington D.C.

8.1 INTRODUCTION

The services from infrastructure systems have, for historical reasons or as a result of specific local contingencies, been totally state-owned in certain countries, entirely privatized in others, and sometimes provided through a mixture of public, private, and self-help arrangements. Many governments are re-evaluating the manner in which services have been provided in the past, and are searching for ways of increasing the efficiency of service delivery. One of the options considered is privatization, whereby a *transfer of ownership of infrastructure assets from the public to the private sector* is undertaken as a measure to increase efficiency. Another option is introducing *multiplicity in the production of infrastructure services* by: introducing competition in and for service production; and devolving responsibilities to regional, state, or local authorities.

The contemplated changes in infrastructure provision policies raise a number of important research issues: (i) which policy leads to higher efficiency in infrastructure provision?; and (ii) is there a sequencing of provision arrangements which is more efficient (e.g., first privatization and then introduction of multiplicity or vice versa)? To answer such questions, we need a methodology relating the "efficiency of service delivery" to the "structure of service production". Such a methodology requires sensitivity to changes in the structure of production, measured in efficiency terms.

Past empirical analyses on the relative performance of services provided under different provision regimes (combinations of ownership and multiplicity structures) have suffered from a number of limitations. First, few of them have accounted for the interacting effects of ownership and multiplicity. Second, past analyses have mostly considered indicators of profitability, with little or no mention of the operational efficiency indicators which contribute to service quality. Finally, the contributing impact of the level of development (and the experience of developing regions) on the performance of infrastructure under different provision regimes has not been systematically studied.

This chapter explicitly explores the relative advantages of one provision regime over another – with respect to a range of efficiency indicators – while controlling for the level of development. A model system relating the provision variables of "ownership" and "multiplicity" to production and service efficiency measures is presented. This model is applied to the provision of power services, using a 100 country data base.

8.2   PROPOSED METHODOLOGY

A simplified relationship between the service provision structure and infrastructure performance is depicted in Figure 8.1. A country's endowment – which is characterized in terms of its achieved level of development and the character of its decision-making structures – is represented as an endogenous effect determining the existing provision structures in a country and regulating or controlling the levels of performance of a typical utility providing infrastructure services. The service provision structures include the types of ownership and the level of multiplicity involved in service provision. Utility performance is measured in terms of production efficiency and service efficiency. In this chapter, we concentrate on the third level of inter-relationships, where the combined effect of a country's endowment and the structure of service provision on attainable levels of utility performance is investigated.

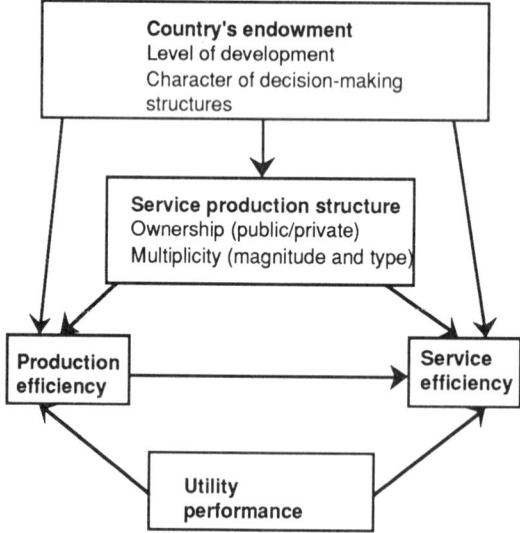

Figure 8.1 Proposed methodology

8.2.1 Utility Performance, Structure of Provision, and a Country's Endowment

Utility performance in Figure 8.1 is determined by the structure of provision, defined along dimensions of ownership and multiplicity, and the country's endowment defined by the achieved level of development (e.g., in terms of per capita GDP) and the decision-making structures within a country.

(i)   Why Ownership Matters?

The ownership structure of infrastructure assets and the nature of entitlement to the proceeds from producing an infrastructure service define the main relationships between the decision taken by the service producers and the beneficiaries from the service and profit flows. Table 8.1 demonstrates this concept using three examples.

Table 8.1 Structure of ownership and the beneficiaries of profit and service flows

Service producer	Beneficiaries	
	Profit	Service
Public entity	Voting public	Users
Private enterprise	Enterprise Shareholders	Users
User group/self-production	Users/self	Users
"Competition"	"Regulation"	"Accountability"

When services are provided by a government department, the producer (e.g., a public enterprise manager) is supposed to act in the interest of the public and user. The degree to which such a manager is *accountable* determines the extent to which the beneficiaries are satisfied. Factors establishing the conditions for accountability are discussed later on in this section. Under such a provision arrangement, the voting public are the beneficiaries of the profit flows, while the users of the service are the beneficiaries of the service flows. When the service producer is a private enterprise, it acts in its own interest or the interest of its shareholders to the extent that it is *regulated*, in *competition* with other service producers, and/or *accountable* to users. Again, in this case, there are factors which determine the environment in which regulation, competition, and accountability are determined – which are depicted as exogenous effects of a country's endowment in Figure 8.1. Finally, in the third case, when the service producer is a user group or when individual households or firms self-produce infrastructure (e.g., owning a power generator) they act in their own interest being beneficiaries of both the profit and service flows. These ownership variables, therefore, dictate the nature of *efficiency* in service production.

It has been argued that while capital, labor, and other inputs necessary for producing infrastructure services as efficiently as possible are important considerations for public entity managers, they are only one of a broad set of social and economic goals that these managers are required to achieve (see for example Chu et al., 1992 and Hatry, 1980). This broader set of objectives affects the choices public entity managers make with respect to production (operational) and service efficiency. Everything else being equal, such entities will display less internal efficiency in infrastructure service production than their private or self-help counterparts who do not face as many objectives. Exceptions, of course, include public enterprises with large managerial and operational capacity such that the extent of their non-service producing obligations does not affect their capacity to provide efficient services.

There is no consensus yet as to the best possible provision regime, from an allocative and internal efficiency point of view. Public policy debates range from claims that privatization tends to improve internal efficiency – but at the risk of worsening allocative efficiency, unless some effects are corrected for by competition and/or regulation (see for example Vickers and Yarrow, 1991) – to arguments that private ownership ensures sustainable efficiency gains (both allocative and internal) over long periods of time (see for example Nellis and Kikeri, 1992 and Bradburd, 1992). This study does not make any a priori assumptions on the relationship between "ownership" and "performance" in Figure 8.1, but develops empirical tests of the directionality and size of the postulated effects of "ownership" on "performance" in Figure 8.1, in comparison to other explanatory variables.

(ii)   Why Multiplicity Matters?

Multiplicity, in Figure 8.1, is defined in terms of magnitude – the number of independent actors involved in service provision – and type, distinguishing between vertically and non-vertically integrated production systems. Multiplicity matters for several reasons. First, the number of actors interacting in service provision affects the nature and integrity of *information* and *decision* flows. Second, multiplicity of producers may lead to competition in and for the market of infrastructure production leading to contests on improving the efficiency of services. Finally, the multiplicity of interactions resulting from administrative processes governing relationships between users and producers, regulators and producers, and users and regulators affects the efficiency, as shown in Spulber (1989). Regulators usually have a protective function with respect to users forcing producers to improve their efficiency to pre-defined benchmarks, and they may also control the nature of entry to and exit from service production functions. The degree of consistency in carrying out administrative functions is a crucial qualifier of the extent to which multiplicity matters.

Everything else being equal, one would expect that the higher the *magnitude of multiplicity*, in terms of the number of actors involved in service production, the more transparent the information and decision flows, and consequently the higher the efficiency of service. However, the size and complexity of interactions may lead to inefficiencies, especially in situations that are rapidly changing. Extreme bureaucratic red tape leading to slower processing of information and decision flows, and hence less efficiency in service production, is an example. It has been observed that in sectors undergoing rapid technological change (e.g., telecommunications) or characterized by extreme uncertainty (e.g., the capriciousness of user demands for air travel services), the size and complexity of administrative functions governing the provision of service is a distinguishing classifier of who succeeds and who fails (see Levy and Spiller, 1993 for a deeper discussion of the effects of size and complexity on performance).

The *type of multiplicity*, as represented by the structure of production, may affect the efficiency of infrastructure services in two main ways: as a result of the information and decision flows argument made above; and based on economies of scale and scope arguments. The degree of multiplicity is low when there is vertical integration, and the activities of an enterprise extend over more than one successive stage of the production process. In the case of power production, a single entity may be involved in the generation, transmission, and distribution phases of service production.

Expected effects favoring vertical integration are reduction in working capital requirements (amount of current assets which are financed from long-term sources of finance), elimination of prohibiting transaction costs, greater price competitiveness, and acquisition of "secure" markets. When the extent of vertical integration leads to monopoly conditions, however, all the inefficiencies expected under monopoly conditions hold. The degree of multiplicity may be increased without losing the positive effects of vertical integration through the introduction of vertically integrated regional monopolies. In such cases, the size of the market served results in maximizing the economies of scale benefits while at the same time providing opportunities for benchmark regulation. In this case, comparable efficiency achievements by "peer" enterprises (e.g., a vertically integrated regional monopoly A) are made public and/or used to regulate the behavior of the remaining peers (e.g., vertically integrated regional monopolies B, C, and D). Water supply in Paris is an example of such a situation.

In summary, therefore, the structure of multiplicity (magnitude and type) affects the transparency of decision flows, the size and complexity of decision structures, and the speed of processing decisions. All of these factors determine the nature and integrity of information flows between producers, consumers, regulators, and policy makers, and hence determine the efficiency with which infrastructure services are provided.

(iii) Factors Affecting the Provision Structure

The model in Figure 8.1 posits linkages between the structure of ownership and multiplicity within a country and the level of development achieved as well as the nature of decision-making within a country.

The level of development achieved within a country determines two important factors affecting the type of provision structures that may exist in a country and their respective efficiency: (i) the amount of resources (labor, capital, and technological know-how) available for allocation among competing provision activities; and (ii) the capacity to manage large scale activities. These two factors determine the efficiency of infrastructure provision to the extent that under-developed economies generally have: (i) lower levels of education and poorer balancing of skill mixes affecting the overall capacity to manage; and (ii) financing limitations (e.g., for carrying out the dual objectives of expanding services and maintaining the quality of existing services) which present constraints to long-term maintenance of high service quality. Therefore, we would expect that, everything else being equal, a public entity in Germany or France would be comparatively more efficient than a public entity in Tanzania or Burkina Faso. In addition, a variety of empirical studies have shown a clear correlation between the level of development (as measured by per capita GNP) and efficiency of service provision. For example, Quieroz and Gautam (1992) show that road condition is highly correlated to the levels of per capita GNP, using cross-section and time-series analysis. For this reason, we have the level of development as an important explanatory variable in Figure 8.1.

Another variable that has been seen to affect not only the level of economic development, but also the nature and degree of accountability and transparency of information and decision flows, is the character of decision-making structures in a country; particularly the nature of liberties (World Development Report, 1991). It has been postulated that a free press and open public debate might expose actions by the government and the private sector that might otherwise hold back development. Alternatively, freedoms can make it more difficult for a government, public, or private (although to a lesser degree) enterprise from taking tough but necessary decisions, from an infrastructure efficiency point of view. It has been shown in Dasgupta (1990) that "political and civil rights are positively and significantly correlated with real national income per head and its growth"; and that after controlling for income growth and regional effects, liberties appear to be strongly and positively associated with measures of overall education (World Development Report, 1991 pp. 50).

Indicators of political and civil liberties have been developed by Gastil (1989). The Gastil index is based on a ranking of countries according to thirty specific tests under two criteria: political rights defined as "rights to participate meaningfully in the political process"; and civil liberties, or the "rights to free expression, to organize and demonstrate, as well as rights to a degree of autonomy".

The political rights index, GAS-POL, is defined by indicators capturing the rights to participate meaningfully in the political process such as: (i) universal suffrage; (ii) the right to compete in the political process; and (iii) the right for elected officials to have a decisive vote on public policy. In order to rank high, a country must have a fully operating electoral procedure, usually including a significant opposition vote. It will likely have had a recent change of government from one party to another, an absence of foreign domination, decentralized political power, and a consensus that allows all segments of the population some power.

The civil liberties index, GAS-CIV, is designed to measure the extent to which people are able to express their opinions openly without fears of reprisals and are protected in doing so by an independent judiciary. Civil liberties are rights to free expression, to organize or demonstrate, as well as rights to a degree of autonomy. Primary attention is given to those liberties which are more directly related to the expression of political rights, with less attention given to those liberties that are expected to affect individuals in their private capacity.

These two indices represent the integrity of the institutional endowment in a country. We expect the GASTIL index to act as a surrogate for the level of accountability of decision flows, the degree of transparency of information flows, and the consistency of the administrative process, alluded to earlier.

8.2.2 Measuring Utility Performance

For analytical purposes, we can distinguish between three aspects of infrastructure performance: (i) at the level of the beneficiaries as measured by service quality or service effectiveness; (ii) at the level of internal operations of the entities producing a service as measured by managerial or operational efficiency; and (iii) at the sectoral level where the size and growth in investments in infrastructure are important. This chapter concentrates mostly on the first two levels.

The efficiency of internal operations of an entity – sometimes termed operational efficiency – can be categorized into measures of labor productivity (e.g., number of customers per employee); proficiency in extending services to customers (e.g., waiting time for service connections, percent with access to service); and responsiveness to new demand (e.g., availability of new service types such as data transmission capabilities in telecommunication).

Service quality indicators are usually more difficult to define because they are related to the degree of satisfaction users may have with a particular service. Precursors to service interruptions and measures of unsatisfied demand can be used as surrogates to service quality. Examples include the percentage of unmet demand for service, the length of the waiting list for service connection, and condition ratings by panels of users (e.g., road condition indicators).

There is a causal relationship between these two aspects of performance. When an entity providing infrastructure services has low operational efficiency, it may result in poor service qualities in the short run and inability to maintain high levels of service quality in the long-run. The size of this effect will depend on the structure of provision, as was demonstrated in Table 8.1. Sustained levels of poor service quality will affect the customers' willingness to pay and their degree of loyalty to the mode of service provided by the entity under consideration. As a result, customers may undertake a variety of options including switching to other modes of provision, to accommodate the poor service quality. Alternatively, depending on the capacity and willingness of the providers to respond to customer complaints and needs – as would exist when an entity is accountable – service quality problems would be rectified, and the customer base would be maintained. Sustained levels of poor service quality would eventually erode the available customer and revenue base of an entity.

Private enterprises or highly autonomous public entities that are operated using commercial principles have an *explicit and direct* relationship between operational efficiency and service effectiveness (by depending on the user for profitability). That is, if an enterprise has low operational efficiency over sustained periods of time, it will not be able to maintain service quality levels, and will eventually (unless subsidized) go out of business. However, if the enterprises are public, and their managers are faced with multiple objectives beyond service provision in the most cost-effective manner, the relationship between operational efficiency and service quality becomes *unexplicit and indirect*. Therefore, everything else being equal, we expect the service quality outcomes under the second provision structure (public enterprises with multiple objectives other than direct service provision) to be low following the causal relationships in Figure 8.1.

The nature of the trade-offs between service quality and operational efficiency is an important qualifier of the true performance of any given provision structure. Therefore, when comparing the performance of infrastructure services under different provision structures, it is crucial to specify the simultaneous and/or independent effects of operational efficiency and the quality of service indicators. Those indicators that jointly represent these two aspects of performance would, in most cases, be preferred.

8.3 MODEL SPECIFICATION AND APPLICATION TO THE POWER SECTOR

The following system of simultaneous equations summarizes the relationships described in Section 8.2.

$$Y = \psi(W)$$
$$S = f(X,Z)+\xi$$
$$X = g(Y,W)+\in$$
$$Z = h(X,Y,W)+\eta \tag{1}$$

where
W = exogenous variables affecting utility performance that derive from a country's or region's endowment (level of development and nature of decision-making environment);
S = performance profile of a service producing enterprise, which is a function of the relative weights given to operational efficiency and service quality;
X = indicators of operational efficiency such as labor productivity and profitability;
Y = indicators of the structure of provision, which may be a combination of ownership and multiplicity, and which may interact with the indicators of a country's endowment (level of development and nature of the decision-making environment);
Z = indicators of service quality or precursors to declines in service quality;
$\xi, \in, \eta$ = random terms; and
f, g, h = suitably specified functions.

There are four types of relationships in equation (1). These are: (i) a structural equation relating the development climate to the structure of service provision within a country – this includes the ratio of public/private ownership of infrastructure assets and the type and consistency of the administrative procedures governing service provision; (ii) a measurement equation relating the indicators of performance and their respective weights to form a performance profile S; (iii) a structural equation separating out the relative contribution of a country's endowment and the structure of provision on the achievable and sustainable level of operational efficiency; and (iv) a structural relationship for evaluating service quality outcomes under different provision structures, development climates, and achieved operational efficiency. Figures 8.2 and 8.3 give a graphical demonstration of these relationships.

The first two equations of the model in equation (1) are the most difficult to specify. A country's endowment, as measured by the level of development achieved and the character of decision-making structures, affects both the observed production structures in a country (e.g., the share of private provision of infrastructure) as well as the efficiency of infrastructure provision. We can generate two reduced form models from Figure 8.2, concentrating on the two dimensions of performance, from the model system in equation (1) and Figure 8.3, as shown below:

$$Z = \alpha + \beta X + \gamma Y + \delta W + \eta \qquad\qquad (2)$$
$$X = \alpha + \gamma Y + \delta W + \epsilon .$$

The relationships in equation (2) include; (i) the measurement of performance through direct variables Z of service outcomes as perceived by a user, and variables affected by decision flows X taken by service producers in day to day operations; and (ii) the limitations imposed on achievable performance by the prevailing structure of provision Y and the country's endowment W. Therefore, the models in equation (2) capture, implicitly, the structural and measurement effects presented in the first two models in equation (1). A graphical demonstration of the model in (2) is presented in Figure 8.4.

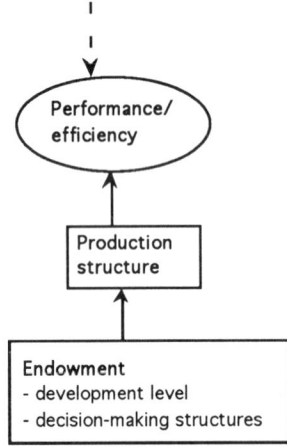

Figure 8.2 Structural relationship

A specific application of this model to the provision of power is shown in Figure 8.5.

Performance is measured by three indicators of operational efficiency and one precursor to poor service quality. The number of customers per employee, denoted by x_1, is used as a measure of utility efficiency from the consumers perspective. Other measures of production efficiency are the generation capacity factor, denoted by x_2, and the number of employees per GWh produced, denoted by x_3. The generation capacity factor indicates the extent to which installed capacity is used in generating electricity. It is computed according to the formula: Gross Output (GWh) times 1000, divided by Installed Capacity (MW), divided by 8 760 hours; expressed as a percentage.

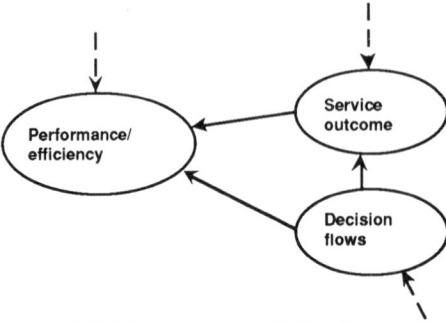

Figure 8.3 Measurement relationship

A variable termed system losses and denoted by z, is used as a surrogate for service quality. System losses are defined as:

$$System\ losses\ =\ \frac{Net\ generation\ \text{-}\ Total\ sales}{Net\ generation}$$

There are two main components of this variable: technical and non-technical losses (see Escay, 1991). Technical losses are due to the electrical characteristics of the power system. They consist mainly of resistance losses which occur during the transmission and distribution process, and are closely correlated to power outages and voltage fluctuations – measures of poor service quality. Non-technical losses consist mainly of unmetered consumption in the distribution process, including billing errors, non-collection of payments, and illegal connections – measures of inefficiency in operations. System losses, therefore, function as an indicator of both service quality and operational efficiency.

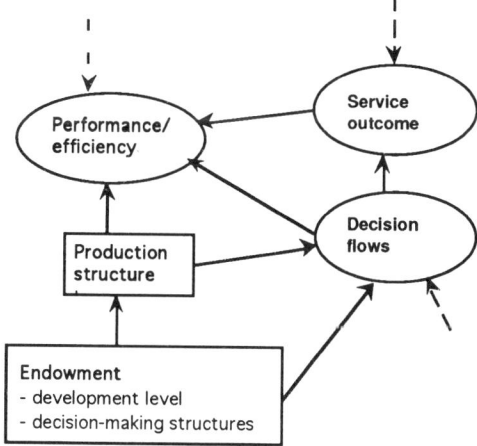

Figure 8.4 Full model specification

The structure of provision in Figure 8.5 is represented by three variables: (i) type of ownership; (ii) magnitude of multiplicity; and (iii) type of multiplicity.

The indicator of ownership is denoted by y_1 and defined by the percentage installed capacity which is publicly owned; where installed capacity refers to the rated capacity as stated on the nameplate of the equipment in a power plant. "Installed capacity" includes the capacity of commissioned equipment, which is already installed, but may not be in service yet. It is differentiated from "available capacity" or "effective capacity" which is usually less than "rated capacity" and typically decreases over time as the equipment deteriorates. The variable to represent ownership, "installed capacity", is therefore free of any efficiency-related effects.

Multiplicity is represented by two variables denoted by: (i) y_2, which represents the magnitude of multiplicity as measured by the number of independent actors involved in service production; and (ii) y_3 representing the type of multiplicity which is based on the industry structure in use. The type of multiplicity that can be found in power production (Besant-Jones, 1992) is summarized in Figure 8.6, and includes:

(1) = national integrated monopoly in charge of generation, transmission, and distribution;

(2) = regionally integrated monopolies in charge of generation, transmission, and distribution;

(3) = national generation and transmission, with regional distribution monopolies;

(4) = competing generation, national transmission with generation, and regional distribution monopolies;

(5) = competing generation, national transmission, and regional distribution monopolies; and

(6) = competing generation, national transmission, regional distribution monopolies competing with generators.

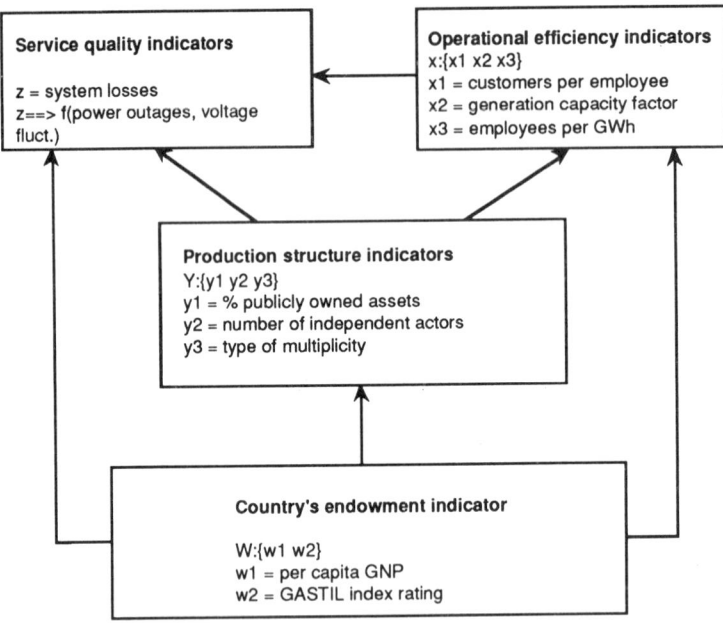

Figure 8.5 Application to the power sector

The endowment variables affecting the structure of provision and included in the analysis are: the level of development achieved, denoted by w_1, and the nature of decision-making in a country denoted by w_2. The level of development is represented by the per capita GNP, while the GASTIL index is used to represent the nature of decision-making. This index takes on the value of one (most democratic/free) to seven (least democratic/free).

8.4   EMPIRICAL INVESTIGATION

The data set used to estimate the relationships in equation (1) and to quantify the relationships in Figures 8.1 through 8.6 included a collection of performance indicators from 100 developing countries. Table 8.2 summarizes the production structures in the power sectors of developing countries for the year 1988. About 22% of these countries depend on the public sector only, 72% have the public sector as the main provider, 5% have the private sector as the main provider, and 1% depend on the private sector alone. In terms of the magnitude of multiplicity, however, up to 58% of the countries have a single entity in charge of power provision (national integrated monopolies).

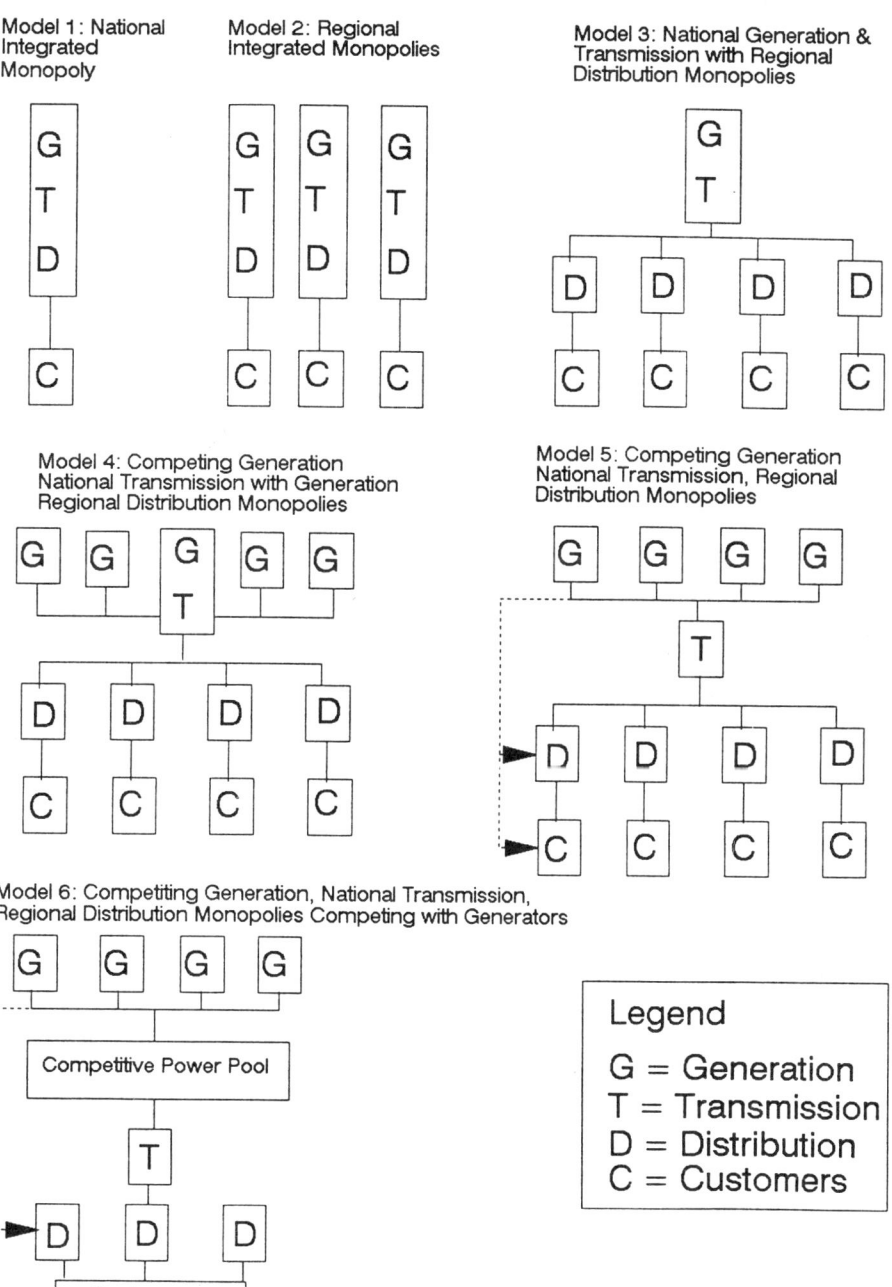

Figure 8.6 Generic models for power industry structure
Source: Besant-Jones (1992)

Table 8.2 Distribution of ownership of power provision

	Public only	Public main	Private main	Private only
Single entity	17	35	5	1
	(29.3%)	(60.3%)	(8.6%)	(1.7%)
Multiple entities	5	37	0	0
	(11.9%)	(88.1%)	(0.0%)	(0.0%)
	22	72	5	1

Sources: Directory of Power Utilities; Power Data Sheets

The data were used for two main purposes: (i) to confirm the structure of the model that postulates a two-level relationship between precursors to poor service quality and operational inefficiency; and (ii) to measure the size and statistical significance of postulated effects. Binary investigations between sets of variables are used for the first objective while two stage-least squares to estimate equation (2) using the indicators defined in section 3 is used for the second objective. The results are summarized in Figures 8.7 through 8.12 and Tables 8.3 through 8.6, respectively.

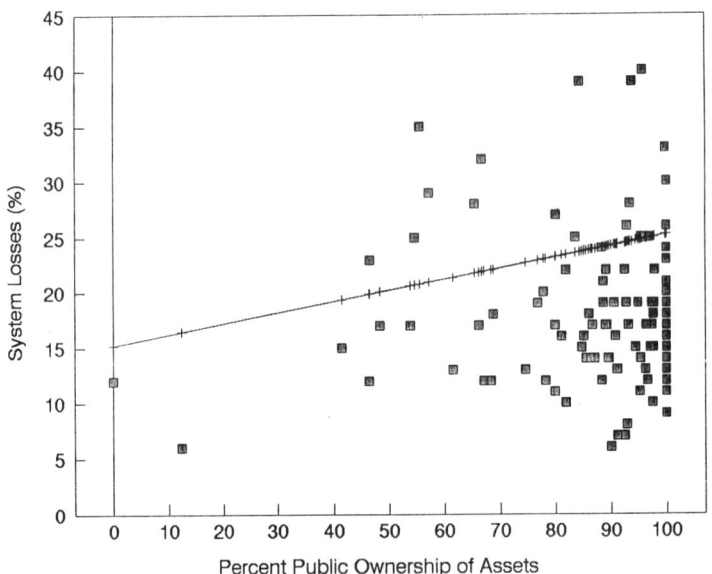

Figure 8.7 System losses and the structure of ownership

8.4.1 Performance and the Structure of Provision

A relationship between system losses (a measure of service inefficiency) and the structure of ownership of power infrastructure is depicted in Figure 8.7. In this figure, we see that despite wide scatter, the percentage system losses decrease as the percentage of public ownership decreases. A similar plot relating the percentage system losses to the magnitude of multiplicity shows the same degree of scatter with a definite declining trend in the losses (see Figure 8.8). This plot indicates that, as the magnitude of multiplicity increases, by having more actors involved in service provision, the degree of inefficiency decreases (lower system losses). The amount of scatter observed in Figure 8.8 could be due to the effects mentioned earlier; that is the size and complexity of decision-making may cause inefficiencies. The type of multiplicity – as measured by the six production

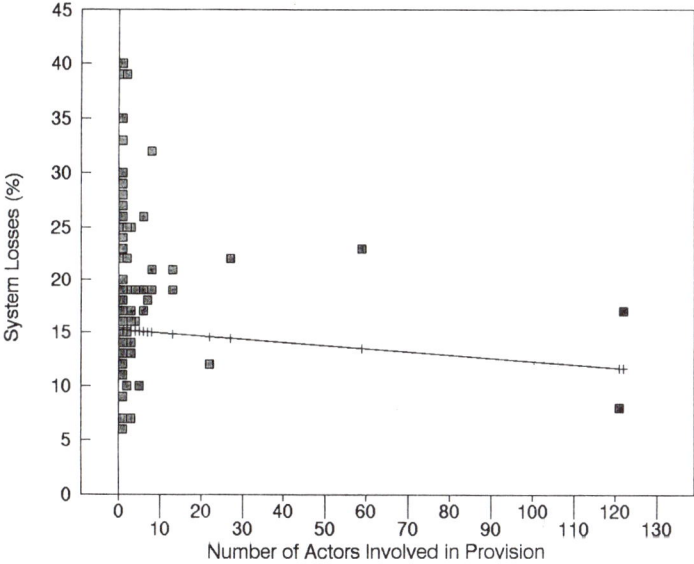

Figure 8.8 System losses and the magnitude of multiplicity

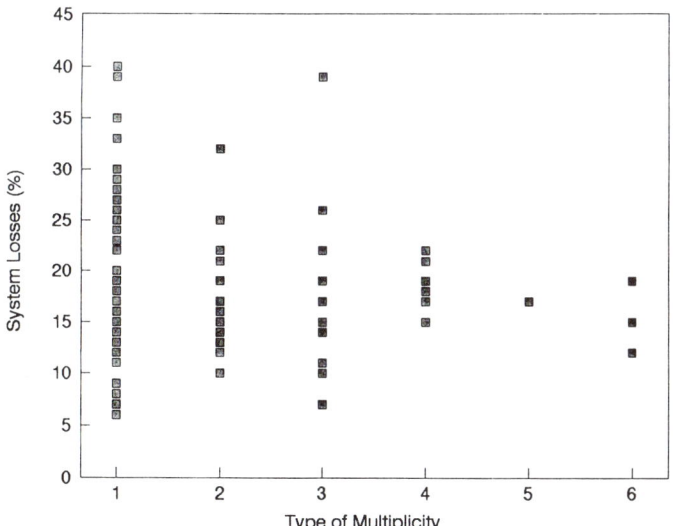

Figure 8.9 System losses and type of multiplicity

structures in Figure 8.6 – does not seem to have an obvious effect on system losses (see Figure 8.9). It is possible that the joint effect of type and magnitude of multiplicity is the important variable affecting performance, a factor that is confirmed in the estimation results. Figure 8.10 shows the effect of the type of multiplicity on production efficiency (as measured by the number of customers per employee). In this figure, as in Figures 8.7, 8.8, and 8.9, there is a lot of scatter.

All these results indicate that a binary relationship between production structure and performance is not sufficient to capture the main effects. A joint estimation of the models in equation (2), as is presented later in this section, allows us to extract the main effects which remain hidden in binary representations such as those shown in Figures 8.7 through 8.10.

8.4.2 Performance and a Country's Endowment

The effect of variables such as per capita GNP and the GASTIL index was also investigated as shown in Figures 8.11 and 8.12, respectively. These figures indicate that the countries with higher levels of development have, with a lot of scatter, more efficient services (see Figure 8.11). Reductions in the transparency of decision-making, as measured by a high GASTIL index, induce declines in performance, as demonstrated by increasing system losses with reductions in the transparency of decision-making (see Figure 8.12).

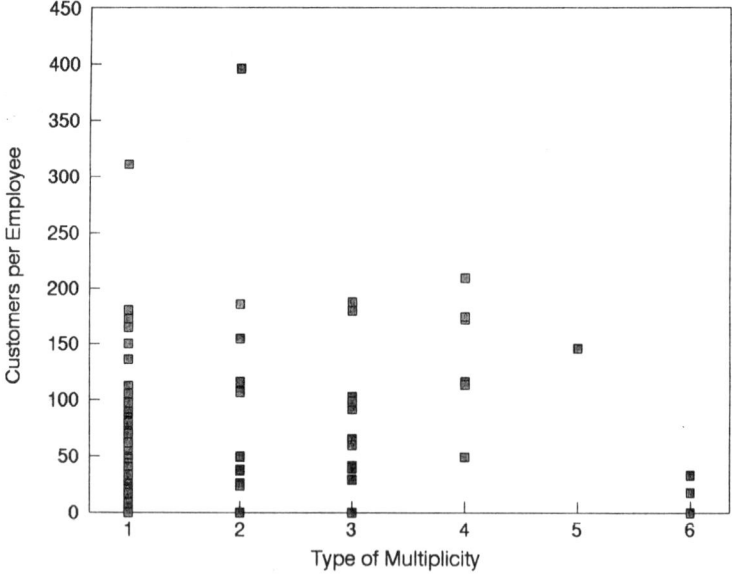

Figure 8.10 Type of multiplicity and production efficiency

8.4.3 Estimation Results

To confirm and explicitly measure the size of the effects depicted in the last two sections, a two-stage least squares estimation of the models in equation (2) was performed. The results are summarized in Table 8.3 and the details of each estimation presented in Tables 8.4, 8.5, and 8.6.

From Table 8.3, we see that the effect of ownership is not that important. Particularly, production efficiency (as measured by generation capacity factor) is not significantly affected by percent public ownership. However, other service related variables such as employees per GWh produced and system losses are negatively affected by increasing percent public ownership. The ownership variable is overshadowed by the variables defining a country's endowment; mainly, per capita GNP and the character of the decision-making environment. If the administrative capacity and transparency of decision-making is high, performance is better. We also see from the summary in Table

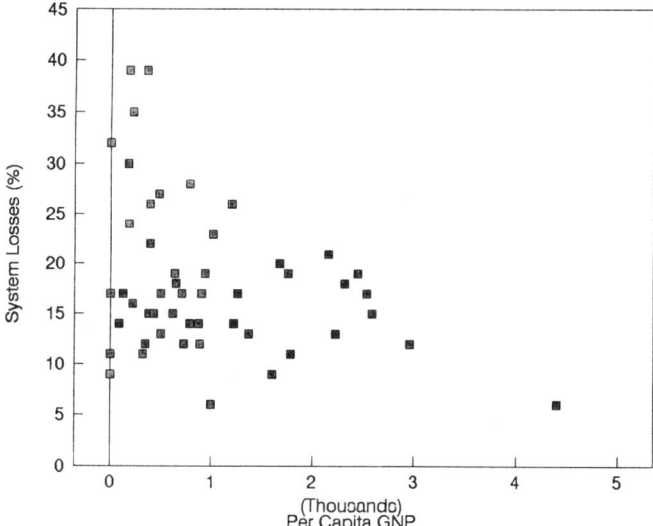

Figure 8.11 Level of development and efficiency

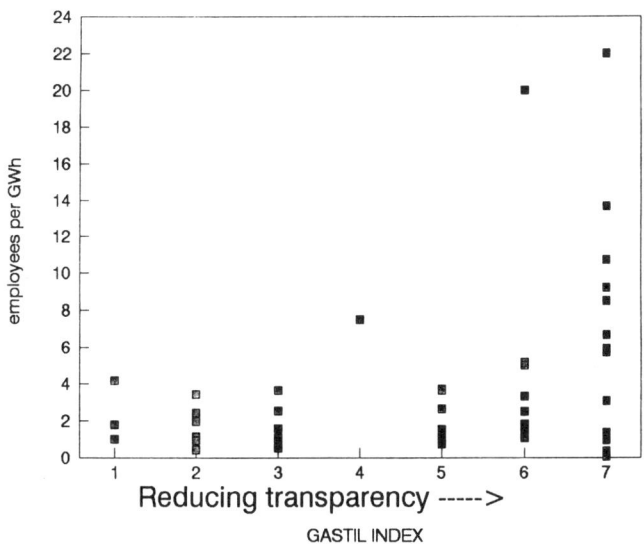

Figure 8.12 Decision-making endowment and production efficiency

Table 8.3 Summary estimation results (t-statistics)

Dep. variabl.	Const.	y1	y2	y3	w1	w2	x1	x2	x3	R-squared
z	17.84 (2.4)	0.09 (1.42)	*	*	-0.005 (-2.40)	0.08 (7.45)	*	*	-0.74 (-1.47)	0.97
x1	45.51 (3.33)	*	0.67 (1.88)	7.79 (1.46)	0.02 (1.54)	*	*	*	-0.47 (-1.02)	0.27
x2	21.72 (2.68)	0.08 (0.86)	0.06 (0.71)	0.74 (0.61)	0.006 (2.55)	-0.007 (-2.30)	*	*	*	0.40
x3	17.94 (2.68)	-0.12 (-1.69)	-0.03 (-0.38)	0.16 (0.15)	-0.003 (-1.72)	*	*	*		0.84

z = system losses
x1 = customers per employee
x2 = generation capacity factor
x3 = employees per GWh produced
y1 = percentage public ownership
y2 = magnitude of multiplicity
y3 = type of multiplicity
w1 = per capita GNP (surrogate for managerial capacity)
w2 = decision-making endowment (regulatory capacity and transparency of decision-making)

8.3, that there are strong effects of multiplicity (magnitude and type) on production efficiency. This is supported by the fact that the number of customers per employee increases with the introduction of multiplicity and the decentralization of production.

Examining the detailed estimation results, we see from Table 8.4 that the two most significant variables affecting the size of service inefficiencies (as measured by system losses) are the level of development (per capita GNP) and the index representing the character of decision-making structures in a country. Recall that a big proportion of system losses (non-technical losses) are due to inefficiencies in billing, collection, and the number of illegal connections. A country which is less democratic and free (high GASTIL index) would have less participation of the public in decision-making, poor accountability of public sector managers, and low capacity to administer. We see that these effects strongly contribute to inefficiencies. More developed economies, on the other hand, would have better management capabilities and hence would exhibit higher efficiencies, as supported by the negative coefficient in Table 8.4 for the level of development variable. Additionally, decreasing the level of public ownership results in increasing efficiency.

An interesting result is that related to the labor productivity variable, employees per GWh. This variable has a negative coefficient (with low significance), meaning that the higher the number of employees per GWh produced, the lower the system losses. Such a result may be indicating that it is necessary to have a large labor force in order to reduce the losses – e.g., due to pilferage and illegal connections to power systems – in service provision. This may be especially valid in countries prone to have corruption.

The customers served per employee, a measure of operational efficiency, increases with increasing multiplicity (both magnitude and type) as shown by positive coefficients in Table 8.5. Similarly, as expected, the number of customers served per employee is higher for more developed economies (positive coefficient for the per capita GNP variable). Interestingly, low labor productivity, as measured by the number of employees per GWh produced, leads to declining service efficiency. However, the significance of these effects is lower than in the case of system losses above. The important difference being that the type of ownership (percent public ownership) is the main provision structure variable affecting system losses, compared with the magnitude and type of multiplicity which affect the customers per employee. The effect of ownership is stronger in determining technical efficiency while multiplicity (through increased competition and transparency perhaps) more strongly influence service coverage and efficiency.

Table 8.4 Impact of provision structure on system losses

$$z=\alpha+\beta_3 x_3+\gamma_1 y_1+\delta_1 w_1+\delta_2 w_2+\eta$$
$$x_3=\alpha_3+\gamma_{31} y_1+\gamma_{32} y_2+\gamma_{33} y_3+\delta_{31} w_1+\delta_{32} w_2+\epsilon_3$$

(Variables as for Table 8.3)

INSTRUMENTAL VARIABLES ESTIMATION
Dependent variable: z

Independent variable	Estimated coefficient	Standard error	t-statistic
One	17.84	7.44	2.40
y_1	0.009	0.007	1.42
w_1	-0.001	0.0002	-2.40
w_2	0.01	0.001	7.45
x_3	-0.74	0.50	-1.47

Number of observations 46
R-squared   0.97
Corrected R-squared   0.97

Table 8.5 Impact of provision structure on customers per employee

$$x_1=\alpha_1+\beta_{13} x_3+\gamma_{12} y_2+\gamma_{13} y_3+\delta_{11} w_1+\epsilon_1$$
$$x_3=\alpha_3+\gamma_{31} y_1+\gamma_{32} y_2+\gamma_{33} y_3+\delta_{31} w_1+\delta_{32} w_2+\epsilon_3$$

(Variables as for Table 8.3)

INSTRUMENTAL VARIABLES ESTIMATION
Dependent variable: x1

Independent variable	Estimated coefficient	Standard error	t-statistic
One	47.51	14.27	3.33
x_3	-0.47	0.47	-1.02
y_2	0.67	0.35	1.88
y_3	7.79	5.34	1.46
w_1	0.01	0.001	1.54

Number of observations 43
R-squared   0.27
Corrected R-squared   0.20

Table 8.6 further confirms the general results described so far. The two most important variables affecting the generation capacity factor are the level of development and the character of decision-making structures in a country. Countries that lack transparency and accountability (high GASTIL index rating) have lower generation capacity factors. More developed economies, on the other hand, display higher generation capacity factors.

Table 8.6 Impact of provision structure on generation capacity factor

$$x_2 = \alpha_2 + \gamma_{21}y_1 + \gamma_{22}y_2 + \gamma_{23}y_3 + \delta_{21}w_1 + \delta_{22}w_2 + \in_2$$

(Variables as for Table 8.3)

INSTRUMENTAL VARIABLES ESTIMATION
Dependent variable: x2

Independent variable	Estimated coefficient	Standard error	t-statistic
One	21.73	8.10	2.68
y_1	0.008	0.009	0.86
y_2	0.006	0.009	0.71
y_3	7.74	1.20	0.61
w_1	0.001	0.0002	2.55
w_2	-0.001	0.0003	-2.30

Number of observations	48
R-squared	0.40
Corrected R-squared	0.33

In Table 8.7 we see again the effect of the decision-making structures on performance. The higher the GASTIL index, the higher the number of employees per GWh, a measure of production efficiency. The level of development also has a positive impact on production efficiency; as the per capita GNP increases the ratio of employees per GWh decreases. A result that contradicts those found in Table 8.4 is that related to ownership; increasing public ownership is seen to reduce production inefficiencies as measured by employees per GWh produced. The reason for this result may be that public entities – because of their size and monopoly power – are better able to capture the benefits of technology, especially in developing economies.

It would be interesting to estimate the same functions using data from industrialized nations in order to clearly separate out the incremental effects of the level of development.

8.4.4 Limitations and Suggestions for Future Research

The results of this research should be interpreted with caution. First, the choice of indicators affects the meaning of the results. For example, the inverse of labor productivity is labor intensity. When comparing across a wide range of countries, presumably with different labor costs and at different levels of development, one may be measuring a policy choice rather than a true inefficiency. Second, the direction of causality assumed in this analysis also affects the interpretation. If one observes that when there are multiple providers services are more efficient by some measures, is this because of multiplicity or that multiplicity has been possible where generation of services is more efficient? Such questions cannot be easily answered by empirical work. Future testing of the relationships developed in this chapter may shed some light as to this argument. To this regard, a "performance profile" hypothesis testing approach was specifically developed to measure the significance and directionality of the effects of interest in this chapter.

Table 8.7 Impact of provision structure on employees per GWh produced

$$x_3 = \alpha_3 + \gamma_{31}y_1 + \gamma_{32}y_2 + \gamma_{33}y_3 + \delta_{31}w_1 + \delta_{32}w_2 + \epsilon_3$$

(Variables as for Table 8.3)

INSTRUMENTAL VARIABLES ESTIMATION
Dependent variable: x3

Independent variable	Estimated coefficient	Standard error	t-statistic
One	17.93	6.70	2.68
y_1	-0.12	0.007	-1.69
y_2	-0.003	0.007	-0.38
y_3	0.16	1.07	0.14
w_1	-0.0003	0.0002	-1.72
w_2	0.002	0.0003	7.83

Number of observations   47
R-squared   0.84
Corrected R-squared   0.82

8.4.5 Performance Profile Analysis

Profile analysis is a statistical procedure for testing the equality of population mean vectors, where a battery of p questions are posited to two or more groups of data. Profiles are constructed, of the average values achieved by each population, and a test of their equality is done based on two main components: (i) the parallelness of the profiles, which is a test of whether the mean vectors of performance forming any two profiles result in the same shape; and (ii) the degree of coincidence of profiles given that they are parallel. The first test measures whether the set of underlying weights determining a typical performance profile are the same, which for our problem is a test whether the mechanisms determining performance outcomes are similar. The second test measures whether any two profiles, derived from the same set of weights, are equal or not. This test allows one to measure the "distance" between two profiles; that is the degree to which one profile is consistently "better" or "worse" than another. It is assumed that the performance of the two or more groups being analyzed is independent from one another, but all performance indicators are measured in similar units. For more detail on the test see Johnson and Wichern (1988). The structure of the hypothesis tests is summarized below. Consider the means of a typical performance profile $\mu'_1 = [\mu_{11}, \mu_{12}, \mu_{13}, \mu_{14}]$ representing the mean performance, say of a group of countries where the provision of infrastructure is through a public monopoly. Consider another group of countries, where the provision of infrastructure is through a number of public enterprises – that is there is multiplicity. This group will display population means which we denote by $\mu'_2 = [\mu_{21}, \mu_{22}, \mu_{23}, \mu_{24}]$ Figure 8.13 shows a plot of these means connected by straight lines, where the four indicators are employees per GWh, number of employees, percentage system losses, and the unit cost of service provision. These broken line graphs are the profiles of populations 1 and 2 respectively; that is performance under monopoly and multiplicity respectively. The hypothesis testing the effect of "multiplicity" on performance can be formulated in two stages:

Component 1: Are the profiles parallel?

$H_{01}: \mu_{1i} - \mu_{2i} = \mu_{2i} - \mu_{2i-1}, \ i = 2,3,..., P$

Test:

$H_{01}: C\mu_1 = C\mu_2$

where C is a constant matrix and the test is an F-test.

Component 2: Assuming the profiles are parallel, are the profiles coincident, or is one profile above or below the other?

$H_{02}: \mu_{1i} = \mu_{2i}, \ 1,2,..., P$

Test:

$H_{02}: 1'\mu_1 = 1'\mu_2$
$1'\mu_1 = \mu_{11} + \mu_{12} + ... + \mu_{1P}$
$1'\mu_2 = \mu_{21} + \mu_{22} + ... + \mu_{2P}$

where profiles are coincident only if the total heights (averages) of each profile are equal. The test is an F-test.

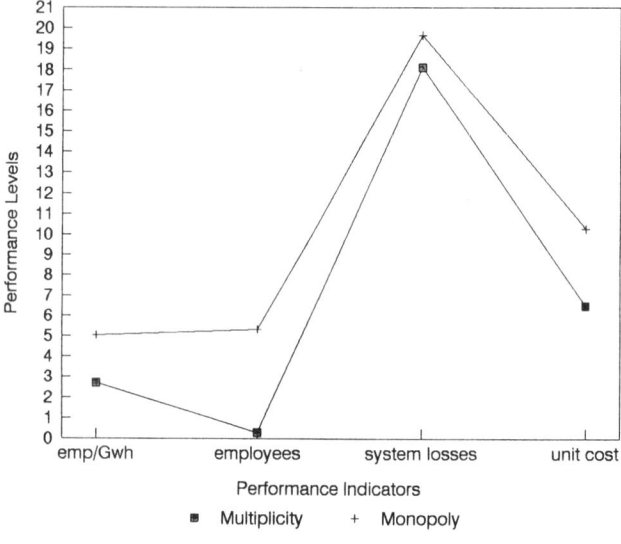

Figure 8.13 Multiplicity under mixed ownership

The results of this test using the profiles in Figure 8.13 are presented in Table 8.8. The table shows that the direct effect of multiplicity is statistically significant (at the 95% level), and that the performance profile in the presence of multiplicity (PMM) is better (meaning higher) than in the presence of monopoly (PMS). The results indicate that multiplicity has a positive effect on performance of infrastructure. The performance profile when infrastructure provision is by a public monopoly (POS) is different from when infrastructure is provided by a private monopoly (PMS). That is, a different set of weights is used to determine operational efficiency under private monopoly and public monopoly. However, the test does not indicate which form is better, and the results may favor either regime. Finally, the joint effects of ownership and multiplicity indicate that the performance of infrastructure is positively enhanced when ownership is mixed and there are multiple actors (PMM), than when a public monopoly provides all services (POS).

Table 8.8 Pairwise performance profile tests

Pair	Test	Parallell profile (95% conf.)	Coincident profile (95% conf.)
PMS-PMM	Multiplicity	Accepted	Rejected
POS-PMS	Ownership	Rejected	Not applicable
POS-PMM	Joint effect	Accepted	Rejected

8.5 SUMMARY AND POLICY IMPLICATIONS

The results of this empirical investigation suggest four points. The first point is that ownership by itself does not matter as much as one would expect – but when it does, we see that decreasing the role of the public in service provision generally results in improvements in performance. The second point is that the magnitude of multiplicity i.e., the number of independent actors, all other things equal, improves performance. So does the type of multiplicity; vertical integration tends to deteriorate performance. Thirdly, the character of the decision-making environment plays a definite role in qualifying the performance outcomes seen in a given setting; democratic and freer countries – which are expected to have more transparent decision-making processes and higher accountability of public decision-makers – exhibit higher performance than others. Finally, the level of development in a country is correlated to the performance of the service delivery enterprises.

The analysis suggests therefore that multiplicity is important if not more important than private ownership, and in particular that reducing the degree of vertical integration is likely to improve performance as much as transfers of ownership. Also found to be important, however, is the nature of endogenous institutions which determine the structure of decision-making environments in a country. So that public ownership in a highly developed, democratic and free country may be more efficient than in an underdeveloped, non-democratic and interventionist country. For the latter type of countries, privatization may be the best mechanism for achieving long-term efficiency gains.

On the methodological side, the models developed to measure the effects of provision structures and the endowment of a country on infrastructure performance were able to capture the important effects. The hypothesis testing procedures also provided a mechanism for jointly testing for the postulated effects as well as a reliable method for establishing statistical significance.

REFERENCES

Besant-Jones, J.E., 1992, "Reforming the Policies for Electric Power in Developing Countries", Industry and Energy Department, The World Bank.
Bradburd, R., 1992, "Privatization of Natural Monopoly Public Enterprises: The Regulation Issue", The World Bank, WPS 864.

Chu, X., G.J. Fielding, and B.W. Lamar, 1992, "Measuring Transit Performance Using Data Envelopment Analysis", *Transportation Research A*, Vol. 26A, 3:223-230.

Dasgupta, P., 1990, "The State and the Idea of Well-Being", *Economic Journal*, Vol. 100, 4: supplement.

Escay, J.R., 1991, "Summary of 1988 Power Data Sheets for 100 Developing Countries", Energy Series Paper No. 40, Industry and Energy Department, The World Bank.

Gastil, R., 1989, *Freedom in the World*, Freedom House, New York.

Hatry, H.P., 1980, "Performance Measurement Principles and Techniques: An Overview for Local Government", *Public Productivity Review*, 4:312-339.

Johnson, R.A. and D.W. Wichern, 1988, *Applied Multivariate Statistical Analysis*, Prentice Hall, Englewood Cliffs.

Levy, B. and P.T. Spiller, 1993, "Regulations, Institutions and Commitment in Tele-communications: A Comparative Analysis of Five Country Studies", presented at a seminar on Institutional Foundations of Utility Regulation: Research Results and Their Operational Implications, The World Bank Group, Watergate Hotel, Washington D.C.

Nellis, J. and S. Kikeri, 1992, "Privatization: The Lessons of Experience", The World Bank.

Queiroz, C. and S. Gautam, 1992, "Road Infrastructure and Economic Development: Some Diagnostic Indicators", Working Paper, The World Bank.

Spulber, D., 1989, *The Market and Regulation*, The MIT Press, Cambridge, Mass.

Vickers, J. and G. Yarrow, 1991, *Privatization: An Economic Analysis*, The MIT Press, Cambridge, Mass.

World Bank, World Development Report: The Challenge of Development, 1991, Oxford University Press.

CHAPTER 9

Ownership, Investment and Pricing of Transport and Communications Infrastructure

Kenneth Button

Loughborough University

9.1   INTRODUCTION

There is mounting concern in many countries about the quantity of transport and communications infrastructure available and the usefulness of what is provided after a period of relatively low maintenance expenditures. Specifically, attention has been focused upon the adequacy of the infrastructure to sustain future economic expansion and development[1]. In many ways, however, remarkably little is known about the importance of transport and communications infrastructure provision in the initiation and simulation of economic development. The aim of this essay is to examine a particular, and indeed small, element of the topic. This concerns the extent to which the current pricing of transport and communications infrastructure in most high-income economies is sub-optimal both from an environmental perspective and from the point of view of more narrowly defined economic criteria. A limitation of much of the literature on infrastructure provision is that it assumes, almost automatically, that public provision is a necessary prerequisite for efficient investment and utilisation to be attained. An underlying theme of the argument presented here is that prices can indeed be inappropriate and investment need not be optimal and that this often stems at least as much from failures in the government process as it does from any notion that markets are failing. Indeed, it could well be argued that a rather more limited role for government in infrastructure provision might reduce some of the problems and lead to a more substantive provision of infrastructure.

The chapter addresses a number of issues in turn. First, it provides a critical look at the some of the main reasons that are advanced for governmental manipulation of the charging for transport and communications infrastructure through national ownership. Ownership is important in this context both because of simple matters of technical competence in managing the system and because of the underlying motivations of those making pricing and ultimately investment decisions. Importantly, since investment decisions are based upon information flows, are the signals emanating from current

---

[1]   In the European Conference of Ministers of Transport countries, for instance, the share of transport infrastructure spending fell from 1.5 percent of Gross Domestic Product in 1975 to 0.9 percent in 1984 leading both to fears of serious legacy effects of inadequate capacity and backlogs of structural maintenance.

pricing practices by nationally owned suppliers helping in the making of rational choices? Secondly, it considers the intrinsic nature of transport and communications infrastructure and thus what efficient pricing structure to adopt and which regulatory framework, if any, to use. Thirdly, it looks at the underlying causes of the current problems with the provision of infrastructure and with the charging of non-economic prices for infrastructure. In particular, it looks at the potential of government intervention failures in the market leading to more serious distortions than are probable with private ownership in a more commercial environment.

9.2   WHY DO WE HAVE SO MUCH PUBLIC OWNERSHIP OF INFRASTRUCTURE?

The provision of adequate infrastructure is often seen as a necessary prerequisite for economic advancement but, while economists are generally rather particular about the ways in which specific goods are categorised, the definition of infrastructure (sometimes equally opaquely referred to as "social overhead capital") tends to be vague and imprecise. Lakshmanan (1989, p.243) talks of the term as, "often employed in a loose impressionistic manner". Where there have been efforts at delineation, the tendency is frequently to look at particular physical features and to offer lists of such characteristics - Nurske (1952), for instance, lists features such as: "provide services basic to any production capacity"; "cannot be imported from abroad" and "large and costly installations". Hirschman (1958, p.83), in defining social overhead capital, lists sectors, *viz.*, "In its widest sense, it includes all public services from law and order through education and public health to transportation, communications, power and water supply as well as such agricultural overhead capital as irrigation and drainage systems. The hard core of the concept can probably be restricted to transportation and power". More recently, these characteristics have tended to be outlined in rather more technical terms and, in particular, the possible relevance of notions such as information flows (Youngson, 1967) and, as a particular case of externalities, of public goods (Andersson, 1989; Andersson and Kobayashi, 1989), have been examined.

While definitions are very important, here we tend to shy away from getting too deeply involved in the issue and adopt the easy way out by following the spirit of Jacob Viner's wisecrack that "Economics is what economists do" and simply treat infrastructure as "what most people consider it to be". From the perspective of providing a strict definition, this may be seen as a form of passing the buck but in practical terms and, given the nature of the chapter, it seems unlikely that it will lead to any substantive degree of confusion.

There has recently been something of an upsurge of interest in the role which transport and other infrastructure plays in stimulating economic development. In part this can, looking back over the literature of the past century or so, be seen to fit in with a cyclical pattern of changing academic interests. A number of key factors can, perhaps, be highlighted as being of specific relevance for the 1990s. There have been major technical advances in telecommunications that require new infrastructure if they are to be fully exploited, although the exact nature of this infrastructure is not always agreed upon. With more conventional forms of transport, rapidly rising demand in the 1970s and 1980s at a time of relatively limited investment and replacement expenditure means that many existing facilities require refurbishment and additional capacity is required under current policies to match forecast demand. Bottlenecks already exist and pressures for improvements for key links in the network are already a reality.

As part of this increased interest, the whole question of the mechanisms of supply and control have come under review. In countries such as the U.K. in particular the role of the state in providing infrastructure has been the subject of detailed debate. Given the historical tendency, at least in recent times, for most, if not all, transport and communications infrastructure to be publicly supplied and operated it is worth considering the economic reasons that have been advanced for this institutional arrangement.

9.2.1 The Economic Development Argument

Good transport infrastructure is frequently cited as a necessary, if not sufficient, condition for economic development[2]. Following on from this, and with confidence in the state's ability to be better informed than the market, public provision has been taken as almost axiomatic. Studies that have attempted to find unambiguous links between transport infrastructure and economic development have not always, however, succeeded in their objective. Certain broad trends have emerged but they are certainly not conclusive in their support for a direct and positive tie between infrastructure supply and economic performance. The literature on the subject is too extensive to explore in detail but a number of general points can usefully be made[3].

First, at the macro level, many observers have pointed to long term trends that indicate close links between transport infrastructure provision, in its most general sense, and economic development. Andersson and Stromquist (1988), however, take an even longer view when looking at four stages of development since the thirteenth century. More quantitative work by Biehl (1991) and Aschauer (1990) has sought to examine the role infrastructure has played in the growth of the E.C. and U.S. economies respectively. The difficulty here, however, is that of defining causation - does the provision of adequate infrastructure allow economic potential to be exploited or does economic expansion lead to resources being generated for investment in transport and communications[4]? The cliometric studies that have been undertaken, for example by Fogel (1964) on U.S. railways, may be indicative in some senses but because of data limitations and technical problems they are certainly far from conclusive.

Secondly, turning to more micro-analysis, and in particular the work that has been undertaken at the regional or local level on the impact of individual pieces of transport infrastructure, the empirical evidence can at best be described as ambiguous. The results of a large number of these types of studies are set down in Table 9.1. Some of the variation in results can be attributed to differences in the methods of analysis used but even making allowance for that, there is significant divergence in the findings reported[5]. A major technical problem, as highlighted by Botham (1980), is that of defining the counterfactual – what would have happened in the absence of the infrastructure? There is also the difficulty that this type of work, which is usually associated with some sort of impact analysis, seldom separates growth creation effects from diversionary effects.

---

2   This type of argument effectively underlays the idea of nationalising much of the U.K.'s infrastructure after World War Two – there was a perceived need to control the 'commanding heights of industry' to maximise economic development.

3   Slater (1992) provides a good overview of much of this literature while Dugonjic (1989), Johansson (1991), Nijkamp (1986), Rietveld (1989) and Blum (1982) review the influence of transport on regional inequalities.

4   The underlying problem is, however, a more general one in that our understanding of what causes economic development is poor. This point was very clearly made by Kindleberger (1958) over a quarter of a century ago: "We have suggested that there is no agreement on how economic development proceeds and have implied that this is because the process is not simple. There are many variables involved, and there is a wide range of substitutability among ingredients – land, capital, and the quality and quantity of labour, and technology can substitute for one another, above certain minima, although there are at the same time certain complementary relationships among them. The will to economise and organisation are probably the only indispensable ingredients. For the rest, none are necessary, and none sufficient".

5   There are implicit assumptions in all these studies that the investments were both the most appropriate and carried through effectively which may well, of course, not have been the case.

Increased production in any particular area, of course, being possible either because aggregate national output rises or because economic activity transfers from elsewhere.

Table 9.1   Summary of findings looking at transport and development in industrialised countries

Author	Geographical scale	Infrastructure	Conclusions
Botham (1980)	28 Zones (U.K.)	Changing nature of highways	Small centralising effect on employment
Briggs (1981)	Non-metropolitan counties (U.S.)	Provision of highways	Presence of interstate highway is no guarantee of county development
Cleary & Thomas (1973)	Regional level (U.K.)	New estuarial crossing	Little relocation but changes in firm's operations
Dodgson (1974)	Zones in North (U.K.)	New motorway	Small effect on employment
Eagle & Stephanedes (1987)	87 counties (U.S.)	New highway exenditure	No increase in employment
Evers et al. (1987)	Regional level (Netherlands)	High-speed rail	Some effects on employment
Forrest et al. (1987)	Metropolitan areas (U.S.)	Light rapid transit	Property blight – good for urban renewal
Judge (1983)	Regional level (U.K.)	New motorway	Small economic impact
Langley (1981)	Highway corridor (U.S.)	Highway	Devalued property in area
Mackie et al. (1986)	Regional level (U.K.)	New estuarial crossing	Small overall effect
Mills (1981)	Metropolitan areas (U.S.)	Interstate highways	No significant effects on location patterns
Moon (1986)	Metropolitan areas (U.S.)	Highway interchanges	Existence of interchange villages
Pickett & Perrett (1984)	Local districts (U.K.)	Light rapid transit	Properties close to the line benefit
Stephanedes (1990)	87 counties (U.S.)	New highway expenditure	Could affect employment – depends on county's economy
Stephanedes & Eagle (1986)	87 counties (U.S.)	New highway expenditures	Some positive association with employment
Watterson (1986)	Metropolitan area (U.K.)	Light rapid transit	Modest growth in land use
Wilson et al. (1982)	Regional level (U.S.)	Existing highways	Transport affects location decisions but not development

Source: Leitham (1993)

A more fundamental point, irrespective of the strength of the evidence linking infrastructure provision and economic development, is whether there is a need for state provision to achieve the desired end or whether regulation through fiscal and command-and-control instruments could attain identical objectives. The issue of public-versus-private provision is a long standing one but in practical terms, the costs and benefits of the alternatives revolve around such matters as relative transaction costs and efficiency levels. These, however, are seldom explicitly addressed.

9.2.2 Transport and Communication Infrastructure have Significant Public Good Attributes

Much is often made of the peculiar nature of transport and communications infrastructure. In particular, the argument is frequently made that such infrastructure is characterised by "public good" attributes and, therefore, will tend to be under supplied if left to market forces[6]. We find this argument, for instance, in Andersson (1991, p.18), "The first and primary characteristic of infrastructure is publicness. To qualify as infra-structure a road must be a public good".

The "public good" nature of infrastructure is often seen as the main *raison d' etre* for the public sector taking a proactive role in directly planning and supplying it. There are secondary reasons, in terms of such things as containing negative externalities, distributional requirements and the provision of merit goods, which are often found, either implicitly or explicitly, in policy statements but the overriding economic rationale for intervention is generally the public good one.

If indeed transport infrastructure is a public good then, left to the market, conventional economic wisdom would support government action either as a direct supplier or as a motivator for expanded supply through such measures as subsidies to the private sector or reciprocal regulations. The difficulty is that in conventional economic terms few forms of transport and communications infrastructure exhibit to any significant extent the characteristics which one normally associates with "publicness". As is well known, and following Musgrave, public goods are goods with a particular kind of externality that embraces the ideas of non-rivalry and non-excludability. Transport infrastructure, however, is frequently congested and, while on parts of a network one user's consumption may have a negligible impact on others, this is certainly not universally the case. (Further, these instances of non-rivalry are not generally the ones of interest to those concerned with capacity constraints and investment.) Equally, it is not difficult to exclude individual users from consuming road space or other forms of transport and communications infrastructure. Indeed the very idea of physical traffic management, and particularly measures such as pedestrianisation, implicitly assumes that such controls can and are very regularly exercised. Seen from an alternative perspective, the exclusion concept is sometimes couched in such terms that the provision of a public good means that all must effectively consume it (national defence covers everyone in the country whether they desire it or not). It is difficult to think of cases where this could be said to apply to either transport or communications infrastructure.

But even if one cannot accept the intuitive line of reasoning that transport and communications infrastructure is much nearer the notion of an economic private good than that of a public good, then there is empirical evidence to draw upon. In countries such as the U.K. and U.S., where a large part of the investment in transport infrastructure has in the past come from private rather than public sources, there appears little empirical evidence of relative under investment when markets were allowed to operate compared to countries where national ownership prevailed and, supposedly, the public good problem of under investment would have been avoided. Indeed, looking at the history of the U.K.'s railways and London's underground system, private investment

---

6   The standard work on public goods is Musgrave (1959). Strictly his definition (p.44) is, "goods the inherent quality of which requires public provision".

based upon commercial criteria actually provided more capacity (some have argued over capacity) than has subsequent public ownership.

9.2.3   Transport Infrastructure is a Merit Good

It is frequently argued that transport and communications provide a social as well as a commercial function, even if the latter is extended to embrace the economic development arguments advanced earlier. Strictly, Musgrave (1959) talks in terms of "merit wants". These are defined as wants "so meritorious that their satisfaction is provided for through the public budget, over and above what is provided for through the market and paid for by private buyers" (p.13). In Britain, for instance, this notion of merit provision was explicit in the designation of "social service obligations" for the railways under the 1968 Transport Act. The "merit good" idea, taken from a standard public finance foundation, also ties in with the notion of "need" (Williams, 1974).

While there may be legitimate reasons for providing services of a non-commercial nature, the need concept is a rather vague one that often involves entwining other notions concerning, for example, public goods and externalities more generally. A careful examination of the specific nature of merit wants, which stripped away elements of publicness, externality and so on, by Charles and Westaway (1981) concluded that only information was a genuine merit want (good). From our perspective, however, the key points are, first, that public ownership is unnecessary to ensure the provision of merit goods and, second, even if private ownership were invoked it would not if correctly operated lead to inadequate capacity – indeed from a strictly commercial and development perspective it would produce excess capacity.

9.2.4   There are Significant Negative Externalities Associated with Transport

As can be seen from Table 9.2, transport is a major contributor to environmental degradation and, in many cases such as the emission of greenhouse gases, its continued growth is posing problems of containment through policies relying on simple technical remedies. While important in quantitative terms, these externalities also represent significant economic costs for the economy. Such costs have been estimated to represent a cost approaching 20 percent of the GDP of high income countries (Quinet, 1990). Government ownership and pricing of infrastructure, it is claimed, provides leverage to manipulate the growth in traffic and to direct traffic to specific, less environmentally damaging modes. Investment in public transport to tempt people from the private car is often cited as being environmentally responsible.

Besides questioning the reality of the argument in terms of the relative levels of public expenditure on different modes, there is very little evidence of infrastructure pricing reflecting social costs to the environment. In particular, most infrastructure pricing regimes for transport have relatively high fixed charges (such as annual licence fees) and comparatively low variable charges (such as fuel taxes) although a substantial amount of environmental damage stems from the use of infrastructure rather than its existence *per se*.

9.2.5   Infrastructure Supply, by its Nature, Contains Monopoly Attributes

Technical reasons, such as conditions of decreasing costs stemming from indivisibilities, mean that roads, railway lines, communications satellites, and so on will most efficiently be provided by a monopoly. Whether this, in practice, will lead to the type of market distortion normally associated with monopoly, however, is not altogether clear. First, as demonstrated, for example, by Joy (1964) in the case of the railways, indivisibilities are often not as great as sometimes supposed and fixed costs can be varied rather more than it is often claimed.

Table 9.2 Some indicators of the environmental impacts of transport

	North America	OECD Europe	Japan	OECD States
		Air		
		Total transport emissions as % of total emission		
Nitrogren oxides (NO$_x$)	47	51	39	48
Carbon monoxide (CO)	71	81	na	75
Sulphur oxides (SO$_x$)	4	3	9	3
Particulates	14	8	na	13
Hydrocarbons (HC)	39	45	na	40
		Noise		
		Population exposed to road traffic noise over 65dBA		
19 million	53 million	36 million	110 million

Secondly, the degree of competition is often greater, especially in the long term when location decisions become a pertinent consideration, than one might suspect. One might also bring in here the matter of potential competition within the framework of contestability theory although such mechanisms, because of the fixed costs involved, are unlikely to function perfectly.

Thirdly, there are Galbraithian style countervailing power arguments. Even if the market for transport infrastructure does naturally lead to monopoly rent seeking potential, this potential is considerably tempered by a variety of countervailing forces. Taking commercial factors, in the ports context, for instance, there is the power of large shipping lines and conferences. But perhaps more potently there is the entire official apparatus of government regulation that exists in all high income countries to contain non-competitive practice – fear of invoking a legal response acts naturally to contain monopoly exploitation. Finally, even if the above arguments do carry little empirical weight, in all cases there is still the question of whether public ownership and the types of price setting that often accompany it are the best solution to the monopoly problem.

9.3   THE CHARACTERISTICS OF TRANSPORT AND COMMUNICATIONS INFRASTRUCTURE IN PRACTICE

The above argument is, in a sense, very negative. It essentially questions many of the economic based arguments that have been advanced from the public provision of transport and communications infrastructure. From a more positive perspective it is useful to consider why infrastructure is a particular economic issue. It certainly often has a number of features that suggest that, without appropriate pricing, its supply (both in terms of quantity and composition) is unlikely to approach optimality. But what is interesting is that much of the current political debate in both North America and Europe[7] evolves around inadequacies in transport networks – the very condition that, as we have seen in the previous sector, has been one of the main driving forces behind government provision of transport and communications infrastructure in the past. The public provision stance would thus seem to be questionable.

One of the major problems is that transport and similar infrastructure is treated as a quasi-public good and thus the idea that standard pricing principles are irrelevant tends to prevail. If one moves away from this position and, instead, recognises that such infrastructure is more akin to a private good, albeit with particular attributes, then many of the problems that have become institutionalised in the way transport and communications infrastructure are treated decrease in magnitude. Interestingly enough, the problems in countries that have in the past looked at it from the private goods perspective seem to have managed to find quite acceptable pricing regimes that generated the investment funds required to sustain and expand the networks at the time.

The key characteristic of infrastructure is, in practice, not publicness but rather that it presents the supplier with a decreasing cost pricing problem[8]. The difficulty is then to reconcile an efficient welfare maximising pricing regime with investment requirements. The elementary case is depicted in Figure 9.1. Quite clearly, a monopolist could make a reasonable profit given the cost curves depicted. However, if a Pareto pricing strategy is pursued and the MC price P* is levied then a subsidy equal to the shaded area is required to cover costs. This subsidy problem has itself been used as a justification for public ownership; namely that expenditure of state money should be closely monitored and public ownership provides the best mechanism for achieving this[9]. Subsidies can, however, of course be avoided in this type of situation. One method is to regulate the infrastructure suppliers so that prices are set to produce an acceptable rate of return. In the case of normal profits this would mean second best prices set equal to average costs (P in the diagram)[10]. The notion of average cost pricing monopoly supplied infrastructure is also one that has gained ground in recent years in a somewhat different context with the upsurge of interest in contestability theory[11]. With a sufficiently open market, it is argued, a monopoly supplier of infrastructure would be obliged to price at average cost rather than at the Marshallian monopoly rent seeking maximising price. The difficulty here, though, is that while subsidies can be avoided, there is still a social loss with average cost pricing due to the non-marginal nature of the pricing structure.

The standard solution to this problem, as for example exemplified in his theoretical paper on the provision of scheduled public transport services by Turvey (1975), is to abandon single prices and to operate a regime of price discrimination. It is then possible, always provided that the cost curves are not significantly higher than the demand curve and that excessive revenue dilution can be avoided, to determine disaggregate demand curves and to have both utilisation consistent with MC pricing principles and to recover full costs of provision[12].

---

[7]   While somewhat advocatory in its tone, a good account of the type of arguments advanced for further investment in infrastructure is contained in Roundtable of European Industrialist (1987).

[8]   The literature on this subject is extensive but Train (1991) provides a clear exposition.

[9]   The notions of the Chicago School that regulators and bureaucrats act as "rational economic beings" and pursue their own interests obviously runs counter to this position.

[10] This approach is standard practice in the U.S.A. in the regulation of utilities and was implicit in the Turnpike system which provided roads in the U.K. from the seventeenth century through to the Victorian era.

[11] See Baumol et al. (1982) for an overview of the necessary technical conditions necessary for the existence of a contestable market.

[12] This type of pricing is remarkably common in transport where airlines and shipping cartels (conferences) have developed sophisticated yield management systems to price the use of their

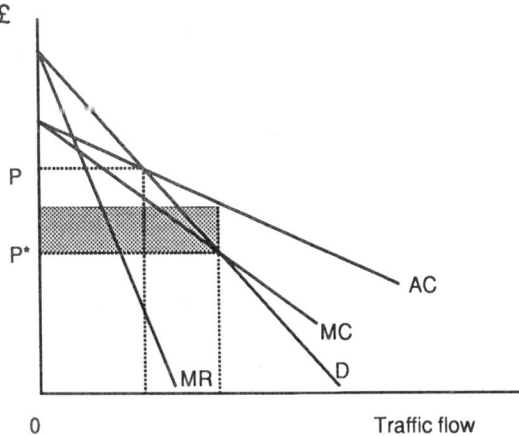

Figure 9.1 Second best pricing

9.4 MARKET AND GOVERNMENT FAILURES IN INFRASTRUCTURE PRICING

The malprovision of transport and communications infrastructure is conventionally blamed on market failures - and, in particular, in the case of under provision on the possible public good nature of such infrastructure. While there are unquestionably market failures in the transport and communications sector, these can often be exaggerated, especially in the relative context of other forms of economic activity. What can often be of equal, if not greater importance, are failures by governments in the types of policy that they pursue.

Government failures occur in this context because government interventions in the provision of infrastructure either create economic failures that would not be serious if the market was allowed full play or worsen imperfections that already exist. A useful way of separating conventional market failures from government intervention failures is to consider the pricing of roads.

Figure 9.2 provides a standard, simplified diagram of the cost curve confronting a user of a congested motorway. The user is aware of his/her own private generalised costs (MPC) that comprise mainly travel times costs plus perceived money costs (possibly of fuel and some other items) but takes no account of the congestion costs the trip is imposing on other road users[13]. If the latter were added in then the full marginal cost of trips is conventionally represented by MSC[14]. What this assumes, however, is that road users are fully cognisant of the track (infrastructure) costs of their trips; in other words

---

infrastructure (i.e. aircraft space and shipping space) so that revenues are maximised within the realm of a contestable environment (Brooks and Button, 1993).

[13] The public sector response to congestion is to impose Pigouvian charges – Hau (1992) offers an account of the current theory in the context of road pricing.

[14] Strictly the diagram is drawn assuming congestion is of the "simple interactive" kind – more complex congestion functions only add to the complexity of the argument while contributing little of substance. One could also add in third party external effects, such as environmental pollution, which would simply change the relationship between the MPC and MSC functions.

that the MPC curve is a genuine reflection of the costs borne by the provider of infrastructure.

In practice, and with the few exceptions of tolled roads (see Table 9.3), road users in Europe are seldom charged directly for their use of infrastructure and, indeed, in many cases much of the revenue is gathered from fixed charges on vehicles. Further there is not even any direct hypothecation to the infrastructure agency of the moneys that road users do pay. In terms of the diagram what this means is that road use is determined by the MPC curve that, in standard theory, results in a dead-weight loss represented by the heavily shaded area. If allowance is made for the misperception of what would normally be private costs if a commercial undertaking were responsible for the road, then the full social cost would rise to MSC' with an additional dead-weight loss shown by the lightly shaded area needing to be taken into account.

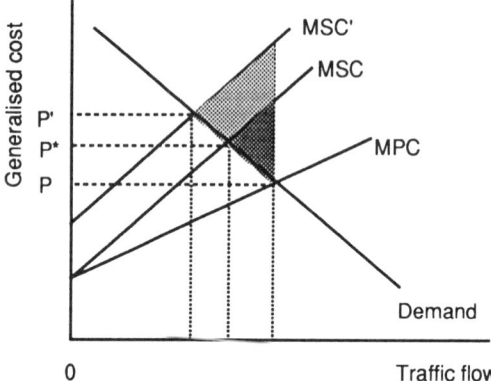

Figure 9.2   The dead-weight losses of market and government failures in road track charging

What brings about this form of government failure is a topic in its own right (Button, 1992)[15]. What concerns us here from the point of view of infrastructure provision is that this failure leads, in the short term, to an over use of the existing infrastructure and, in the longer term, to the potential of under investment in new infrastructure (either in a quantitative or qualitative sense).

The short term problem is that much transport infrastructure is over used with excessive congestion the result. A simple examination of the congestion costs associated with road traffic in the U.K. (Table 9.4) and of the associated social costs of high levels of congestion (in this case for the U.S. – Table 9.5) provides an indication of the extent to which road users in particular underpay for the facilities that they use. Part of this underpayment is obviously due to the externality factor but, equally, the inadequacy of track cost charging mechanisms must inevitably worsen the situation. The arguments for resolving such problems through such devices as road pricing and a shifting of user charges to tolls and away from annual taxation and fuel duties are well rehearsed in the literature and provide a rational economic response to the short term problem (See Appendix 1).

---

[15]   They can usefully be divided between those due to inappropriate pricing or use of command-and-control instruments and to administrative failures. They do not include misdirected policy brought about by poor or incomplete information.

Table 9.3 Sources of revenue from road users in European Union countries in 1985

Country	Percentage revenue from		
	Fuel tax	Vehicle tax	Tolls
Belgium	76	24	-
Denmark	62	38	-
Germany	75	25	-
Greece	83	17	-
France	74	12	14
Irish Republic	92	8	-
Italy	82	7	11
Luxemburg	86	14	-
Netherlands	59	41	-
Portugal	93	7	-
United Kingdom	71	29	-

Source: Organisation for Economic Co-operation and Development (1987)

Table 9.4 Estimated congestion costs by road type in the U.K.

Road type	Marginal cost (pence per km)
Motorway	0.26
Urban central peak	36.97
Urban central off-peak	29.23
Non-central peak	15.86
Non-central off-peak	8.74
Small town peak	6.89
Small town off-peak	4.20
Other urban	0.08
Rural dual carriageway	0.07
Other trunk and principal	0.19
Other rural	0.05

Source: Newbery (1990)

Table 9.5 Estimation of financial costs of urban traffic congestion in U.S.

Social costs	Cost per vehicle mile (1982 prices)
Travel time	$0.1152
Air pollution	$0.0256
Noise pollution	$0.0037
Excess fuel consumption	$0.1105
Traffic accidents	$0.1265
Total	$0.3815

Source: Khisty and Kaftanski (1986)

The longer term problem of inadequate or inappropriate capacity stems largely from two sources. First, appropriate charging for infrastructure provides signals as to investment needs and priorities. Without an effective pricing mechanism priorities are difficult to determine and, even if commercial criteria are not deemed the most appropriate to employ, important benchmarks for assessing opportunity costs are lacking. Secondly, appropriate pricing generates revenue that provides the basis for the funding of new infrastructure and the maintenance of existing facilities. While there are limitations, the Public Choice's School of argument favouring earmarking of revenues has clear advantages if there is the opportunity for them to be captured – in the case of publicly owned transport and communications infrastructure – by the political process (Buchanan, 1963).

An interesting question is to what extent the problems of current infrastructure mis-pricing might be avoided by privatisation measures. Poole (1988) and others have argued that privatisation of infrastructure would bring about the internalisation of congestion costs and, at the same time, lead to optimal long term capacity provision. In practice the idealised conditions which would bring this about are unlikely to materialise. It can be demonstrated that a monopolist would choose capacity to minimise total costs, including those borne by the user, but the prices then levied may not yield social welfare maximising usage (Arnott et al., 1993). In other words appropriate investments would be made but then the facilities would not be optimally utilised.

In particular, a profit maximising monopolist while charging prices to users that would cover all congestion costs would, nevertheless, tend to charge prices above marginal costs at times when such costs were low simply to keep on the elastic part of the demand schedule. For socially optimal pricing and investment, as Knight (1924) pointed out many years ago, the demand schedule would need to be perfectly elastic and this, from the empirical studies conducted, is certainly not the situation[16].

While this analysis suggests that the congestion externality is internalised, and also that monopolist private suppliers of infrastructure would be concerned to use all resources, including users of their facilities at minimum cost, there would be concern over the mark-up levied[17]. This, however, is hardly a justification for public provision of the infrastructure, although it may be seen as providing a basis for economic regulation[18]. Whether it would automatically result in a large change in the scale and nature of infrastructure provision is unclear. It does, however, provide a logic framework for decision-making and removes many of the problems generated by short term considerations of a political nature (see Appendix 2).

---

[16] The intuition of the technical arguments follows (see Arnott et al., 1993) if we show the monopoly price for a given time period, on the assumption that time periods are independent of each other, as: $p_h = SRMC_h \{e_h/(e_h-1)\}$ where: p_h is the user perceived price for period h; $SRMC_h$ is the short run marginal cost including the user's time and other costs; e_h is the absolute value of the own-period price-elasticity of demand ($e_h > 1$ for monopoly pricing). The monopolist thus charges a fee taking social costs (in this case congestion costs) into account but also marks up to recover long run costs and extract economic rent. With $e_h = 1$ then SRMC pricing occurs.

[17] The prices charged to use the infrastructure may also prove either too high or too low to optimise congestion if the monopolist is non discriminating when the value of travel time varies between users. The intuition here is that the monopolist is only concerned with the marginal user while optimality also concerns the infra marginal user (Mills, 1981).

[18] Indeed, in other cases where there have been transfers of ownership from the public to private sector there is evidence of enhanced efficiency, for example the case of electricity (Button and Weyman-Jones, 1993a). Meta studies across a range of sectors looking at efficiency under different regulatory and ownership regimes are contained in Button and Weyman-Jones (1992; 1993b). The question of the efficiency of various types of regulatory regimes applied to transport is addressed in Button and Keeler (1993).

9.5   THE ENVIRONMENTAL DIMENSION

A major shift in policy priorities in the last two decades has been brought about by the increased attention that is being paid to the environmental implications of policy decisions[19]. In terms of transport and communications infrastructure, much of the attention has been on developing better techniques for including environmental externalities in investment decision making frameworks (e.g. Wood, 1993). The development of procedures that more fully embrace such things as pollution and noise nuisance within a cost-benefit style framework will inevitably have implications on future transport and communications infrastructure provision. While unlikely, given the large social benefits that seem to be associated with mobility and communications[20], to reduce the overall level of investment such changes will probably influence the design and type of infrastructure provided. It may well, for instance, lead to a shift toward tele-communications in some instances and away from personal transport.

The problem with this approach is that while reasonable estimates of externalities may improve investment decision making they will have minimal impact on the use made of this infrastructure once constructed. Government intervention to contain externalities associated with the use of transport and communications infrastructure are already in existence both in terms of command-and-control instruments (the fitting of catalytic converters and so on) and, more limited, through fiscal measures (taxation differentials between leaded and unleaded fuel)[21]. Additionally, because of the high correlation which often exists between congestion and environmental externalities, there are important externality synergy effects that often mean that environmental improvements coincide with reduced congestion.

Making users aware of the environmental costs of the infrastructure they use *per se* (such as visual intrusion, nature effects, impacts of quarrying and extractive sites and loss of bequest value) is a far more difficult task. The problem with current practice is that with many forms of infrastructure, without hypothecation of revenues collected from infrastructure users, there is often actually no direct link between payments and costs[22]. The difficulty should not be seen as a purely institutional one. An important feature of infrastructure is that the demand for it is a derived demand and often, as in the case of transport and communications this demand is at one stage removed. In the case of roads, for example, the facility is demanded by buses and their services are demanded by passengers. The potential for distortions inherent in the messages that currently pass between supplier and user are thus compounded.

Bringing the costs of the environmental damage caused by infrastructure into the calculus of potential road users in a private sector model could, though, be achieved in a number of possible ways.
•   First, the government could treat the environment as state property and "lease" it out to road or other infrastructure owners at an annual rent that would then be reflected in the rates paid by the user of the infrastructure. Estimating this rent, however, despite

---

[19]   One reason for this is an increased appreciation that there are important links between economic efficiency and environmental efficiency. For example a recent E.C. report argued that, "...a general deterioration in transport conditions due to inefficient use of the networks and the saturation of certain infrastructures (especially road and air). Also – albeit not so immediately noticeable – there is an on-going increase in the nuisance caused by transport. The culprit here is not so much network saturation as the actual increase in traffic" (Group Transport 2000 Plus, 1991).

[20]   In the U.K. the rate of return calculated without an explicit environmental component with the COBA framework is well above the cut-off rate and effectively infrastructure investment is rationed through the availability of funds. Inclusion of environmental costs may change rankings but the number of schemes which would fail to meet the NPV=0 criteria would be negligible.

[21]   Button (1993) offers an outline of current policy and approaches in this field.

[22]   Although countries such as the U.K. do often say that the excess of road user taxation over the track costs incurred is in part a sumptuary tax and in part a surrogate environmental charge.

advances in the valuation of environmental resources with the advent of contingent valuation and other techniques, is still not anywhere near an exact science as far as most of the relevant externalities are concerned.

• An alternative, and one that could be of particular relevance in the urban context, is that those developing infrastructure must post a bond to cover the cost of ultimately returning the facility to its original form[23]. The interest payments involved in tying up this money would then be passed on through user fees. The limitation of the approach is that while it may provide a mechanism to internalise items such as bequest and existence factors, it is not designed to handle the on-going costs such as visual intrusion and community severance.

• Marketable permits have been employed to reduce atmospheric emissions of such chemicals as lead in the USA and these may be developed to internalise within a private sector framework the costs of infrastructure. Essentially permits would be allocated, possibly through a lottery system, to use elements of the scarce environment. Ensuing trading of these permits between those interested in developing further infrastructure links and those concerned with environmental protection should provide a system that ensures infrastructure is constructed in socially optimal locations and that its full costs (since the costs of acquiring permits would be passed to users through the fees levied) are included in final prices. The difficulties are those of deciding upon the mechanism for the initial allocation, both in terms of the number of permits to issue and who gets them, and the subsequent insurance that competitive markets prevail without any monopoly (or monopsony) power evolving.

Clearly none of these schemes is ideal and, even in concert, they do not provide a solution for handling the direct environmental costs of transport and communications infrastructure. For one thing they all need rather more rigorous development at the theoretical level and, for another, the transactions and administrative costs need fuller consideration. What they do suggest, however, is that there may be mechanisms that will allow not only the environmental externalities associated with infrastructure use to be brought within a coherent pricing structure but also the environmental costs associated with the infrastructure itself. This would have a number of advantages.

It would provide a more consistent framework for investment appraisal and financing which could well, and this may seem perverse, lead to more infrastructure becoming available and becoming available more rapidly. Explicit incorporation of full environmental costs would remove at least part of the capture prone public debate surrounding the desirability of new investments. It would also mean more effective use of what is available. Since congestion of existing facilities has tended to lead to considerable latent demand (Small et al., 1989), willingness to pay for this higher quality of service seems likely to provide resources for network expansion.

Such an approach may well also change the nature of the infrastructure demanded. Within the narrow confines of transport full social cost pricing set in the context of a competitive framework would provide a stimulus to rail investment. Perhaps of more importance, in the longer term the environmental advantages of electronic communications[24] that are currently not realised because of government intervention failures as much as through any technical or market imperfection, may shift the focus of infrastructure investment away from transport modes. At present their potential social benefits are not reflected in the market place and government involvement in their provision has limited in some instances their potential development.

---

[23] A discussion of how a scheme like this may work in practice is contained in Button and Pearce (1989).

[24] An examination of the environmental benefits associated with a significant up take of videoconferencing, for instance, is found in Button and Lauder (1992).

9.6   CONCLUDING COMMENT

This chapter has been concerned with the role of transport and communications infrastructure in economic development and, most particularly, with how the pricing of this infrastructure could be improved. Much has recently been written about the need for improved and extended infrastructure in high income countries and equally the question of sources of financing has been continually raised. The debate, however, has tended to focus around rather narrow, albeit pressing issues, namely the financing of new investment, and the matter of pricing and maintaining existing facilities has, with some exceptions, been given rather more cursory treatment. The argument in this chapter is that if investment is to be satisfactorily carried through, and all costs are to be recovered, then there is a need to treat infrastructure in very much the same way as other economic goods. This involves consistency across the entire decision making framework. A focus on private provision within a regulated environment may not produce the optimal outcome but there are reasonable grounds for supposing that it will result in an improvement over current conditions.

APPENDIX 1

It should be emphasised that the problem of infrastructure pricing, especially with respect to roads, has little to do with the total amount that users pay. In many cases this is well in excess of the attributed costs and, as illustrated by the U.K. roads situation, the difficulty is in terms of the incidence of the charges.

Vehicle class	Tax to cost ratios
Cars/light vans/taxis	3.4:1
Motorcycles	2.3:1
Buses and coaches	1.1:1
Goods vehicles over 1.525	
Tonnes unladen:	
Not over 3.5 tonnes GVW	3.1:1
Over 3.5 tonnes GVW	1.3:1
Other vehicles	2.4:1
All vehicles	2.6:1

APPENDIX 2

Implicit in recent work from the Brookings Institution (Small et al., 1989) is evidence that private sector provision of roads would increase short term prices to users but lead to superior quality roads (e.g. thicker pavements) with subsequent reductions in user costs. The table below offers some illustrative calculations derived from the study. Comparisons between columns 2 and 4 indicate the difference between current charges on U.S. roads for a number of user categories and the ultimate charges if infrastructure had been optimally constructed.

Vehicle	Taxes (cents per mile)		
	Current cost	Marginal cost existing roads	Marginal cost improved roads
2-axle single unit			
26000lbs	2.5	9.2	3.6
33000lbs	3.0	23.8	9.3
5-axle tractor-trailer			
33000lbs	4.0	1.2	0.5
80000lbs	7.2	41.3	16.2

REFERENCES

Andersson, Å.E., 1991, "Infrastructure and the Transformation of the C-Society" in R. Thord (ed.), *The Future of Transportation and Communication*, Swedish National Road Administration, Borlänge.

Andersson, Å.E. and K. Kobayashi, 1989, "Some Theoretical Aspects of Spatial Equilibria with Public Goods", in Å.E. Andersson, D.F. Batten, B. Johansson and P. Nijkamp (eds.), *Advances in Spatial Theory and Dynamics*, North Holland, Amsterdam.

Andersson, Å.E. and U. Strömquist, 1988, "The Emerging C-Society", in D.F. Batten and R. Thord (eds.), *Transportation for the Future*, Springer-Verlag, Berlin.

Arnott, R., A. de Palma and R. Lindsey, 1993, "A Structural Model of Peak-Period Congestion: A Traffic Bottleneck with Elastic Demand", *American Economic Review*, 83:161-179.

Aschauer, D.A., 1990, "Why is Infrastructure Important?", in A.H. Munnell (ed.), *Is There a Shortfall in Public Capital Investment?*, Conference Series 34, Federal Reserve Bank of Boston.

Baumol, W.J., J.C. Panzar and R.D. Willig, 1982, *Contestable Markets and the Theory of Industrial Structure*, Harcourt, Brace, Jovanovich, San Diego.

Baxter, R.D., 1866, "Railway Extension and its Results", *Journal of the Statistical Society*, 24:549-595.

Biehl, D., 1991, "The Role of Infrastructure in Regional Development", in R.W. Vickerman (ed.), *Infrastructure and Regional Development*, Pion, London.

Blum, U., 1982, "Effects of Transportation Investments on Regional Growth: A Theoretical and Empirical Analysis", *Papers of the Regional Science Association*, 49:151-168.

Botham, R.W., 1980, "The Regional Development Effects of Road Investment", *Transportation Planning and Technology*, 6:97-108.

Briggs, R., 1981, "Interstate Highway System and Development in Non-Metropolitan Areas", *Transportation Research Record*, 812.

Brooks, M. and K.J. Button, 1993, "Yield Management: A Phenomena of the 1980s and 1990s", in *A Look Back from the Year 2000*, CTRF, Fredericton, pp. 218-230.

Buchanan, J.M., 1963, "The Economics of Earmarking", *Journal of Political Economy*, 71.457-459.

Button, K.J., 1992, *Market and Government Failures in Environmental Policy: The Case of Transport*, OECD, Paris.

Button, K.J., 1993, *Transport, the Environment and Economic Policy*, Edward Elgar, Aldershot.

Button, K.J. and T.E. Keeler, 1993, "The Regulation of Transport Markets", *Economic Journal*, 104:1017-1028.

Button, K.J. and D. Lauder, 1992, Videoconferencing, U.K. Department of Trade and Industry, London.

Button, K.J. and D.W. Pearce, 1989, "Improving the Urban Environment: How to Adjust National and Local Government Policy Instruments for Economic and Environment Gain", *Progress in Planning*, 32:135-184.

Button, K.J. and T. Weyman-Jones, 1992, "Ownership Structure, Institutional Organisation and Measured X-Efficiency", *American Economic Review, Papers and Proceedings*, 82:439-445.

Button K.J. and T. Weyman-Jones, 1993a, "X-Inefficiency and Regulatory Regime Shift in the U.K.", *Journal of Evolutionary Economics*, 3:269-284.

Button, K.J. and T. Weyman-Jones, 1993b, "X-Efficiency and Technical Efficiency", *Public Choice,* 80:80-104.

Charles, T.S. and A.J. Westaway, 1981, "Ignorance and Merit Wants", *Finanzarchiv*, 39:74-78.

Cleary, W.J. and R.E. Thomas, 1973, *The Economic Consequences of the Severn Bridge and its Associated Motorways*, Bath University Press, Bath.

Dodgson, J.S., 1974, "Motorway Investment, Industrial Transport Costs and Sub-regional Growth: The M62 Case-Study", *Regional Studies*, 8:75-91.

Dugonjic, V., 1989, "Transportation: Benign Influence or an Antidote to Regional Inequality?", *Papers of the Regional Science Association*, 66.61-76.

Eagle, D. and Y.J. Stephanedes, 1987, "Dynamic Highway Impacts on Economic Development", *Transportation Research Record*, 1116.

Evers, G.H.M., P.H. van der Meer, J. Oosterhaven and J.B. Polak, 1987, "Regional Impacts of New Transport Infrastructure: A Multi-Sectoral Potentials Approach", *Transportation,* 14:113-126.

Fogel, R. W., 1964, *Railroads and American Economic Growth, Essays in Econometric History*, Johns Hopkins University Press, Baltimore.

Forrest, D., J. Glen and R. Ward, 1992, "Both Sides of the Track are Wrong: A Study of the Effect of an Urban Railway System on the Pattern of House Prices", Proceedings of UTSG 24th Annual Conference, University of Newcastle-upon-Tyne.

Group Transport 2000 Plus, 1991, *Transport in a Fast Changing World* (No place of publication).

Hau, T.D., 1992, Economic Fundamentals of Road Pricing – A Diagrammatic Analysis, World Bank WPS 1070, Washington

Hirschman, A.O., 1958, *The Strategy of Economic Development,* Yale University Press, New Haven, Conn.

Johansson, B., 1991, "Transportation Infrastructure, Productivity and Growth", in R. Thord (ed.), *The Future of Transportation and Communication*, Swedish National Road Administration, Borlänge.

Joy, S., 1964, "British Railways Track Costs", *Journal of Industrial Economics*, 13:74-89.

Judge, E.J., 1983, "Regional Issues and Transport Infrastructure: Some Reflections on the Effects of the Lancashire-Yorkshire Motorway", in K.J. Button and D. Gillingwater (eds.), *Transport, Location and Spatial Policy*, Gower, Aldershot..

Khisty, C.J. and P.J. Kaftanski, 1986, "The Social Costs of Traffic Congestion During Peak Hours", Presented to the 66th Annual Meeting of the Transportation Research Board, Washington.

Kindleberger, C.P., 1958, *Economic Development*, McGraw-Hill, New York.

Knight, F., 1924, "Some Fallacies in the Interpretation of Social Cost", *Quarterly Journal of Economics*, 38:582-606.

Lakshmanan, T.R., 1989, "Infrastructure and Economic Transformation", in Å.E. Andersson, D.F. Batten, B. Johansson and P. Nijkamp (eds.), *Advances in Spatial Theory and Dynamics*, North Holland, Amsterdam.

Langley, C.J., 1981, "Highways and Property Values: The Washington Beltway Revisited", *Transportation Research Record*, 812.

Leitham, S., 1993, "Predicting the Economic Development Effects of Transportation Projects", Proceedings of UTSG 25th Annual Conference, University of Southampton.

Mackie, P.J. and D. Simon, 1986, "Do Road Projects Benefit Industry?", *Journal of Transport Economics and Policy*, 20:377-384.

Mills, D.E., 1981, "Ownership Arrangements and Congestion-Prone Facilities", *American Economic Review*, 7:493-502.

Moon, H.E., 1986, "Interstate Highway Interchanges as Insignigators of Non-metropolitan Development", *Transportation Research Record*, 1125:8-14.

Musgrave, R., 1959, *The Theory of Public Finance*, McGraw-Hill, New York.

Newbery, D.M., 1990, "Pricing and Congestion: Economic Principles Relevant to Road Pricing", *Oxford Review of Economic Policy*, 6:22-38.

Nijkamp, P., 1986, "Infrastructure and Regional Development: A Multi-Dimensional Policy Analysis", *Empirical Economics*, 11:1-21.

Nurske, R., 1952, *Problems of Capital Formulation in Developing Countries*, Basil Blackwell, Oxford.

Organisation for Economic Cooperation and Development, 1987, Toll Financing and Private Sector Involvement in Road Infrastructure Development, Paris.

Pickett, M.W. and K.E. Perrett, 1984, "The Effect of the Tyne and Wear Metro on Residential Property Values", *TRRL Supplementary Report* SR 825.

Poole, R.W., 1988, "Resolving Gridlock in Southern California", *Transportation Quarterly*, 42:499-527.

Quinet, E., 1990, The Social Costs of Land Transport, Environment Monograph 32, OECD, Paris.

Rietveld, P., 1989, "Infrastructure and Regional Development: A Survey of Multi-regional Economic Models", *Annals of Regional Science*, 23:255-274.

Roundtable of European Industrialists, 1992, *Missing Networks: A European Challenge*, ERI, Brussels.

Small, K.A., C. Winston and C.A. Evens, 1989, *Road Works - A New Highway Pricing and Investment Policy*, Brookings Institution, Washington.

Slater, D.W., 1992, "Transportation and Economic Development: A Survey of the Literature", in Royal Commission on National Passenger Transportation, *Directions*, Volume 3, Ottawa.

Stephanedes, Y.J., 1990, "Distributional Effects of State Highway Investment on Local and Regional Development", *Transportation Research Record*, 1274:156-164.

Stephanedes, Y.J. and M.E. Eagle, 1986, "Time-Series Analysis of Interactions between Transportation and Manufacturing and Retail Employment", *Transportation Research Record*, 1074.

Train, K., 1991, *Optimal Regulation*, MIT Press, Cambridge, Mass.

Turvey, R., 1975, "A Simple Analysis of Optimal Fares on Scheduled Transport Services", *Economic Journal*, 85:1-9.

Watterson, W.T., 1986, "Estimating Economic and Development Impacts of Transit Investments", *Transportation Research Record*, 1046.

Williams, A., 1974, "'Need' as a Demand Concept (with Special Reference to Health)", in A.J. Culyer (ed.), *Economic Policies and Social Goals*, Martin Robertson, London.

Wilson, F.R., A.M. Stevens and T.R. Holyoke, 1982, "Impact of Transportation on Regional Development", *Transportation Research Record*, 851.

Wood, D., 1993, "Environmental Quality and Value for Money in British Roads Policy", in D. Banister and K.J. Button (eds.), *Transport, the Environment and Sustainable Development*, E. & F.N. Spon., London.

Youngson, A.J., 1967, *Overhead Capital, A Study in Development*, Edinburgh University Press, Edinburgh.

PART C: THE COMPLEXITY OF ECONOMIC DEVELOPMENT

CHAPTER 10

Complexity, Adaptability and Flexibility in Infrastructure and Regional Development:
Insights and Implications for Policy Analysis and Planning

Jonathan L. Gifford[1]

George Mason University, Fairfax

10.1   INTRODUCTION

The concept of order is a powerful and appealing inspiration for the planning and development of urban infrastructure. Those engaged in the planning process derive professional identity and satisfaction from the notion that they are somehow working out or contributing to the realization of order.

We conceptualize order in multiple ways. One is the Renaissance notion of the city and its infrastructure as a realization of "the order of God's creation" (Kemp, 1991). This concept of the city plan was articulated as early as the fifteenth century by architect, art theorist and writer Leon Battista Alberti: "The principal ornament of any city lies in the siting, layout, composition and arrangement of its roads, squares and individual works; each must be properly planned and distributed according to use, importance and convenience. For without order there can be nothing commodious, graceful and noble".[2] The vestiges of this conceptualization of order are clear in the American Progressive Era (see Hays, 1959; Wiebe, 1967) and the City Beautiful Movement.

A second and related conceptualization of order is neoclassical economics, with its emphasis on marginal utility and Walrasian equilibrium. If the economic system is left undisturbed, a determinate general equilibrium will emerge, with a steady-state price and quantity for each input and output.

A third conceptualization of order is the rational decision model, with its embrace of a systematic process for defining goals, identifying evaluation criteria, generating alternatives, evaluating alternatives against the criteria and selecting the optimal alternative. This concept of order is powerfully reflected in the Fordist system of production (see Hounshell, 1984) and in the time and motion studies of Taylorism.

These concepts of order and equilibrium are reflected in the methodologies that guide infrastructure planning and development decisions. Planning processes typically embrace some variant of the rational model, with more or less recognition of the uncertainties associated with various future states.

---

[1]   This chapter draws from the author's forthcoming book Flexible Urban Transportation Systems. A related paper (Gifford, 1995) extends this work to examine behavior and environmental policy.

[2]   Leon Battista Alberti, De re aedificatoria (On the Art of Building), quoted in Kemp (1991).

Relatively naive versions of the rational model simply predict values for important planning variables (e.g., levels of traffic, demand for water). These point estimates are then used as the basis for design decisions about capacity levels. This approach fails to capture the fact that the point estimates are uncertain, sometimes with significant consequences.

Nineteenth century *ingenieurs des ponts et chaussees,* for example, assumed that France's well developed canal system would serve far into the future as the principal mode for freight movement and that rail would never succeed in undercutting canals' low cost. Thus, they designed the famous French "star" of rail routes emanating from Paris, well suited to carrying passengers to and from the capital. Shipping freight on a star network, which has followed from the obsolescence of the canal, is very inefficient, however (Smith, 1990). Post-World War II American highway engineers, for another example, assumed that a systematic and comprehensive metropolitan transport plan could anticipate and provide for urban transportation "needs", only to discover that the very notion of need is somewhat arbitrary, and that social "constants" like the labor force participation rate could give way with breathtaking speed as women entered the paid (and commuting) labor force (see Seely, 1987; American Association of State Highway and Transportation Officials, 1991; Gifford, 1984 and Pisarski, 1987).

More sophisticated versions of the rational model attach probability distributions to design values instead of point estimates and propagate uncertainty through the decision model to derive probability distributions for selected performance estimates (e.g., net benefits) (see, e.g., Haynes et al., 1984). These more sophisticated approaches assume that a probability distribution is known or can be approximated without violating the integrity of the analysis.

While useful in many applications, probabilistic approaches also have some limitations. First, probabilistic models require as a starting point a model of the basic nature of the problem domain, what affects what and in what way. But often there is significant uncertainty about the appropriate model for a particular problem. Such "model uncertainty" is often not amenable to probabilistic treatments (Morgan and Henrion, 1990).

A more serious problem with probabilistic approaches arises when the planning domain is *adaptive* in the sense that demand for particular infrastructure facilities or services is determined by the way in which they are provided. If water is abundant and affordable, then society "discovers" multiple ways to use it: to quench thirst, to convey sewage, to clean cars and driveways. If highway transportation is cheap and widely available, society tends to develop lots of ways to use it to provide value. If infrastructure demand really is endogenous, then the planner's role shifts from being a working out or revelation of some predetermined level of social preference to a process of social construction (see, e.g., Bijker et al., 1987).

Recent years have witnessed an increasing awareness that the concept of order itself is problematic. Uncertainty, disorder, chaos and complexity are present in many fields of inquiry. Much of this awareness derives from the work of Nobel laureate Ilya Prigogine (see, e.g., Schieve and Allen, 1982). The recent appearance of popular non-mathematical treatments of the topic (Waldrop, 1992; Lewin, 1992) has elevated complexity to something approaching cult status.

At the risk of indulging in fad, this chapter inquires about the relevance and implications of complex adaptive system behavior to the planning and design of urban infrastructure, with particular emphasis on urban transportation infrastructure. The central question is how should decisions about infrastructure be made? Much of the rationale for contemporary planning and decision approaches is strongly conditioned by assumptions about order and equilibrium. But perhaps the effects of urban infrastructure location and design decisions cannot be anticipated and evaluated systematically under the rubric of scientific or technical rationality alone because of the complexity, adaptiveness and dynamic nature of the urban environment.

If the urban infrastructure domain is not in equilibrium or equilibrium-tending, if it is an adaptive system, then what is the appropriate scope for public action? What is the appropriate role for government in imposing or enabling or facilitating order? On what basis should a particular order be selected from the range of all possible orders? And what role should individual preference play?

In some respects, these are not new questions. Philosophy, art and literature have long asked, "Is there an underlying order?" One observer has characterized the conflict between "Dirty Neoplatonists" and enlightened Aristotelianism as follows: "Plato, profoundly influenced by mathematics, thought of the world in terms of ideal and abstract perfect forms that lay behind the sloppiness of sensory experience. Aristotle, the biologist, elbow deep in dissections, thought of the world in terms of experimental categories and inductive generalizations. At its extreme, Platonism finds reality by deriving the observed world from abstract ideas. Aristotelianism at its extreme finds reality by deriving the essences from the observed world" (Morowitz, 1993).

A similar conflict is found in the debates surrounding Darwinian natural selection. Is the universe and all that is within it the result of a mindless process of evolution and natural selection, or has development been informed and influenced by some superior power?[3] Existentialism rejects such an underlying order. Deconstruction questions the validity of any externally referenced concept of order or meaning.

While it is not our purpose to explore these themes here, it is important to recognize that questioning the appropriateness and legitimacy of Cartesian order and efficiency are rooted in a centuries-long debate about the nature of the world and man's role in it.

Our discussion will proceed by first reviewing some of the recent work in increasing returns economics. We start with increasing returns economics because it provides a means for understanding in economic terms the nature of complex, adaptive systems. We then assess the applicability of increasing returns to the domain of urban infrastructure planning and development. A concluding section then explores the implications of complex, adaptive system behavior to the planning and design process.

10.2 COMPLEXITY, TECHNICAL CHOICE AND INCREASING RETURNS ECONOMIC

One of the most exciting developments in contemporary social thought is the recognition and development of concepts to describe complex adaptive systems. By complex we mean systems that operate far from equilibrium, steady state or global optima, that are subject to improvement and anticipation by agents or decision making units that adapt their behavior to changes in their surrounding environment.[4] Complex adaptive systems are of particular interest because most systems that social scientists study are complex and adaptive. Social, economic, technological and environmental conditions are continuously in flux, continuously adjusting and adapting, in simultaneous interaction with their surroundings. Most neoclassical economics focuses on understanding systems as tending toward some Walrasian equilibrium. Much of the contemporary world, however, appears not to be equilibrium-tending at all.

The relevance of these insights into urban infrastructure systems is that most of the economic thought that has informed the development and understanding of infrastructure systems and their urban environment is firmly rooted in neoclassical economics. The models of von Thünen, for example, explain the relationship between transportation and land development. They were developed to explain the rather static world of an agrarian economy with a single market center surrounded by an undifferentiated field of agricultural land (von Thünen, 1826). To explain seventeenth and eighteenth century

---

3   Daniel C. Dennett developed some of these ideas in Dennett (1993).
4   This definition draws on John Holland (1993).

agrarian economies, of course, such models were useful because the subject systems were fairly static and did exist in fairly stable equilibrium. As a result, the assumptions of stasis and equilibrium implicit in traditional economic theory were largely applicable to describe the major economic resources of that era.

Conditions in contemporary industrialized high-income countries are far from static, however. On the contrary, technological, economic, environmental and social conditions are in a state of rapid flux. But applying decisions based on static analysis to a complex adaptive system may give rise to puzzling results, since the results predicted by the static model may often fail to materialize. A famous paradox of dynamic network analysis, Braess's paradox, demonstrates that improvements to a single link of a network, which by static analysis would appear to be beneficial, may instead reduce overall network performance (Knodel, 1969; Murchland, 1970).

In order to understand the implications of complex adaptive system behavior, we start with a short primer on increasing returns economics, which addresses matters associated with complex adaptive systems in the economic domain.[5] We then apply these notions to the urban transportation setting to establish that there is an increasing returns process operating in urban development. We then examine methods for selecting appropriate infrastructure investments, both the traditional selection process and more flexible approaches.

10.3   BASIC CONCEPTS OF INCREASING RETURNS ECONOMICS

Increasing returns processes are those where the benefits of adopting a particular course of action increase with the number of people adopting that course of action. Examples abound. Being the only person with a telephone is not very useful. The benefits of having a telephone increase with the number of people who get telephones, since each new subscriber to the telephone system gets the benefit of access to all of the previous subscribers.

Our discussion of increasing returns is in three parts. First, we discuss the sources of increasing returns. Second, we discuss the properties of systems subject to increasing returns. And third, we discuss the policy dilemmas raised by the existence of systems subject to increasing returns. These issues are particularly salient in the area of technology standards, and hence much of the literature on increasing returns derives from concerns in that domain. But the issues and processes are quite relevant to urban transportation planning and development.

10.3.1 The Sources of Increasing Returns

There are generally four sources of increasing returns: (1) coordination effects (also called network externalities), as in the telephone case cited above; (2) large set-up or fixed costs, which provide economies of scale; (3) learning effects, "which act to improve products or lower their costs as their prevalence increases"; and (4) adaptive expectations, "where increased prevalence on the market enhances beliefs of further prevalence".[6]

Coordination Effects. Coordination effects or network externalities refer to the technical interrelatedness of the components of a particular system. Technically interrelated components cannot be evaluated in isolation of the system of which they are a part, since their performance is contingent in some degree on the rest of the system. Congestion impacts are a common example in the urban transportation domain. Under congestion,

---

5   We will not dwell on the mathematics of this process, although its behavior can be described mathematically.

6   This formulation of four sources is from Arthur (1988).

the addition of one unit to a traffic stream reduces the system's overall performance. This would be a source of decreasing or diminishing returns. Frequent travelers will be familiar with the network externalities of the runway separation at Stapleton International Airport in Denver, Colorado. In low visibility conditions that require the closing of one runway, the effects are felt throughout the national air system due to delayed flights and missed connections.

But coordination effects can also be positive. The imposition of a single truck width standard, for example, may lower overall costs for shippers and shift the split between trucking and other freight modes. Similarly, the expansion of a single bottleneck, say the new Denver International Airport, may improve the overall performance a system, thereby reducing costs and benefiting other suppliers in that system.

A related coordination effect has to do with technologies that offer greater benefits as the number of users who make the same choice increases. An example is the choice to subscribe to a telephone service. The more people elect to subscribe to the telephone, the greater value there is to subscribe. If only one user subscribes, the system has no value at all. A similar example is the fax machine. Another is language.

A third type of coordination effect has to do with the cost of complementary products and services, which may be more readily or cheaply available if a large number of users elect to purchase the original product. Hence, the availability of a broad range of computer software for a particular operating system depends on the overall level of demand for that operating system. Similarly, the availability of a wide range of refueling and repair locations for automobiles is dependent on a large number of automobiles. This subgroup of coordination effects would also include traditional spatial agglomeration economies whereby there is an economic advantage for two firms to locate near each other in order to take advantage of common external resources, like law firms, specialized labor pools, and the like.

Large Setup Costs/Economies of Scale. A second important source of increasing returns is economies of scale, specifically the economies that redound to a single firm from having a larger scale operation. The most familiar economy of scale is engineering economies, that is, the technical efficiency that comes from a larger scale of production. Often this takes the form of a large up-front fixed cost that allows lower variable costs of production. This might be attributable to, say, the fluid mechanical properties of the production machine. For example, the sidewall resistance in a pipe increases only in the first order of its diameter, while its carrying capacity increases in the second order, so that twice as large a pipe will have twice as much sidewall resistance but approaching four times as much carrying capacity.

Scale economies also derive from production economies, which result from the lumpiness of capital investments and the possibility of redundancy in larger scale production operations. The use of one widget processing machine in a factory would leave that factory vulnerable to a 100 percent loss of capacity if that machine failed, whereas a larger factory that had four widget processors of equal reliability would be much less likely to lose 100 percent of its capacity.

Scale economies also derive from economies of scope, which are internal economies deriving from needing only one payroll or personnel office for a wide range of production lines, for example. Essentially, these are to human and organizational resources what engineering economies are to capital assets. A small company would need some personnel expertise which may be difficult to find in combination with the needed expertise in, say, information systems, in just the right combination.

Learning by Doing. Another important source of increasing returns derives from learning by doing (Arrow, 1962; Rosenberg, 1982). Here the notion is that a production organization gains experience in the process of production that allows it to produce the same product more cheaply and possibly to produce related or improved products more quickly or more cheaply than a firm just entering a production sector. As an example, Japan is said to have built upon its early expertise in precision instruments in order to gain a foothold in the consumer electronics market and, subsequently, the integrated circuits that they contain (Arthur, 1990, p. 93).

In the presence of uncertainty about the relative merits of two possible technological formats, the cost reductions gained through learning by doing can make it very unlikely that the untried technology will ever be pursued, even if its ultimate or long-term costs would be lower than the one that was tried (Cowan, 1991). For example, there may have been a competition of this sort between steam and petroleum fired internal combustion engines for automobile propulsion. If we had chosen steam and were as far down the learning curve with steam as we now are with internal combustion, we might well have preferred steam. Yet clearly the costs of a conversion to steam at this point in time, given the uncertainties about its long-term efficacy, would make it very difficult to justify (Beasley, 1988; Cowan, 1989). An important characteristic of increasing returns from learning is that they are not retroactive, that is, the benefits of that learning cannot be applied to decisions made before it occurs.

Adaptive Expectations. The final important source of increasing returns is adaptive expectations. These refer to choice situations where the presumed dominance of a particular alternative among consumers reinforces its adoption to the point that it becomes the dominant alternative. By some accounts, for example, the prevalence of the DOS operating system is largely attributable to the widespread assumption by consumers that IBM would become a *de facto* standard, thereby leading it to occur. In cases where increasing returns due to adaptive expectations are present, the sponsors of competing alternatives sometimes engage in strategic behavior in order to establish an installed base or early market presence that will lead consumers to believe that a particular format will eventually prevail.[7]

10.3.2 The Properties of Increasing Returns Systems

Increasing returns give rise to four properties of interest to us: (1) multiple equilibria; (2) possible inefficiency, which may occur when one equilibrium is superior to another but fails to win out; (3) lock in, which occurs when one of the solutions or equilibria, once it becomes dominant, is difficult to exit from; and (4) path dependence, whereby the "selection" of a particular equilibrium may depend on relatively small chance events.

Two of these – multiple equilibria and inefficiency – are relatively well acknowledged in the literature. Lock in and path dependence are less well known and have only recently begun to be the subject of study.

Multiple Equilibria. One of the most interesting properties of increasing returns systems is that they can evolve into a number of steady states, equilibria or configurations. This possibility means that there is no single system optimum. Each of these states may have a different level of social welfare associated with it, but it is possible for a system to "settle down" into more than one possible configuration or trajectory. This is a significant departure from the single general equilibrium state associated with neoclassical economics.

Economists have long recognized the possibility of multiple equilibria.[8] International trade theory has acknowledged since the 1920s a problem of multiple equilibria, as for example when two countries can each produce in two possible industries, both of which have large set-up costs (e.g., aircraft and automobile). Given economies of scale, it may make sense for one country to produce the aircraft and the other the automobiles and to trade with each other to achieve their preferred consumption mixture. But which commodity is produced in which country cannot be determined by economic logic alone.

---

[7] For a literature review, see David and Greenstein (1990).

[8] The following examples are taken from Arthur (1988).

Spatial economics has recognized a similar problem in the concentration of industries in particular regions. When firms benefit from locating close to similar or complementary firms, the allocation of industries among regions may depend on historical accident, since several possible equilibrium allocations may exist (Krugman 1991).

A similar problem exists in industrial organization. There may be several stable market shares of competing products, say between VHS and Betamax video cassettes or IBM compatible and Macintosh microcomputers.

Possible Inefficiency. Inefficiency may exist because one or more of the possible steady states may be optimal from a social welfare standpoint. Emergence of any but an optimal steady state would be inefficient, but as noted above, there is no reason to expect this optimum to occur.

Lock In. Lock in refers to the difficulty of deviating or exiting from a particular steady state condition or stable attractor once it has been entered. Familiar examples abound. To return to the international trade and spatial economics example above, once these two hypothetical countries have settled which will supply autos and which aircraft and have developed their industries, the energy and effort required to change that arrangement would be formidable indeed. They would be "locked in" to their particular steady state. Extraordinary effort would be required to finance and develop new plant and equipment in the upstart area, as well as establishing the labor force, supplier firms and regulatory environment that would be conducive to that particular industry. Similarly, the effort required to convert from VHS to Betamax video formats if Betamax were judged to be superior on some grounds would be extraordinary. Sunk costs in VHS equipment among households is extremely large, complementary institutions such as video cassette distribution and outlets are well established.

It should be noted that concerns about lock in on an inferior alternative due to increasing returns must be tempered by the recognition that it is not inexorable. Increasing returns due to large fixed costs may be mitigated by the depreciation of those assets. If an alternative is superior enough, by this reasoning, it will afford someone an opportunity to switch and exploit that opportunity. Thus Japan's "lean production" process displaced "Fordism", and superior computer technology frequently renders older technology obsolete.[9] If an alternative is not sufficiently superior to generate such exploitation, by this reasoning it probably does not matter very much.

On the other hand, some theoretical work has identified circumstances of "excess inertia" where the net benefits of switching can outweigh the net benefits of not switching and yet because of the distribution of those benefits no switch will occur. The reason is that no single agent may benefit sufficiently to start the band wagon, and so no band wagon ever gets started (Farrell and Saloner, 1985). (There is also a complementary concern over "excess inertia", whereby switching can occur even when it is not beneficial.)

Path Dependence. Path dependence refers to the fact that selection among possible equilibria might well turn on rather small-scale events and choices. There is a large and growing literature on this particular topic. One of the favorite cases is that of the so-called "QWERTY" keyboard and its path to market dominance. The QWERTY keyboard was developed in the 1870s in order to reduce the frequency of key clashes. It also allowed the product name, "Type Writer", to be spelled out using only the keys on one row. A competing configuration, "The Ideal", had keys composing seventy percent of English text on the "home" row of keys. Since then, another format, "Dvorzak", has also been suggested. But QWERTY's dominance has so far been difficult to dislodge (David, 1985).

If QWERTY were objectively the "best" keyboard configuration, then its market dominance would be of only limited interest. But some argue that it is in fact objectively inferior to competing alternatives available at the time of its adoption and to the since-

---

9   I am indebted to Brien Benson for articulating this point.

developed Dvorzak. Its dominance is attributable not to any technical superiority, according to this line of reasoning, but rather to historical "accidents" that occurred at the time of its development and marketing. Specifically, QWERTY's inventor, James Densmore, promoted his product through training programs that taught touch typing. As QWERTY-trained clerks proliferated, the manufacturer of the competing configuration started making QWERTY available as an option on its machines, and QWERTY emerged as the predominant configuration. Thus, the reasoning goes, QWERTY's adoption is attributable to the merits of the training program, not the technology itself. Its selection was path dependent.

10.4   POLICY DILEMMAS FOR INCREASING RETURNS SYSTEMS

Increasing returns systems raise significant and thorny issues about the appropriate role of government. Some conclude from the QWERTY case and others that since a *laissez faire* process can give rise to an inferior technology, the appropriateness of *laissez faire* approaches in the selection of a particular technology is therefore in question and that some sort of state intervention to protect the public interest is thereby indicated. Others question the presumption of QWERTY's technical inferiority and conclude that the case does not offer a reason to reject the *laissez faire* approach (see, e.g., Krauss, 1992).

There are many, many examples where one technology wins out over another for reasons seemingly unrelated to its technical merit, like how it was packaged and marketed or which particular firms picked it up and aggressively pursued it. The Betamax-VHS competition comes to mind.

What is interesting about these cases is not the merits of different keyboards or other technical details, obviously, but rather the selection process itself. The "selection problem", to use Arthur's terminology, is how a particular steady state is arrived at. That is, given the existence of several possible steady states, how is the particular steady state that emerges selected? And is that selection process a fair or otherwise appropriate process?

The economic literature has focused on whether inferior alternatives can theoretically emerge as *de facto* standards under various conditions, and what that implies for governance and social welfare. There seems to be a consensus that inferior technology can emerge under particular *laissez faire* conditions. But there is much less consensus on the implications of that finding for governance and social welfare, and specifically on whether or under what conditions government can do any better (see, e.g., Cowan, 1991; David, 1985 and Krauss, 1992).

The alternatives to *laissez faire* selection are two. First are voluntary standards. With voluntary standards, the parties interested in a particular selection process would convene and agree to adhere to a set of specifications set forth in a publicly available form. Voluntary standards resemble *laissez faire* in many respects since they are based on voluntary adherence to a specification and involve no government coercion. But they differ in an important respect because the standard is a public good insofar as it is nonexcludable and nonrivalrous. Under *laissez faire,* a *de facto* standard may not be a public good, indeed, it may subject to patent or property rights. It was, for example, the refusal of Sony to make publicly available its Betamax specifications that purportedly gave rise to the opportunity for Philips and others to enter the VCR market with a competing format (VHS) that was public (Krauss, 1992).

But voluntary standards are not always feasible. In some cases, the length of time required to create a viable standard is too great for them to be useful, as when a technology is evolving rapidly, or after most of the relevant decisions have already been made. In other cases, one party may have a disproportionate influence due to market share in related sectors that allows it to proceed independently. In still other cases, it may be difficult to find representatives of all interested parties, as for example, when environmental externalities are in question.

A second alternative to *laissez faire* is outright government sponsorship of a particular alternative. Government can effect sponsorship in three ways: (1) statutory or regulatory sponsorship of a standard (i.e., mandating it in law or regulation); (2) direct procurement; and (3) indirect procurement (i.e., grant restrictions). All of these involve one form or another of coercion. Statutory and regulatory authority involve the authority to mandate or restrict particular activities. Direct and indirect procurement involve use of compulsorily collected tax revenues.

Government sponsorship raises three rather profound policy dilemmas, which have been given the catchy titles: (1) narrow windows; (2) blind giants; and (3) angry orphans (David, 1987). The narrow windows dilemma refers to the fact that the ability of a central authority to influence the path of development, say the selection of a particular format, is limited in time. Once things have started to move in the direction of a particular steady state, government may not be able to redirect to a preferred steady state without exercising some sort of extraordinary police power. Thus, selection is sensitive to small, perhaps random or arbitrary actions at the early stages, but increasing returns produces powerful forces to pursue a particular selected steady state once things get going.

The blind giant dilemma refers to the fact that the actors with sufficient authority and self-conscious interest in affecting selection – presumably governments – are unable to discern a clear path because of the uncertainties associated with any single path. Uncertainty about the benefits and costs associated with a single path is so great that scientific rationality alone cannot select a particular course of action. Hence, the central authority is faced with the unseemly choice of choosing arbitrarily among competing courses of action or allowing *laissez faire* processes to choose between those courses of action. Deferring a decision is not an option because of the narrow windows phenomenon – by the time there is enough information to make a rational decision, it is too late to effect it.

The angry orphans dilemma emerges from the fact that early adopters of a technology may be disgruntled if the format they choose does not emerge as the *de facto* standard. Again, the Betamax-VHS example is apt. Those who invested in Betamax technology were "orphaned" by the market shift to VHS, so they were losers in the sense that they would probably have had higher net benefits if they had chosen VHS, at least in situations where the availability of complementary products was important. This premise is not absolute, however. In some applications, access to complementary products is far less significant. For example, a student relates that his Betamax was fine for recording and replaying broadcast programming, even though the selection of prerecorded video cassettes for Betamax was limited by the predominance of VHS.

Another caveat to the angry orphans dilemma is that sometimes the payoffs from a particular technology are so powerful that even though they may become obsolete, they pay for themselves so quickly that it is better to invest and replace later than it is to wait until a standard technology emerges. Some analyses of electronic highway toll collection technology, for example, estimate payback periods of eight months. In a case like that, it is better to invest now in full recognition that one might have to completely replace in two years in order to adopt the ultimate industry standard.

These three dilemmas – narrow windows, blind giants and angry orphans – pose severe challenges to students of technology selection. For while it is fairly clear that *laissez faire* approaches to selection can lock in on inferior alternatives, the efficacy of the alternatives to *laissez faire* is problematical. And if neither *laissez faire* nor governmental choice is clearly indicated, what is an appropriate selection policy?

Stated another way, path dependence suggests that decisions early on in the deployment of a technology or development of an entity can have powerful self-reinforcing consequences that are difficult or impossible to predict confidently *ex ante*. It is likely, for example, that Densmore knew or suspected that he could sell more of his Type Writer if there were secretaries and clerks in the labor force who knew how to touch type using QWERTY and sought to exploit that complementarity through his training program. Yet he could not have known or suspected the continuing effects of his ultimate success on the nature of text processing a century later, nor could any central authority

that was attempting to assess the merits of QWERTY vis-a-vis the competing configuration of the time or such configurations as might be invented in the future – the blind
giant dilemma.

So it is difficult to be confident that a technology assessment of keyboard configurations undertaken in 1880 would have yielded a superior outcome. And indeed, the delay
imposed by such a study would have led to the irretrievable loss of benefits that firms
would have gained from using the technology during the course of the study.

Students of decision making have long recognized the presence of bounded rationality
and so-called satisficing behavior (March and Simon, 1958, esp. Ch. 6). The notion of
path dependence raises the stakes considerably, however. For now boundedly rational or
satisficing decisions may have path selection effects that yield lock in on a particular
technology or configuration that is not strictly speaking optimal. What is a rational
decision maker to do?

One answer has come from advocates of market processes, most notably Hayek, who
described in 1945 how the price system and free and voluntary commerce maximized
social welfare (von Hayek, 1945). Yet Hayek's insights and the body of research it has
spawned do not address the issue of increasing returns and its features of lock in and path
dependence.

An important element of this set of decisions is that in his attempts to impose order,
there are two rational strategies. One is to share or pool risk, as in an insurance pool. The
other is to manipulate the selection process itself. Densmore clearly sought to influence
selection through training. But another strategy is to win sponsorship from actors with
significant market or police power. By some accounts, this is how DOS and IBM
compatibility gained a significant market share, displacing what had begun to be a fairly
steady state movement towards CPM (Andersen and Dawes, 1991). In the area of
intelligent vehicle highway systems, some manufacturers are currently advocating the
adoption of a single "architecture" to help coordinate and form a national market for
IVHS products and services.[10] And historically, government has played an important
role in establishing standards for television, color television (Crane, 1979), cellular telephones and other technologies. On the other hand, many telecommunications and
computer standards have been agreed to through voluntary consensus among interested
parties.

10.5 INCREASING RETURNS IN URBAN TRANSPORTATION AND DEVELOPMENT

The conditions giving rise to increasing returns, and the associated properties, are widely
present in the urban environment. We will start with a discussion of the sources of
increasing returns, then turn to how the properties of increasing returns manifest themselves in the urban domain.

10.5.1 Sources of Increasing Returns

Earlier, we identified four sources of increasing returns: coordination effects, large set-up
or fixed costs, learning effects and adaptive expectations. To what extent are these
sources of increasing returns operative in the urban transportation environment?

Coordination Effects. Coordination effects refer to the technical interrelatedness of the
components of a system. The metropolitan transportation arena is clearly one that exhibits
high interrelatedness of its component parts. Economic activity may be loosely defined as
the production, consumption and distribution of material, energy and information among

---

[10] For a review of standards issues in the area of intelligent vehicle highway systems, see Gifford
(1992).

households and firms and other economic units. A wide range of infrastructure systems play a role in economic activity so defined. Indeed, most of the built environment – infrastructure, buildings, parks – plays some role.

A high level of coordination and interrelatedness exists among these units. Households engage in distribution and consumption through the use of transportation systems, which requires accessibility, either by foot or some other conveyance, to the points of product sale, be they strip shopping centers or neighborhood shops in a "walking city". Similarly, manufacturers distribute their products to points of sale through the use of technical components that must be compatible. Distribution via rail cannot occur unless points of sale are accessible to rail heads. Distribution by truck cannot occur if streets are too narrow to allow their passage. While this is all fairly obvious to even the casual observer, we stress it here because of the significance of technical interrelatedness and coordination effects as a source of increasing returns.

Another dimension of coordination effects has to do with an increase in benefits the more people or firms adopt a particular alternative. These, too, are important in the urban transportation domain. The benefits to a household of having a car increase as the number of retail opportunities that are car-accessible increase, subject to transportation costs. The benefits to a retailer of being car accessible increase as the number of households owning cars increases, again subject to transportation costs. Similarly, the benefits of living in a pedestrian friendly neighborhood increase with the number of shops locating in that neighborhood, subject to competition for space within walking distance. The benefits to a retailer of locating in a pedestrian friendly neighborhood increase with the number of people living within walking distance, subject to competition for space.

A third dimension of coordination effects derives from the availability of complementary goods and services. Such effects are also widely present in the urban transportation/land use domain. Most clearly, the more people that elect to own automobiles, the greater the diversity of auto-related services that is feasible, like service stations, tire outlets, etc.

Large Setup Costs/Economies of Scale. Economies of scale and large setup costs operate widely in the urban transportation domain. Indeed, the very nature of most infrastructure, transportation and otherwise, is associated with economies of scale. At its most general, infrastructure is a capital investment the purpose of which is to produce services at lower costs than would be possible without it. We identified three kinds of scale economies in our earlier discussion: engineering economies, production economies and economies of scope.

One important form of urban transportation scale economy derives from the pure technical or engineering characteristics of the system. An investment in a lane of concrete between two points yields lower operating costs for moving vehicles between those points. Purchase of a vehicle (fixed cost) yields lower marginal costs of travel (excluding externalities for a moment).

In the case of providing guideway (a lane or a steel track), congestion does impose decreasing returns beyond some level of traffic. With highways, the onset of congestion can sharply reduce the flow of traffic on a facility. With rail, capacity on a single line can increase to a maximum, but typically flow does not diminish due to congestion, delay simply rises.

Auto users impose significant external costs in the form of congestion, air pollution and dependence on foreign oil, however, the full economic value of which is not known.[11] Further, there is some current debate that consumer purchase of insurance in an annual or semi-annual contract further distorts the driver's perceived cost function,

---

[11] Estimates abound, but are at best problematical. See, e.g., Hanson (1992) and Lowe (1993).

since a significant portion of risk of loss derives from the use of the car, rather than from its mere ownership.[12]

The second class of scale economies is production economies, which derive from the redundancy and robustness of a larger system. An example of these from the urban transportation domain is route redundancy in a dense network. A large scale provider, for example, can efficiently support multiple routes in a particular region, lessening the likelihood of total system shutdown due to the failure of a single link. For another example, a large scale freight carrier will on average have lower unit costs for any particular pick-up or delivery because of the likelihood of having other nearby pick-up or deliveries for any particular request.

The third class of scale economies is economies of scope, which provide economies from being able to specialize particular parts of the production force. For a highway supplier, economies of scope would derive from being able to share maintenance garages across a wide range of facilities and service vehicle fleets. For a large fleet operator like a courier or taxi company, for example, such economies would derive from the ability to have a single service garage and single dispatch operation.

Learning by Doing. Increasing returns due to learning by doing are also operative in the urban transportation domain. At one level, the process of everyday life is shot through with learning by doing. Which bakery has the freshest croissants? Which dry cleaner gives best service? Which mode and route to work is most reliable? Most economical? Most secure? Anyone who has ever relocated into a new city knows that discovering alternatives and assessing them involves matters of choice, experimentation and learning that are irreversible and non-retroactive, in the sense that one cannot recapture expenditures made on wrong choices. At this level, households and firms are clearly subject to powerful decreasing returns due to learning by doing.

Certainly these learning-by-doing returns affect matters associated with urban transportation. Habit, custom and routine are all manifestations of learning by doing. This is not to say that households and firms are unwilling or incapable of adapting to changing circumstances. Quite the contrary! Households and firms seem to adapt with breathtaking speed when it serves their interests. But it does indicate that in order to induce a departure from routine, it is necessary for them to be convinced that the alternative is worth the trouble of trying out.

In a similar way, agencies and governmental units are also creatures of habit, routine and tradition. For sometimes rather obscure historical reasons, a particular policy or procedure is adopted. Even if that policy or procedure could never be justified starting from first principles today, yet it is necessary to show convincingly that an alternative will lead or is likely to lead to superior outcomes in order to justify departing from it.

Adaptive Expectations. The final source of increasing returns is adaptive expectations, whereby the presumed dominance (or failure) of a particular alternative causes that alternative to become dominant (or to fail). Adaptive expectations exert powerful influence in many elements of the urban transportation domain. One important aspect of adaptive expectation is the irreversibility or quasi-irreversibility of particular decisions such as construction of a road or location of a military base. While current military base closing activities in the U.S. provide a stark reminder that such large scale decisions are not completely irreversible, nonetheless, households and firms often incorporate assumptions about the irreversibility of such actions into their decision making.

---

[12] A counter argument is that shifting insurance from a periodic to a per-mile cost would still obscure significant variation in risk exposure due to time and place of travel that may exceed the variations caused by miles of travel alone. For example, driving a hundred miles at posted speed limits on a rural Interstate during daylight is significantly safer than driving the same distance at over the speed limit on city streets on a Saturday night, even for the same driver.

10.5.2 Manifestations of the Properties of Increasing Returns

The presence of these sources of increasing returns give reason to explore the extent to which the properties of increasing returns systems are present in the urban transportation environment. Earlier, we identified four properties of systems with increasing returns: multiple equilibria, possible inefficiency, lock in and path dependence.

Multiple Equilibria. The presence of multiple equilibria or steady states is certainly extant. Different cities demonstrate that patterns or structures or organizations of urban forms do exist and continue for long periods of time. While they are hardly static or in equilibrium, they do have stability. Indeed, there is a large literature that documents the existence of significant variations in the form and transportation characteristics of metropolitan areas (see, e.g., Newman and Kenworthy, 1989). In simple terms, we see evidence of multiple steady states in discussions of the different types of cities, the walking city, the garden city, the automobile city, the edge city. And for centuries there has been a conscious attention to the vernacular vs. the designed city.

Possible Inefficiency. The question of possible inefficiency relates to the notion that various forms or equilibria may have rather different efficiency characteristics. Indeed, there is a rather considerable literature on the topic of the efficiencies of various urban forms, including a series of studies on the costs of sprawl.[13] Possible inefficiency may arise because it is possible to select something other than the most efficient steady state.

Lock In. The notion of lock in is particularly relevant for understanding the nature of urban development processes (Konvitz, 1985). Even casual observation suggests that once an area has undergone development, redevelopment that differs very much is a very difficult enterprise. Indeed, in her study of the impact of great fires and disasters, Christine Rosen found that to a striking extent, cities were rebuilt in much the same pattern as that which had existed before the disaster (Rosen, 1986). The reason lies partially in the tenure of land and the regulations and legal restrictions placed upon its use and treatment, which does not change as dramatically in the event of a disaster as the improvements built upon the land. Once it is platted and subdivided, it establishes a structure of ownership rights and responsibilities that are in many respects extremely rigid (see Johnson, 1976).

History provides many instances of the magnitude of effort required to exit from locked in states. The experiences of the urban renewal programs of the 1950s and 1960s were explicitly aimed at reassembling parcels of land with clear titles in order to allow the financing and construction of buildings with a substantially different character. In terms of increasing returns, urban renewal was an attempt to exit from a steady state that was judged to be suboptimal. The construction of the grand boulevards of Paris between 1852 and 1870 was the result of an extraordinary exercise of the power of the state to demolish large corridors in the interests of achieving a harmonious and technically efficient configuration of streets and vistas. Baron Haussmann could only execute such a plan with the power and authority of Napoleon III behind him (Saalman, 1971, p. 16). In the U.S., Robert Moses exercised tremendous power in order to introduce new transportation technologies into the New York metropolitan area (Caro, 1974).

Path Dependence. Also important in urban transportation and land development is the issue of path dependence. The events precipitating the location of a settlement or the particular layout of a city or street system are highly site specific and enigmatic in many instances. It is not that these were random events in the sense of being drawn from a probability distribution. They may well have been quite conscious and systematic from the standpoint of the decision maker who initiated the precipitating event. But the consequences of these decisions have extended far beyond the considered expectations of the decision makers who originally took them, just as Densmore's selection of QWERTY, while perhaps internally consistent and technically rational at the time he

---

[13] For a review of the literature, see Frank (1989), Newman and Kenworthy (1989).

selected it, has had consequences that he never could have considered. Furthermore, the conditions have changed. The possibility frontier is now much different than it was.

10.6   SELECTION IN URBAN TRANSPORTATION AND LAND DEVELOPMENT

The presence of increasing returns and its properties in the urban transportation and land development policy domain raises some interesting and rather daunting questions. The basic question is what is the appropriate mode of selection or blend of modes for urban transportation systems: *laissez faire,* voluntary standards or government sponsorship?

The selection problem is at the heart of much of the controversy about urban transportation policy. In simple terms, the alternative steady states that exist are: (1) auto-dependent conventional suburban sprawl; and (2) transit and pedestrian friendly urban form. Between these two states, overall social welfare is seen to differ significantly, with auto oriented development scoring high on individual autonomy but perhaps low on land consumption and air quality; and transit/pedestrian-friendly development scoring high on land use efficiency and air quality, but lower perhaps on individual autonomy.

The selection process that has operated in most American cities is basically selection through sponsorship that is seen by some as favoring auto-dependent development and compromising social welfare (see, e.g., Lowe, 1993). Others view the selection process as simply an expression of consumer sovereignty (Gordon and Richardson, 1989).

These views of the selection process then inform debate and policy development for "reform". Our purpose here is not to endorse one or the other of these views. Rather, it is to meld this debate over transportation "selection" policy with the tools and insights of complex adaptive systems and increasing returns economics in order to use the insights from the latter to inform discussions of the former. In specific, we will identify and examine alternative selection approaches and the issues associated with selecting selection processes, that is, meta-selection, and of switching between selection processes. This raises an increasing returns problem in and of itself, since the steady state of the *status quo* selection process is difficult to convince people to abandon in favor of something much less certain. That is, it may be difficult to get people to abandon selection through exercise of police power in favor of selection through competitive rivalry and historical accident, even if we are convinced that it would likely yield superior social welfare outcomes.

In our earlier discussion of the policy dilemmas deriving from increasing returns systems, we identified three basic dilemmas: narrow windows, blind giants and angry orphans. To what extent are these policy dilemmas relevant to the discussion of urban transportation systems?

In the context of urban development, the narrow windows dilemma would seem to be present in a wide variety of situations. As noted earlier, the difficulty of redeveloping or restricting established development once it has occurred or gotten moving in a particular direction is certainly present. The popular perception might be characterized in the sentiment that, "Once the developers have moved in, it's too late to plan". A similar sentiment is that once a county has learned how to plan it's too late. The notion here is that development on the fringe of metropolitan areas occurs in jurisdictions that have only primitive planning capacity, and that by the time that capacity has been brought up to speed, it is too late, much of the development has been set into motion. The character of this process is very similar to the notion of "tipping" in technology choice, or David's "narrow windows" in the development of standards. Once a particular alternative begins to take hold, it is very difficult to dislodge or redirect it.

The second dilemma, blind giants, is also very relevant to the processes involved in the planning of urban transportation and land use, although perhaps it is less widely acknowledged. For in the narrow window when the overall shape of urban development can be influenced, central authority has only very limited information on which to base its decisions. Uncertainty is pervasive about the consequences of particular choices, about the future character of technology, economic conditions, environmental constraints, social preferences. As a result, decisions that seek to identify any sort of optimal or even satisfactory urban development formats come to be, ultimately, fundamentally arbitrary and value laden. They are not expressions of a rational, objective synthesis of future conditions but instead become the idiosyncratic impositions of a particular individual with his or her own history, lodged in an institutional setting and operating under policies and procedures that are to some extent accidents of history, seeking to impose order on a chaotic, unpredictable environment. This is a significant distance from "scientific planning".

The third dilemma, angry orphans, also operates in the urban transportation environment, to a large extent through the tyranny of the orphan. The issue of angry orphans was that early adopters of an alternative are dissatisfied if the alternative they choose does not later emerge as a *de facto* standard (if a *de facto* standard does indeed emerge). How does this play out in the urban transportation environment?

The closest analog to the Betamax orphan in the urban transportation environment is the speculator or developer who purchases or develops a piece of land in anticipation of some future event that fails to materialize. A former head of the Bureau of Public Roads during the late 1950s when the Interstate was being laid out once said that everyone would be better off if the whole Interstate system were moved one mile south. His point, of course, was that everyone wanted the system to be moved just a mile nearer or further from them.

To some extent, we tolerate the losses of these angry orphans. Speculators cannot always win. They knowingly gamble on the basis of local or special knowledge and information about the location of facilities, interchanges, etc. When they win, they may win big. When they lose, we let them lose.

At another level, however, the law introduces some significant asymmetries and irreversibilities into the decision process. Once access to a public road is granted, it cannot be revoked without compensation to the landowner or his assigns. And even if a landowner does not have a property right vested in a particular decision, he may well seek to influence public (or for that matter, private) actions that affect his interests, as well he should. In this sense, the parties to an urban development process or an urban transportation development process exert much greater influence over that process than, say, the private consumers of a VCR. There are good reasons for the openness of this process on the basis of principles of open, democratic government. Yet it is also the case that it introduces significant complications and biases into the provision of urban transportation services.

Because of the unique character of the state, a public decision to act on a particular matter or in a particular way can have an immediate impact on the decisions of a large number of other actors. Through adaptive expectations, other actors assume or wager that government will follow through. Once government puts its imprimatur on a particular development plan, other interests can immediately capitalize on those decisions and then exert a claim against any changes in the plan, either on the basis of legal standing or through political action.

As a result, a "blind giant" develops a plan, which is then immediately converted through adaptive expectations into a set of rights and vested entitlements. Any deviation from the plan has extraordinary impacts on associated parties. This is a tyranny of the orphans because by granting such high standing to those who would be potentially orphaned by a change from planned development, we increase the extent to which particular situations are locked in.

10.7   CONCLUDING REMARKS

These policy dilemmas – narrow windows, blind giants and angry (or tyrannical) orphans – are manifest in many of the most fundamental debates about urban infrastructure policy. For centuries, man has struggled with the notion of how to establish order and predictability in his environment. "Chaos is the law of nature", as Henry Adams observed, "order is the dream of man" (Adams, 1907, 1931).

Twentieth century experience with the urban planning and transportation planning traditions has yielded metropolitan areas that are deeply troubling to many. Yet many of these derived from the application of scientific or technical rationality. If increasing returns undermine the validity of scientific rationality for determining which order is socially preferable, what scope is there for public action?

This is the fundamental dilemma that is posed by an understanding of the urban transportation domain as one that is shot through with multiple equilibria, inefficiencies, path dependencies and lock in. If the scientific rationality that provides the fundamental rationale and justification for public action is suspect, then what is the appropriate role for action by democratic government? How ought selection to proceed if government sponsorship based on scientific rationality is not clearly a superior mode?

Each approach has its own problems. *Laissez faire* in the presence of multiple equilibria, path dependency and lock in leaves open the possibility of selecting the "wrong" steady state. Voluntary standards have only limited applicability in highly dynamic environments. Government sponsorship faces the "blind giant" dilemma.

Therein lies the dilemma for those engaged in the planning and development of urban infrastructure systems. For if infrastructure planning is in fact little more than coercive realization of a self-fulfilling, self-reinforcing dream of order, then its critics have every reason to challenge that particular vision of the future with visions of their own. An enlightened hybrid approach might seek to use government authority to preserve options and flexibility, to delay lock in on a particular alternative while the merits of available alternatives are being explored, and to maintain a diversified portfolio of possible alternatives to be drawn upon if and when conditions that favor them arise.

The development of such flexible approaches poses a challenge to the professions of infrastructure planning and development. Such approaches are markedly different from conventional ideas about infrastructure planning and development. They demand a different orientation towards thinking about the future, and pose different opportunities for those societies that succeed in learning to adapt.

REFERENCES

Adams, H., 1931, *The Education of Henry Adams*, Modern Library, New York.
American Association of State Highway and Transportation Officials, 1991, *The States and the Interstates: Research on the Planning, Design and Construction of the Interstate and Defense Highway System,* Washington, D.C.
Andersen, D.F. and S.S. Dawes, 1991, *Government Information Management*, Prentice Hall, Englewood Cliffs.
Arrow, K., 1962, "The Economic Implications of Learning by Doing", *Review of Economic Studies*, 29:155-173, cited in Arthur, W.B., 1988, "Self-Reinforcing Mechanisms in Economics", in P.W. Anderson, K.J. Arrow and D. Pines (eds.), *The Economy as an Evolving Complex System*, Addison-Wesley, Redwood City, p.10.
Arthur, W.B., 1988, "Self-Reinforcing Mechanisms in Economics", in P.W. Anderson, K.J. Arrow and D. Pines (eds.), *The Economy as an Evolving Complex System*, Addison-Wesley, Redwood City, p.10.
Arthur, W.B., 1990, "Positive Feedbacks in the Economy", *Scientific American*, 93:92-99.

Beasley, D.R., 1988, *The Suppression of the Automobile: Skulduggery at the Crossroads*, Greenwood Press, New York.

Bijker, W.E., T.P. Hughes and T.J. Pinch (eds.), 1987, *The Social Construction of Technological Systems: New Directions in the Sociology and History of Technology*, MIT Press, Cambridge, Mass.

Caro, R.A. 1974, *The Power Broker*, Knopf, New York.

Cowan, R., 1989, "Review of The Suppression of the Automobile: Skulduggery at the Crossroads", by D.R. Beasley, *The Journal of Economic Literature*, 27:1682-1684.

Cowan, R., 1991, "Tortoises and Hares: Choice Among Technologies of Unknown Merit", *The Economic Journal*, 101:801-814.

Crane, R.J., 1979, *The Politics of International Standards: France and the Color RV War*, Ablex Publishing, Norwood.

David, P.A. and S. Greenstein, 1990, "The Economics of Compatability Standards: An Introduction to Recent Research", *The Economics of Innovation and New Technologies*, 1:3-41.

David, P.A., 1985, "Clio and the Economics of QWERTY", *American Economic Review*, Vol. 75, 2:332-337.

David, P.A., 1987, "Some New Standards for the Economics of Standardization in the Information Age", in P. Dasgupta and P. Stoneman (eds.), *Economic Policy and Technological Performance*, Cambridge University Press, Cambridge.

Dennett, C.D., 1993, "Evolution as an Algorithm – The Ultimate Insult?", Proceedings of *The Mind, the Brain and Complex Adaptive Systems*, George Mason University, Fairfax, May 24-26.

Farrell, J. and G. Saloner, 1985, "Standardization, Compatibility and Innovation", *Rand Journal of Economics*, Vol. 16, 1:70-83.

Frank, J.E., 1989, The Costs of Alternative Development Patterns: A Review of the Literature, The Urban Land Institute, Washington, D.C.

Gifford, J.L., 1984, "The Innovation of the Interstate Highway System", *Transportation Research*, 18A: 319-332

Gifford, J.L., 1992, "Standards for Intelligent Vehicle Highway System Technologies", *Transportation Research Record*, 1358:22-28.

Gifford, J.L., 1995, "Urban Infrastructure Systems, Behavior and Environmental Policy", in M. Rolén, ed., *Urban Policies for an Environmentally Sustainable World*, The OECD-Sweden Seminar on the Ecological City, June 1-3, 1994, Report 95:7, FRN, Forskningsrådsnämnden (FRN, The Swedish Council for Planning and Co-ordination of Research), Stockholm.

Gordon, P. and H. Richardson, 1989, "Notes from Underground: The Failure of Urban Mass Transit", *The Public Interest*, 94:77-86.

Hanson, M.E., 1992, "Automobile Subsidies and Land Use: Estimates and Policy Responses", *Journal of the American Planning Association*, Vol. 58, 1:60-71.

Haynes, K.E., A. Krmenec, D. Whittington, W.F. Echelberger, Jr., and T.D. Georgianna, 1984, "Planning for Capacity Expansion: Stochastic Process and Game-Theoretic Approaches", *Socio-Economic Planning* Science, Vol. 18, 3:195- 205.

Hays, S.P., 1959, *Conservation and the Gospel of Efficiency: The Progressive Conservation Movement, 1890-1920,* Harvard University Press, Cambridge, Mass.

Holland, J., 1993, "Can There Be a Unified Theory of Complex Adaptive Systems?", Proceedings of *The Mind, the Brain and Complex Adaptive Systems,* George Mason University, Farifax, May 24-26.

Hounshell, D., 1984, *From the American System to Mass Production, 1800-1932: The Development of Manufacturing Technology in the United* States, The Johns Hopkins University Press, Baltimore.

Johnson, H.B., 1976, *Order Upon the Land: The U.S. Rectangular Land Survey and the Upper Mississippi Country*, Oxford University Press, New York.

Kemp, M., 1991 "The Mean and Measure of All Things", in J.A. Levenson (ed.), *Circa 1492: Art in the Age of Exploration,* National Gallery of Art, Washington, D.C.

Knodel, W., 1969, *Graphentheoretische Methoden und ihre Anwendungen*, Springer Verlag, Berlin.

Konvitz, J.W., 1985, *The Urban Millennium: The City-Building Process from the Early Middle Ages to the Present*, Southern Illinois University Press, Carbondale.

Krauss, M.I., 1992, "Command vs. Spontaneous Coordination in the Development of Standards: The Case of Intelligent Vehicle Highway Systems", in J.L. Gifford, T.A. Horan and D. Sperling (eds.),*Transportation, Information Technology and Public Policy: Institutional and Environmental Issues in IVHS,* The Institute of Public Policy, George Mason University, Fairfax, and The Institute of Transportation Studies, University of California, Davis.

Krugman, P., 1991, "Increasing Returns and Economic Geography", *Journal of Political Economy*, Vol. 99, 3:483-499.

Lewin, R., 1992, *Complexity: Life at the Edge of Chaos*, Macmillan Pub. Co., New York.

Lowe, M.D., 1993, "Rediscovering Rail", in *State of the World*, Worldwatch Institute, Norton, New York, pp. 120-138.

March, J.G. and H.A. Simon, 1958, *Organizations*, John Wily & Sons, New York.

Morgan, M.G and M. Henrion, 1990, *Uncertainty: A Guide to Dealing with Uncertainty in Quantitative Risk and Policy Analysis*, Cambridge University Press, New York.

Morowitz, H., 1993, *Entropy and the Magic Flute*, Oxford University Press.

Murchland, J.D., 1970, "Braess' Paradox of Traffic Flow", *Transportation Research*, 4:391-394, cited in L.J. LeBlanc, 1975, "An Algorithm for Discrete Network Design", *Transportation Science*, 9:183-199.

Newman, P.W.G. and J.R. Kenworthy, 1989, *Cities and Automobile Dependence: A Sourcebook*, Aldershot, Hants., and Gower Technical, Brookfield.

Pisarski, A.E., 1987, *Commuting in America: A National Report on Commuting Patterns and Trends*, Eno Foundation for Transportation, Westport.

Rosen, C.M., 1986, *The Limits of Power: Great Fires and the Process of City Growth in America*, Cambridge University Press, New York.

Rosenberg, N., 1982, *Inside the Black Box: Technology and Economics*, Cambridge University Press, Cambridge.

Saalman, H., 1971, *Haussmann: Paris Transformed*, Braziller, New York.

Schieve W.C. and P.M. Allen, 1981 (eds.), *Self-organization and Dissipative Structures: Applications in the Physical and Social Sciences*, University of Texas Press, Austin.

Seely, B.E., 1987, *Building the American Highway System: Engineers as Policy Makers*, Temple University Press, Philadelphia.

Smith, Jr., C.O., 1990, "The Longest Run: Public Engineers and Planning in France", *American Historical Review*, Vol. 95, 3:657-692.

von Hayek, F.A., 1945, "The Use of Knowledge in Society", *American Economic Review*, 35:519-530.

von Thünen, J.H., 1826, *Der Isolierte Staat*, Hamburg, English Translation P. Hall (ed.), 1966, *The Isolated State*, Pergamon Press, Oxford.

Waldrop, M.M., 1992, *Complexity: The Emerging Science at the Edge of Order and Chaos*, Simon & Schuster, New York.

Wiebe, R., 1967, *The Search for Order: 1877-1920*, Hill & Wang, New York.

CHAPTER 11

Production Milieu and Competitive Advantages

Börje Johansson

Jönköping International Business
School (JIBS)

Rune Wigren

Uppsala University

11.1   INTRODUCTION

In agricultural societies the population tends to concentrate on sites in response to the fertility of land. In postagricultural societies we find new forms of "fertility" differentiation over space. Both within and across urban regions of various sizes one can observe how the competitive advantages differ between locations. We relate such distributions of location advantages to the variation of attributes of each location's production milieu. In this chapter we present a series of Swedish studies examining how the production milieu influences the performance of manufacturing and service industries, as well as the entire regional economy. This introductory section emphasises how certain persistent observations demand a modification or renewal of economic theory. We also outline the types of models employed in the Swedish analyses of the production milieu during the period 1970-1995.

11.1.1 Observations in Conflict with Economic Theory

Differences between regions as regards their production milieu provide opportunities for specialisation in accordance with the advantages of each region. This type of analysis was initiated by Ricardo and was developed by Heckscher and Ohlin to the theory of comparative advantage. In this model an equilibrium implies a pattern of specialisation such that each region makes use of its relative advantages – as given by those fixed resources which constitute the region's production milieu.

Following the above description, the production milieu is defined by those location attributes which are regionally trapped and which influence the production possibilities. Some of these regional attributes are given by nature – such as mineral deposits, the existence of other raw materials, the fertility of the soil, the climate, etc. Other attributes are created by investments of different kinds – including the experiences, knowledge and competence of the labour force in the region, assuming that households display a low degree of mobility. The built environment including infrastructure constitutes another set of regional attributes.

Our observations and our theoretical framework emphasise several phenomena which cannot be understood without modifications of established economic theory. First, we suggest that production factors and regionally located resources in general adjust on slower time scales than are normally assumed in neoclassical analysis. Second, we argue that the regional resources included in the concept of production milieu affect production possibilities in a fundamental way and influence location dynamics as well. Third, we observe that the production milieu also comprises agglomeration economies which implies that it evolves in a self-organising and self-reinforcing way. Moreover, we try to demonstrate that the production milieu should be given a fundamental position in economic theory. Another observation is that production functions (for the same type of output) differ between regions, partly because the closing down of old techniques is a delayed process in many regions, partly because new techniques and products are developed and introduced much faster (earlier) in certain regions than in the average type of region. Finally, if the influence from the production milieu is disregarded in the specification of a sectoral production function, it will differ accordingly between regions.

Our observations tell us that differentials between milieu attributes of regions remain over decades. For example, we shall illustrate how one category of municipalities persistently has experienced a high relative growth of jobs, while another is characterised by a distinct relative decline. Similar observations can be made with regard to income as well as regional gross product per capita and productivity in various sectors. Table 11.1 illustrates that to a certain extent the regional differences are size related (agglomeration phenomena). However, the variation within the size-clustered groups of regions in the table is considerable.

Table 11.1   Index for income per capita and changing population share in size-clustered groups of municipalities (Stockholm = Index 100)

Type of region	Income per capita 1967 (Index, %)	Income per capita 1990-91 (Index, %)	Population increase as a share of the region's population 1973-92,%
The Stockholm region	100	100	12.1
The Göteborg & Malmö regions	87	82	9.1
Middle range regions	68	73	7.7
Small regions	65	70	-1.8

Remark: Income per capita refers to "earned income" (and excludes government transfers).
Sources: SOU 1970:15, appendix 5 to LU95.

Table 11.1 indicates that the labour market regions associated with Stockholm, Göteborg and Malmö (Sweden's three small metropolitan regions) are strong attractors for labour force mobility. The rigidity of this adjustment process is, however, considerable. In 1965 these three regions hosted 32.5 percent of the country's working population. Twenty-five years later this figure had risen to 35.8 percent.

11.1.2 The Production Milieu in Economic Models in Swedish Research

One may include production milieu aspects in several categories of economic models. In Swedish research, we may distinguish (i) the specification of production functions which include location attributes as arguments, (ii) interregional trade models of the comparative advantage type including spatial price equilibrium models (SPE-models), (iii) location models which focus on how the location of different activities and how land values adjust to transportation conditions and other location attributes.

Production functions which use infrastructure features or location attributes as arguments can be specified for individual sectors or aggregates of industries and the regional economy as a whole. Overviews of this approach can be found in Rietveld (1989). In Swedish research we recognise Andersson (1970), Åberg (1974), Wigren (1976, 1984), Andersson et al. (1990).

The SPE-model adheres to the Heckscher-Ohlin framework. It was outlined by Samuelson (1952) and further developed by Takayama and Judge (1964, 1971). In its pure form the model explains location as a consequence of transportation costs in combination with a fixed pattern of located demand. With a continuous representation of a homogeneous space Beckmann and Puu (1985) generate a set of various SPE-results (with minimal assumptions). The SPE-model has also been associated with putty-clay assumptions in models where each production unit has a specific technology vintage, and where already located as well as optional units compete for a multiregional market (Johansson and Westin, 1987). In its pure form, this model generates trade patterns which (for many types of commodities) do not fit observations in an acceptable way (Westin, 1990). Hence, location aspects are also problematic in pure versions of this model.

Location models of the Weber type as well as a class of spatial oligopolistic models can be directly related to the SPE-model (Beckmann and Thisse, 1986; Gabszewicz and Thisse, 1986). The von Thünen class of location models describe variations in the milieu within an urban region as the consequence of accessibility patterns. This class of model has also been related to spatial product cycle models (Hirsch 1967; Andersson and Johansson, 1984). In the latter class of models the requirements as regards the production milieu vary over the life cycle of each specific product. Applied nation-wide, multiregional location models in Swedish research are represented by Snickars and Granholm (1981), Johansson and Strömqvist (1981) and Lundqvist (1981).

In Swedish research there are few examples of multiregional, general economic equilibrium studies in which the allocation of resources and price formation, as well as trade patterns and the location of activities adjust to the characteristics of each region's production milieu. Such models are outlined and assessed in Westin (1990), who also relates them to SPE-models.

In our subsequent presentation we will focus on selected Swedish contributions applying (i) production functions and (ii) analyses of location patterns. In both cases we provide examples of static and dynamic formulations, i.e., cross-sections and time-series as well as combined approaches.

11.2   THE CONCEPT OF A PRODUCTION MILIEU

Infrastructure forms an important part of the regional production milieu. However, it is the consequences of the infrastructure rather than the size or value of the capital stock which constitute the regional milieu. For example, the milieu is characterised by its capacity for economic interaction, generalised costs of interaction and time distances in general. Formally, the production milieu comprises those properties (location attributes) of a region which are durable, and those (i) which the individual firm cannot control, (ii) for which there are no market prices and no direct charges, (iii) which influence the firm's input deliveries, production activity, distribution and sales activities, management and innovation activities. In addition, the location attributes should vary across regions.

In this section we identify the time scales of change processes in a region, specify the activity categories of a firm and examine how such categories are affected by the production milieu. Moreover, the concepts of regional efficiency and competitive advantages are defined and related to location attributes. While discussing the expected consequences of efficiency differentials among regions we formulate model predictions (hypotheses) which in principle are testable.

11.2.1 Time Scales of Regional Characteristics

Consider the following model of an economic system, represented by a system of differential equations:

$$\dot{z}_i = F_i(z_1, z_2, ...) + f_i(t), \ i = 1, 2, ... \tag{1}$$

where t denotes time, all z-variables are endogenous and the $f_i(t)$-variables are exogenous driving forces. The z-vector comprises variables which adjust at different speeds like infrastructure, production capacity and current production and sales. The objective of this section is to decompose the z-vector according to the time scale of every variable. In this way we are able to discuss the time scale and type of equlibrium to which we want to confine our empirical studies.

The system in (1) may refer to a single region. However, by expanding the i-indexes it can represent a multiregional economy. In vector form we have

$$\dot{z} = F(z) + f(t).$$

Referring to a short discussion by Samuelson (1947) and following frameworks outlined in Westin (1990) and Johansson (1989) we decompose the vector z = (w, y, x) and the pertinent system into three coupled systems such that

$$\dot{x} = H(w, y, x) + h(t)$$
$$\dot{y} = G(w, y, x) + g(t) \tag{2}$$
$$\dot{w} = E(w, y, x) + e(t)$$

where x is a vector of slow, y of medium speed and w of fast variables. This speed characterisation tells us how quickly each type of variable responds to the system's vector *(w,y,x)* almost all the time.

First we recognise that according to our previous assumptions the vector x will include those variables which describe the production milieu. Consider next a medium-term time interval $T = [t_0, t_1]$. During this interval we can assume that the slow vector remains almost invariant which means that $\dot{x} \approx 0$, and then $H(w, y, x) \approx -h(t)$. Given this restriction, one can introduce the approximation $x(t) = \bar{x}$ for $t \in T$ which allows for the following parametrisation of the G- and E-functions while reducing the system in (2) to (3):

$$G_{\bar{x}}(w, y) = G(w, y, \bar{x})$$
$$E_{\bar{x}}(w, y) = E(w, y, \bar{x}) . \tag{3}$$

Consider now the vector of fast adjusting variables w. According to standard assumptions in economic theory it will include quantity and price variables referring to current inputs such as energy, intermediaries and transportation as well as output. The quantity adjustments remain fast provided that capacity constraints are not binding. These variables can be assumed to adjust with very short delay as demand conditions and production decisions change. The w-vector adjusts faster to its equilibrium than the y-vector does iff $\dot{w} / w \ll \dot{y} / y$. This implies that if $y(t)$ and $w(t)$ are disturbed away from their respective equilibria $w^*(t)$ and $y^*(t)$, then $w(t)$ returns more quickly to $w^*(t)$ than $y(t)$ approaches its equilibrium position $y^*(t)$. The equilibrium $w^*(t)$ satisfies $E_{\bar{x}}(w^*,y) + e(t) = 0$. We may then conclude that for the time interval T we can set $\dot{w} = 0$ and make the following adiabatic approximation (Haken, 1983, pp. 35-36; 187-216):

$$w^* = \tilde{E}(y,t, \bar{x}), \ t \in T$$
$$\tilde{E}(y,t, \bar{x}) = E(w,y, \bar{x}, \ w = w^*) + e(t).$$

$$(4)$$

The approximation implies that the w-vector is slaved by the slower y-vector. The path $w^*(t)$ can then be embedded into the $\tilde{G}$-function in the following way:

$$\tilde{G}(y,t, \bar{x}) = G(\tilde{E}(y,t, \bar{x}),y, \bar{x}) + g(t)$$
$$\dot{y} = \tilde{G}(y,t, \bar{x}).$$

$$(5)$$

The y-vector comprises variables describing (for firms in distinct sectors) slowly adjusting factor inputs such as employment categories, equipment and other forms of production capital. These factors constitute the capacity of the pertinent firms.

Suppose that $\bar{x}$ remains invariant in the medium term perspective, i.e., as $t \in T$. One may then empirically study two related phenomena. In the first case one investigates how the capacity variables (y-vector) change in the form of investment and location dynamics. In the second case one examines how the output, costs and profits (w-vector) are influenced by the $\bar{x}$-vector, given the capacity constraints at each point in time.

The nature of the process $\dot{y} = \tilde{G}(y,t, \bar{x})$ determines the possibilities of empirically estimating the relation between the y-vector and the $\bar{x}$-vector. The dynamics may, for example, come to rest in the form of (i) a point y^* or (ii) a steady state $y^*(t)$ such that $\dot{y}^*/y^*$ remains constant or (iii) a cyclic fluctuation around a steady state. In all these cases one can formulate appropriate estimation approaches. Of course, the adjustment of the y-vector may also exhibit complex dynamics with associated complications.

Components of the w-vector refer to production output, costs and profits. In this case formula (4), $w^* = \tilde{E}(y,t, \bar{x})$, directly suggests how one might go about empirically examining the relation between production or productivity and the $\bar{x}$-vector.

11.2.2 Activity Categories of a Firm

Any firm may be described by specifying its various activities and how they are organised as a system. In our analysis we follow Wigren (1976) by identifying four separate but interlinked categories of activities or functions. These are (i) the organisation of input flows and personnel management, (ii) production, (iii) distribution and sales activities, (iv) administration and management.

The efficiency of a firm is determined by the efficiency with which it performs the activities enumerated above. Our next concern is how the performance of the four activities is influenced by the production milieu. The following descriptions summarise our general assumptions:

(i)   The control of input flows comprises the purchase of current inputs, equipment and production services, and the hiring of personnel. The production milieu should by definition influence the various transaction costs associated with these input markets. In particular, input efficiency increases with increasing accessibility to the supply of labour and production services.

(ii)   Standardised production activities of a manufacturing firm are often considered to be invariant with respect to variations in the production milieu. However, service production and customised production in general require customer contacts as an integral part of the production activity as such. In cases like these milieu differentials are assumed to influence the production efficiency .

(iii) The production milieu comprises the accessibility to customers and market potentials. As such it influences the efficiency of the distribution and sales activities. This impact is accentuated with regard to customised production and deliveries which tend to be contact intensive.

(iv) The management and administration function comprises all activities not included in the three categories described above. It controls and develops the technical, organisational and commercial knowledge associated with the firm. Hence, it includes innovation activities which generally are stimulated by accessibility to deliverers, customers, competitors and R&D-resources.

Each of the four types of activities described above relate to both activities and inter-actions within the firm, as well as external interaction. As regards the internal activities the production milieu may allow positive scale effects to be realised. In addition, the size of the economic environment will in general bring about non-linear scale effects on the transaction costs. When these scale phenomena are positive, they all correspond to the economies of scale argument put forward by Krugman (1991).

11.2.3 Regional Efficiency and Competitive Advantages

In the subsequent analysis regional efficiency is a central concept. We may think of a firm's efficiency (or total productivity) as its capability to make use of its internally controlled resources. Given this formulation, the regional efficiency is that part of the firm's efficiency which depends on the characteristics of the production milieu. This is emphasised by Figure 11.1 in which the regional efficiency is influenced (i) primarily by geographic conditions, as well as infrastructure and support systems oriented towards firms and households, and (ii) secondarily by the supply of land and premises, as well as the supply of employment categories. Naturally, the secondary factors are themselves affected by the primary aspects of the production milieu.

How can we explain that one firm is more efficient, and has a higher total productivity than another competitor? The first firm may have a more clever management, a better composition of its labour competence, younger vintages of the production technique embodied in the production capital and organisation, a larger scale of the activities, and a better capacity utilisation. In individual cases such a favourable position may be due to random phenomena. However, in a statistical sense we can expect all the above conditions to be positively influenced by the production milieu.

Marshall (1920) identified three specific conditions which explained why firms in a certain sector tended to be localized, i.e., why they could function more efficiently when located nearby each other. The same conditions can also be applied to explain why the multiplicity and richness of a specific production milieu (agglommeration diversity) brings benefits to firms in many sectors. Marshall's three factors are associated with the labour market, the provision of nontraded inputs and the acquisition of technological information. First, an industrial centre and, in particular, a diversified urban region with several industrial centres allows a pooled (and robust) market for workers with specialised skills such that the robust market benefits both workers and firms. Second, the same urban region can provide nontraded inputs specific to each of its localised industries at lower costs. Third, new and subtle information can spread more easily and accurately in a local environment than in distant networks, and this generates market and technology spillovers.

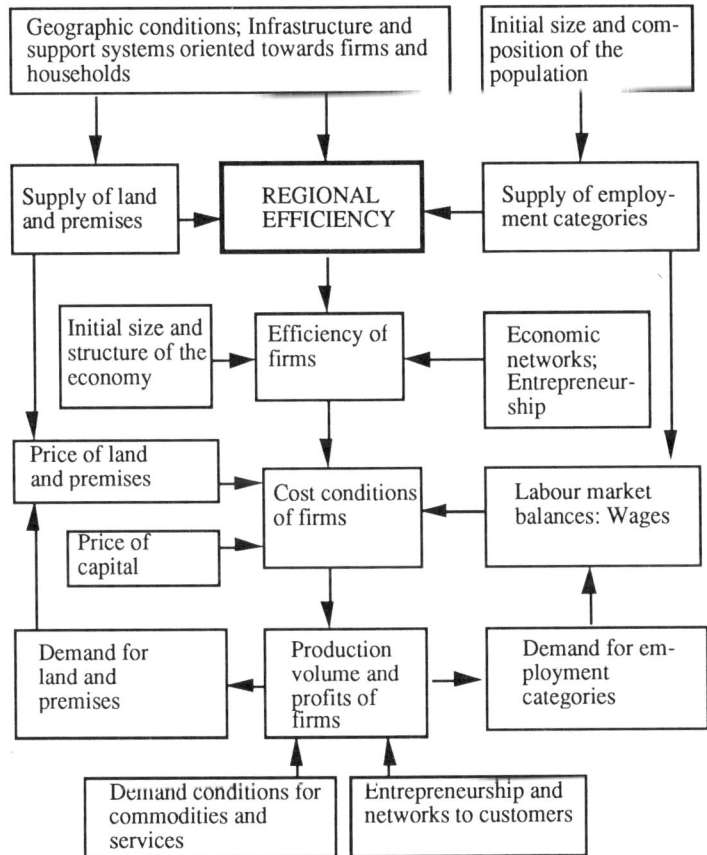

Figure 11.1 Regional efficiency and interregionally oriented firms

The Marshall inspired arguments above indicate that a specialised industrial centre can self-reinforce its location advantages for a specific industry. In addition, a vital and multifaceted urban region can do even better. It can provide a creative milieu (Andersson, 1985); a diversified supply of various producer services; an intraregional network for information flows about new production techniques, products, suppliers and customers (Johansson, 1991); and a differentiated supply of labour categories. Our enumeration of location attributes tends to emphasise intraregional accessibility and the associated infrastructure. It also implies that firms may mutually reinforce each others production milieu characteristics. To this we should simply add the importance of interregional interaction links and pertinent accessibility properties.

11.2.4 Consequences of Efficiency Differentials

Let us investigate the interdependencies in Figure 11.1. As an initial step we can examine the properties of a solution that approximates the short term equilibrium specified in (4). The regional efficiency influences the efficiency of individual firms together with the existing set of other firms, the existing economic networks and networks between entrepreneurs in the region. The efficiency of the individual firm determines its cost conditions (cost function) together with the existing wage levels, capital price and prices of land and premises. These elements together with the demand for each firm's output and the existing networks to customers determine the realised output, and the associated cost and profit of each firm.

To illustrate the short-term nature of the above situation, let us introduce the following production function referring to a specific industrial sector or firm in region r:

$$Y_r = f(L_r, K_r; A_r) \tag{6}$$

where L_r and K_r represent the labour and capital employed in the industry, and where A_r refers to the regional efficiency, partly determined by infrastructure (public capital). Next, we introduce the price variables w_r, ρ_r which denote the wage level and the capital price in region r, where the latter includes the price of premises. Let us assume neoclassical regularity of (6). Then we can express the dual cost function associated with the production function as follows:

$$C_r = C(w_r, r_r, Y_r, A_r). \tag{7}$$

Using Shepherd's Lemma one obtains the shadow price, $P(A_r)$, of the public infrastructure

$$P(A_r) = -\frac{\partial C_r(w_r, r_r, Y_r, A_r)}{\partial A_r} \tag{8}$$

where $P(A_r)$ signifies the willingness to pay for additional services from the regional infrastructure. It reflects the savings in the industry's production cost as the characteristics of the production milieu are improved. When the costs of such improvements are smaller than $P(A_r)$ the system has not come to rest in a long-term equilibrium (cf. Seitz, 1993).

However, we should first consider the medium-term adjustment processes. Expanding demand and a growing number of customers provide incentives to increase production capacity, and as a consequence the demand for labour as well as for land and premises will grow. This pushes wages and the price of land and premises upwards. The latter constitute equilibrating changes which counteract or counterbalance the attractivity of an urban area with a favourable regional efficiency.

Broadening the perspective further, we may deliberate upon other adjustment processes such as the inmigration of households and increased supply of employment categories in response to increasing demand and higher wages, the location of new firms in response to regional efficiency effects which are not offset by correspondingly high land values, and stimulation to supply more land and premises in response to increasing price levels. These responses are reflected by equation (5), according to which $\dot{y} = G(y, t, \bar{x})$. One may also contemplate modelling the investment in infrastructure and the supply of infrastructure services as well as other support services as adjustments initiated by observed disequilibrium gaps. However, in this latter case we are dealing with very slow adjustments.

11.3   PRODUCTION AND EFFICIENCY POTENTIALS

The milieu advantages in urban regions are described by Hägerstrand (1970) who emphasises that they facilitate considerably the contacts between decision-makers, between experts, between sellers and buyers. Many of the results presented in this section verify that the costs associated with contacts between persons are a main efficiency factor for the manufacturing industries. We start by presenting studies by Wigren which are focused upon a large set of sectors within the manufacturing industry, and show how they vary in their dependence on the characteristics of the production milieu. Next, we describe the results from a study which utilises an aggregate production function referring to the total production in a region (Andersson et al., 1990). As a final step we present a quasi-dynamic model which has been applied to estimate how the production milieu in municipalities influences the production in different manufacturing industries (Johansson, 1993a). We also compare the conclusions about the importance of different characteristics of the production milieu.

11.3.1 Wigren's Sectoral Production Functions

In Wigren (1976, 1985) the manufacturing industry is differentiated into around 15 sectors. The firms of each sector are separated into two categories – complete and incomplete. Complete firms perform all necessary functions in a market economy, while processing activities have a more pronounced role in the incomplete firms. Among the latter we find subsidiary establishments but also formally independent firms which are dominated by a larger company. A similar approach is also found in Wigren (1984) which focuses specifically on one single sector, i.e., fabricated metals. The production output, Q_r, of this sector in region r is assumed to depend on (i) the inputs of production factors $v_r = (v_{1r},...,v_{mr})$, (ii) firm specific characteristics $u_r = (u_{1r},...,u_{nr})$, and (iii) regional characteristics $x_r = (x_{1r},...,x_{hr})$. The components of the last vector refer to characteristics of the production milieu which are common to all firms in the same region. These location attributes are assumed to be unaffected by the individual firm. From this a regional production function is specified as follows

$$Q_r = F(v_r, u_r, x_r) = A_r f(v_r, u_r)$$
$$A_r = A(x_r).$$

(9)

In (9) it is assumed that the F-function can be decomposed such that a regional efficiency factor A_r may be identified. Observe also that the functions f and A are explicitly assumed to be the same in all regions. Consider now $A^* = A(x^*)$, where x^* represents the most favourable composition of location attributes observed in any region. In this way A^* signifies an "optimal" value and we can define the relative regional efficiency as

$$a_r = A(x_r) / A^*.$$

(10)

One may note that (10) is based on a condition of Hicks neutrality. Suppose that we want to express regional efficiency without assuming Hicks neutrality. Then formula (11) should be substituted for (10) as follows

$$\hat{a}_r = F(v_r, u_r, x_r) / F(v_r, u_r, x_r^*).$$

(11)

Firm-specific characteristics and the inputs of factors will be described in the next subsection. With regard to the regional characteristics we note that they comprise as many as 62 variables. In order to transform this rich information set to useful arguments in the production function introduced in (9), factor analysis was carried out (principal components). The first seven factors collected more than 73 percent of the variation with regard to the complete firms and about 70 percent for the incomplete firms. As regards the complete firms, the first factor collected 40, the second another 12, and the third an additional 11 percent of the variance. As a consequence, in the next subsection we focus on the content of these three factors.

In Table 11.2 we describe the three most important regional factors with regard to complete firms. Table 11.3 presents the two most important factors with regard to incomplete firms. Each factor is characterised by those x-variables (location attributes) which determine the properties of the factors by having high factor loadings. In practice, the table enumerates all x-variables with factor loadings larger than 0.8 in absolute values. One should observe that some of the location attributes are measured for functional regions. Each municipality belongs to a functional region, often formed by 3-4 municipalities, although the metropolitan regions are formed by a larger number of municipalities.

Table 11.2   The three most important factors in regard to the regional production milieu for complete firms

ACCESSIBILITY PROPERTIES	(I) 10 variables which describe the location in the Swedish market landscape, (II) 3 variables which describe the location of the municipality in the export landscape, (III) relative supply of office (white collar) personnel in functional regions, (IV) relative supply of business services measured for functional regions, (V) travel time to the nearest of Stockholm, Göteborg and Malmö, (VI) the total number of persons employed in the municipality.
THE SIZE OF THE MUNICIPALITY AND ITS BUDGET	(I) the municipality's expenditures on streets and buildings, (II) its expenditures on harbours, communications and industry
THE DEGREE OF INDUSTRIA- LISATION	(I) the relative supply of female workers in the functional region

Table 11.3   The two most important factors in regard to the regional production milieu for incomplete firms

ACCESSIBILITY PROPERTIES	(I) 5 variables describing the location in the Swedish market landscape, (II) relative supply of male technical and (male & female) office personnel recorded for functional regions, relative supply of business services in functional regions, (III) estimated distance to the main establishment of the firm, (IV) travel time to the nearest of the three metropolitan regions.
THE SIZE OF THE MUNICIPALITY AND ITS BUDGET	(I) total number of persons employed in municipalities, (II) the municipality's expenditures on streets and buildings, (III) its expenditures on harbours, communications and industry.

The export landscape is described by market potentials with regard to (i) the Nordic countries, (ii) the U.K., U.S.A. and countries where Germanic languages are spoken, and (iii) other countries. The potential expresses the size of the demand in each group discounted by the travel-time distance. The market landscape is described by distances to harbours and domestic market potentials. In particular the following variables characterise profoundly the contact landscape for both complete and incomplete firms: (i) travel time to Stockholm, (ii) travel time to the closest of the three metropolitan regions Stockholm, Göteborg and Malmö, (iii) travel time to the town hosting the provincial government, and (iv) travel time to the nearest university, and the road distance in kilometers from the centre of a municipality to the centre of its functional region.

By inspection one can see that to a large extent the incomplete firms are dependent on the same type of factors as the complete ones. However, the variables that describe the accessibility conditions are fewer for the incomplete firms. A noteworthy difference is that the link distance between an incomplete firm and its super ordinate complete firm (often head office) matters.

11.3.2 Sectoral Differentials as Regards Milieu Dependency

In his early study Wigren (1976) used a rather coarse spatial resolution with 24 counties. In later analyses by Wigren (1984, 1985) the counties are subdivided into 275 municipalities. The observation period is the three years 1973-1975. Wigren's material is unique in the sense that the observation units are individual establishments, with information about the type of output, consumption of production resources, sales value, costs of intermediary inputs, value added, wages etc. The available information also makes it possible to distinguish between complete and incomplete firms, as defined earlier.

The regional efficiency is that part of the total factor productivity which can be explained by the characteristics of the production milieu (location attributes). Other factors which affect the factor productivity are the scale of output, the technology vintage of the capital equipment, and factor allocation in general. For all firms the analysis is initiated by estimating sector-specific production functions of the following type:

$$
\begin{aligned}
ln(q / v_1) &= b_0 + b_1 ln(B / v_1) + b_2 ln(v_2 / v_1) + \\
&+ b_3 ln(v_3 / v_1) + b_4 ln(v_4 / v_1) + b_5 ln v_1 + \varepsilon
\end{aligned}
\tag{12}
$$

where (12) refers to observations of individual firms, j, in particular regions, r. Hence, the random error term is observed with the specification ε_{jr}. The variables are defined as follows:

$$
\begin{aligned}
q \quad &= \text{value added} \\
v_1 \quad &= \text{number of male production workers} \\
V_2 \quad &= \text{number of female production workers} \\
v_3 \quad &= \text{number of supervisors} \\
v_4 \quad &= \text{consumption of electric energy} \\
B \quad &= \text{gross profit (capital income = value added - total labour costs)}
\end{aligned}
\tag{13}
$$

In the subsequent step the observed residuals $\tilde{\varepsilon}_{jr}$ are confronted with the factor values, k_{sr}, obtained from the principal components analysis mentioned above, and where s =1,2,... This confrontation is accomplished by means of the following estimation, specified for each firm j in each region r:

$$
\tilde{\varepsilon}_{jr} = \beta_o + \sum_s \beta_s k_{sr} + \gamma_{jr}.
\tag{14}
$$

The regression in (14) is carried out for each individual sector. A statistical test may be used to decide for each sector whether one should use 3 or 7 factors, i.e., whether s = 1,2,3 or s = 1,...,7. When the parameters of (14) have been estimated the following index, $\hat{a}_r$, can be calculated to express the relative value of the regional efficiency in r:

$$\hat{a}_r = 100 \sum_s \beta_s k_{sr}. \tag{15}$$

We should note that the type of index described in (15) is calculated with respect to each industrial sector. Hence, we obtain sector-specific information about the regional efficiency.

As regards R^2-values and other measures of statistical significance for the equations described in (12) and (14), a detailed discussion of one specific sector is provided in Wigren (1984) with a sectoral overview in Wigren (1986). On the basis of statistically significant results we now turn to the comparison between different manufacturing sectors. Compiling the results for all different sectors one can conclude (with regard to the observation period 1973-1975) that roughly one third of the industries reveal a strong dependence on the production milieu, one third displays a medium dependence, and the remaining third shows no sensitivity at all vis-a-vis the regional milieu. We should expect that this type of sectoral sensitivity will gradually change as time goes by and the technology develops. The important observation is that the sensitivity varies. Moreover, the differences observed in Wigren's studies can be interpreted in general terms. Industries characterised by standardised products and production methods tend be less dependent on the production milieu than others.

Table 11.4 Differences between sectors as regards their sensitivity to characteristics of the production milieu 1973-1975

Industrial sector	Share of the value added in manufacturing
STRONGLY DEPENDENT SECTORS: Metal products; machinery products; transportation equipment – complete firms (excl. shipyards); electrical products – incomplete firms.	37 percent
MEDIUM LEVEL DEPENDENT SECTORS: Food & beverage products; shoes, leather & fur products; non-metal mineral products; metal works products; textile products – complete firms; transportation equipment – incomplete firms (excl. shipyards).	32 percent
NONDEPENDENT SECTORS: Wood products; paper & pulp products; chemical & plastic products; textile, fertilising, rubber & electrical machinery products – incomplete firms.	31 percent

11.3.3 Total Production and Regional Characteristics

Wigren's investigations in the 1970's were initiated in a climate of equity discussions like – how can the production milieu be improved in disadvantaged regions by means of public policy (Wigren, 1976)? In the 1980's the Swedish policy focus changed and researchers were asked to answer questions of the type – in which regions should the production milieu be improved in order to stimulate national economic growth and increase overall productivity. Another difference is that in the 1980s there is a stronger focus on R&D and knowledge-intensive sectors, inside and outside the manufacturing industry. In this intellectual atmosphere Andersson et al. (1987, 1990) estimated production functions using characteristics of the regional milieu as explanatory variables. Their production function is specified as follows:

$$Q_r = A(x_r)f(v_r) \tag{16}$$

where Q_r represents the value of production in a functional region r = 1, ..., 70, v_r is a vector representing the size of the labour input and its knowledge intensity, and x_r is a vector referring to the regional milieu. In the estimations, the value of production and other variables (except the accessibility measure) are normalised by means of division by the size of the entire area of the functional region. The A-function has the Cobb-Douglas form, while the f-function is assumed to adhere to Frisch's regular ultra passum law which implies that when inputs increase proportionally the output increases along a sigmoid path.

The intial work by Andersson et al. (1987) contains studies of both the entire economy of regions and individual sectors. The presentation here is restrained to the contribution from 1990 which focuses on the production capability of the economy as a whole in regions, represented by the observable "total regional income". The authors argue that the production milieu in a functional region should be thought of as regional infrastructure. As a basic aspect in the definition of infrastructure they require publicness in space and time. All capital that influences conditions of production beyond the spatial and dynamic limits of the decision-making firm is regarded as infrastructure. In addition they add that land without infrastructure is useless.

One particular feature of the f_i-*function* is that it distinguishes between standard and knowledge-intensive labour. Table 11.5 presents the econometric results which are presented in qualitative form with regard to 1970 and 1980. Variable 2, which is a true accessibility variable, is strongly significant in both years. The length of roads and railroads divided by the land area indicates the capacity for intraregional interaction and – to a certain extent – also long distance interaction. The airport and R&D variables each reflect in their own way the region's capacity to interact as regards long distance personal contacts and knowledge based contacts.

Table 11.5 The production milieu described by infrastructure variables included in the A-function in formula (16)

INFRASTRUCTURE OF EACH REGION	1970	1980
1. Value of the building capital	+	+
2. Travel time to the nearest metropolitan region	-	-
3. Airport capacity	(0)	(+)
4. R&D capacity *	-	(-)
5. Airport capacity multiplied by R&D capacity	+	+
6. Length of main roads **	(-)	(+)
7. Length of railroads	+	(+)
LABOUR INPUTS		
8. Standard employment categories	+	+
9. Knowledge-intensive employment categories	+	+

Remark: Parameters which are not significant at the 95 percent level are given within parentheses. For 1970 variable 6 has the wrong sign. The negative sign for variable 4 is compensated by the positive sign for variable 5.

The authors present six other estimations in which the variables are not normalised by the land area. Instead the developed (built) land area is included as a new variable. In all essence these alternative specifications support the result in Table 11.5. Moreover, these equations all include an additional accessibility variable expressing interregional accessibility to population concentrations across the country.

11.3.4   A Quasi-Dynamic Model of Regional Production

Sections 11.3.1 and 11.3.2 present two quite different approaches which emphasise similar characteristics of the production milieu. Further support can be found in a study by Johansson et al. (1991) based on information about aggregate sectors in muni-cipalities. In the sequel we follow the presentation in Johansson (1993a) and Forslund and Johansson (1995). The approach is characterised by formulating a quasi-dynamic econometric model in which the production potential in each municipality is a function of the municipality's accessibility to different resources. These accessibility measures are assumed to reflect the production milieu of existing and potential firms in that municipality.

A set of alternative functions are estimated for several different sectors of the manufacturing industry in order to establish how the production potential is determined (Johansson, 1991, 1993a). In this presentation we will focus on the analysis of the manufacturing industry as a whole. The general form of the function referred to is:

$$\tilde{Q}_r = A\left(x_r\right)f\left(K_r, L_r\right); \hat{f}(K_r / L_r)L_r = f(K_r, L_r) \tag{17}$$

where $\tilde{Q}_r$ represents the potential output in municipality r, x_r is a vector of variables characterising the infrastructure in r, K_r and L_r refer to the recorded capital and labour inputs to the industry of municipality r. As described in Forslund and Johansson (1995) this type of aggregate function refers to an "average" or "typical" firm. As an alternative interpretation we may assume that formula (17) represents a "typical composition of firms". The function A is increasing in its arguments. Thus, when the x-variables increase by Δx_r, the value $A(x_r)$ increases to $A(x_r + \Delta x_r)$ and in this way $\tilde{Q}_r / L_r$ moves upwards as described in Figure 11.2.

$\tilde{Q} / L_r$

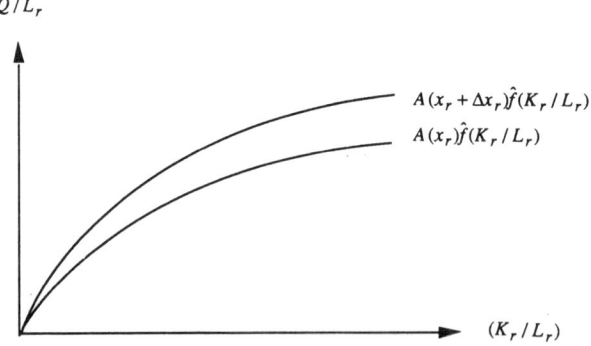

Figure 11.2 Effects of Δx_r on potential output per labour input

The characteristics of the production milieu (location attributes) of a municipality are described by infrastructure variables referring to (i) the quality of the local built environment, (ii) intraregional accessibility, and (iii) interregional accessibility. The general form for depicting the accessibility, T_{rj}, to a resource j with capacity or value A_{sj} in municipality s is given in formula (18)

$$T_{rj} = \sum_s A_{sj} \exp\{-\gamma_j t_{rs}\}. \tag{18}$$

Among recorded variables of the A_{sj}-type one should observe (i) the capacity of international harbours, (ii) the potential labour supply with a normal, college and university education, respectively, and (iii) the population concentrations.

In which way can we expect the G-function in (17) to affect the $\tilde{Q}$-value? Referring to the literature on infrastructure one should assume that the G-function has a sigmoid form. Beyond a certain point the effect of improving each category of location attributes flattens out. For example, if one improves the road network the traffic speed cannot increase beyond a certain level.

How has equation (9) been estimated? The regression approach is based on the overall assumption that the production potential $\tilde{Q}_r$ will increase as Δx_r is augmented. As time goes by the realised and observed production Q_r is assumed to gradually approach the value $\tilde{Q}_r$.

In order to capture this type of dynamic adjustment the functions f and A are estimated by means of a quasi-dynamic model called DYN (Johansson, 1991; 1993a). This formulation has been inspired by Mills and Carlino (1989) and Holmberg and Strömqvist (1988). Formally, the regression analysis attempts to explain the difference $\Delta Q_r = Q_r(t+\tau) - Q_r(t)$ in each municipality, where $Q_r(t+\tau)$ and $Q_r(t)$ denote the observed value added in year $t+\tau = 1988$ and $t = 1980$, respectively. The estimation strategy is to show how ΔQ_r depends on the potential $Q_r = A(x_r) f(K_r(t+\tau), L_r(t+\tau))$, where

$$f(K_r(t+\tau), L_r(t+\tau)) = K_r(t+\tau)^{\alpha_1} L_r(t+\tau)^{\alpha_2}$$
$$A(x_r) = x_{r1}^{\beta_1} \dots x_{rm}^{\beta_m}. \tag{19}$$

The variables $K_r(t+\tau)$ and $L_r(t+\tau)$ are observed at time $t+\tau$. The value of $A(x_r)$ should represent the infrastructure properties during the entire 8-year period. Hence, the vector x_r is assumed to remain approximately unchanged during the estimation period. This approach reflects the assumption that the x_r-variables adjust at a slow pace compared to the normal adjustment speed of the somewhat "faster" variables K_r and L_r.

The DYN-model relates the observed change ΔQ_r to the potential $A(x_r) f(K_r(t+\tau), L_r(t+\tau))$ in the following way:

$$\Delta Q_r = \lambda[f(K_r(t+\tau), L_r(t+\tau)) A(x_r) - Q_r(t)] \tag{20}$$

where $0 < \lambda \leq 1$ is a parameter which indicates how far the adjustment has developed during the 8 years. We may observe that (20) has to be estimated by means of non-linear regression techniques. In the estimation process the equation is normalised by dividing the left and right hand sides by $L_r(t+\tau)$. Some of the estimation results are presented in Table 11.6. It should be observed that the α and β-coefficients of the f-function are almost completely invariant across the various alternative specifications of the A-function.

We may emphasise that the implicit dynamics in (20) are driven by the size of the gap between $\tilde{Q}_r$ and $Q_r(t)$. The change process is a movement which gradually closes the gap. If we divide λ by τ, the value λ/τ indicates the average annual speed of this process. In a series of alternative specifications of the production potential function, the average value of λ comes out as $\lambda \approx 0.5$, which corresponds to 16 years of adjustment (e.g. Johansson, 1993a).

We may observe that Table 11.6 contains four location attributes which characterise intraregional aspects of the production milieu. Of these, variables I, III and IV relate to the municipality, while variable II refers to the county region which includes the municipality, since public transport is organised in such a larger framework. Location attributes V, VI and VII describe the interregional accessibility of the municipality. Each estimated equation is restricted to contain only 3-4 location attributes. The reason for this is that there is a high degree of multicollinearity among the characteristics of the production milieu. In that sense one cannot claim that the study allows for any precise statements about which of the characteristics are more important than others. However, it shows which characteristics belong to the group of potentially important regional efficiency factors and which do not.

Table 11.6 Alternative specifications of the A-function associated with robust estimation results

	EQUATION NUMBER					
LOCATION ATTRIBUTE	1	2	3	4	5	6
I. Flow capacity of the road system in the municipality		x		x	x	x
II. Capacity of regional public transport	x		x			x
III. Value and density of the built environment				x		
IV. Population density	x		x			
V. Accessibility by car to population concentrations	x		x			x
VI. Accessibility by truck to international harbours		x		x	x	
VII. Accessibility to airport capacity	(x)	x				

Remark: A parenthesis signifies parameters which are not significant at the 95 percent level. Robust results refer to the fact that α – coefficients remain invariant when the A-function is varied.

With the above background as inspiration Table 11.7 compares the overall patterns of the three studies presented in Section 11.3. The table illustrates a fairly consistent pattern, which partly reflects that the studies are founded in the same theoretical framework, partly that the availability of data constrains the possible model formulations. The main difference between the studies is that (1) and (3) use data about production and location attributes from municipalities and formulate accessibility measures, while (2) uses data from functional regions, i.e., more aggregate data.

One may ask why the intraregional attributes in study (3) do not include the accessibility to the labour force in the functional region or to a labour supply with a college and university education. The reason for this is that the iterative, nonlinear solution algorithm did not converge when these variables were included, basically due to effects from "multicollinearities". A municipality's accessibility to the supply of different employment categories exhibits a rather strong correlation with the flow capacity of the main road system within the municipality. It is also correlated with the regional capacity of public transport. As regards study (2) we should observe that the share of knowledge-oriented employment categories is an argument in the aggregate production function. This prevents the inclusion of similar labour supply variables in the set of regional characteristics.

Table 11.7 Comparison between three studies

	STUDY (1)	STUDY (2)	STUDY (3)
INTERREGIONAL ACCESSIBILITY	(a) ten variables describing the municipality's accessibility in the Swedish market landscape, including labour markets; (b) three variables describing the municipality's accessibility to export markets; (c) travel time to metropolitan regions in Sweden.	(a) time to the nearest metropolitan region; (b) airport capacity of the functional region.	(a) accessibility to population concentrations; (b) accessibility to international export and import markets; (c) accessibility to airport capacity
REGIONAL ATTRIBUTES	(a) the municipality's size and expenditures on streets, buildings, harbours and communications; (b) regional supply of office personnell and business services	(a) combination of airport and R&D capacity; (b) length of main roads and railroads in the region; (c) value of the building capital.	(a) capacity of the main road system; (b) capacity of public transport; (c) value and density of the built environment; (d) population density

Remark: (1) = studies in Sections 11.3.1 - 11.3.2 (Wigren, 1985); (2) = studies in Section 11.3.3 (Andersson et al., 1990); (3) = studies in Section 11.3.4 (Johansson, 1993a).

11.4   LOCATION DYNAMICS

Consider the set of regional characteristics exposed in Table 11.7. In this section we present empirical models which refer to the same characteristics, while the models at the same time focus on location dynamics in an explicit and pronounced way.

11.4.1 Household and Job Mobility

Population changes in the period 1980-1989 vary strongly among the Swedish municipalities. The median value is zero, while the upper quartile contains growth rates between 4 and 37 percent, and the lower quartile rates of decline between -3 and -11 percent. Hence, the location dynamics of households should be appreciated as a "heavy" change process. We may observe that compared to the median, 110 municipalities experienced fast growth both with regard to jobs and inhabitants, 112 experienced a correspondingly slow development for both variables, while 24 were characterised by an unproportionally fast job expansion and 24 a correspondingly fast population increase.

Swedish studies of the above process of change have been inspired by a study by Mills and Carlino (1989) in which they collect a vector of structural variables from all counties in the U.S. (about 2500) for the years 1970 and 1980. In a quasi-dynamic econometric model they use these structural characteristics of each region to explain the population change across counties during the decade. The results support the hypothesis that the gradual relocation of households among regions is influenced by the attributes of the regional milieu in the beginning of the period. These attributes comprise infrastructure, the built environment and accessibility properties.

A study by Holmberg and Strömqvist (1988) follows the above Mills-Carlino approach. In the Swedish study the following equilibrium conditions are introduced:

$$L^* = H(B,x)$$
$$B^* = G(L,x) \tag{21}$$

where L^* and B^* denote the equilibrium of jobs and population in a municipality, given the infrastructure (location attributes) of the municipality as specified by the vector x and the current values of B (population) and L (jobs). According to model assumptions, the system in (21) continues to change as long as $B^* \neq B$ and $L^* \neq L$. The adjustment towards equilibrium is assumed to be gradual and slow. In order to detect this kind of change process with limited data, the econometric analysis is based on observations of B and L from year $t = 1980$ and $t+\tau = 1988$. The model is specified as follows:

$$L(t + \tau) = L(t) + \lambda(L^* - L(t)$$
$$B(t + \tau) = B(t) + \mu(B^* - L(t) \tag{22}$$

where L^*, B^*, λ and μ are dependent variables and hence estimated, and where λ and μ denote the speed at which the gaps $(L^* - L(t))$ and $(B^* - B(t))$ are closed, given that the process is allowed to come to rest without further disturbances or incitement. We may first note that the econometric results imply that both λ and μ have low values, corresponding to an adjustment period longer than two decades. The strongest influence on L comes from B and vice versa. Table 11.8 summarises the results.

Table 11.8 Overview of results from the study by Holmberg and Strömqvist (1988)

Location attributes which influence the adjustment processes in municipalities, and which appear as significant in one or several alternative model specifications are specified below:	
CHANGE OF POPULATION	CHANGE OF JOBS
Number of jobs in the municipality	Number of inhabitants in the municipality
Number of jobs in neighbouring municipalities	Number of inhabitants in neighbouring municipalities
Supply of public transport	Supply of public transport
Local supply of single-family houses	Supply of air traffic
Accessibility by car to population concentrations	Frequency of intercity train departures
Flow capacity of main roads in the municipality	Flow capacity of main roads in the municipality

11.4.2 Location Dynamics of Jobs

The study reported on in the previous subsection deals with the location of the aggregate of all jobs or all work-places. What can be said about work-places in the manufacturing industry as a whole? The total number of these work-places diminished in almost all municipalities during the assessed period 1980-1988. In Section 11.3.4 we presented an analysis of how the regional milieu affects the production potential of the manufacturing sector. Here we continue to assess the same data by asking if there is any covariation between changes in manufacturing output and changes in jobs in the manufacturing industry.

Let ΔQ_r denote the change in manufacturing production in municipality r, and ΔL_r the corresponding change in jobs. By referring to a study by Holmberg and Johansson (1992) we can conclude that ΔQ_r tends to be low when ΔL_r is high and vice versa. This is illustrated in Table 11.9. The same pattern also obtains if we match the productivity change, $\Delta(Q_r / L_r)$, and ΔL_r. Hence, in municipalities where the manufacturing production and productivity is growing, the number of jobs in the manufacturing industry shows a stronger tendency to reduce than elsewhere. The chi-square value associated with Table 11.9 shows that this tendency is significant.

Table 11.9 Contingency table showing the relative frequency of municipalities in each contingency cell

	ΔL_r is strongly negative	ΔL_r is larger than average	SUM
ΔQ_r is small	20	30	50
ΔQ_r is above average	30	20	50
SUM	50	50	100

Remark: Chi-square = 9.8

Recognise that in general the production value grows faster in municipalities with regional characteristics according to Table 11.6. In fact, the empirical results in Holmberg and Johansson (1992) indicate that in municipalities with location attributes which are favourable with regard to the manufacturing production potential, the number of manufacturing jobs tends to reduce at a faster speed than in the average municipality.

The reported findings are consistent with various aggregate observations of economic development across regions in Europe during the period 1970-1990 (e.g. Cheshire and Hay, 1989; Rodwin and Sazanami, 1991). Essentially these observations indicate that vital regions with a high level of expected regional efficiency have a more rapid reduction of persons employed in the manufacturing industries than average. In order to shed some light on this issue we now present some econometric experiments carried out in Holmberg and Johansson (1992). They examine the following two aggregates of service activities in detail: (i) the WT-sector comprising wholesale and transport, and (ii) the CB-sector comprising various forms of consulting and all kinds of bank services. For each of these sectors, j, a variable, V_{rj}, is introduced to express the degree of concentration (or localisation) in municipality r. The regional concentration is specified as follows:

$$V_{rj} = W_{rj} / H_r \tag{23}$$

where W_{rj} denotes the sum of wages in sector j and municipality r, and where H_r signifies the potential labour supply in municipality r. The study by Holmberg and Johansson indicates that the examined service sectors are concentrated on municipalities in which the infrastructure facilitates personal contacts and mobility. Moreover, a large share of these municipalities have experienced a higher than average growth rate as regards the number of jobs. These conclusions are based on the following econometric equation:

$$V_{rj} = aA(x_r) \tag{24}$$

where a denotes the intercept and where $A(x_r)$ is a function of the following x_r-variables describing the production milieu of r: (i) the flow capacity of the road system, (ii) the value of premises per job, (iii) accessibility to a labour supply with a college education, (iv) the frequency of interregional trains, (v) the size of the public sector relative to the number of jobs, and (vi) travel time to Arlanda airport outside Stockholm. Only the last of the these variables is not significant at the 5 percent level.

Given the results presented above, Holmberg and Johansson continue to study the change in the total number of jobs, $\Delta L_r = L_r(t + \tau) - L_r(t)$, in each municipality between t+τ =1990 and t=1980. They show that the following econometric model can describe the spatial variation in the change of jobs:

$$\Delta L_r = \lambda(L_r^* - L_r(t)$$
$$L_r^* = A(x_r)^\alpha H_r(t)^\beta \tag{25}$$

where L_r^* can be interpreted as the equilibrium number of jobs, $H_r(t)$ denotes the potential total labour supply in the initial year, and where λ shows at which speed the gap $(L_r^* - L_r(t))$ is being closed. $A(x_r)$ may refer to either the WT or the CB–sector. The estimation is characterised by significant parameters and high F-values in both cases. Hence, location attributes which favour the concentration of these two service sectors also seem to stimulate the location of jobs over time.

11.4.3 Relative Shares of Sectoral Employment in A-regions

Table 11.10 describes how the share of total employment has developed during the 25 year long period 1965-1990 for clusters of Swedish A-regions. The table reveals large discrepancies between different parts of the country and between types of regions. Before we assess the processes behind the observed pattern, we recall that an A-region is a group of municipalities which forms an integrated labour market, so that we do not have to distinguish between where a person resides and works.

The patterns of change in the table refer to the processes analysed in Sections 11.4.1 and 11.4.2. As can be seen, the overall increase of total employment is without comparison largest in those regions with a university. Second in the hierarchy we find the middle sized primary centres, often hosting a regional university college, while regional centres have lost in relative terms in all parts of Sweden.

The preceding sections describe location attributes in municipalities which have functioned as location attractors during the 1980s. In general we find high values of such location attributes in regions with a university. However, we can shed some further light on the associated process of location changes by presenting results from a study by Wigren (1995), which relies on a subdivision of the economy into 19 sectors and observations during the 25 year period, 1965-1990.

Table 11.10 Changing shares of total employment 1965-1990. Percent.

REGIONS	TOTAL	UNIVERSITY REGIONS	PRIMARY CENTRES	REGIONAL CENTRES
Upper Norrland	+5.9	+23.1	+3.0	-14.7
Middle Norrland	-9.0		-1.0	-21.9
Northern Mid-Sweden	-9.6		-2.5	-17.4
Eastern Mid-Sweden	+5.7	+20.9	-2.9	-13.4
Stockholm		+12.9		
Småland + Islands	-3.6		+1.3	-8.1
Southern Sweden	-4.5	+2.1	-6.1	-13.3
Western Sweden	+0.9	+9.7	-8.2	-0.5

Remark: Malmö-Lund and Göteborg are the university regions of southern and western Sweden, respectively.
Source: Wigren (1995).

Wigren's empirical approach is based on the framework outlined in Figure 11.1. Regional efficiency is treated as a relative or comparative phenomenon by using the relative share, l_{rj}, of each region r's employment in every sector j as a central variable, such that

$$l_{rj} = L_{rj} / L_j \qquad (26)$$

where L_{rj} denotes the employment in sector j and region r and L_j denotes the employment in sector j in the whole country. As the dependent variable in his regression equations Wigren introduces the change, $\delta_{rj} = \Delta l_{rj} / l_{rj}$. The regression equation may be summarised as follows:

$$\delta_{rj} = H(x_r, s_{rj}, \varepsilon_{rj}) \qquad (27)$$

where the vector x_r denotes location attributes (characteristics of the regional milieu), the vector s_{rj} denotes sector j's initial competitive power in region r and contains variables describing the relative size of various sectors including the i-th sector, and where ε_{rj} is a random error term. For different sectors the x_r-vector comprises variables reflecting (i) accessibility, (ii) the type of region, and (iii) the size of regional public support sectors. These variables are presented briefly in Table 11.11.

The x_r-vector contains 7 accessibility variables and 8 variables classifying the type of region. The competitive power of a sector in a region is reflected by 4 variables. Of the 19 sectors initially studied, Wigren excludes 3, i.e., agriculture, forestry and mining.

According to the regression analysis, the size of a region and its density has had a significant influence on the change pattern of 11 sectors. No influence can be verified for public administration, education and research, and health care.

As many as 6 of the 16 sectors studied seem to develop invariantly with respect to the region's accessibility, while the change process of all national sectors such as manufacturing, wholesaling, hotels and restaurants, banking and insurance, and consulting activities are statistically affected by the region's accessibility features.

Referring to the 16 sectors included in the regression analysis, a high relative concentration of sector i is negatively correlated with the growth of the δ_{rj}-variable as regards 15 sectors. The only exception is retail trade.

Table 11.11 Variables characterising the regional milieu

ACCESSIBILITY	TYPE OF REGION	REGIONAL SUPPORT
Travel time to Stockholm	The region's share of Sweden's total population	High relative concentration of education and research
Changed travel time to Stockholm between 1965 and 1985	The region's share of urban population	High relative concentration of energy, culture and public administration
Regions adjacent to Stockholm	The share of the region's population living in its largest urban node	High relative concentration of regional commercial employment
Travel time to the closest metropolitan region	The region's share of persons below 15 and above 65 years of age, respectively	High relative concentration of public production (adminstration, health care and education)
Regions adjacent to a metropolitan region	Metropolitan region	
Peripheral regions	University region	
Accessibiity to regional income concentrations	Primary centre	
	Regional centre	

Remark: Relative concentration of a sector denotes for a region the employment share of the sector divided by the sector's employment share in the whole country.

11.5   THEORY IMPLICATIONS

This chapter introduces the concept of a production milieu which is comprised of the attributes of a region which affect the production possibilities and the efficiency of firms; the attributes adjust on a slow time scale, and are not controlled by individual firms; there are no direct charges for them. The Swedish studies surveyed in this chapter show that one can identify a set of variables which reflect such location attributes both for municipalities and for groups of municipalities forming an integrated labour market (A-region).

The survey includes studies which demonstrate, for given points in time, a correlation between productivity differentials and location attributes. Other studies show that differences as regards economic development in regions are associated with the varying size and composition of the location attributes among the regions.

Although the modern network economy contains activities which have a low distance friction in certain respects, it is still true that economic activities in general occur in local and regional environments which influence the efficiency of production and transaction efforts. A conclusion from the Swedish studies presented in this chapter is that models of economic growth and development should distinguish between coupled time scales according to the suggestions in Section 11.2. This conclusion refers to both pure theory and the design of econometric models. A further implication is that for many research issues the borders of the regional milieu are more relevant for delineating an economy than the national borders.

Our second theory consideration concerns the modelling strategy as regards aggregation. Different location attributes in two regions imply that they will have different specialisation opportunities and may experience disparate product cycles. Hence, even if the two regions have a similar sector composition at a certain level of aggregation, a further disaggregation may reveal that productivity and growth differentials are explained by unequal opportunities for fostering expanding economic activities. We may then apply the same production function to the two regions and use a location attribute vector to explain their different performance. However, a more precise microeconomic approach would be to identify each region's product mix (activity composition) in detail and to use the location attribute vector to explain why specific activities are more profitable and expansive in one of the regions.

REFERENCES

Andersson, Å.E., 1970, "Storstadsproblematiken" (The Metropolis Problem), Särtryck ur *SOU 1970:15*, Allmänna förlaget, Stockholm.

Andersson, Å.E., 1985, *Kreativitet: Storstadens framtid* (Creativity: The Future of the Metropolis), Prisma, Stockholm.

Andersson, Å.E., C. Anderstig and B. Hårsman, 1990, "Knowledge and Communication Infrastructure and Regional Economic Change", *Regional Science and Urban Economics*, 20:359-376.

Andersson, Å. E. and B. Johansson, 1984, "Knowledge Intensity and Product Cycles in Metropolitan Regions", WP-84-13, IIASA, Laxenburg, Austria.

Appendix 5 of LU95, 1994, Sveriges ekonomiska geografi (The Economic Geography of Sweden), Bilaga 5 till LU95, Finansdepartmentet, Fritzes offentliga publikationer, Stockholm.

Beckmann, M. and J.-F. Thisse, 1986, "The Location of Production Activities", in P. Nijkamp (ed.), *Handbook of Regional and Urban Economics vol I*, North-Holland, Amsterdam.

Beckmann, M. and T. Puu, 1985, *Spatial Economics: Density, Potential and Flow*, North-Holland, Amsterdam.

Cheshire, P.C. and D.G. Hay, 1989, *Urban Problems in Western Europe*, Unwin Hyman, London.

Forslund, U.M. and B. Johansson, 1995, "Assessing Road Investments: Accessibility Changes, Cost Benefit and Production Effects", *The Annals of Regional Science*, 29:155-174.

Gabszewicz, J.J. and J.-F. Thisse, 1986, "Spatial Competition and the Location of Firms", in R. Arnott (ed.), *Location Theory*, Harwood Academic Publishers, Chur.

Haken, H., 1983. *Advanced Synergetics*, Springer-Verlag, Berlin.

Hirsch, S., 1967, *Location of Industry and International Competitiveness*, Oxford University Press, Oxford.

Holmberg, I. and B. Johansson, 1992, "Growth of Production, Migration of Jobs and Spatial Infrastructure", Arbetsrapport 1992-6, Regional Planning, The Royal Institute of Technology, Stockholm.

Holmberg, I. and U. Strömqvist, 1988, "LOSE – Länstrafik och samhällsekonomi" (Economic Assessment of Public Transport in Counties) bil.3 Transportforskningsberedningen, Stockholm.

Hägerstrand, T., 1970, "Tidsanvändning och omgivningsstruktur" (The Allocation of Time and Local Environment), *Bilaga 4 i SOU 1970:14*, Allmänna Förlaget, Stockholm.

Johansson B., 1989, "Economic Development and Networks for Spatial Interaction", CWP-1989:28, CERUM, University of Umeå.

Johansson, B., 1991, "Economic Networks and Self-Organisation", in E.M. Bergman, G. Maier and F. Tödtling (eds.), *Regions Reconsidered – Economic Networks, Innovation and Local Development in Industrialized Countries*, Mansell, London.

Johansson, B., 1993a, "Infrastructure, Accessibility and Economic Growth", *International Journal of Transport Economics*, Vol. XX, 2:131-156.

Johansson, B., 1993b, "Economic Evolution and Urban Infrastructure Dynamics", in Å.E. Andersson, D.F. Batten, K. Kobayashi and K. Yoshikawa (eds.), *The Cosmo-Creative Society*, Springer-Verlag, Berlin.

Johansson, B., A. Anderstig, I. Holmberg and U. Strömqvist, 1991, "Infrastruktur och produktivitet" (Infrastructure and Productivity), *Expertutredning Nr 9 till Produktivitetsdelegationen*, Allmänna Förlaget, Stockholm.

Johansson, B. and U. Strömqvist, 1981, "Regional Rigidities in the Process of Economic Structural Development", *Regional Science and Urban Economics*, 11:363-375.

Johansson, B. and L. Westin, 1987, "Technical Change, Location and Trade", *Papers of the Regional Science Association*, 62:13-25.

Krugman, P., 1991, *Geography and Trade,* Leuven University Press, Leuven.

Lundqvist, L., 1981, "A Dynamic Multiregional Input-Output Model for Analyzing Regional Development, Employment and Energy Use", TRITA-MAT-1980-20, The Royal Institute of Technology, Stockholm.

Marshall, A., 1920, *Principles of Economics*, Macmillan, London.

Mills, E. and G. Carlino, 1989, "Dynamics of County Growth", in Å.E. Andersson, D.F. Batten, B. Johansson and P. Nijkamp (eds.), *Advances in Spatial Theory and Dynamics*, North-Holland, Amsterdam.

Rietveld, P., 1989, "Infrastructure and Regional Development", *Annals of Regional Science*, 23:255-274

Rodwin, J. and H. Sazanami, 1991, *Industrial Change and Regional Economic Transformation*, Harper Collins Academic, London.

Samuelson, P., 1947, *Foundations of Economic Analysis*, Harvard University Press, Cambridge, Mass.

Samuelson, P., 1952, "Spatial Price Equilibrium and Linear Programming", *American Economic Review*, 42:283-303.

Seitz, H., 1993, A Dual Economic Analysis of the Benefits of the Public Road Network, *Annals of Regional Science*, 27:223-239.

Snickars, F. and A. Granholm, 1981, "A Multiregional Planning and Forecasting Model with Special Regard to the Public Sector", *Regional Science and Urban Economics*, 11:377-404.

SOU 1970;15, 1970, See Andersson (1970)

Takayama, T. and G.G. Judge, 1964, "Equilibrium among Spatially Separated Markets: A Reformulation", *Econometrica*, 32:510-524.

Takayama, T. and G.G. Judge, GG, 1971, *Spatial and Temporal Price and Allocation Models*, North-Holland, Amsterdam.

Westin, L. 1990, *Vintage Models of Spatial Structural Change*, Umeå Economic Studies, No. 227, Umeå university.

Wigren R., 1976, "Analys av regionala effektivitetsskillnader inom industribranscher. En teori med tillämpning på svenska förhållanden". (Analysis of Regional Efficiency Differentials within Industrial Sectors), Memorandum 58, Dept. of Economics, University of Gothenburg.

Wigren, R., 1984, "Measuring Regional Efficiency – A Method Tested on Fabricated Metal Products in Sweden 1973-75", *Regional Science and Urban Economics*, 14:363-379.

Wigren R., 1985, "Productivity and Infrastructure: An Empirical Study of Swedish Manufacturing Industries and their Dependence on the Regional Production Milieu", in F. Snickars, B. Johansson and T.R. Lakshmanan (eds.), *Economic Faces of the*

Building Sector, Document D20:1985, Swedish Council for Building Research, Stockholm.

Wigren, R., 1995, "Trender och trendbrott – Sysselsättningen 1965-2015 i Gävle/Sandvikens A-region" (Trends and Switching Trends – Employment Patterns in the Labour Market Region Gävle/Sandviken), mimeo, Dept of Housing Research, University of Uppsala.

Åberg, Y., 1973, "Regional Productivity Differences in Swedish Manufacturing", *Regional and Urban Economics,* 3:131-156.

Åberg, Y., 1974, "Regionala produktivitetsskillnader" (Regional Productivity Differentials), *Bil 9 till SOU 1974:3,* Allmänna Förlaget, Stockholm.

CHAPTER 12

A Review of Infrastructure's Impact on Economic Development

Christine Kessides

The World Bank, Washington, D.C.

12.1 INTRODUCTION

This chapter summarizes some of the economic benefits from infrastructure in the context of developing countries, and considers the necessary conditions for these benefits to be realized. Infrastructure is defined here as the long-lived engineered structures, equipment, and facilities, and the services they provide, that are used both in economic production and by households. This grouping of "economic" infrastructure comprises public utilities (electric power, piped gas and heating, telecommunications, water supply, liquid and solid waste disposal), public works (major dam and canal works for irrigation, as well as roads), and other transport sectors (railways, urban transport, ports and waterways, and airports).

Infrastructure's linkages to an economy are multiple and complex, because it affects production and consumption directly, creates many positive and negative externalities, and involves large flows of expenditure. The sections below provide evidence to illustrate the main theme of this chapter – the notion that the flow of infrastructure services is the main measure of economic benefits from these sectors, and that an efficient allocation of resources in this area should be in response to the effective demand for services. Although private markets must therefore be relied upon to a greater extent to achieve this allocation, government will need to retain a role in managing these markets and ensuring, especially through interventions in investment planning, regulation, and financing, that major development goals of efficient growth, equity, environmental sustainability and macroeconomic stability are served.

12.2 INFRASTRUCTURE'S IMPACT ON ECONOMIC DEVELOPMENT - AN OVERVIEW

Infrastructure contributes to economic development both by increasing productivity and by providing amenities that enhance the quality of life. The services generated by infrastructure investment lead to growth in the production *of firms* in two ways:
(i) infrastructure services are *intermediate inputs* to production, and any reduction in these input costs raises the profitability of production, permitting higher levels of output, income, and/or employment;

(ii)   infrastructure services *raise the productivity of other factors* (labor and other capital)
       – for example, by permitting the transition from manual to electrical machinery,
       reducing workers' commuting time, and improving information flows through
       electronic data exchange. Infrastructure is thereby often described as an "unpaid
       factor of production", since its availability leads to higher returns obtainable for
       other capital and labor. The existence of infrastructure in a given location may attract
       flows of additional resources ("crowding-in" private investment); this can lead to
       reduced factor costs and transaction costs at that site. The resulting economies of
       agglomeration are the great advantage of urbanization. However, when the available
       infrastructure becomes congested or begins to create a predominantly negative
       impact on the environment, the quality of services declines and their contribution to
       productivity suffers.

Both effects contribute to economic growth by stimulating aggregate supply as well as
demand.

The consumption of infrastructure services *by households* contributes to economic
welfare because many of these services, notably clean water and sanitation, create
environmental amenities, while others (recreational transport, residential telecommunications) are valued items of consumption in their own right . Also, these services provide
access to jobs and other consumption opportunities, and promote the health of
individuals. Thus, reductions in the cost and improvements in the quality of infrastructure
services to households can have the beneficial effects of increasing their real income and
consumption, raising the productivity of their labor, and freeing time of individuals for
higher-value activities – analogously to the benefits realized by firms.

It is worth emphasizing that *all of the above contributions of infrastructure to
economic growth and the quality of life, which are long recognized in economic theory,
derive not from the mere existence or creation of the physical facilities but from their
efficient operation and the value that users perceive from the services generated.*

Much of the literature on infrastructure's macroeconomic impact (defined here as
based on industry-wide as well as nation-wide data) was generated in the 1980s with
respect to developed countries. Much of this literature seeks to capture infrastructure's
direct and indirect (externality) effects by observing the relationship between public
capital expenditure (as a proxy for increases in the stock of infrastructure), or a measure
of physical capital stocks, and some measure of growth in aggregate output or
productivity. Among the most provocative of these studies are those by Aschauer (1989)
and Canning and Fay (1993). Munnell (1992) provides a review of mainly U.S.
literature, and Rietveld (1989) surveys more European studies of infrastructure's impacts
on regional development. Many of the findings reported in these studies have
demonstrated correlations, but the range of results is large and thus, conclusions are far
from robust. The main shortcomings of much of this research are the following:

(i)   simultaneity of effects is not accounted for adequately (economic growth can lead to
       investment in infrastructure as well as result from it), and therefore causality cannot
       be inferred from time series correlations;

(ii)   even where efforts are made to identify the direction of causality, the results are still
       often inconclusive because of other econometric issues (such as the possible
       omission of variables that might explain both output and infrastructure growth, and
       poor model specification - for example, the effect of private investment in
       infrastructure is not always accounted for).

(iii) the variables used (e.g., public capital expenditure, or the level of physical
       infrastructure stocks) are often too aggregated to be meaningful for policy
       conclusions. Most of the studies do not differentiate among quality, location and
       composition of infrastructure, or among levels of the stock (e.g., expenditure to
       expand a sparse network versus improvement of quality or decongestion of a mature
       network). Blum (1982) and Andersson et al. (1990) do examine the issue of
       infrastructure bottlenecks in studies of Germany and Sweden, respectively.

(iv) finally, most of the available research does not examine the efficiency of utilization of the infrastructure, that is, the flow of services actually generated from the investment orponditure.

A more revealing line of research has examined the effects of differences in the stocks of public capital across regions or sectors of individual countries, while controlling for other factors potentially affecting differences in productivity. These studies have produced considerable variation in their specific findings, for example, regarding the elasticities of output with respect to different factors (public capital, private capital, and labor), and the complementarity or substitutability among these factors. Most of these studies are not exactly comparable either in the type of economy studied (developed or developing), in definitions of the dependent variable (aggregate or sectoral production, or private investment), or in definitions of the variable representing infrastructure. However, overall it can be said that most studies find a positive and significant effect of public capital on output (both variously defined).

Among the interregional studies in the U.S., those best represented by Hulten and Schwab (1991) indicate that infrastructure capital acts as an "unpaid" factor of production by raising the returns to private capital in a given area, which then stimulates an inflow of capital and labor. Interregional differences in the growth of manufacturing are then found to be related mainly to differential growth rates of labor and capital.

A well-designed study of India by Binswanger et al. (1989) has found that a large part of the inter-district differences in infrastructure capital (roads, electricity, canal irrigation) is explained by the observable agro-climatic differences between districts – thus showing that infrastructure cannot be treated as an exogenous variable. Once these agro-climatic differences are accounted for, it is found that certain types of infrastructure have significant effects on only certain output variables. One conclusion reached is that roads, for example, have less impact on private investment directly than on promoting marketing opportunities and reducing transactions costs generally in the local economy.

Among other research which distinguishes among regions of different economic performance, there is evidence from studies on Mexico (Looney and Frederiksen, 1981), Japan (Mera, 1973) and the U.S. (Eberts, 1986) that the effect of public capital appears stronger in the more developed or rapidly growing regions, compared to those that are lagging or declining.

In summary, most of the formal empirical research supports the broad conclusion that infrastructure capital is important in economic growth or productivity. However, there is need for a more refined theoretical understanding of the mechanisms of this linkage, and for empirical studies of microeconomic data which capture the effects of particular kinds of infrastructure services on various activities of firms and households. Some findings from these types of studies are briefly discussed in the next section.

There is also a set of important economic effects which do occur specifically from the *flows of expenditure on investment,* as opposed to the *operation or generation of services* from infrastructure. The *first* is the multiplier effect of the expenditure on wages and other inputs used in the construction of physical infrastructure facilities, and the derived demand thus generated for the output of other sectors. Under certain conditions (such as where labor markets are rigid), the demand generated by infrastructure investment may "crowd out" private investment by bidding up the cost of labor and other inputs. The *second* linkage to investment concerns the way in which the expenditure is financed. Infrastructure investment affects the availability of financial capital for other uses; it may also affect fiscal balance and external creditworthiness, and therefore macroeconomic stability. The potential of infrastructure investment to raise the cost of capital is described as financial "crowding-out". It should be noted that both the multiplier effect and financial crowding-out may apply to government expenditure on any sector, and not only infrastructure; moreover, crowding-out is not limited to investment, and could also occur to the extent that operation and maintenance (O&M) are financed by taxation (budgetary subsidies) or borrowing rather than revenues from the services generated. These effects of infrastructure expenditure are also briefly illustrated in the section below.

12.3   THE NATURE OF INFRASTRUCTURE'S EFFECTS ON ECONOMIC DEVELOPMENT: LESSONS OF EXPERIENCE

This section illustrates and analyzes the various effects outlined above through reference to both formal and informal research and country studies. None of the individual evidence discussed here is generalizable to all circumstances, but taken as a whole it portrays a fairly clear picture of the factors which matter most in determining the economic impact of infrastructure.

12.3.1 Contributions to Growth Through Reductions in Costs

(i)   Effects on Production, Investment and Employment

If enterprises are unable to realize the benefit of efficient generation of infrastructure services, either because the services are absolutely unavailable or provided so unreliably as to be virtually unavailable, the firm is forced to seek higher cost alternatives which may have unfavorable impacts on profits and level of production achieved. The economic costs of infrastructure unreliability (e.g., power outages, call interruptions, erratic water pressure, poor road passability) are multiple. They include, first of all, the direct costs of production delays, loss of perishable raw materials or outputs, and damage to sensitive electronic equipment. In their totality, these costs lead to underutilization of existing productive capacity, and constrain short-run productive efficiency and output growth. Secondly, unreliability or lack of access to infrastructure services requires users to invest in alternative sources, thus raising their capital costs. Third, the resulting higher costs and disruptions of output have ripple effects on other sectors, creating bottlenecks and slack capacity utilization elsewhere in the economy.

A 1987 study of primarily the first of these multiple effects of power outages in Pakistan estimated that the direct costs of load shedding to industry during a year, coupled with the indirect multiplier effects on other sectors, implied an 1.8 percent reduction in GDP and a 4.2 percent reduction in the volume of manufactured exports. In India, a 1985 study concluded that power shortages were a major factor in low capacity utilization in industry, and estimated the total production losses in 1983-84 at 1.5 percent of GDP. Neither of these studies estimated the value of foregone infrastructure services to commercial or residential users, nor the dynamic long-term costs, for example of delays in application of new technology which depends on reliable power (USAID, 1988). Bottlenecks of rail transport capacity, leading to shortages of coal deliveries to power plants, were estimated to result in a loss of GNP of one percent in China in 1989.

Problems with undermaintenance of facilities and poor service quality shift the burden of infrastructure provision and often increase the overall costs of production by firms. A survey of 179 manufacturing establishments in Nigeria has documented the costs of unreliable infrastructure for firms of different sizes, as well as the costs of their investments in alternative sources. The study found that because of the pervasive failures of publicly-provided infrastructure, 92 percent of the firms surveyed owned electricity generators. The impact of infrastructure deficiencies of all types was consistently higher for the small firms. Private infrastructure provision (for generators, boreholes, vehicles for personnel and freight transport, and radio communications equipment) constituted 15 percent of total machinery and equipment costs for large firms (over 50 employees), but 25 percent for small firms. Small firms were found to generate a larger percentage of their power needs privately than did larger firms, and to pay a higher premium for doing so, as measured by the excess costs of privately-generated power over that publicly provided (Lee and Anas, 1992). A similar survey in Indonesia found likewise that manufacturers relied heavily on own investment in power generators and boreholes, with the smaller firms facing higher unit costs for privately-provided power than the large firms (Lee et al., 1993).

Studies in several Latin American countries, including Chile and Costa Rica, have concluded that each dollar not spent on needed road maintenance can increase vehicle operating costs by three dollars, and lead to an additional $2-3 dollars for premature reconstruction. These incremental (preventable) capital expenditures amount to 1-4 percent of GDP. Moreover, two-thirds of the additional vehicle operating costs are in foreign exchange and represent a substantial drain on this scarce resource. In the water sector, various studies have documented the considerable private investment incurred to compensate for an unreliable public supply. In Lima, Peru, households have been investing in pumping and water storage facilities at costs 40-80 times higher than those of the public utility. And in Tegucigalpa, Honduras, the amount invested by households in such systems is comparable to what it would have cost to double the city water supply from deep wells (Gyamfi et al., 1992). This is truly "demand-driven" infrastructure development with an admirable degree of private resource mobilization, but it may not represent efficient use of capital resources for the sector overall, and is particularly burdensome to the poor.

The finding that self-provision of infrastructure poses a particularly heavy cost to small firms could also have major implications for the growth of industries and the generation of employment. New firms tend to start up near urban centers with easy access to good utilities and relocate to peripheral areas as they expand production. Small companies generate between 60 to 80 percent of the new jobs created in large cities in Asia and Latin America (Lee, 1989), and much of the supply response to structural adjustment in many countries and systemic reform in former socialist countries is expected to come from the small/medium-scale enterprise sector.

(ii)   Impact on International Competitiveness

Inadequate and unreliable infrastructure cripples the ability of countries to engage in international trade, even of traditional export commodities. The fight for *new* export markets is even more dependent on infrastructure. In the last two decades, the globalization and intensified competition in world trade has resulted not only from the liberalization of trade policies in many countries, but also from major advances in communication, transport, and storage technologies. These developments have transformed the traditional organization of production and marketing to focus on the management of *logistics*[1] to achieve cost savings in inventory and working capital and permit rapid response to changing consumer demands. During the 1980s, order cycle times in the OECD countries have been reduced by up to 80 percent; more than 60 percent of production and sales in these markets are now processed directly to order, and "just in time" (JIT) delivery to customers is projected to increase continuously. About one-quarter of logistics costs in industry are due to transport. Virtually all the improved practices reducing logistics costs have been based in some way on information technologies using telecommunications infrastructure. Trade and industry managers in OECD countries report that a one percent reduction in logistics costs is equivalent for them to a ten percent increase in annual sales (Peters, 1992).

---

[1] Logistics may be defined as the "orchestration of purchasing, production, and marketing functions in order to obtain the least cost combination of all activities involved in these processes, while maintaining a high level of customer service" (Peters, 1992).

The exigencies of modern logistics management in developed industrial countries pose similar requirements for developing countries wishing to compete in these markets. The share of manufactured exports directed to OECD countries has increased significantly for both low- and middle-income developing countries during the past two decades. Global sourcing has created interwoven networks of international trading and industrial relations, in which businesses in several countries produce different goods and services components of the same final product. The ability of developing countries to provide the transport and communications services essential for modern logistics management will increasingly determine their ability to compete for export markets and direct foreign investment. Although provision of infrastructure is clearly not a sufficient condition for attracting private investment to a given location, differences in the quality of infrastructure can be an important factor at the margin in determining the choices among potential sites (Wheeler and Mody, 1992).

(iii)   Impact on Domestic Market Development

Various research studies in developing countries have concluded that rural (farm to market) roads have a major effect in improving marketing opportunities and reducing transaction costs. The marketing of agricultural commodities, excluding the stages of processing, can account for 25-60 percent of final prices for foodstuffs in developing countries, with about half of the marketing costs attributable to transport (Beenhakker, 1987). Adequate road infrastructure in rural areas could both raise farmers' incomes and lower the prices of food to urban consumers. This outcome would be more likely to occur as improved transport facilitates the adoption of productivity-enhancing technology on farms (see below), reduces transport costs, and makes markets more competitive by increasing access to market information.

12.3.2 Contributions to Growth Through Structural Change

(i)   Economic Diversification

Infrastructure has direct effects on production costs and profitability of agriculture which are similar to those for industry discussed earlier, and also create profound structural changes on the rural economy. These latter changes have been found in various studies to affect income levels, the availability of alternative sources of income, the composition of consumption, and the health of the population. Research studies of the impact of infrastructure (irrigation and roads) on rural villages find that it has both direct and indirect effects: by raising the demand for labor both on the farm, as well as in nonfarm activities (for India – Lanjouw and Stern, 1993, and Epstein, 1962 and 1973; for Colombia – van Raalte, cited in Evans, 1990). Improved rural transport can also ease the introduction of improved farming practices by lowering the costs of modern inputs such as fertilizer, as shown by Ahmed and Hossain (1990) in Bangladesh.

(ii)   Impact on Technological Innovation

In a fundamental sense, and today more than ever before, infrastructure provides the key to modern technology in practically all sectors. The changes in markets and production brought about by the railroad and electric power in the past are significant enough, but are dwarfed by the "information revolution" of recent decades which is based on telecommunications. Electronic information systems (informatics) using the technology and services of telecommunications underlie a very large share of production and distribution activities in secondary and tertiary sectors of the modern economy, including banking, government, and culture.

(iii)   Impacts on Structure of Production and Consumption

Infrastructure is central to the basic patterns of demand and supply, and to the economy's ability to respond to changes in prices or endowments of other resources. In the United States, for example, it is observed that the expansion of service, high technology, and financial sectors relative to manufacturing and goods-producing industries increases the demand for telecommunications, but decreases the relative requirements for transportation of manufacturing inputs and outputs, and infrastructure for industrial waste disposal (U.S. Department of Commerce, 1987). In many other countries – including most strikingly those in Europe and Asia which are shifting from socialist to market principles – infrastructure will have to undergo fundamental changes to serve the economy-wide restructuring of demand and supply.

12.3.3 Impacts of Infrastructure on Personal Welfare

Infrastructure relates to personal welfare (and to poverty) in three broad respects: first, infrastructure services have a basic consumption value; second, they affect labor productivity and access to employment, and thus the capacity to earn future income; and third, infrastructure affects real wealth. The main focus here is on the implications of inadequate or low quality infrastructure services for the reduction of welfare and persistence of poverty.

(i)   Infrastructure's Value in Household Consumption

The availability of services such as clean water and sanitation, transport, power and communications is itself a measure of welfare; in this sense, individuals *are* poor because (insofar as) they do not have access to services of the necessary quality. In India, over 1981-91, the population living in slums (settlements lacking basic infrastructure) grew, even while poverty fell as measured by indicators of income and food consumption. Thus, the dimensions of poverty and likewise, the policies needed to address it, are changing in developing countries and infrastructure is becoming a central poverty issue.

Besides their direct value in the "consumption basket" of households, infrastructure services provide a means to acquiring other goods and services. In addition, the price of infrastructure services relative to other items affects the level of overall consumption which households can achieve within a given budget constraint.

The value to households of any infrastructure can be inferred from information on willingness to pay, allocation of income, and allocation of time. Numerous studies of informal sector water vending in developing countries (e.g., Ghana and Nigeria) reveal that the population not serviced by the municipal system purchase water from private vendors at prices that can be 20 times those of the public utility (Whittington et al., 1991 and 1992; World Bank Water Demand Research Team, 1993). In some cases, poor households spend up to 20 percent of their income on water. Other research conducted in rural Pakistan found that women who had access to an improved water supply spent 70-80 percent less time collecting water than those without (Read and Kudat, 1992). This extra time saved was spent mainly on income-generating or domestic activities.

Recent research on households' responses to the unreliability of public water supply in Istanbul (Turkey), Faisalabad (Pakistan), and Jamshedpur (India) reveals the range of alternatives used to meet the need for water in the face of an unreliable public supply.

This research shows that households incur high costs of coping with unreliability. Lower income households (and households headed by women) have fewer options to deal with unreliability, and pay higher portions of their income to cope, than higher income groups.

In all three cities, households used multiple sources of water, but the access to a source increases with income – so that poorer households bear a disproportionate burden of deficient infrastructure. In Istanbul, the poorest households surveyed spend a larger share of their income (about 5 percent) to supplement inadequate water supply than do wealthier ones (which spend about 1 percent). These expenditures on informal sources (wells and storage facilities) are in addition to the user charges for publicly-supplied water, which amount to 1-2 percent of annual income. Despite the existence of a piped water system in Jamshedpur, at least 17 percent of the population meets 90 percent of its water needs from wells and handpumps. Over and above the monetary costs that consumers bear, households in Jamshedpur spend on average two hours per day fetching and storing water. *The burden of these activities falls in nearly all cases on women.* The pattern of private augmentation of the public water supply at substantial private costs to consumers is observed also in Faisalabad, Pakistan. Less than 20 percent of the households which have piped water use this source exclusively - 70 percent have motor pumps and 14 percent have hand pumps (Bell et al., forthcoming; Humplick et al., 1993).

The benefits of improved transport facilities include personal mobility and the access it provides to other goods and services, including education and health care. Recent research in Sub-Saharan Africa documents the extensive practice of "headloading" of firewood, water, and crops due to the absence of road infrastructure for motor vehicles and of intermediate means of transport such as carts and bicycles (Riverson and Carapetis, 1991). Thus, where the poor have little access to modes of transport other than walking, they have to forego time which could be spent on activities with higher utility to them. When distortions in urban housing markets require the poor to be concentrated on the periphery, as in many developing countries, the costs and availability of public transportation become critical factors in determining their ability to search for, and retain, employment and to maintain adequate levels of household consumption. As noted earlier, inadequate transport and communications impede the efficient functioning of markets, and thus have highly unfavorable impacts on prices faced by the poor either as producers or as consumers.

(ii)   Infrastructure and Labor Productivity

Whether households *remain* poor can depend on the availability of employment – which is affected by infrastructure through the costs of job creation, job search, and commuting – and on the productivity of labor. Part of the link to labor productivity is seen through infrastructure's role in raising the returns to the "paid" factors of production as indicated earlier. Infrastructure also has an impact on personal health, and thereby on the individual's capacity to work as well as his or her quality of life.

A large body of research has documented that improvements in water supply and sanitation have a large measured impact in reducing morbidity from major water-borne diseases (ranging from 25-78 percent), reducing child mortality, and reducing the severity of disease when it occurs (Esrey et al., 1990). However, the health benefits are not assured merely by access to the physical infrastructure for water supply. Adequate sanitation is critical to the reduction in incidence and severity of diseases, and thus planning for both water supply and sanitation needs to be better integrated. Moreover, the research has found that a sufficient minimum per capita quantity of water, as well as consistent and reliable operation of the facilities are necessary to obtain the health benefits – for example, they must not fail during seasonal transmission periods of the diseases.

(iii)   Infrastructure and Wealth

Since investments in infrastructure are most often fixed in place, they affect land values and consequently wealth. The irrigation and drainage sector is an obvious example of the implication for poverty. In many countries (e.g., Nepal), publicly financed-investments in land improvement benefit most directly the wealthier farmers who own or use this land, often without paying for the services. In urban areas, water and sanitation infrastructure, access to roads and public transit routes, and connection to power and telephone lines can have a major impact on real estate values. In Karachi, Pakistan, researchers found that the provision of infrastructure doubles land values after controlling for the distance of plots from the city center (Dowall, 1991).

12.3.4 Impacts of Infrastructure on the Environment

Infrastructure's linkages to the environment, as to poverty, are felt both through its effects on the quality of life and on economic productivity. These effects may be positive as well as negative, depending on the nature of each infrastructural development and what the alternatives are. While there may be trade-offs between the economic benefits and the environmental impacts involved in particular cases, there is a wide scope for "win-win" strategies through which both the infrastructure services and environmental quality can be enhanced.

Negative environmental impacts often result, or become more serious, from a failure to take account of interdependencies among infrastructure sectors. For example, underinvestment in sewerage relative to water supply in many places has led to harmful contamination of water reserves, exacerbated flooding, and reduced the health benefits from water investments alone. Poor management of solid waste complicates wastewater disposal and urban street drainage. The lack of safe water requires users to boil contaminated supplies, with a considerable cost in energy – in Jakarta, energy consumption for this purpose is estimated to amount to one percent of the city's GDP (World Bank, 1992b). The inefficient burning of biomass fuel (plant and animal waste) for household energy contributes to erosion and loss of soil nutrients. In many countries, overuse of water for irrigation has damaged soils and severely constrained its use for urban areas, where it would have higher economic returns and more positive environmental effects. Finally, the dearth of telephone connections in many cities requires businesses and individuals to increase their use of transport facilities – with the consequent traffic-related air and noise pollution – for necessary communications. There are also many positive opportunities for synergism among activities in infrastructure and other sectors to increase both environmental and economic benefits (Kalbermatten and Middleton, 1992). For example, many countries, such Egypt, India, and Indonesia are experimenting with the conversion of organic solid waste materials into commercially usable compost as part of a municipal program of solid waste management to reduce the need for landfills and incinerators.

Much has been learned about assessing the potential harmful environmental effects of infrastructure activities such as power generation and road construction, and about ways of mitigating such effects as ozone depletion, soil erosion, deforestation, and other issues of the "green agenda". The environmental problems within urban areas (the "brown agenda") have even more immediate and serious implications for health and productivity, particularly for the poor. These issues include the lack of safe water supply, sanitation and drainage; inadequate solid and hazardous waste management; uncontrolled emissions from cars and low-grade domestic fuels; accidents linked to transport congestion and crowding; and the occupation and degradation of environmentally-fragile or hazard-prone land. Addressing issues of the urban environmental agenda requires, in part, improved infrastructure and better infrastructure services such as through substitution of "dirty" fuels for cleaner-burning power generation, safe water supplies and sanitation systems, and support for public transport, low-polluting transport modes, and traffic management. In most countries, better maintenance of facilities is also a strategy with clear environmental benefits: in the power sector, for example, inadequate maintenance leads to inefficient thermal generation which accounts for a substantial share of energy-related pollution; likewise, inadequate upkeep of water and sewerage lines results in contamination of water supplies. Environmentally-sound practices can also be introduced in the management of existing infrastructure, for example, by appropriate disposal of wastes from port dredging and railway maintenance workshops.

12.3.5 Infrastructure and Macroeconomic Stabilization

(i)   Infrastructure Investment as a Countercyclical Tool

Investment in infrastructure creates employment in construction and generates purchasing power. This "multiplier" aspect of infrastructure is well understood by macroeconomic managers and politicians, for whom it can be a valuable counter-cyclical instrument in periods of slack demand and a magnet for political support. Some empirical work on this effect (e.g., Duffy-Deno and Eberts, 1991) suggests that the multiplier effects dampen quickly and are completely realized within the short period when investment expenditures are made. Public spending on investment in infrastructure (or other sectors) can also "crowd out" private investment, and this is most likely to occur where there are supply rigidities in the local market. As a stimulus to growth during a protracted recession, infrastructure investment requires a sustained source of financing. Many developing countries cannot rely on public deficit spending (as used prominently in the Great Depression era by the presently industrialized countries), nor substantial access to foreign savings for this purpose. It is therefore the longer-term effects of infrastructure on growth which should guide investment policy in this sector.

The experience with labor-intensive public works is important to consider in this context. Public works programs usually involve a combination of objectives including poverty alleviation, employment generation, and asset creation. The projects can have an impact on employment and incomes both during the construction stage, and from the operation of the assets. In evaluating such programs, the effects in both stages need to be considered and compared to the benefits the economy would have gained from the alternative uses of the resources (labor and capital) absorbed by the public works projects.

The quality of infrastructure created by public works programs in developing countries – and thus the longer term economic benefits to be derived from it – is varied. Many of the projects have had respectable rates of return and compare favorably to investments in other sectors. However, as a rule there is a trade-off between an emphasis on short-term benefits (through quick creation of employment and assets) and longer term benefits (through more careful project selection, creation of higher quality assets, and more emphasis on training of workers). Programs which emphasize labor intensity focus on works such as unpaved roads and often demonstrate poor project implementation. By contrast, projects which entail higher proportions of skilled labor and materials (e.g., for irrigation, land reclamation, paved roads) sometimes have higher economic returns (Burki et al., 1976; Ravaillon, 1990).

In contrast to the traditional, rural-oriented public works, many of the programs set up in the late 1980s are of a different design and focus on urban areas. In some Latin American and African countries, "social action/investment" funds have been established to support small-scale infrastructure interventions, among other compensatory measures, in the context of structural adjustment (the prototype was the "Emergency Social Fund" in Bolivia). As a similar model in Africa, a nonprofit, nongovernmental entity (the prototype is called AGETIP in Senegal) has been set up in several donor-assisted projects to contract-out small-scale public works to private sector contractors. Significantly, both types of programs derive project proposals from local communities and nongovernmental organizations in a "demand-driven" approach; both also depend on the private sector contractors to execute the works and hire the labor, and thus the nature of employment and wages provided are entirely market-determined. Although the experience of these new types of public works programs is still very limited, indications are that both models are relatively successful at developing local capacity in contracting and construction. In both project selection and implementation, the programs have been designed to maximize responsiveness to expressed needs of the community institutions and to the labor market.

The reviews of past experience with the variety of public works programs in developing countries suggests the following conclusions and lessons of interest for infrastructure policy. First, public works programs can be effective in generating significant amounts of short-term employment and income transfer where these are important policy objectives. However, the extent of their broader economic impact in terms of stimulating domestic demand in the surrounding economy, influencing structural unemployment, or increasing incomes and employment in the longer term are more questionable. Second, the infrastructure is clearly of higher quality when projects are designed and selected to produce the highest economic returns, not to maximize employment during construction. Third, the projects should be integrated into other development programs of the local area to generate the greatest benefit, and public works alone cannot be expected to create employment and income in the post-construction phase in regions which do not have development potential. Fourth, to ensure that projects meet effective demand, beneficiary communities should identify and contribute to the costs of investment as much as possible, and should take responsibility for financing operation and maintenance. User charges, where feasible, are the most efficient and equitable means of financing operations and maintenance of public works – although rarely a feature of such programs in past experience.

(ii) Budgetary Financing of Infrastructure

As suggested above, whether expenditure in this sector "crowds out" private investment is only a concern to the economy if the infrastructure involved has a lower economic productivity than alternative uses of the same resources. The attention of policy should therefore be focused on ensuring that investments in this sector respond to effective demand, preferably as expressed by users' willingness to pay.

Following this reasoning, it is not possible to determine whether the form or level of public expenditure on infrastructure is "adequate" in a given country without considering the efficiency of its allocation. Some attempts to analyze trends in public investment in infrastructure across countries reveal that this investment is a slightly higher share of GDP in low income countries (averaging 3.3 percent) than in middle income countries (averaging 4.3 percent); and that infrastructure absorbs about 20 percent of *total* investment in both groups, but a higher share of *public* investment for middle income countries (57 percent) than for the poorer countries (37 percent). The same study also shows that the composition of infrastructure stocks changes with country income level, as middle income countries tend to concentrate on accumulating more power and telecommunications capacity, while low income countries focus their infrastructure investment more on roads, irrigation and water supply (World Bank, 1994; Ingram and Fay, 1994). However, these broad trends do not suggest what is the appropriate rate or composition of infrastructure investment in any given country. There are, of course, specific cases (e.g., Cote d'Ivoire and Philippines during the 1980s) where public investment on infrastructure has borne a heavy share of fiscal adjustment, and where the effect has been not only to curb the obviously "white elephant" projects but also to defer system improvements which are essential for renewed growth.[2] As indicated below, appropriate financing policies are necessary to ensure that the infrastructure expenditures required for development do not threaten macroeconomic stability.

The existence of net transfers from government to infrastructure entities often reflects inappropriate policies on internal cost recovery and expenditure, and poor management by the entities or the government. Policy and institutional reforms aimed at making the entities more commercial and financially autonomous, including by shifting financial responsibility to the private sector, would reduce or eliminate many of these transfers. However, some of the transfers are desirable (e.g., targeted subsidies from the budget to entities which perform certain nonremunerative social services; and payments by infrastructure entities of taxes and dividends to the state for its share of ownership). For these kinds of transfers, the aim of reform would be to increase their amount or improve their structure in the interest of greater efficiency.

Net financial transfers have been calculated for a number of countries for the transport sector. An analysis for transport in fourteen countries in Latin America, Asia, Africa, and EMENA between 1982 and 1987 indicated that none of the railways delivered positive fiscal flows to the government. In only six of the countries did the aggregate results of the public transport sector show a profit. A consistent pattern in many other countries is that of net subsidies to railways and often to the airline (Heggie and Quick, 1990). In Zambia, the total cash shortfall in the transport sector in fiscal 1991 (mainly due to the airline and railway) absorbed 12 percent of the government's total current revenue (World Bank, 1994). Financing of transport was thus one of the country's main macroeconomic problems. Similar situations are seen in the power sector (World Bank, 1993b).

The heavy burden of subsidies often reflects the dominance of socio-political rather than commercial objectives in infrastructure. A comparative study of utility companies in Sub-Saharan Africa reveals that their operating losses in 1987-89 were proportional to the expressed importance of social objectives. The water/sewerage, urban transport and (to a lesser extent) electricity sectors, for which universal service is an important social value, together registered a net operating loss of 7 percent, in contrast to a net operating profit of 4 percent for telecommunications (French Ministry of Cooperation, 1991). Some subsidies can indeed be justified for certain kinds of infrastructure services, but they must be financed without creating serious fiscal imbalances and be properly targeted. Analysis of budgetary subsidies to consumers for transportation, power and heating, water and sanitation in several countries indicate that they can be unsustainably high (up to 5 percent of the government budgets in Central European countries in the late 1980s) (Holzmann, 1991). In many cases, according to studies in Bangladesh, Egypt, Poland, and Hungary, these subsidies are also highly regressive – particularly those for passenger rail transportation, utilities in subsidized housing, and irrigation. Large consumer subsidies to infrastructure divert public funds which could be used more effectively on other programs to alleviate poverty, and can discourage other suppliers from competing in the market for the same services.

The potential for some infrastructure activities, in particular telecommunications and power, to provide fiscal revenues to government is often abused when the entities lack financial and managerial autonomy from government budgets. The roads sector provides a relatively inexpensive source of revenues from vehicle-related charges, and they represent a significant share of total government tax revenues in developing countries (up to 30 percent). However, the portion of road receipts which can be considered strictly as "user charges" is much lower, typically around 10-25 percent. For roads, a recent review

---

2   A 1993 World Bank study showed that in countries that received intensive structural adjustment lending during the 1980s, central government expenditure on "economic infrastructure" (transport and communications), measured both as a share of GDP and of the total budget, declined over the decade. However, these expenditure shares fell even more sharply for the countries that did not receive adjustment lending (World Bank, 1993a).

found that user charges were adequate to cover maintenance in all but 4 of 40 countries, and total expenditures in about half of them (Heggie, 1995). However, because road user charges are not linked to maintenance expenditures, the latter remain too low in many countries. Increasing the allocation of road-related taxes to necessary maintenance, through commercialized management of roads, is an important issue for improving the performance of the sector.

The trend of fiscal and administrative decentralization to subnational levels of government is now apparent throughout the former socialist countries of Central/Eastern Europe and the former Soviet Union, and in a large number of countries in Latin America, Africa, and Asia. This development underlines the importance of governments at all levels limiting their involvement in infrastructure to those activities which require a public role, and leaving the remainder to the private sector; as well as the importance of appropriate financial policies to recover the costs of public infrastructure provision.

(iii)   Linkages with Credit Markets

Borrowing by local governments is especially underdeveloped in many countries, and appropriate policies in this area should be put in place in the context of the decentralization process noted above. In a number of countries, specialized financial institutions ("municipal credit institutions" or "infrastructure development banks") have existed for some years to channel funds raised through bond issues, government transfers, and external donor support to municipalities for housing and infrastructure investment. In an unfortunate number of cases, especially in Latin America, such funds have engaged heavily in government-guaranteed lending at below-market interest rates, which has contributed to undermining the soundness of the financial system and to macroeconomic destabilization. Quite often the institutions have not made worthwhile investments or maintained financial viability, because criteria for project selection have been too political, the entity has not had to compete for funds, nor been concerned with recovering its costs (Davey, 1988).

An initial step in creating financial autonomy for public enterprises in many countries has been to cut their access to budgetary financing for investment and require them to obtain bank loans. A high degree of bank borrowing by infrastructure entities can be a sign of mature financial policy in the sector; however, the borrowing in many cases indicates an inadequate degree of internal revenue mobilization, and frequently appears in the non-creditworthy enterprises. Large infrastructure enterprises have been implicated in the external debt problems of some countries as well. The Philippines in the late 1970s-early 1980s was a particularly striking case of foreign borrowing by public infrastructure enterprises, a factor which contributed to the macroeconomic repercussions of the external debt crisis in 1983-85.

Many infrastructure enterprises have made less use of debt or equity financing than would be efficient for them, in some instances (e.g., Brazil's TELEBRAS in the 1980s) because of a general credit shortage in the country and a macroeconomic climate that was unfavorable for foreign investment. In other cases, the performance of infrastructure entities has made them no longer creditworthy. In a recent survey of electricity enterprises in 60 developing countries, for more than half of the respondents net revenues over 1979-88 were inadequate to cover debt service by a factor of 1.5 times; one-fifth of the countries did not even show a coverage of 1.0 times, and were thus insolvent (unable to cover their costs of borrowing without government support or loan guarantees). Due to this internal lack of creditworthiness and compounded by the external debt crisis, supplier credits and private commercial financing together accounted for only 12 percent of total financing under Bank-financed power projects during the same period (World Bank, 1993b). This type of situation represents highly inefficient mobilization and allocation of financial resources in infrastructure, and results ultimately in poor performance of services and high levels of unmet demand.

12.4   LESSONS FROM EXPERIENCE: IMPLICATIONS FOR INFRASTRUCTURE POLICY

The preceding discussion suggests that infrastructure policy involves high stakes for developing economies: there are multiple benefits to be gained, but likewise high potential costs (economic and financial) from mistakes in these sectors. A number of conditions appear necessary for infrastructure to have the favorable impacts on economic development described above. *As a first and basic condition, there should be a macroeconomic policy climate which is favorable to efficient allocation of resources.* It is particularly important to avoid pricing rigidities in factor and goods markets so that infrastructure draws other resources to productive activities and does not crowd out more attractive investments. Macroeconomic policy issues such as inappropriate budgetary subsidies of infrastructure and distortions in financial and foreign exchange markets can seriously handicap the sectors' access to financing and undermine incentives for efficiency.[3] This implies that major infrastructural investments should be accompanied or preceded by macroeconomic structural adjustment; and that where severe macroeconomic distortions persist, even "strictly hardware" projects may not be a productive use of resources.

Second, infrastructure projects can only raise the productivity of other resources when there is a sufficient complement and basic productive level of other resources. Infrastructure investments cannot create economic potential, only help develop it. A review of the evolution of theory and experience regarding "new towns" and "growth poles" has found these developments to be very disappointing; such investments proved to have low returns where the underlying conditions for potential economic growth were unfavorable. Similarly, a recent evaluation of export processing zones (EPZs)[4] in developing countries concluded that their success in trade promotion depended on two types of factors: (i) favorable macroeconomic policies, along with access to managerial and marketing know-how, and (ii) appropriate location, generally in a major urban area already having good access to trade infrastructure (international transport systems and communications). Zones located in backward regions with the intention of accelerating their development have yielded poor returns, as have zones in small cities far from major centers of activity (World Bank, 1992a).

Third, infrastructure having the most significant and durable benefits to both productivity and consumption is that which provides the degree of reliability and quality of services needed by users. Reliability is found to be particularly essential to infrastructure's impact on international trade, production costs for small enterprises, and even for the health benefits from water supplies. Achieving such reliability will require institutional arrangements with strong accountability, which are capable of assessing changes in demand quickly and accurately, and are flexible and innovative in response.

Finally, infrastructure is likely to be provided more efficiently, and have more favorable impacts on the environment, when it is subject to user charges. These charges should reflect both costs of supply and demand considerations (willingness to pay). In

---

3   Relevant to this point, an empirical study conducted in 1991 of a large sample of World Bank Group projects over twenty years found that the ex-post economic rates of return of projects in "public non-tradable sectors" (a proxy for infrastructure) were significantly reduced in the presence of macroeconomic policy distortions, although generally less so than projects in tradable sectors (Kaufmann, 1991).

4   EPZs consist of two components: an industrial estate with links to international transport and communications infrastructure and utilities, and policy instruments providing a suitable trade and regulatory regime.

order to obtain the greatest benefits from infrastructure's ability to raise the returns to other factors of production, resources for infrastructure should be priced to reflect their scarcity value (e.g., the cost of capital used in financing projects should be realistic). User charges are also necessary to elicit effective demand, and to discourage wasteful consumption of infrastructure services and natural resources. The absence of user charges has usually not promoted access to services by the poor, but rather reduced availability and worsened inequalities.

ACKNOWLEDGEMENTS

The author would like to thank the following persons for very helpful comments provided on earlier drafts of this paper: Patricia Annez, Esra Bennathan, Michael Cohen, Harvey A. Garn, Frannie Humplick, Gregory Ingram, Arturo Israel, and an anonymous referee.

REFERENCES

Ahmed, R. and H. Mahabub, 1990, "Developmental Impact of Rural Infrastructure in Bangladesh", Research Report 83, International Food Policy Research Institute, Washington, D.C.

Andersson, Å.E., C. Anderstig and B. Hårsman, 1990, "Knowledge and Communications Infrastructure and Regional Economic Change", *Regional Science and Urban Economics*, 20:359-376.

Aschauer, D.A., 1989, "Is Public Expenditure Productive?", *Journal of Monetary Economics*, 23:177-200.

Beenhakker, H.L., 1987, "Issues in Agricultural Marketing and Transport Due to Government Intervention", Transportation Issues Series. Discussion Paper No. TRP7, World Bank, Transportation Department, Washington, D.C.

Bell, M., J. Boland, F. Humplick, A. Kudat, S. Madanat and N. Mukherjee, "Reliability of Urban Water Supply in Developing Countries: The Emperor Has No Clothes", *World Bank Research Observer*, forthcoming.

Binswanger, H.P, S.R. Khandker and M.R. Rosenzweig, 1987, "On the Determinants of Cross-Country Aggregate Agricultural Supply", *Journal of Economics*, 36:111-131.

Binswanger, H.P., S.R. Khandker and M.R. Rosenzweig, 1989, "How Infrastructure and Financial Institutions Affect Agricultural Output and Investment in India", Policy, Planning and Research Working Paper No. 163, World Bank, Latin America and the Caribbean Country Department II, Washington, D.C.

Blum, U., 1982, "Effects of Transportation Investments on Regional Growth: A Theoretical and Empirical Investigation", *Papers of the Regional Science Association,* 29:169-184.

Burki, S.J., D.G. Davies, R.H. Hook and J.W. Thomas, 1976, "Public Works Programs in Developing Countries: A Comparative Analysis", Staff Working Paper No. 224, World Bank, Washington, D.C.

Canning, D. and M. Fay, 1993, "The Effect of Transportation Networks on Economic Growth", Columbia University Working Paper, New York.

Davey, K., 1988, "Municipal Development Funds and Intermediaries", Policy, Planning and Research Working Paper No. 32, World Bank, Development Economics, Washington, D.C.

Dowall, D., 1991, "The Land Market Assessment: A New Deal for Urban Management", United Nations Development Program (UNDP)/United Nations Center for Human

Settlements (UNCHS)/World Bank Urban Management Program Discussion Paper, Washington, D.C.

Duffy-Deno, K.T. and R.W. Eberts, 1991, "Public Infrastructure and Regional Economic Development: A Stimulation Equations Approach", *Journal of Urban Economics*, 30: 329-343.

Eberts, R.W., 1986, "Estimating the Contribution of Urban Public Infrastructure to Regional Growth", Working Paper No. 8610, Federal Reserve Bank of Cleveland.

Epstein, T.S., 1962, *Economic Development and Social Change in South India*, Manchester University Press, Manchester.

Epstein, T.S., 1973, *South India: Yesterday, Today and Tomorrow*, Macmillan, London.

Esrey, S.A., J.M. Potash, W. Roberts and C. Shiff, 1990, *Health Benefits from Improvement in Water Supply and Sanitation: Survey and Analyses of the Literature on Selected Diseases*, Technical Report No. 66, Water and Sanitation for Health Project (Wash), CDM and Associates and United States Agency for International Development (USAID), Arlington, Virginia.

Evans, H.E., 1990, "Rural-Urban Linkages and Structural Transformation", Infrastructure and Urban Development Department, Discussion Paper No. INU 71, World Bank, Washington, D.C.

French Ministry of Cooperation and Development, 1991, "Urban Public Utilities in Africa: Technical and Financial Data, 1987-89", (Synthesis), Paris.

Gyamfi, P., L. Gutierrez and G. Yepes, 1992, "Infrastructure Maintenance in LAC: The Costs of Neglect and Options for Improvement", Regional Studies Program Report No. 17, World Bank, Latin America and Caribbean Technical Department, Washington, D.C.

Heggie, I.G., 1995, "Management and Financing of Roads: An Agenda for Reform", World Bank Technical Paper No. 275, Africa Technical Series, World Bank, Washington, D.C.

Heggie, I.G. and M. Quick, 1990, "A Framework for Analyzing Financial Performance of the Transport Sector", Infrastructure and Urban Development Department Working Paper No. 356, World Bank, Washington, D.C.

Holzmann, R., 1991, "Budgetary Subsidies in Centrally Planned Economies in Transition", Fiscal Affairs Dept., WP/91/11, International Monetary Fund, Washington, D.C.

Hulten, C.R. and R.M. Schwab, 1991, "Is There Too Little Public Capital? Infrastructure and Economic Growth", American Enterprise Institute, Washington, D.C.

Humplick, F., A. Kudat and S. Madanat, 1993, "Modeling Household Responses to Water Supply: A Service Quality Approach", Working Paper 4, World Bank, Transport, Water and Urban Development Department, Washington, D.C.

Ingram, G. and M. Fay, 1994, "Valuing Infrastructure Stocks and Gains from Improved Performance", Background paper for *World Development Report 1994*, World Bank, Washington, D.C.

Kalbermatten, J.M. and R.N. Middleton, 1992, *Challenges in Environmental Protection in Cities: New Approaches and Strategies for Urban Environmental Management*, Kalbermatten Associates, Inc., Washington, D.C.

Kaufmann, D., 1991, "The Forgotten Rationale for Policy Reform: The Productivity of Investment Projects – Preliminary Findings and Implications of Research-in-Progress", Background Paper to *World Development Report 1991*, World Bank, Washington, D.C.

Lanjouw, P. and N.H. Stern, 1993, "Agricultural Change and Inequality in Palanpur, 1957-84", in K.A. Hoff and J. Stiglitz (eds.), *The Economics of Rural Organization*, Oxford University Press, Oxford.

Lee, K.S., 1989, *The Location of Jobs in a Developing Metropolis: Patterns of Growth in Bogota and Cali, Colombia,* Published by Oxford University Press for the World Bank, New York.

Lee, K.S. and A. Anas, 1992, "Costs of Deficient Infrastructure: The Case of Nigerian Manufacturing", *Urban Studies,* Vol. 29, 7:1071-1092.

Lee, K.S., A. Anas and S. Verma, 1993, "Infrastructure Bottlenecks, Private Provision, and Industrial Productivity: A Study of Indonesian and Thai Cities", World Bank, Transport, Water and Urban Development Department, Washington, D.C.

Looney, R. and P. Frederiksen, 1981, "The Regional Impact of Infrastructure in Mexico", *Regional Studies,* 15:285-296.

Mera, K., 1973, "Regional Production Functions and Social Overhead Capital", *Regional and Urban Economics,* 3:157-185.

Munnell, A.H., 1992, "Policy Watch: Infrastructure Investment and Economic Growth," *Journal of Economic Perspectives,* Vol. 6, 4:189-198.

Peters, H.J., 1992, "Service: The New Focus in International Manufacturing and Trade", Policy Research Working Papers No. 950, World Bank, Infrastructure and Urban Development Department, Washington, D.C.

Ravallion, M., 1990, "Reaching the Poor Through Rural Public Employment: A Survey of Theory and Evidence", World Bank Discussion Paper No. 94, World Bank, Washington, D.C.

Read, G. and A. Kudat, 1992, "Why a Women in Development Component Should be Part of a Rural Water Project and What Such A Component Should Comprise: The Case of Sindh, Pakistan", Infrastructure Note No. WS-8, World Bank, Infrastructure and Urban Development Department, Washington, D.C.

Rietveld, P., 1989, "Infrastructure and Regional Development: A Survey of Multi-regional Economic Models", *Annals of Regional Science,* 23:255-274.

Riverson, J.D.N. and S. Carapetis, 1991, "Intermediate Means of Transport in Sub-Saharan Africa: Its Potential for Improving Rural Travel and Transport", World Bank Technical Paper 161, Washington, D.C.

United States Agency for International Development (USAID), 1988, "Power Shortages in Developing Countries: Magnitude, Impacts, Solutions, and the Role of the Private Sector", USAID Report to Congress.

United States Department of Commerce, 1987, "Effects of Structural Change in the U.S. Economy on the Use of Public Works Services", A Report to the National Council on Public Works Improvement, Washington, D.C.

Wheeler, D. and A. Mody, 1992, "International Investment Location Decisions: The Case of U. S. Firms", *Journal of International Economics,* 33:57-76.

Whittington, D., D.T. Lauria, A.M. Wright, K. Choe, J.A. Hughes and V. Swarna, 1992, "Household Demand for Improved Sanitation Services: A Case Study of Kumasi, Ghana", Water and Sanitation Report 3, UNDP-World Bank Water and Sanitation Program, Washington, D.C.

Whittington, D., D.T. Lauria, A.M. Wright, K. Choe, J.A. Hughes and V. Swarna, 1991, "A Study of Water Vending and Willingness to Pay in Onitsha, Nigeria", *World Development,* 19:2/3.

World Bank, 1992a, "Export Processing Zones", Policy and Research Series No. 20, Washington, D.C.

World Bank, 1992b, *World Development Report 1992: Development and the Environment,* Published for the World Bank by Oxford University Press, New York.

World Bank, 1993a, "Adjustment Lending and Mobilization of Private and Public Resources for Growth", Policy and Research Series 22, Washington, D.C.

World Bank, 1993b, "The Bank's Role in the Electric Power Sector: Policies for Effective Institutional, Regulatory and Financial Reform", A World Bank Policy Paper, Washington, D.C.

World Bank, 1994, *World Development Report 1994: Infrastructure for Development*, Oxford University Press, New York.

World Bank Water Demand Research Team, 1993, "The Demand for Water in Rural Areas: Determinants and Policy Implications", *World Bank Research Observer*, Vol. 8, 1:47-70.

CHAPTER 13

Infrastructure and Urban Development: The Case of the Amsterdam Orbital Motorway

Frank Bruinsma   **Gerard Pepping**   **Piet Rietveld**

Free University of Amsterdam

13.1   INTRODUCTION

The first European motorways were realized in countries such as Germany and Italy in the 1920s. In the 1930s these motorways were extended into interregional networks connecting cities at considerable distances. During this period the first orbital motorways were also planned around cities such as Berlin, Munich and London. It took a long time to complete these orbital motorways, and some of them were never completed. As Hall (1990) indicates the major reason for the planning of the European orbital motorways was not just the desire to remove traffic congestion. At that time roads were not yet very congested in Europe. Other motivations for building orbital motorways were the desire to reveal and reinforce the organic spatial structure of cities, and to make monumental artifacts which could serve nationalistic purposes.

After the Second World War road traffic started to grow at a very rapid rate in many European countries and this has induced the creation of orbital motorways in many countries. Orbital motorways have various types of impacts on metropolitan areas including direct impacts on traffic and impacts on the spatial structure of activities. We know much more about the first type of effect than the second type of effect (cf. Bruinsma, 1994). It is for this reason that we have decided to focus on the second type of effect in this contribution.

This chapter is structured as follows. In Section 13.2 we present a concise survey of research results in the field of impacts of orbital motorways. Section 13.3 provides information about the completion of the Amsterdam orbital motorway in 1990 and the observed effects on traffic flows since then. Expert opinions concerning the impact of the orbital motorway are given in Section 13.4. Effects of the orbital motorway on office rents are discussed in Section 13.5. Responses of firms, based on a stated preference approach are discussed in Section 13.6. Concluding remarks are made in Section 13.7.

13.2   ANALYZING IMPACTS OF ORBITAL MOTORWAYS

Changes in highway networks lead to various types of changes in the behavior of (potential) network users:

– timing of trips
– routing of trips
– choice of transport mode
– choice of origin or destination of trip (trip distribution)
– trip frequency
These changes which take place in the sphere of transport will in their turn have wider economic and spatial impacts. A reduction in generalized transport costs will lead to a higher productivity in economic activities, not only because transport costs as such decrease, but also since indirect gains can be realized by adjustments in logistics and because it leads to a better functioning of the labor market. The increase in productivity leads to lower consumer prices, higher factor prices (including prices of land) or combinations of these. Spatial effects will occur since the accessibility gains due to the improvement of the transport network are not distributed evenly in space. One may expect spatial relocations of economic activity, accordingly (Rietveld, 1994).

A useful summary of research on impacts of highway improvement is given by Bonsall (1992). He finds that the impacts depend strongly on a number of important conditions such as the size of the improvement, the pre-existence of suppressed demand, present levels of congestion, present network density and local economic conditions. For these reasons one may not expect simple generally applicable answers to questions concerning the effects of highway improvements. For the transport behavior components mentioned above Bonsall finds the following effects of road transport improvement:
– In previously congested areas it is not uncommon that substantial numbers of drivers return to the peak period.
– Route changes may vary from zero to as much as 60% in particular cases.
– Changes in transport modes depend strongly on the pre-improvement share of public transport.
– Short term changes in the choice of origin or destination are limited; maybe around 5% of the trips using the improvement have changed in origin or destination.
– Changes in trip frequencies (new traffic) are expected to come about in the long run. There is much uncertainty about their exact size, however.
– Uncertainty about land use effects is even greater because it is often difficult to say to what extent observed changes in land use are really caused by network improvements.

The above results relate to highway improvements in general. In the case of orbital motorways the type of improvement is more specific so that one may hope to arrive at more definite results. An important feature of orbital motorways is that they make route choice much more flexible. When traffic is blocked on one part of an orbital motorway one can still use the other parts of this road to reach any destination desired. In the case of orbital motorways one can distinguish three types of use:
1. use for intra-urban trips,
2. use for trips from outside the urban area to inside, or vice versa,
3. use for trips with both origin and destination outside the urban area.
With type 1 use effects the attention is focused on the role of orbital motorways within the urban network. These effects depend strongly on the existing intra-urban network. In the case of type 2 use effects the accessibility of the urban area from the surrounding regions is the major concern. In the case of type 3 use effects the role of an orbital motorway in a larger interregional network is taken into account.

The relative importance of the three types of use will vary considerably between cities. In some cases an orbital motorway may be of major importance for the accessibility of regions in a large interregional network. In other cases its dominant importance may be as a relief for congestion within cities. The balance between the two effects depends strongly on the radius of the orbital motorway: when it is small type 1 use will be most important, when it is very large type 3 use will become important. The lack of attention paid to the radius of orbital motorways may be one of the reasons why research on the effects of the construction of these motorways does not lead to unambiguous outcomes.

Another important factor which has to be taken into account is that the way one measures the impact of an orbital highway is not always well defined. Does one take the impact of the whole motorway into account, or only that of the last part which was completed many years after important parts of the motorway were already taken into use. In some countries the time between the use of the first part and the final completion of an orbital motorway may be as long as 25 years. Still another factor which makes it difficult to compare the impacts of orbital motorways at different places is that the zero-situation may vary strongly. In one case there may already have been a reasonable road connection before the orbital motorway was constructed. In other cases the construction of an orbital motorway may have a much more revolutionary impact, for example when it involves the replacement of ferry services by a tunnel or bridge.

Choice of transport mode is an interesting theme in the case of the construction of orbital motorways. Rail transport connections usually have a star-shaped structure. As a consequence many rail transport users have to travel via the center which gives rise to substantial detour factors and time losses when one has to change trains. The construction of orbital motorways leads to an adjustment of the road network away from a star-shaped structure. This means that travel time gains may be substantial, especially when the destination of the trip is not in the center of the city. Thus the construction of orbital motorways leads to a deterioration of the competitive position of rail transport, especially in criss-cross trips.

A study on the accessibility effects of the M25 London Orbital Motorway was carried out by Linneker and Spence (1992). The M25 was built between the years 1975 and 1986. It is located in the green belt around London and with a radius of some 26 kilometers it clearly has the character of an outer ringroad. In terms of accessibility based on travel times, the construction of the M25 has led to relatively large improvements in those parts of South East England through which the road passes (increase more than 10%). For inner London there has been almost no change in accessibility. For regions further away a moderate but certainly not negligible improvement can be observed (1-5%). Changes in route choice due to the construction of the M25 usually lead to longer though quicker routes so that when generalized transport costs are taken into account the improvements in accessibility are less pronounced and may even become negative. These results depend strongly on the coefficients for time and vehicle operating costs used in the generalized transport cost calculations.

Given the result that accessibility changes due to orbital motorways may be substantial, one may wonder what relocation effects will occur. Such effects are not studied by Linneker and Spence (1992), but in other studies attempts have been made to estimate them. Guiliano (1986) reports about a broad survey of effects of beltways in U.S.A. metropolitan areas. The effects are on average smaller than one might expect: the strongest conclusion possible is that beltways can have small though significant effects on regional development patterns and the economies of central cities.

Rather indecisive results are found in a comparative study of integrated transport-land-use models (Webster et al., 1988). Simulations with models developed for cities in a number of countries (Germany, Great Britain, Japan, Spain) indicate that the overall decentralizing effects of orbital motorways on the location of residences and workplaces is small compared with the effects of autonomous changes in land use patterns. The uncertainty in the outcomes may be due partly to the differences in the radius of the ringroads in the cities.

A more precise analysis is carried out in Dasgupta and Webster (1992), where a distinction is made between an outer ringroad with a large radius and an inner ringroad with a small radius. Based on a comparative study in three cities (Leeds, Bilbao and Dortmund) the authors find no clear results confirming a centralizing or decentralizing effect of an outer ringroad on the distribution of employment or population (see Table

13.1). A possible explanation is that the results of the model simulations depend on where the new road is located in relation to the boundary of the study area. This underlines the importance of having a sufficiently large study area in analyses of this type. An inner ringroad appears to have a weak centralizing tendency. As Dasgupta and Webster note, these rather small effects may be due to the fact that the three cities considered already have relatively well developed orbital links. One should be aware that the effects reported in Table 13.1 relate to the average outcome for the whole area. Thus, although ringroads only have small effects on the average degree of decentralization in an urban area, their effects on particular zones may of course be much larger.

Table 13.1 Effects of ringroad investments (percentage change)

	New investment in	
	Outer ringroad	Inner ringroad
Mode share:		
car	0.3	0.2
public transport	-0.2	0.0
walk	-0.8	-0.3
Mean trip:		
distance	0.9	0.0
time	-1.2	-0.7
road speed	0.2	-0.1
Distribution of:		
population	?	?
employment	?	weak centralization

Source: Dasgupta and Webster (1992)

The result for trip distances and trip times indicates that outer ringroads lead to longer trips in terms of distances travelled, but to shorter travel times, so that average road speeds increase.

Much larger impacts of a ringroad project on urban development are found by Morisugi et al. (1993) for the city of Gifu, Japan. In this case, the modelling simulations indicate that quite substantial changes will take place in urban land prices, leading to a high benefit incidence to absentee land owners at the expense of households and private firms. In spatial terms, the construction of the ringroad, of which the radius is about 4 kilometers, leads to a substantial change in structure. The model predicts a suburbanization of population and a growth of employment in the central part of the area.

Lathrop and Cook (1990) indicate that the spatial distribution of economic activities in the U.S.A. has been influenced by major factors such as the desire to live in spacious single-family houses and the growth in car ownership. This has induced suburbanization tendencies which would have occurred even if no beltways had been built, but beltways certainly have acted as catalysts for such a development.

13.3   THE AMSTERDAM ORBITAL MOTORWAY

13.3.1 Introduction

Like most of the capital cities in European countries Amsterdam suffers from traffic problems. Not only is the city confronted with large flows of traffic but in the peak hours in particular the roads near Amsterdam are also heavily congested. During recent decades the inner city of Amsterdam with its rings of canals has provided insufficient capacity for the growing car traffic. Partly as a result of these traffic problems companies have moved out of the inner city areas to the suburbs, where large office buildings have been constructed. The south-eastern, southern and south-western parts of the agglomeration were especially in favour as locations for those companies. Government policies to guide the suburbanization of the population went in another direction, however. For over two decades the government planned – by creating its own housing programs and restricting allowances to build anywhere else – complete residential cities at some distance from the large cities already existing in the Netherlands. Locations north of Amsterdam, in particular, were selected for the construction of large numbers of dwellings. However, the growth of employment in these new cities remained far behind the expectations of the government. This led to an increasing imbalance on local labor markets and an increase in commuting distances. As a consequence, one of the main traffic problems has been the crossing of the river IJ which splits Amsterdam into two parts just north of the inner city. This crossing is important since a large flow of commuters travels daily from the residential areas north of the river IJ to the employment center in the southern part of the agglomeration. But severe traffic problems have also arisen on other roads giving access to Amsterdam.

So, both the housing program and the shift of employment from the center of the city to the southern part of the agglomeration caused the need for an orbital motorway in the Amsterdam region to make the necessary cross agglomeration trips possible. The orbital motorway was constructed in several phases, partly using existing motorways. Major parts were already completed in the 1970s and 1980s. In September 1990 the last part of the Amsterdam orbital motorway – the Zeeburger tunnel under the river IJ – was completed (see Figure 13.1). With a radius of about 5 kilometers, the Amsterdam orbital motorway has the character of an inner ringroad: important parts of the agglomeration are located outside the ringroad circle.

The orbital motorway has three functions:
– improvement of the accessibility of Amsterdam and the province of North Holland to the region north of the river IJ
– relieving the secondary road network in the Amsterdam region
– creating improved conditions for the economic development of the Amsterdam region.

In this section we will concentrate on the first two functions. They concern effects which can be measured in the short run. Research on these functions has been completed by several institutes and traffic consultants under the supervision of the Ministry of Transport and Public Works. Sections 13.4 and 13.5 focus on the third function and contain results of our own research. In this section the following effects of the completion of the orbital motorway on traffic flows will be discussed[1]:
– effects on traffic volumes
– effects on travel behavior
– effects on congestion.

These results are based on large scale measurements in the road network in Amsterdam before and after the opening of the orbital motorway. In addition, several surveys have been carried out among residents in the region.

---

[1]In this section intensive use has been made of Rijkswaterstaat (1992).

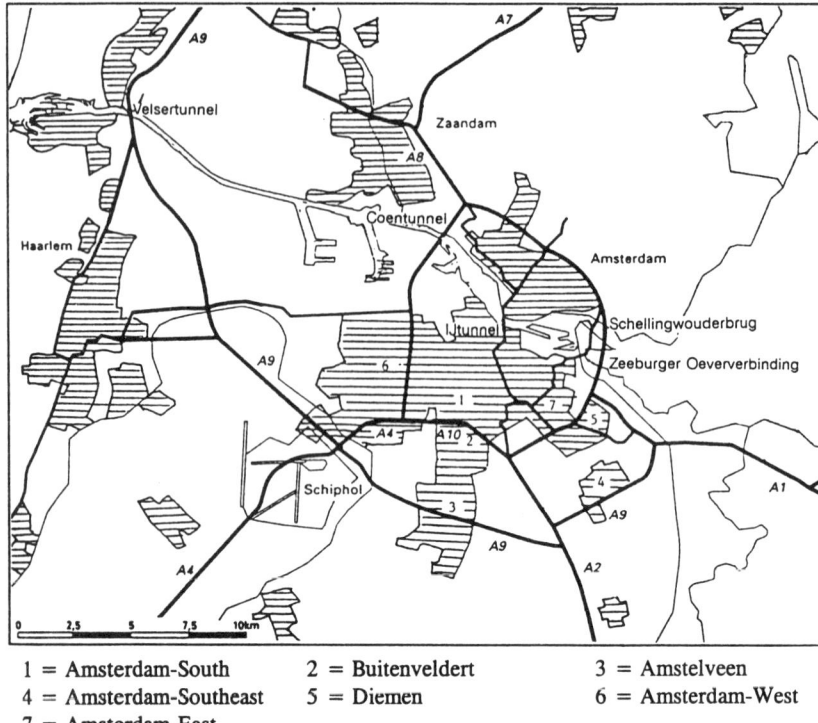

1 = Amsterdam-South   2 = Buitenveldert   3 = Amstelveen
4 = Amsterdam-Southeast   5 = Diemen   6 = Amsterdam-West
7 = Amsterdam-East

Figure 13.1 Map of the Amsterdam agglomeration

13.3.2   Effects of the Opening of the Orbital Motorway on Traffic Volumes

The opening of the Zeeburger tunnel as the final part of the orbital motorway has led to a huge increase in capacity of the regional road network, especially in relation to the crossing of the river IJ. The new connections make it possible to pass Amsterdam on the eastern side. For a number of reasons this means a decrease in travel distance and/or travel time.

The total number of kilometers driven in the Amsterdam region has increased slightly faster than the induced traffic volume for the whole of the Netherlands (0.5 to 1.0% in the Amsterdam region compared with 0.1 to 0.2% in the Netherlands as a whole). This increase is the result of an increase in the number of kilometers driven on the main road network. The secondary road network of the Amsterdam region has been relieved. For instance, the number of kilometers covered by traffic crossing the river IJ on the highways increased by 13%, while the number of kilometers by traffic crossing the river on other roads decreased by 33%.

In the Amsterdam region one can observe a clear shift of traffic flows in easterly and northerly directions. The traffic density on the southern and western highways decreased by 9 to 29%. On all the existing river IJ waterway crossings traffic density has dropped as a result of the opening. 58,000 motor vehicles per day go through the new Zeeburger tunnel.

13.3.3 Effects of the Opening of the Orbital Motorway on Travel Behavior

The possibility to pass Amsterdam on the eastern side has led to a major shift in route choice. Of the car drivers who cross the river IJ 25% have changed their choice of waterway crossing point. The Zeeburger tunnel now has 19% of the share of all motor vehicles that cross the river IJ. Because of the change in routes towards the use of the orbital motorway, Amsterdam's city road network has been relieved.

Of the car drivers who cross the river IJ, 31% have changed their time of departure (either earlier or later). Before the opening they were forced to travel at times less suitable for them, mainly because of congestion. Since the opening of the orbital motorway they can select their time of departure more in accordance with their individual preferences. This means that, individually, drivers are benefitting. The changes in departure times have led to a 16% increase in the number of crossings of the river IJ by drivers in the morning rush hour between 7.00 and 9.00, the so-called 'return-to-the-peak' effect.

The opening of the orbital motorway has caused minor changes in the frequency of journeys, the destination of journeys and the transport mode choice for journeys crossing the river IJ. For instance the opening has led to an increase of 1% for commuter traffic and 5% for traffic with other purposes (shopping, leisure, social visits).

The opening of the orbital motorway has made visible a latent demand for crossings of the river IJ in the rush hour. This largely concerns changes within existing traffic patterns. Travellers have mainly adjusted their route and time of departure, often in combination. The number of daily journeys on the waterway crossings has increased by 4.5% due to the opening. Of this 1.5% are journeys which existed before the opening; 3.0% are journeys generated by the opening.

Only small changes have been observed in the use of different transport modes (car driver, car passenger, user of public transport). This limited change in transport mode corresponds to daily changes in behavior that would have occurred without the opening. The public transport traffic flows across the river IJ have hardly been influenced or uninfluenced by the opening of the orbital motorway.

13.3.4 Effects of the Opening of the Orbital Motorway on Congestion

Considerable journey time gains have been recorded for through journeys using the main road network in the Amsterdam region. The largest gains refer to journeys between the Province of North Holland north of the river IJ and the Center of the Netherlands. Travel via the 'old' routes also takes less time as a result of a congestion level that has decreased almost everywhere.

The reduction in the total time lost due to congestion on the entire main road network in the region is 20%. This is the result of extra capacity and of the changes of route due to the opening. Because of the changes in the choice of departure time ('return-to-the-peak' effect) this reduction is less than what might have been expected on the basis of the increase in capacity. In the existing tunnels – Coen, Velser and IJ – the total loss of time due to congestion decreased by 39%, 58% and 100% respectively.

One must bear in mind however that the total journey time losses due to congestion are relatively small in the Amsterdam region; we guess that they are not greater than 5% of total travel time (Bruinsma et al., 1993). Thus, the gain in total journey time due to the reduction of congestion is about 1%. One interpretation of this outcome is that it is rather low. On the other hand, the reduction in time losses due to congestion of 20% may be considered as rather high. From interviews with road users in the area it appears that many of them perceive the change as substantial (see also Section 13.5).

13.4   THE EFFECTS OF THE ORBITAL MOTORWAY ON THE OFFICE MARKET

An indication of the potential of suburban areas to attract new firms and to develop in a broader economic sense can be found in their popularity as location sites for offices. The development of prices of absorbed office space is a proper indication of this popularity because it reflects to a certain extent the willingness to pay of entrepreneurs for specific sites. The advantage of analyzing prices of absorbed office space relative to office construction decisions lies in the fact that the first prices reflect the latest changes in market preferences while the latter are in this respect delayed in time. The opening of the orbital motorway might increase the willingness to pay in some specific areas along it, because of cost reductions due to improved logistic organization, more punctuality in deliveries of goods, an extension of the geographical labor market, promotional advantages in the case of sites that are visible from the motorway (sight locations), and so on.

For a series of three years, two before the completion (1987 and 1989) and one after the completion of the orbital motorway (1991), data on transaction prices of offices larger than 500 m^2 on the Amsterdam office market were collected. These prices were analyzed in relation to the distances of the buildings to the nearest entry to the orbital motorway. It would have been more accurate if the accessibility had been measured using both travel costs and travel time and combining different modes. Unfortunately the data required for such a measure were not available.

Two techniques to measure the impact on office prices were used: an impact analysis and a regression analysis. In order to assess the effects of the orbital motorway on office prices, it is important to make a distinction between suburban districts in which (a part of) the orbital motorway was already located before the completion, and suburban districts that were made accessible by new parts of it. The first group of districts includes Amsterdam-West, -South, Buitenveldert and Amstelveen; the second group includes Amsterdam-North, -East, -South-East and Diemen (see Figure 13.1).

The areas in which distances to the orbital motorway did not change average prices of office space – classified according to the distance by road from the respective sites to the nearest ramps of the orbital motorway – are given in Table 13.2. A distinction has been made between locations less than 2 kilometers and locations more than 2 kilometers from the orbital motorway.

Table 13.2   Number of transactions and average prices per m^2 (in Dutch guilders) of new offices in locations in which the distance by road to the orbital motorway did not change after the opening, per city district

Distance to the orbital motorway	1987		1989		1991	
	No.	Price	No.	Price	No.	Price
< 2 km.	22	250	35	256	28	294
> 2 km.	36	212	61	220	53	264
Total	58	230	96	239	81	273

In the areas where distances did not change, office space absorbed between the years 1987 and 1991 shows a significantly higher price at sites within a limited distance from the orbital motorway compared with sites further away. Office prices increased considerably in these areas between 1989 and 1991, i.e. during the period in which the orbital motorway was opened.

The development of office prices in zones where the distance to the orbital motorway had changed due to its completion is given in Table 13.3. This table shows the average office prices for various zones distinguished according to the decrease in distance to the orbital motorway.

Table 13.3 Number of transactions and average rent per m^2 (in Dutch guilders) of new offices in locations in which the distance to the orbital motorway decreased after its completion

Decrease in distance 1991 compared with 1987	1987		1989		1991	
	No.	Price	No.	Price	No.	Price
< 1 km.	7	125	9	204	4	147
1-2 km	12	237	27	238	16	238
> 2 km.	4	197	7	211	7	217
Total	23	208	43	222	27	224

What strikes most in Table 13.3 is the fact that office prices in zones that profited most from the new orbital motorway rose insignificantly between 1989 and 1991, when it was completed. They lagged behind the development in areas in which the accessibility was not affected by the new segment of the orbital motorway. Apparently, an improvement in the accessibility of certain areas due to the ringroad construction has until now not led to a stronger competitive position for these areas in relation to the western and southern parts of the agglomeration. However, as mentioned, the timing of this research may have been too early after the completion to detect these effects.

One might argue that an anticipation of office prices may already have taken place in the construction phase of the orbital motorway. Indeed the possibility of such behavior is quite relevant for multi-year contracts on renting office space. However, if one compares the totals of Tables 13.2 and 13.3 no sign of such anticipation is found for the three years before the opening. The increase in office prices of locations for which the distance to the orbital motorway decreased is of about the same order as for those locations for which the distance to the orbital motorway did not change. It is hard to expect that any anticipation of office prices took place before 1987 .

The conclusion to be drawn is that as far as the completion of the orbital motorway has influenced office prices, this influence is not observable in those areas where the new segments were constructed.

The impact of infrastructure on office prices can also be studied by means of regression analysis on the basis of individual transactions on the office market. Together with the influence of the orbital motorway, the influences of the existing rail infrastructure and the metro network have been also analyzed, including the extension of the metro network in 1990. In the regression model an assumption has been made that office prices are dependent on the following location factors:
− the distance by road from the office location to the nearest orbital motorway ramp
− the walking distance from the office location to the nearest railway station
− the walking distance from the office location to the nearest metro station.

One has to take into account the influence of status aspects. Also, the quality of office buildings is an important factor determining office prices. In this respect the following factors must be mentioned:
− quality of the construction
− possible alternative use of the building
− the ratio between gross and net office space

- the representativeness of the building
- the level to which the building meets specific user requirements. For example, telematics infrastructure places a new dimension upon the user value of the building.

The last two factors have become increasingly important in recent years. Together with governmental policies like subsidies and land taxes, these factors may lead to high variations in office prices in the Amsterdam area.

A simple linear regression model that has only the distance by road to the nearest orbital motorway ramp as an explanatory factor for office prices, has the following form:

$$y_n = \alpha_0 + \alpha_1 x_n$$

whereby

y_n = price per m^2 of office space taken into use on site n
x_n = distance by road from site n to the nearest orbital motorway ramp.

In Figure 13.2 the variation in office prices relative to their proximity to the orbital motorway is shown for the years 1987, 1989 and 1991. Except for the fact that the variation becomes wider in the investigated period, it appears that in all three years office prices are negatively correlated with the distances to the orbital motorway. The angle of the regression line slightly increases in this period, which could stress a growing influence of the orbital motorway. In 1991, when larger price differences occur than in 1989, top level prices clearly increase when distances to the orbital motorway decrease.

A more sophisticated regression model incorporates the influences of the rail and metro networks in Amsterdam. In order to correct for the influence of non-infrastructure factors on office prices, the quality of office buildings and area status influences are also accounted for. The age of the buildings has been taken as an indicator for the quality of office buildings. In this respect a distinction has been made between (old) existing buildings that get new users and (new) buildings, either newly constructed or renovated. In order to deal with status aspects, a distinction has been made according to the various districts. These factors can be added to the model by formulating them as dummy variables. The resulting model then has the following form:

$$y_n = \quad \alpha_0 + \alpha_1 x_{1n} + \alpha_2 x_{2n} + \alpha_3 x_{3n} + \alpha_4 d_{1n} + \alpha_5 d_{2n} + \alpha_6 d_{3n} + \alpha_{7d} d_{4n} +$$
$$\alpha_8 d_{5n} + \alpha_9 d_{6n} + \alpha_{10} d_{7n} + \alpha_{11} d_{8n}$$

whereby

y_n	=	price per m^2 of office space at site n (in Dutch guilders)
x_{1n}	=	distance by road from site n to the nearest ramp of the orbital motorway (in kilometers)
x_{2n}	=	walking distance from site n to the nearest railway station (in meters)
x_{3n}	=	walking distance from site n to the nearest metro station (in meters)
$d_1..d_7$	=	dummy variables that determine the location of the sites in one of the respective districts Amsterdam-South, Buitenveldert, Amstelveen, Amsterdam-South-East, Diemen, Amsterdam-West and -East
d_8	=	dummy determining whether the concerned buildings are (old) existing or newly constructed/renovated buildings.

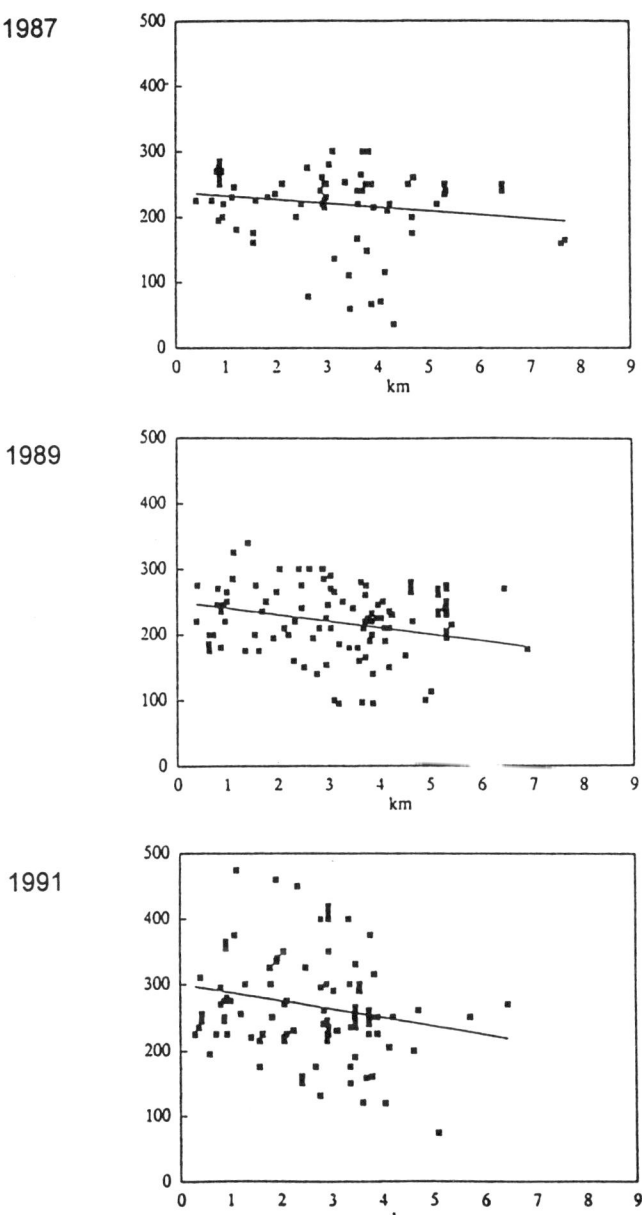

Figure 13.2 Variations in office prices at locations in the Amsterdam agglomeration for the years 1987, 1989 and 1991, by road distance to the nearest ramp of the orbital motorway

The more complete model is superior to the simple model formulated above (see Table 13.4), although not all variables appear to be significant and the R^2 values are rather low.

The orbital motorway appears to be a robust explanatory factor. The coefficient of -23 in 1991, for example, means that – other factors kept constant – the price of office space near to a ramp of the orbital motorway is 23 guilders per m² higher than in locations 1 kilometre away. The role of public transport networks is not clear. In 1991 railway stations have a slightly negative coefficient, while metro stations have a positive coefficient. Standard errors of both coefficients are high. The coefficients of the dummy variables for the various districts confirm the higher status of Amsterdam-South, Buitenveldert and Amstelveen in relation to other office sites in the Amsterdam area. For example, the average office price per m² in Amsterdam-South in 1991 is 63 guilders higher than in the Center, other factors kept constant. The influence of the quality of office buildings is also clearly confirmed. In 1991 the average price of new (or renovated) office buildings is 37 guilders higher than the price of existing offices.

Table 13.4 Regression results for office prices

	1987		1989		1991	
	Coeff.	Stand. error	Coeff.	Stand. error	Coeff.	Stand. error
Constant	245.27*	51.16	231.35*	41.14	299.16*	58.80
Orbital motorway	-17.27*	10.72	-10.49	6.53	-23.21*	9.15
Railway Station	0.42	11.87	3.23	5.32	-0.19	10.18
Metro stops	1.81	10.60	-4.09	4.34	8.62	6.96
Dummy variables:						
South	7.64	31.37	57.87*	15.55	63.26*	23.25
Buitenveldert	7.87	38.00	43.07*	22.74	-1.81	26.25
Amstelveen	46.23	46.96	54.99*	23.95	68.37*	32.02
South-east	53.80*	29.94	25.51	18.39	6.52	33.29
Diemen	16.66	29.54	-12.63	19.41	-58.52*	33.81
West	-46.08	56.43	-18.86	22.91	-92.76*	32.04
East	-21.01	30.73	-5.85	20.21	-45.23	29.76
New buildings	24.12*	12.77	31.55*	8.49	36.86*	12.77
R²		0.27		0.46		0.44

* = significant at 10% level

The overall conclusion to be drawn from this quantitative analysis of prices on the Amsterdam office market is, that although the effects are not directly visible in the areas where the new segments were constructed, in general the orbital motorway is an important location factor for office firms.

13.5 THE EFFECTS OF THE ORBITAL MOTORWAY ACCORDING TO ENTREPRENEURS

13.5.1 Introduction

In the spring of 1992 a questionnaire was sent to 516 entrepreneurs – each with a labor force of at least 10 persons – located across three types of zones. The first zone consists of areas which are located near parts of the orbital motorway which already existed before the final completion. The second zone consists of areas which became accessible after the opening of new segments of the orbital motorway. The third zone consists of areas which are rather located at a distance from the orbital motorway (either the inner city or the remote suburbs). The first zone is subsequently entitled the *old accessible zone*, the second zone the *new accessible zone* and the third zone the *remote zone*.

The questionnaire was sent to entrepreneurs in four economic sectors: industry, distribution, services and the office sector. The first two sectors have a strong orientation towards the transportation of goods, the others towards business and commuting traffic.

The net response of 25% was evenly spread across zones and sectors. In an over-surveyed area like the Amsterdam region a net response rate of 25% is relatively high. Nevertheless, this response rate does not give a full guarantee of the representativeness of the questionnaire for the economic sectors involved in the survey. In the old accessible and remote zones the office sector is the dominant sector with shares of 74 and 59% respectively. In the new accessible zones the industrial sector (41%) and distribution sector (30%) are the main economic sectors. These shares are close to the overall sectoral composition in those zones. Results will be presented for the whole agglomeration as well as the zonal and sectoral levels.

13.5.2 The Use of the Amsterdam Orbital Motorway

The first part of the questionnaire deals with the actual use of the orbital motorway. It seems that all 44 companies in the old accessible zone, 44 out of the 45 companies in the new accessible zone and 30 out of the 41 companies in the remote zone make use of the orbital motorway. The least use of the orbital motorway is made by the service sector in the remote zone. An explanation might be that those companies are oriented towards the local market and thus make no use of the orbital motorway which is at some distance. A second argument concerns the activities of the service sector in general. The service sector generates traffic in the form of customers instead of their own traffic.

Table 13.5 shows that the use of the orbital motorway for all traffic activities distinguished is high, especially for commuting and contacts with customers.

At the zonal level (Table 13.5.A) the scores of the new accessible zone are above the average use for all activities except commuting. This can be explained by the strong specialization of this zone in the distribution and industry sector. As shown below commuting is relatively unimportant for those sectors. The scores of the remote zone are below average for all traffic activities. The scores of the old accessible zone are more diverse: above average for commuting and contacts with customers and below average for the delivery of goods. In the old accessible zone – and the remote zone – the office sector is dominant. This explains the importance of commuting for this zone. The use of the motorway for visits by customers, business travel and commuting in the old accessible zone is substantially higher compared with the remote zone. These differences explain the lower use of the orbital motorway in the remote zone compared with the old accessible zone.

At the sectoral level (Table 13.5.B) some interesting results are found. The relatively low use of the orbital motorway for the delivery of goods is explained by the low scores of the office sector for these activities, which is the dominant sector in our sample. All other sectors score above average for the delivery of goods. The scores of the sectors for the use of the orbital motorway for the activities distinguished are fairly robust. For instance, the scores for the delivery of goods are low for the office sector and the service sector has a low score for visits to customers and business travel.

Table 13.5 The importance of the orbital motorway for several transport activities (in %)

A. ZONAL	All respondents			New accessible		
	Imp.	Neutral	Unimp.	Imp.	Neutral	Unimp.
Inflow of goods	60	9	31	81	5	14
Outflow of goods	58	8	34	80	3	18
Visits by customers	72	16	12	74	19	7
Visits to customers	71	13	16	74	14	12
Business trips	66	18	16	67	19	14
Commuting	78	12	10	72	143	14
	Old accessible			Remote		
	Imp.	Neutral	Unimp.	Imp.	Neutral	Unimp.
Inflow of goods	47	10	43	38	14	48
Outflow of goods	41	14	45	38	10	52
Visits by customers	83	5	12	50	31	19
Visits to customers	73	11	16	63	15	22
Business trips	67	19	14	59	15	26
Commuting	88	12	0	73	10	17

B. SECTORAL	Industry			Distribution		
	Imp.	Neutral	Unimp.	Imp.	Neutral	Unimp.
Inflow of goods	68	16	16	89	5	5
Outflow of goods	75	13	13	84	11	5
Visits by customers	76	20	4	78	11	11
Visits to customers	88	13	0	75	10	15
Business trips	88	8	4	60	35	5
Commuting	72	12	16	76	10	14
	Offices			Services		
	Imp.	Neutral	Unimp.	Imp.	Neutral	Unimp.
Inflow of goods	26	6	69	92	8	0
Outflow of goods	26	6	69	70	0	30
Visits by customers	68	16	16	67	20	13
Visits to customers	71	13	17	33	17	50
Business trips	66	16	18	36	21	43
Commuting	85	12	4	67	20	13

13.5.3 Hindrances Before the Opening

When asked about the hindrances that the companies had experienced over two thirds of the companies had complaints about the use of the infrastructure network before the opening of the motorway in 1990. The complaints were highest in the new accessible zone (which was not accessible by motorway before the opening) and by the distribution sector.

In Table 13.6 the scores for different kinds of hindrances are given. At the zonal level (Table 13.6.A) the fact that the new accessible zone scores below the average except for the lack in punctuality of deliveries is interesting. It seems that the companies incorporated the expected delays in their behavior. This is something which cannot be said for the companies in the old accessible zone. They give very high scores for time delays, late arrival of personnel and staff and the lack of punctuality for appointments. The remote zone companies also give a high score for delays in travel time.

At the sectoral level (Table 13.6.B) it seems strange that the office sector scores higher for time delays than the distribution sector. However, the transport activities of the office sector mainly concern commuting which is within the peak hours. The activities of the distribution sector are more evenly spread over the day. In addition, the distribution sector makes more detours to avoid congestion spots. The concentration of the activities of the office sector in the rush hours also explains the relatively high scores for late arrivals of staff and personnel. The lack of punctuality of deliveries has serious consequences for the productivity of the distribution and industry sectors.

Only 40% of the companies took measures to relieve the hindrances. Most measures were taken in the new accessible zone and by the industry sector. The least measures were taken in the old accessible zone. Over two thirds of the measures concern adjustments in route planning, working hours or a combination of both.

Table 13.6 Hindrances before the opening of the orbital motorway (in %)

A. ZONAL	Total	New accessible	Old accessible	Remote
Delays in travel time	90	79	100	94
Detours	58	59	56	59
Lack of punctuality for appointments	50	44	56	53
Personnel too late for work	46	35	67	35
Lack of punctuality for deliveries	27	35	22	18
Staff too late for work	14	6	26	12

B. SECTORAL	Industry	Distribution	Offices	Services
Delays in travel time	88	76	97	90
Detours	59	65	56	40
Lack of punctuality for appointments	29	65	56	30
Personnel too late for work	29	41	59	40
Lack of punctuality for deliveries	24	47	9	60
Staff too late for work	0	18	25	0

13.5.4 The Effects of the Opening for the Companies

Most companies stated that the opening of the orbital motorway relieved the traffic problems for their company (Table 13.7). A clear majority noticed a reduction in travel time, better accessibility and/or a decrease in annoyance experienced in using the infrastructure network. Although the effect reported by the majority is neutral, a substantial percentage of companies still experienced a rise in turnover, a decrease in the costs per unit product and/or improved punctuality in the delivery of goods.

Table 13.7 Effects of the orbital motorway (in %)

A. ZONAL	All respondents			New accessible		
	Imp.	Neutral	Worsen.	Imp.	Neutral	Worsen.
Accessibility	80	9	2	91	10	0
Travel time	76	14	10	76	12	12
Annoyance in traffic	75	20	5	74	19	7
Inflow/outflow of goods	43	50	7	64	28	8
Costs per unit product	19	78	3	23	71	6
Turnover	12	87	1	15	85	0
	Old accessible			Remote		
	Imp.	Neutral	Worsen.	Imp.	Neutral	Worsen.
Accessibility	74	24	2	72	24	3
Travel time	71	21	7	83	7	10
Annoyance in traffic	78	20	3	72	21	7
Inflow/outflow of goods	24	74	3	35	52	13
Costs per unit product	9	89	3	28	72	0
Turnover	16	82	3	4	96	0
B. SECTORAL	Industry			Distribution		
	Imp.	Neutral	Worsen.	Imp.	Neutral	Worsen.
Accessibility	80	20	0	84	16	0
Travel time	80	12	8	80	10	10
Annoyance in traffic	73	23	4	74	11	16
Inflow/outflow of goods	50	38	13	65	18	18
Costs per unit product	32	68	0	31	63	6
Turnover	10	86	5	18	82	0
	Offices			Services		
	Imp.	Neutral	Worsen.	Imp.	Neutral	Worsen.
Accessibility	75	22	4	87	13	0
Travel time	76	18	6	64	14	21
Annoyance in traffic	79	21	0	75	17	8
Inflow/outflow of goods	24	74	2	60	40	0
Costs per unit product	9	86	5	9	91	0
Turnover	9	91	0	27	73	0

At the zonal level (Table 13.7.A) only a few differences in this general pattern occur. As before, the major contrasts are between the new and the old accessible zone. For instance, in the new accessible zone 64% of the companies noticed a rise in the punctuality of the delivery of goods, whereas in the old accessible zone 74% noticed no difference at all.

At the sectoral level (Table 13.7.B) it is important to note that a relatively high percentage of companies in the industry and distribution sectors experienced a decrease in the costs per unit product. These sectors are – more than the other sectors – used to assessing costs per unit product and could actually notice changes in the cost structure of their products. A relatively large number of companies in these sectors also noticed an improvement in the punctuality of the delivery of goods. On the other hand a relatively high number of companies experienced a decrease in punctuality. The fact that the office sector is not used to working with physical products leads to very neutral scores for changes in costs per unit product and in the delivery of goods.

The developments in the service sector are interesting. The relatively high score for the rise in turnover could result from better accessibility leading to a rise in the number of customers. Second, the strong reduction in travel time has led to an expansion of the market area. So reach has improved as well as accessibility. And third, the rise in the punctuality of the delivery of goods has led to more efficient operations.

13.5.5 Expected Consequences if the Orbital Motorway had not been Completed

In Table 13.8 impressions about the effects which would have occurred if the orbital motorway had not been completed are recorded.

Table 13.8 Expected effects if the orbital motorway had not been completed[a]

A. ZONAL	Total	New accessible	Old accessible	Remote
Firm closed	1	-	1	-
Firm smaller	4	1	1	2
Firm relocated	7	2	3	2
Less invested	11	8	2	1
Less personnel	6	4	0	2
Total	130	45	44	41

B. SECTORAL	Total	Industry	Distribu-tion	Offices	Services
Firm closed	1	-	-	1	-
Firm smaller	4	-	1	3	-
Firm relocated	7	-	1	6	-
Less invested	11	2	4	4	1
Less personnel	6	-	2	3	1
Total	126	26	22	60	18

[a] = * since no entrepreneur mentioned an enlargement of their firm, or expected that their investment or employment figures would have been higher if the orbital motorway had not been constructed, these factors are not included in the table.
* four observations have been deleted in part B because the sector is unknown.
* in some cases a firm may have indicated more than 1 option (for example: firm smaller, less invested).

As shown, this would have had especially strong effects on the investment behavior of the companies. About 10% stated that they would have invested less. A minor number of companies expected that they would have had less personnel or stated that they would have moved to another location. These negative effects would have been felt hardest in the new accessible zone and in the office or distribution sectors.

13.6   CONCLUSIONS

The completion of the Amsterdam orbital motorway has had substantial impacts on the choice of routing and timing of trips. The impact on modal choice and trip frequencies has been small. Time losses due to congestion in the Amsterdam area have been reduced by about 20%.

There are no indications that office prices in zones directly benefitting from the completion of the orbital motorway increased more strongly than in other zones. On the contrary, office prices at locations near existing parts of the orbital motorway displayed the largest increase after the completion. Thus, the ringroad seems to have reinforced the position of zones which already had a strong competitive position in the region.

A statistical analysis of office rents reveals that distance to the nearest orbital motorway ramp has a significant negative impact on office prices. For the railway and metro system no such effects are found.

In a survey of entrepreneurs some 60-70% indicated that the orbital motorway is important for transport activities such as the inflow and outflow of goods, visits of customers and commuting. Before the motorway was completed firms experienced various hindrances in the form of delays (90%), lack of punctuality for appointments (50%) and personnel arriving too late (40%). According to about 80% of the respondents the completion of the ringroad led to an improvement of accessibility. Some 10-20% of the firms indicated that they had experienced an increase in turnover and/or productivity as a consequence of this. Almost 10% of the firms indicated that they would have invested less had the ringroad not been completed.

ACKNOWLEDGEMENTS

This study is based on Bruinsma, Pepping and Rietveld (1993). The research project was funded by the Transportation and Traffic Research Division, Rijkswaterstaat, Rotterdam.

REFERENCES

Bonsall, P.W., 1992, Feasibility of Measuring Responses to Highway Improvement, Institute of Transport Studies, Leeds.

Bruinsma, F.R., 1994, De Invloed van Transportinfrastructuur op Ruimtelijke Patronen van Economische Activiteiten, Ph.D. thesis, Free University, Amsterdam.

Bruinsma, F.R., G. Pepping and P. Rietveld, 1993, Economische Uitstraling Opening Ringweg Amsterdam, Rijkswaterstaat, Rotterdam.

Dasgupta, M. and V. Webster, 1992, Land Use/Transport Interactions: Policy Relevance of the ISGLUTI Study, World Conference in Transportation Research, Lyon.

Guiliano, G., 1986, "Land Use Impacts of Transportation Investments: Highway and Transit", in S. Hanson (ed.), *The Geography of Urban Transportation*, New York, The Guildford Press, New York, pp. 247-279.

Hall, P., 1990, "Keynote Address on Orbital Motorways", in D. Bayliss (ed.), *Orbital Motorways,* Thomas Telford, London, pp. 1-31.

Lathrop, G.T. and K.E.Cook, 1990, "The Effects of Beltways on Urban Development: a Discussion of US Experience", in D. Bayliss (ed.), *Orbital Motorways*, Thomas Telford, London, pp. 143-156.

Linneker, B.J. and N.A. Spence, 1992, "An Accessibility Analysis of the Impact of the M25 London Orbital Motorway on Britain", *Regional Studies*, 26:31-47.

Morisugi, H., E. Ohno and T. Miyagi, 1993, "Benefit Incidence of Urban Ring Road: Theory and the Case Study of Gifu Ring Road", *Transportation*, 20:285-303.

Rietveld, P., 1994, "Spatial Impacts of Transport Infrastructure Supply", *Transportation Research A,* 28:329-341.

Rijkswaterstaat (1992) Effects of the Opening of the Amsterdam Orbital Motorway: Final Report Phase 1, Transportation and Traffic Research Division, Rijkswaterstaat, Rotterdam.

Webster, F.V., P.H. Bly and N.J. Paulley (eds.), 1988, *Urban Land-Use and Transport Interaction: Policies and Models,* Aldershot, Avebury.

CHAPTER 14

Innovative Capacity, Infrastructure and Regional Policy

Luis Suarez-Villa
University of California, Irvine

14.1 INTRODUCTION

Few items are as important for a national or regional economy's long term viability as the development of its technological potential, and the human capital resources that support it. Infrastructural investment is a decisive factor in the development of that technological potential, given its enormous quantitative and qualitative impacts on the kinds of human and physical capital needed to support invention and innovation. Among the most important investments in the future of any regional or national economy are those which seek to promote a higher level of endogenous technological capabilities, through enhancements of the human and physical capital infrastructure that can lead to the expansion of invention and innovation (Andersson, 1985; Kuhn, 1962; Schmookler, 1966; Rosenberg, 1972; Rubin and Huber, 1986; Ayres, 1988; Davelaar and Nijkamp, 1990; Lee and Reid, 1991; Nelson and Wright, 1992).

The rapid globalization of technological capabilities is making it necessary to re-think how nations promote and support the scientific and technological skills of their populations. As the twentieth century closes, it appears that invention, as the single most important source of innovation, will necessarily receive increasing attention at the policy-making level, if national and regional technological competitiveness is to be preserved and improved. More and more, the technological competitiveness of whole industries, regions and nations may be determined by endogenously-generated inventive productivity. In this rapidly changing global panorama, infrastructural support for invention is bound to acquire greater relevance than ever before, as nations and regions strive to improve access to information, advanced skills, networks, and the diffusion of new ideas and discoveries (see, e.g., Andersson, 1986; Andersson and Batten, 1988; Snickars, 1987; Lakshmanan, 1989; Håkansson, 1989; Johansson, 1991; Vickerman, 1989; Haynes and Stough, 1988; Machlup, 1980; Rogers and Shoemaker, 1971; Hägerstrand, 1967).

This chapter will provide, first, a brief definition of the concept of *innovative capacity* and its measurement, based on U.S. invention patent data. The relationship between invention and infrastructural investment will then be explored through a concise analysis of infrastructural and patent age cycles. This analysis will provide insights on any possible convergence in the long term upswings and downturns of both infrastructural investment and innovative capacity. The analysis of infrastructural investment and innovative capacity will then be followed up with a discussion of several policy programs that can take into account the modes and means of invention, and the kinds of infrastructural investment that will be needed to raise the national and regional innovative capacity.

14.2   INVENTION, INFRASTRUCTURE AND INNOVATIVE CAPACITY

Invention involves discoveries of new processes, products, or combinations that can lead to some practical application. Innovation involves the application of inventions, as a discovery or new product is refined and made suitable for marketing. This fundamental difference between invention and innovation has been lost to most of the literature on technological change, where invention and innovation tend to be used synonymously, without regard for the contrasting levels of risk and uncertainty, or the very different kinds of work processes, that are involved in these two activities (Suarez-Villa, 1990, 1993).

Patenting is the common institutional mechanism applied to protect the property rights and to guarantee the originality of an invention, before innovation and diffusion occur. The patent system is by far the most important legal and institutional mechanism along the way from discovery to innovation and diffusion. It is also a powerful incentive for scientist-entrepreneurs since it can ensure, better than any other existing safeguard, that some appropriation of returns will occur. Where relatively competitive markets exist, and where trusts or monopolies are largely outlawed and imports are accessible, as in the case of the United States, the patent system provides the single most important legal means for appropriating the returns to invention, if or when usage occurs (Griliches, 1990; Fischer et al., 1991; Cornish, 1981; Schmookler, 1966).

While questions may be raised about whether the patenting of any given invention will lead to innovation and usage, or whether any returns may eventually occur, at the very least patenting provides an important property right that helps reduce the uncertainty of appropriation, if any successful diffusion occurs. Without patenting, then, the uncertainty of appropriating returns is much greater than if a patent award is obtained. The propensity to patent new discoveries is therefore quite high, even in large corporate organizations that control a substantial share of their product markets. Few discoveries today, regardless of their expected economic impact, risk being left unpatented, even when the prospects of obtaining any economic returns are very uncertain. The increasing globalization of information systems and networks, of technological knowledge, and the widespread diffusion of production capabilities, have contributed to the importance of patenting, as a means of safeguarding the property rights to any ideas or discoveries (Griliches et al., 1987; Horstmann et al., 1985; Beggs, 1984; Scherer, 1983).

14.2.1 Innovative Capacity and Technological Potential

Innovative capacity is a potential measure of the innovation possibilities available through invention (Suarez-Villa, 1990, 1993). It represents the actual stock of all inventive knowledge available as patents, that can be used by the corporate or individual awardees, or by others through licensing. Clearly, invention patenting does not include all of the technological innovation possibilities available to an economy. Organizational and process-oriented innovations are introduced in many organizations on an ad-hoc (or trial) basis which, when found satisfactory, are adopted until better ways or arrangements replace them. Many of those ad hoc innovations then diffuse out nationally, regionally or internationally through an industry's productive structure, as experience is gained and publicized, or as personnel change positions and employers.

Nevertheless, invention patenting remains the single most reliable historical indicator of the endogenous inventive knowledge available to an economy. It incorporates consistent evaluation standards over long periods of time, with respect to the originality of ideas and discoveries. Patenting also introduces a uniform temporal parameter for the use of an invention, by allowing a 17-year term of legal validity, which is rarely ever extended. Patent statistics are therefore one of the very few historically reliable, consistent and precise data resources available in the United States over a very long period, providing a basis on which to build analyses of invention trends (Griliches, 1990; Acs and Audretsch, 1989; Basberg, 1987; Narin et al., 1987; Pavitt, 1978, 1988; Comanor and Scherer, 1969).

The measurement of innovative capacity for any given year is based on the number of new patents awarded in that year (of age zero or less than one) added to the total of patents whose legal life term is still in effect (ages 1 through 17). More details on the measurement and conceptual definition of innovative capacity are provided in Suarez-Villa, (1990, 1993) and in Suarez-Villa and Hasnath (1993) and, for the sake of brevity, will not be replicated in this chapter. The national or regional innovative capacity is therefore a cumulated variable comprising the total number of invention patents that are legally available for usage at any given time. Long term changes in innovative capacity are influenced by the number of both new patent awards and those with expiring life terms at any point in time. Consecutive deficits over a prolonged period, in the net number of new patent awards entering the pool of available patents, will cause a decline in the national or regional innovative capacity. Conversely, increases in the number of inventions that are successful in obtaining patenting, will offset the withdrawal of expiring patents, causing the innovative capacity to increase if the rise of new inventions can be sustained over time.

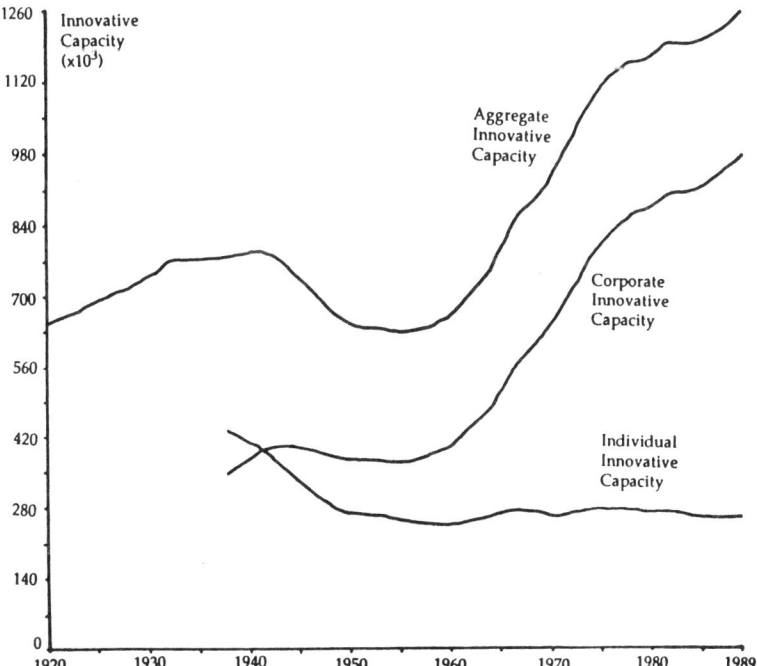

Figure 14.1 Innovative capacity: Aggregate, corporate, individual
Source: Suarez-Villa and Hasnath (1993)

Innovative capacity trends for the United States, in Figure 14.1 (for 1920-89), show the rising importance of corporate invention over the postwar era (U.S. Patent and Trademark Office, various years; U.S. Bureau of the Census 1975, various years). Corporate invention virtually determined the aggregate innovative capacity trend from 1950 onwards, while individual invention stagnated. These contrasts are a result of the emergence of R&D operations as an integral component of corporate structures and organization (Suarez-Villa, 1990; Hounshell and Smith, 1988; Bound et al., 1984; Pakes and Griliches, 1984; Mansfield, 1971). Corporate R&D contributes to both invention and innovation. Although it is impossible to estimate precisely which of these two sets of activities receive greater emphasis in corporate R&D, it is quite probable that innovation, being less risky and uncertain, may take a higher corporate priority, all things considered (Suarez-Villa, 1993).

A prolonged decline of innovative capacity can be assumed to have serious negative implications for any national or regional economy. Endogenously-generated invention and its derivative, innovation, are essential for the creation of new technologies and industries, and for domestic and international trade competitiveness (Schmookler, 1966; Jorgenson et al., 1988; Baumol et al., 1989; Mowery and Rosenberg, 1989; Adams, 1990; Derian, 1990; Malecki, 1991; Suarez-Villa, 1990, 1991). The endogenous generation of a strong invention dynamic is also crucial for the development of the human capital infrastructure, as scientific and technological education are key components of any regional or national development trajectory. A sustained decline of the innovative capacity can also have serious negative implications for the public resource base, since a less competitive position can cause economic contractions that end up reducing public revenues. Downturns of public investment in education and human capital development that are sustained over several iterations, can then result in a much diminished human capital infrastructure, making it more difficult for a regional or national economy to recover over time (Wozniak, 1987; von Hippel, 1988; Mensch, 1979; Ben-Porath, 1967; Berry, 1991).

A downward innovative capacity trend can be compounded by the outmigration of highly skilled scientists and technicians, causing an area's human capital infrastructure to decline further, as more attractive opportunities are found elsewhere. In the United States, for example, the migration of scientific talent from the industrial heartland (the Northeast and Midwest) toward some Sunbelt states, such as California and Texas, compounded the decline of the human capital resources and the educational-scientific infrastructure of various Northeastern and Midwestern states over the past thirty years (Suarez-Villa, 1993). One of the clearest indications of this trend is the fact that membership in the National Academy of Sciences, which was overwhelmingly concentrated in the Northeastern states only forty years ago, is now evenly split geographically between East and West (National Academy of Sciences, 1991). Over time, this trend favoring some Sunbelt states has seriously reduced the scientific human capital infrastructure of heartland states, such as New York, Pennsylvania, Ohio, Michigan and Illinois, causing a decline in their technological competitiveness (Suarez-Villa, 1993).

14.2.2 Infrastructural Investment and the Rise of Innovative Capacity

Keeping the innovative capacity on an increasing path should be a major policy objective, if a region's endogenous inventive potential and its human capital resource base are to be supported and developed. While various factors can influence any area's inventive performance and its human capital resources, infrastructural investment (broadly conceived) is a crucial component of any region's or nation's rise as an important source of scientific and technological knowledge (Andersson, 1986; Haynes and Stough, 1988; Lakshmanan, 1989; Nakicenovic, 1991). Because of its characteristics, infrastructure is one of the most permanent, long-term investments that can be made in a region's future development. At the same time, infrastructure is a very policy-sensitive instrument, with impacts that strongly affect an area's access to human capital upgrading, and to scientific and technological skilling. Few other investments can promote the long-term transformation of a regional economy as infrastructure can, with impacts that can help determine such phenomena as quality and access to education, the competitiveness of economic activities, the migration of highly skilled professionals, and the very balance between development, growth, or backwardness (American Public Works Association, 1976; Vickerman, 1989; Aschauer, 1990; Eberts, 1990; Hasnath and Chatterjee, 1990; Munnell, 1990; Chatterjee and Hasnath, 1991).

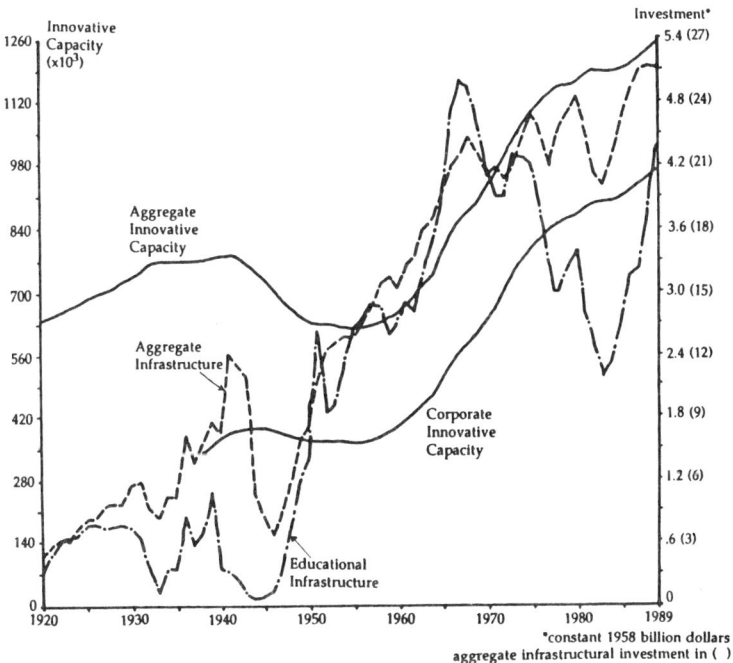

Figure 14.2 Innovative capacity and public infrastructural investment
Source: Suarez-Villa and Hasnath (1993)

Data on infrastructural construction expenditures, in Figure 14.2 and Table 14.1, show substantial fluctuations over most of the twentieth century (U.S. Bureau of the Census, 1975, 1981, various years). Only between the late 1940s and the late 1960s are there continuously rising trends for both aggregate public infrastructure and public educational infrastructure spending. Deeper fluctuations and a substantial downturn over the 1970s can be observed for educational infrastructure spending in Figure 14.2. Comparing infrastructural spending with the innovative capacity trends in Figure 14.2, however, it is unclear to what extent any positive association may be found between infrastructure spending and changes in Innovative Capacity. Some coincidence (with some lags) between the sustained increases in both infrastructural spending and innovative capacity over the postwar era may be observed, but this cannot be considered a convincing indication that a positive association between the two variables exists. A look at the deeper structure of the changes that occurred in both the infrastructure spending and innovative capacity trends is therefore necessary to provide clearer answers on this point.

Table 14.1 Innovative capacity and public infrastructural investment, 1920-89

Interval[a]	Aggregate innovative capacity[b]	Corporate innovative capacity[b]	Aggregate public infrastructure[c]	Public educational infrastructure[c]
1920-24	661.74	n.a.	3.02	.56
1925-29	709.40	n.a.	4.59	.76
1930-34	761.93	n.a.	5.16	.44
1935-39	777.48	354.70[d]	7.42	.72
1940-44	776.82	392.84	9.70	.22
1945-49	693.72	389.09	5.13	.52
1950-54	637.79	370.73	11.50	2.05
1955-59	635.96	376.88	14.42	2.76
1960-64	702.54	436.22	17.05	3.04
1965-69	857.16	566.59	21.28	4.63
1970-74	1005.52	713.44	21.11	4.12
1975-79	1141.43	840.20	22.71	3.45
1980-84	1188.64	896.13	21.85	2.64
1985-89	1225.92	944.50	24.95	3.48

[a]Interval estimates are annual means for each interval, based on annual data.
[b]Innovative capacity estimates $\times 10^3$.
[c]Infrastructural investment estimates in constant 1958 billion dollars.
[d]Based on 1938 and 1939 data.
Estimates are based on data obtained from U.S. Patent and Trademark Office (various years), U.S. Bureau of the Census (1975, 1981, various years), U.S. Department of Commerce (various years).

Source: Suarez-Villa and Hasnath (1993).

The *age cycle* dynamics of both infrastructural investment and innovative capacity can provide insights on the temporal association between these two processes (Suarez-Villa, 1990, 1993). To estimate the age cycle dynamics, infrastructural investment and invention patents are grouped in age segments, with a temporal parameter limited by the 17-year legal life term of invention patents. Three age segments (0-5, 6-11, 12-17 years) are then analyzed for the innovative capacity and public infrastructural investment, noting any correspondence in the upward or downward turns of each age segment's cycle, and the time lags that may occur between them. Further details on the estimation of invention patent age cycles and their dynamics may be found in Suarez-Villa (1990, 1993) and in Suarez-Villa and Hasnath (1993).

The expected rank-order of the age segments' relative share, for a rising innovative capacity or infrastructural investment trend to occur, is younger-to-oldest age segment (0-5, 6-11, 12-17 years in that order, largest to lowest share). A complete inversion of this rank-order would signal declining innovative capacity or infrastructural investment trends in future years (Suarez-Villa, 1990). Corporate invention patenting and public education infrastructural investment were found to have the strongest correspondence, in terms of their age cycle dynamics. In general, public educational infrastructural investment provided a better association than aggregate infrastructural investment, with both aggregate and corporate innovative capacity. Their graphed age cycles, shown in Figure 14.3, reveal temporal convergences at various points, indicating a positive association between their trends.

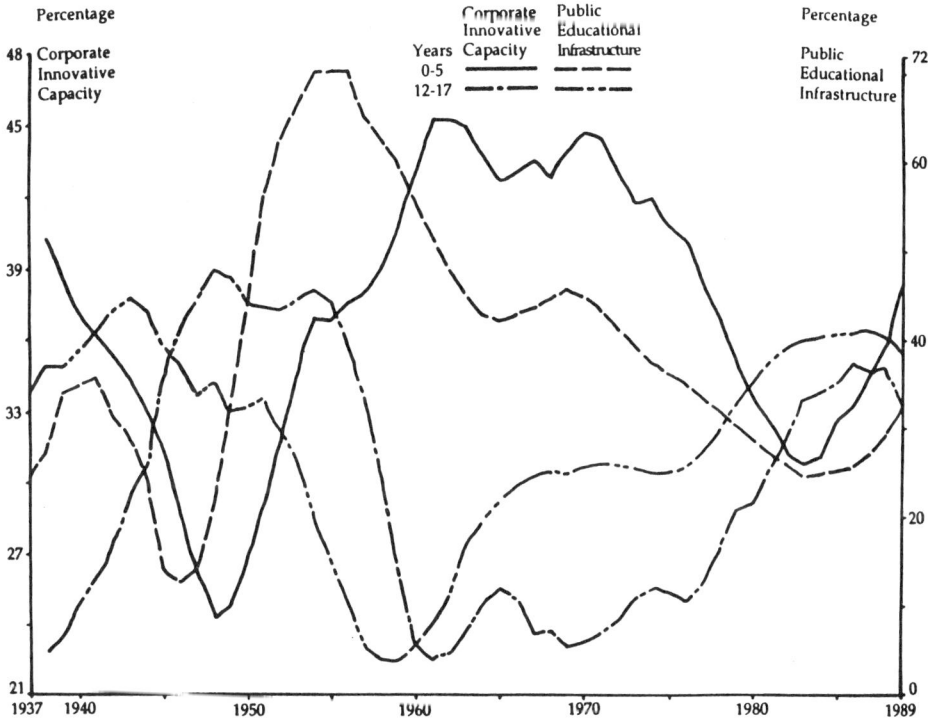

Figure 14.3
Source: Suarez-Villa and Hasnath (1993)

Peaks in the educational infrastructure's newer age segment (0-5 years) occur initially in 1955 and then again in 1969 (see Figure 14.3). The corporate innovative capacity's corresponding (though lagged) peaks for the same age segment (0-5 years) occur in 1961-62 and again in 1970. In turn, the troughs of the educational infrastructure's newer age segment occur in 1946, 1964 and in 1983, corresponding with the corporate innovative capacity's bottoming out in 1948, 1965 and 1983. Similar convergent turns are provided by the older age segments (12-17 years), with the educational infrastructure peaking initially in 1943 and in 1985-86, while the corporate innovative capacity's corresponding high points occur in 1948 first and then again in 1986. The dynamic of the oldest age segment, shown in Figure 14.3, reveals troughs in 1949, 1958-59, 1968 and 1974-75, corresponding (with lags) with the corporate innovative capacity's bottomings of 1950-52, 1961, 1969 and 1976. The expected rank orders of the age segments (0-5, 6-11, 12-17 years, largest to lowest share) are also remarkably similar, leading to rising trends over 1955-74 (educational infrastructure investment) and 1958-78 (corporate innovative capacity).

It may be noted from the previous analyses and Figure 14.3, that a progressive reduction of the temporal lags between the peaks or troughs of the educational infrastructure investment and corporate innovative capacity age cycles occurred over time. Lags of as much as six years can initially be found, for example, between the newer age segment's first peak for educational infrastructure (1955) and that of the corporate innovative capacity's (1961). The corresponding lag is then reduced to approximately one year, in the subsequent maximal upturn of the oldest age segment for educational infrastructure (1969) and corporate innovative capacity (1970). Clearly, lagged effects of infrastructural investment on innovative capacity can be expected, although it should be recalled that the cumulated character of the innovative capacity variable can conceal lags of greater magnitude. For example, both infrastructural investment and innovative capacity can be weighted toward the earlier or later years within any age segment, depending on when the largest proportionate stream of investments and patent awards entered the stock (see Suarez-Villa and Hasnath, 1993). In some cases, however, the completion of certain educational facilities, such as specialized research laboratories, can have an immediate impact on inventive performance while others, such as technical university facilities, have a longer gestation period before they can have appreciable impacts on a region's innovative capacity. Also, the construction of certain facility types can have a significant link to demographic characteristics as, for example, the aging of the "baby boom" segment of the population in the United States generated greater demand for higher education and specialized technical education facilities over the 1970s and 1980s (Suarez-Villa and Hasnath, 1993; Berry, 1991; Berry et al., 1993).

Tests with infrastructural investment and innovative capacity data, beyond the analyses of age cycle dynamics, showed a significant statistical association over the post-World War II era (Suarez-Villa and Hasnath, 1993). Regression estimates utilizing the Durbin serial correlation correction method, provided a statistical association of as high as 63.5 percent between infrastructural investment and corporate innovative capacity (the dependent variable). Most of the effect of infrastructural investment on corporate innovative capacity was accounted for by educational infrastructural investment, however. The stronger association between educational infrastructure investment and innovative capacity can be expected, since the aggregate infrastructural investment variable typically includes many other facilities, such as roads, hospitals or airports, that may not be as directly linked with human capital development and inventive performance as educational facilities.

14.3   POLICY-TARGETING, INNOVATIVE CAPACITY, AND INFRASTRUCTURAL DEVELOPMENT

Much has been written about invention and innovation without any precise clues as to what needs to be supported, promoted or measured, how it is to be done, or what the spatial and temporal dimensions of such policy support should be. All too often the modes and means of invention and innovation tend to be confused, leading to policy formulations that are seriously flawed or, at best, ineffective. Equally confusing is the use of the term infrastructure, which all too often tends to be a catch-all phrase devoid of specifics, with little indication of just what sorts of infrastructural investments are to be made, what modes and means of invention and innovation they will support and how, and the policy programs that are needed to implement them.

Linking policy programs with the infrastructural investments that can best promote invention must be a crucial objective, if public resources are to be effective in the goal of raising the regional and national innovative capacity, through endogenously-generated invention. Understanding the inventive resource base of any area or nation, where human capital is a most important factor, must be a key element of the policy formulation process. Policy programs that support infrastructural investment, and their human capital benefits, must be coordinated to prevent long-term downturns in the innovative capacity dynamic.

Spatially, invention can be most effectively promoted and supported at the regional level. The institutions that most closely affect the human capital resources needed for invention, such as research laboratories and advanced educational institutions, tend to have their greatest impacts through their regional scope. The contact systems, the networks, and access structures that infrastructure supports tend to be articulated, operate best, or are in turn rendered dysfunctional at the regional level. The scope of infrastructural investments and policies is also best addressed at the regional level, given the effects of distance on the personal contact movements, collaboration, and diffusional interaction that are so important for invention.

14.3.1 Modes and Means of Invention: A Policy Perspective

Policy programs aiming to raise any region's or nation's innovative capacity through infrastructural investments, must address differences in the modes and means of invention. How the modes and means of invention contribute to changes in the innovative capacity is vital for the formulation of effective policy mechanisms. Targeting infrastructural investments to a given mode or means is important for the success of any policy effort, in raising the innovative capacity and the human capital resources that support it.

The two basic modes of invention in operation today are the corporate one, occurring mainly through the structuring of R&D in corporate organizations, and the individual mode, which was predominant up to the first third of the twentieth century (Suarez-Villa, 1990). As was shown previously, corporate invention has accounted for most of the changes occurring in the United States' innovative capacity over the past five decades. An understanding of the importance of this mode of invention is therefore vital for any policy initiatives aimed at generating innovative capacity endogenously, through fixed capital outlays.

The means of invention refer to how the process occurs, in terms of the generation of discoveries and ideas that can pass the definitive test of patenting. The various means of invention can occur through either the individual or corporate mode, although the latter should be of greatest interest insofar as any policy efforts are concerned. Three types of means can be outlined. The first one occurs within a single firm or, in the individual invention mode, through one individual's efforts. A second type is the collaborative one, involving, say, two or three firms (or individual inventors) that decide to selectively share their resources in one or more ways to achieve a mutually beneficial inventive outcome, in the form of one or more patent awards. The third type may be defined as "collective", in the sense provided by Allen (1983); its structure would be closest to that of a consortium, involving more than a handful of firms. One or more firms may take the lead for various components of their larger cooperative arrangement, or they may rotate leadership roles at various stages, in flexible arrangements designed to optimize opportunities and resources.

Collaborative and collective invention between firms may well become the most important means of endogenously-generated invention and innovative capacity in the twenty-first century. Trends favoring substantial cooperation and collaboration are already evident among many advanced technology firms (see, e.g., Hansen, 1992; Alter and Hage, 1992; Håkansson, 1989). All indications are that the sharing of corporate resources to achieve greater inventive productivity may well become one of the most important benefits of networking in the R&D field.

Strategic R&D alliances can effectively capture the benefits of inventive cooperation, especially when an emphasis is placed on basic invention and innovation rather than on simple incremental innovation or development. Such alliances can be of two different forms. One is the collaborative type, alluded to earlier, and the second is a more complex but potentially richer one, "collective" or consortia-based strategic alliances, occurring with the participation of numerous firms. The potential benefits of the latter depend more on the quantity of resources invested in the strategic alliance, which can be quite substantial and can therefore be qualitatively oriented more toward basic invention and innovation. At the same time, the possibilities for the cross-fertilization of ideas and of creative networking can be enormous, if the whole effort is organized in ways that facilitate direct communication, rapid testing, and lean bureaucratic procedures.

Networking possibilities may be most intense (and effective) at the regional level, once an agglomeration threshold of inventive firms is present, or when the human capital resources of an area can sustain a rapid incubation of invention-oriented firms. It is primarily at the regional level where collaborative and collective invention may become important sources of patenting and innovative capacity. In the United States, for example, the agglomeration of invention-oriented firms in Southern California and in Silicon Valley, turned California into the most important source of endogenously-generated innovative capacity in less than three decades (Suarez-Villa, 1993). As the agglomeration of new invention-oriented firms increased, supported by much public investment in the human capital infrastructure, access to cooperation and collaboration became significant localization advantages that attracted more invention-oriented venture capital to these areas.

An important objective of policy efforts aimed at raising the local and regional innovative capacity may therefore be to capture the self-reinforcing dynamic of technological development. One of the most important long-term benefits of expanding an area's technological base is that technology can serve, in and of itself, as a source of knowledge on which to base further discoveries. This cumulative dynamic is determined to a great extent by the local and regional human capital base, by the influx of highly skilled individuals attracted by the externalities that are provided, and by the institutional infrastructure that is directly linked to the area's technological base. The impact of this cumulative and self-reinforcing dynamic tends to be greatest whenever basic inventions and innovations can be generated in a continuous and cumulative way. Such continuity and cumulativeness then become the key on which the self-reinforcing dynamic turns, where invention and technology themselves become the keys to further discoveries, making a locale or region a world-class source for the diffusion of innovations.

The strategic selection of sectors for which inventions and innovative capacity will be generated, through the various modes and means, must also be considered by any policy-making program. Clearly, the selection of sectors involves decisions which are best left up to the corporate actors or individual inventors involved; nevertheless, once certain sectors are targeted by invention-oriented firms or individuals, policy support, in the form of infrastructural investment and better access to information and venture capital, must be considered essential. It is in the targeting of inventions for primary use in some sectors, that the future competitiveness of nations and industries lies. The growth of innovative capacity and inventive productivity of some nations, and their targeting of certain sectors, can reveal where the future dominance of technologies and of entire industries may lie. A brief look at the data on patenting emphasis by country of origin in Table 14.2, and the patenting volume data of Figure 14.4, may prove revealing in assessing where the competitive strengths of some nations may be over the first three decades of the twenty-first century. Japanese dominance of the crucial information technology field may seem assured, while Western European and American emphasis has shifted toward chemicals and biotechnology.

Table 14.2 Comparative patenting emphasis of technologies in the United States, 1990

| Patent class[a] | Patent class name | Country of origin[b] | | | |
		US	Japan	Germany	UK
208	Mineral oils: Processes and products	GREATER	Lesser		
166	Wells	GREATER	Lesser	Lesser	
252	Compositions	GREATER			GREATER
354	Photography	Lesser	GREATER	Lesser	Lesser
355	Photocopying		GREATER	Lesser	Lesser
360	Dynamic magnetic information storage or retrieval		GREATER		Lesser
369	Dynamic information storage or retrieval	Lesser	GREATER	Lesser	Lesser
365	Static information storage and retrieval		GREATER	Lesser	
400	Typewriting machines	Lesser	GREATER		
84	Music	Lesser	GREATER	Lesser	Lesser
180	Motor vehicles	Lesser	GREATER		
346	Recorders		GREATER	Lesser	
123	Internal combustion engines	Lesser	GREATER		
102	Ammunition and explosives		Lesser	GREATER	
532-570	Organic compounds (part of class 532-570 series)			GREATER	GREATER
71	Chemistry, fertilizers			GREATER	GREATER
106	Compositions, coating or plastic			GREATER	GREATER
244	Aeronautics		Lesser		GREATER

[a]U.S. Patent Classification System
[b]Classified by country of residence of first-named inventor, regardless of whether the patent is assigned to a firm or to an individual inventor.

Country emphasis categories were determined by dividing the proportion of invention patents granted in a class by the proportion of all invention patents granted in all classes (specific to a given country of origin). Only classes for which a minimum of 200 invention patents were granted were included in the estimates above.

Source: U.S. Patent and Trademark Office (1991, 1992).

Policy support for invention-intensive, targeted sectors must be evaluated not only in terms of their future competitiveness, but also on the basis of the upgrading of human capital resources that they can generate. Impacts on a region's human capital may well be a function of the means through which invention occurs. For example, it is likely that for many projects collaborative invention may be able to both use and develop more of an area's human capital resources, than for those which would occur solely within a single firm. Similarly, forms of collaborative and "collective" invention which enlist the human capital of research institutions (public and private), such as universities and technical centers, may provide greater benefits to an area's endogenous, inventive human capital than those that have more restrictive participatory scopes (see, e.g., Brett et al., 1991; Haynes and Stough, 1988).

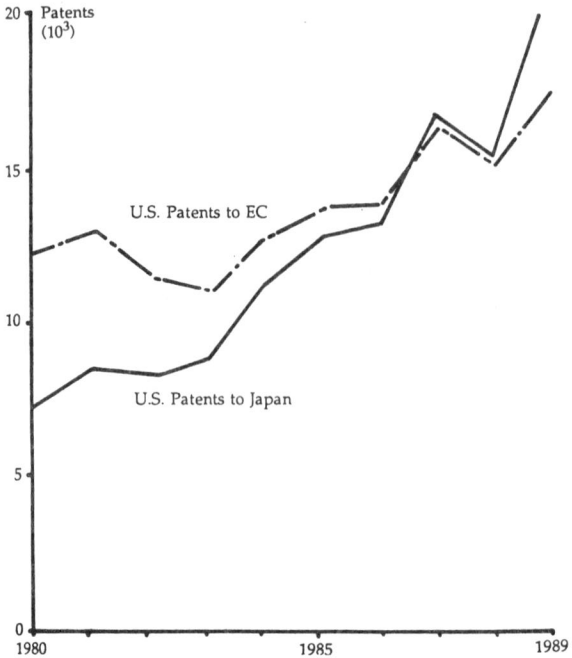

Figure 14.4 U.S. patents issued to Japan and the EC, 1980-89

14.3.2 Policy Programs: Outlines and Agendas

Several premises underlie the policy programs that are outlined in this chapter. One is that invention will occur most effectively by private initiative and creativity, through either the corporate or the individual modes. The policy programs' function is therefore one of support for those initiatives and creativities, by providing public goods and services that would be very difficult for private capital to sustain, at least initially, because of the high uncertainties involved, high initial capital investment requirements, or because of low short-term profitability.

The provision of infrastructure, targeted to support invention and the growth of the innovative capacity, is a vital component of the policy programs. Infrastructure's role must be thought of in terms of the human capital needs that are directly linked to the development of endogenous inventive capabilities. These can include, for example, the construction of joint public-private facilities where invention, through laboratory experiments, mechanical construction, theoretical research, simulation, or advanced education and interaction, may occur. Infrastructure that can support extensive forms of networking, within a region and with other areas, by providing better access to advanced communications, sources of information, and to specific "invention-idea" nodes and outlets, should also be included. These infrastructural improvements can provide what may be referred to as "information-interaction freeways", that should be easily accessible, with minimal hardware and link-up costs, to anyone with inventive interests.

At the same time, a policy program supporting invention and the growth of the innovative capacity must provide some basic financing, in the form of seed capital, to allow a start of inventive processes for which private capital may not be readily available, because of their perceived riskiness and uncertainty. A key component of this aspect is that infrastructural investments provide for the accelerated diffusion of the potential uses of inventions, as a means to recover the seed capital outlays incurred by the public sector. Such rapid diffusion possibilities can themselves become important incentives to invent, by potentially increasing the returns to inventors, as diffusion and adoption occur more rapidly. Without strong infrastructural support to facilitate access to information, interaction, experimentation and diffusion, even the best thought-out and implemented policy programs may fall short of their objectives, especially when strict public accountability guidelines are enforced.

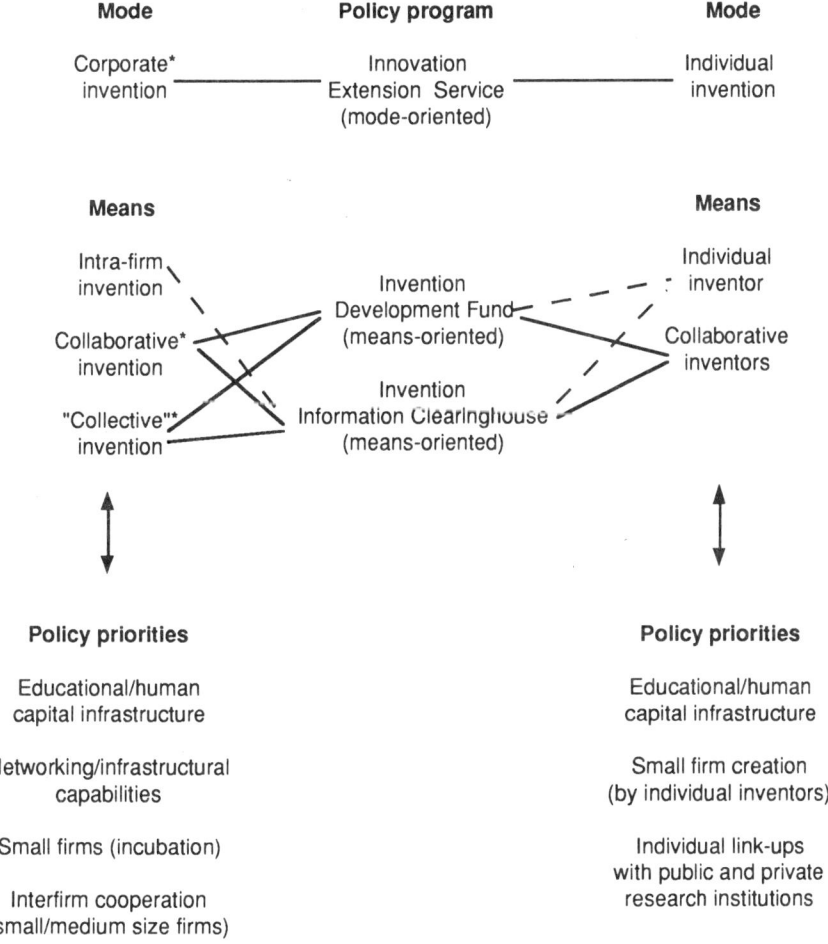

* of greater priority for innovative capacity growth

Figure 14.5 Invention modes, means, and policy programs

The first component of the policy program, the Innovation Extension Service, is mode-oriented and has the primary objective of demonstrating uses for inventions developed by either the corporate or individual modes (see Figure 14.5). The licensing of inventions that are put to use, and making it easier to obtain returns, could also be within its scope. The sectoral scope of the Innovation Extension Service should be multi-faceted, providing information and instruction to firms and to individual entrepreneurs in services, manufacturing, agriculture, or to government agencies. This policy program could operate through a variety of regional centers (as mini-campuses), where work-shops, classes, demonstration sessions, and other events related to invention and innovation diffusion would be held. Geographically, the regional centers would be tactically located where they could provide maximum exposure to attract and accommodate interested parties.

Clearly, some firms producing inventions may prefer to retain control over the patents that they acquire, curtailing their diffusion at least within the same industry or sector of operation. In such cases, the Innovation Extension Service could provide assistance in seeking licensees and usage outside a firm's main sector of operation, if such possibilities are viable. Individual inventors and small firms may potentially become strong beneficiaries of this program, since it can provide a much-needed market access for their ideas and discoveries. Increasing the rate of usage of invention patents may also be an important outcome of this policy program; a large proportion of patents in the United States has always remained unutilized throughout their life terms.

The Invention Development Fund should have as its primary goal the provision of seed venture capital, to allow invention projects to start or proceed over their various stages, until a patenting application can be submitted (see Figure 14.5). This policy program would contribute to raise the regional and national innovative capacity, especially in cases where sufficient individual or corporate resources cannot be marshalled, because of a lack of private venture capital, or because of the inherent riskiness of the projects. The Invention Development Fund could also provide seed capital for the micro-infrastructure required to start and carry through invention projects to the patent application stage. Specific laboratory facilities, equipment, hardware to link-up with networks, and other limited fixed capital would be examples of such support. One of its main outcomes could be to generate a larger number of invention ventures, among small firms and individual inventors.

Collaborative and collective invention, especially among small and medium size firms, should be a priority for the Invention Development Fund program. A key assumption is that both of these means of invention can contribute more to increase an area's innovative capacity, by promoting greater inventive productivity as well as more significant discoveries. Small and medium size firms may require greater attention because of their limited resources; such firms may also become the future entrepreneurial lifeblood of a regional economy, as they expand and mature with new technologies. This policy program would also help individual inventors to start their own (small) firms, utilizing and marketing their inventions. In some advanced nations, such as the United States, small and medium size firms are the most important employment creators.

The third component of the policy program, the Invention Information Clearinghouse, would have the primary objective of providing current and would-be inventors with information about on-going or proposed projects that may lead to collaboration (see Figure 14.5). In several ways, this program would have a nodal function, linking up inventors (as individuals or in firms) to create and expand a network that may enrich the idea base for a particular range of invention projects. The infrastructural investments required by this policy program would be more at the level of communication links and facilities, that can provide easier and lower-cost user access to information and contact networks. This means-oriented program could contribute to raise an area's innovative capacity significantly, as better-informed inventors, working individually or in corporate organizations, become more productive. At the same time, it may be argued that better informed invention-oriented firms and individuals could produce qualitatively more significant ideas and discoveries.

The Clearinghouse program may provide the equivalent of an information or networking "freeway", that can expand and link-up with interregional and international channels. Favoring collaborative arrangements would probably have a greater quantitative and qualitative impact on the innovative capacity over the medium and long term, especially insofar as the corporate invention mode is concerned. This program could also have much impact on individual inventors, since link-ups with extensive networks may allow individuals to set up their own firms, in association with other individual inventors. At the same time, better networking access could allow greater interaction with public and private research institutions, and with the innovation extension service centers.

The policy programs discussed in this section are intended to complement each other in two dimensions. The means-oriented programs (Invention Development Fund, Invention Information Clearinghouse) would act on the process of invention itself, providing resources in the form of infrastructure, information access, or capital outlays, that can further both productivity and quality, while raising an area's innovative capacity over the medium and long term. The mode-oriented program (Innovation Extension Service) would then act on the usage diffusion side, providing greater opportunities for improving efficiency and productivity, through technological substitution in the adopting sectors and activities.

14.4   CONCLUSION

Three aspects related to the process of technological development have been addressed in this chapter. The first one dealt with the measurement of invention, as the single most important source of endogenous technological development and innovation. For this purpose, the concept of innovative capacity was defined, utilizing U.S. historical invention patent data. A second facet then examined the relationship between infrastructural investment and innovative capacity, to determine whether a positive causal association might be occurring. A direct, positive relationship between public educational infrastructure investment and the growth of innovative capacity can be assumed to occur, based on previous empirical research. Patent and infrastructural investment age cycles were found to have a remarkable convergence, in terms of the cyclical upswings and downturns that contribute to medium and long term changes in any region's or nation's innovative capacity.

The third facet of this chapter then dealt with the policy programs that may be implemented to promote invention, and increase the innovative capacity over the medium and long term. Three policy programs dealing with access to information and networks, the usage and diffusion of inventions, and seed or short-term financing, were outlined. Infrastructural support, closely related to the development of human capital resources at both the macro and micro levels, was considered essential for the success of each policy program. Specifically targeting the policy programs to either allow new firm formation by individual inventors, or to support inventive initiatives by small and medium size firms, was considered an important objective, along with the promotion of collaborative research.

Relating each policy program to the modes and means of invention is vital for targeting the specific mechanisms, that should be applied to deal with regional or national underinvestment in technology and in its support infrastructure. Each means may require different approaches, if any policy effort is going to be effective in raising an area's endogenous innovative capacity, through investments in the human capital infrastructure. The support of collaborative and "collective" invention are thought to be important in promoting greater inventive productivity. Collaborative and collective invention may well become the most important means of generating invention, quantitatively and qualitatively, in future years and decades, as many inventive processes become more complex or rely on a greater diversity of skills and information.

Underinvestment in infrastructure must be viewed in terms of the regional and national priorities served by infrastructural development. In view of the increasing globalization of technology, and the need to support national and regional competitiveness, technological development, in the form of endogenously-generated invention, should be at the top of the policy-making agenda. Infrastructural development, targeted to support the human capital resources needed for invention, must be a central component of any effort aimed at improving long term economic performance. A consideration of the indicators provided by the concept of innovative capacity and the policy programs outlined in this chapter, should help in formulating better policy mechanisms and strategies, to support technological and human capital development at this particular juncture. The end of the twentieth century will very likely witness the most intense globalization and diffusion of technological knowledge ever seen by mankind, with dire consequences for nations that neglect their technological and human capital infrastructures.

REFERENCES

Acs, Z.J. and D.B. Audretsch, 1989, "Patents as a Measure of Innovative Activity", *Kyklos*, 42:171-180.

Adams, J. D., 1990, "Fundamental Stocks of Knowledge and Productivity Growth", *Journal of Political Economy*, 98: 673-702.

Allen, R.C., 1983, "Collective Invention", *Journal of Economic Behavior and Organization*, 4:1-24.

Alter, C. and J. Hage, 1992, *Organizations Working Together: Coordination in Inter-organizational Networks*, Sage, Newbury Park, Ca.

American Public Works Association, 1976, *History of Public Works in the United States, 1776-1976*, Public Works Association, Chicago.

Andersson, Å.E, 1985, "Creativity and Regional Development", *Papers of the Regional Science Association*, 56:5-20.

Andersson, Å.E., 1986, "The Four Logistical Revolutions", *Papers of the Regional Science Association*, 59:1-12.

Andersson, Å.E. and D. Batten, 1988, "Creative Nodes, Logistical Networks and the Future of the Metropolis", *Transportation*, 14:281-293.

Aschauer, D.A., 1990, "Why is Infrastructure Important?", in A.H. Munnell (ed.), *Is There a Shortfall in Public Capital Investment?*, Federal Reserve Bank of Boston, Boston.

Ayres, R.U., 1988, "Technology: The Wealth of Nations", *Technological Forecasting and Social Change*, 33:189-202.

Basberg, B.L., 1987, "Patents and the Measurement of Technological Change: A Survey of the Literature", *Research Policy*, 16:131-141.

Baumol, W.J., S.A.B. Blackman and E.N. Wolff, 1989, *Productivity and American Leadership: The Long View*, M.I.T. Press, Cambridge.

Beggs, J.J., 1984, "Long-run Trends in Patenting", in Z. Griliches (ed.), *R&D, Patents and Productivity*, University of Chicago Press, Chicago.

Ben-Porath, Y., 1967, "The Production of Human Capital and the Life Cycle of Earnings", *Journal of Political Economy*, 75:352-365.

Berry, B.J.L., 1991, *Long-Wave Rhythms in Economic Development and Political Behavior*, Johns Hopkins University Press, Baltimore.

Berry, B.J.L., H. Kim and H.-M. Kim., 1993, "Are Long Waves Driven by Techno-Economic Transformations? Evidence from the U.S. and the U.K.", *Technological Forecasting and Social Change*, 43:111-136.

Bound, J., C. Cummins, Z. Griliches, B.H. Hall and A. Jaffe, 1984, "Who does R&D and Who Patents?", in Z. Griliches (ed.), *R&D, Patents and Productivity,* University of Chicago Press, Chicago.

Brett, A., D.V. Gibson and R.W. Smilor, 1991, *University Spin-Off Companies: Economic Development, Faculty Entrepreneurs, and Technology Transfer,* Rowman and Littlefield, Boston.

Chatterjee, L. and S.A. Hasnath, 1991, "Public Construction Expenditures in the United States: Are There Structural Breaks in the 1921-1987 Period?", *Economic Geography,* 67:42-53.

Comanor, W. and F.M. Scherer, 1969, "Patent Statistics as a Measure of Technical Change", *Journal of Political Economy,* 77:329-398.

Cornish, W.R., 1981, *Intellectual Property: Patents, Copyrights, Trademarks and Allied Rights,* Sweet and Maxwell, London.

Davelaar, E.-J. and P. Nijkamp, 1990, "Technological Innovation and Spatial Transformation", *Technological Forecasting and Social Change,* 37:181-202.

Derian, J.-C., 1990, *America's Struggle for Leadership in Technology* (translated by S. Schaeffer), M.I.T. Press, Cambridge.

Eberts, R.W., 1990, "Cross-sectional Analysis of Public Infrastructure and Regional Productivity Growth", Working Paper 9004, Federal Reserve Bank of Cleveland, Cleveland.

Fischer, M.M., S. Fröhlich and H. Gassler, 1991, "An Exploration into the Determinants of Patent Activities", Presented at the 31st European Congress, Regional Science Association International, Lisbon.

Griliches, Z., 1990, "Patent Statistics as Economic Indicators: A Survey", *Journal of Economic Literature,* 28:1661-1707.

Griliches, Z., A. Pakes and B.H. Hall, 1987, "The Value of Patents as Indicators of Inventive Activity", in P. Dasgupta and P. Stoneman (eds.), *Economic Policy and Technological Performance,* Cambridge University Press, Cambridge.

Hägerstrand, T., 1967, *Innovation Diffusion as a Spatial Process,* University of Chicago Press, Chicago.

Håkansson, H., 1989, *Corporate Technological Behaviour: Co-operation and Networks,* Routledge, New York.

Hansen, N.M., 1992, "Competition, Trust, and Reciprocity in the Development of Innovative Regional Milieux", *Papers in Regional Science,* 71:95-106.

Hasnath, S.A. and L. Chatterjee, 1990, "Public Construction in the United States: An Analysis of Expenditure Patterns", *Annals of Regional Science,* 24:133-145.

Haynes, K.E. and R.R. Stough, 1988, "Infrastructure Investment for Basic Research: U.S. Patterns in University Science and Technology", in L.J. Roborgh, R.R. Stough and T.A.G. Toonen (eds.), *Public Intrastructure Redefined,* Leiden University Press, Leiden.

Horstmann, I., G.M. MacDonald and A. Slivinski, 1985, "Patents as Information Transfer Mechanisms: To Patent or (Maybe) Not to Patent", *Journal of Political Economy,* 93:837-858.

Hounshell, D.A. and J.K. Smith, 1988, *Science and Corporate Strategy,* Cambridge University Press, New York.

Johansson, B., 1991, "Infrastructure and Productivity Growth", Presented at the 38th North American Meetings, Regional Science Association International, New Orleans.

Jorgenson, D., F. Gollop and B. Fraumeni, 1988, *Productivity and U.S. Economic Growth,* Harvard University Press, Cambridge.

Kuhn, T.S., 1962, *The Structure of Scientific Revolutions,* University of Chicago Press, Chicago.

Lakshmanan, T.R., 1989, "Infrastructure and Economic Transformation", in Å.E. Andersson, D.F. Batten, B. Johansson and P. Nijkamp (eds.), *Advances in Spatial Theory and Dynamics,* Elsevier – North Holland, New York.

Lee, T.H. and P.P. Reid, 1991, *Prospering in a Global Economy: National Interests in An Age of Global Technology,* National Academy Press, Washington, D.C.

Machlup, F., 1980, *Knowledge: Its Creation, Distribution, and Economic Significance,* Princeton University Press, Princeton.

Malecki, E.J., 1991, *Technology and Economic Development,* John Wiley, New York.

Mansfield, E., 1971, *Research and Innovation in the Modern Corporation,* Norton, New York.

Mensch, G.O., 1979, *Stalemate in Technology,* Ballinger, Cambridge.

Mowery, D. and N. Rosenberg, 1989, *Technology and the Pursuit of Economic Growth,* Cambridge University Press, New York.

Munnell, A.H. (ed.), 1990, *Is There a Shortfall in Public Capital Investment?,* Federal Reserve Bank of Boston, Boston.

Nakicenovic, N., 1991, "Diffusion of Pervasive Systems: A Case of Transport Infrastructures", *Technological Forecasting and Social Change,* 39:181-200.

Narin, F., E. Noma and R. Perry, 1987, "Patents as Indicators of Corporate Technological Strength", *Research Policy,* 16:143-155.

National Academy of Sciences, 1991, *Organization and Members, 1991,* National Academy Press, Washington, D.C.

Nelson, R.R. and G. Wright, 1992, "The Rise and Fall of American Technological Leadership: The Postwar Era in Historical Perspective", *Journal of Economic Literature,* 30:1931-1964.

Pakes, A. and Z. Griliches, 1984, "Patents and R&D at the Firm's Level: A First Look", in Z. Griliches (ed.), *R&D, Patents and Productivity,* University of Chicago Press, Chicago.

Pavitt, K., 1978, "Using Patent Statistics in Science Indicators: Possibilities and Problems", in *The Meaning of Patent Statistics,* National Science Foundation, Washington.

Pavitt, K., 1988, "Uses and Abuses of Patent Statistics", in A.F.J. van Raan (ed.), *Handbook of Quantitative Studies of Science and Technology,* North Holland, Amsterdam.

Rogers, E.M. and F. Shoemaker, 1971, *The Communication of Innovations,* Free Press, New York.

Rosenberg, N., 1972, *Technology and American Economic Growth,* Harper and Row, New York.

Rubin, M.R. and M.T. Huber, 1986, *The Knowledge Industry in the United States, 1960-80,* Princeton University Press, Princeton.

Scherer, F.M., 1983, "The Propensity to Patent", *International Journal of Industrial Organization,* 1:221-225.

Schmookler, J., 1966, *Invention and Economic Growth,* Harvard University Press, Cambridge.

Snickars, F., 1987, "The Transportation Sector in the Communications Society: Some Analytical Observations", in P. Nijkamp and S. Reichmann (eds.), *Transportation Planning in a Changing World,* Gower, Aldershot.

Suarez-Villa, L., 1990, "Invention, Inventive Learning, and Innovative Capacity", *Behavioral Science,* 35:290-310.

Suarez-Villa, L., 1991, "Regional Evolution and Entrepreneurship: Roles, Eras and the Space Economy", *Entrepreneurship and Regional Development,* 3:335-347.

Suarez-Villa, L., 1993, "The Dynamics of Regional Invention and Innovation: Innovative Capacity and Regional Change in the Twentieth Century", *Geographical Analysis,* 25:147-164.

Suarez-Villa, L. and S.A. Hasnath, 1993, "The Effect of Infrastructure on Invention: Innovative Capacity and the Dynamics of Public Construction Investment", *Technological Forecasting and Social Change,* 44:333-358.

U.S. Bureau of the Census, 1975, *Historical Statistics of the United States,* U.S. Government Printing Office, Washington, D.C.

U.S. Bureau of the Census, 1981, *Construction Reports: Value of New Construction Put in Place in the United States 1964 to 1980,* U.S. Government Printing Office, Washington, D.C.

U.S. Bureau of the Census, (various years), *Statistical Abstract of the United States,* U.S. Government Printing Office, Washington, D.C.

U.S. Department of Commerce, 1980, *Technology Assessment and Forecast,* 7th report, U.S. Government Printing Office, Washington, D.C.

U.S. Department of Commerce, (various years), *Construction Review,* U.S. Government Printing Office, Washington, D.C.

U.S. Patent and Trademark Office, 1991, *Technology Assessment and Forecast,* U.S. Government Printing Office, Washington, D.C.

U.S. Patent and Trademark Office, 1992, *Highlights in Patent Activity,* U.S. Government Printing Office, Washington, D.C.

U.S. Patent and Trademark Office, (various years), *Annual Report,* U.S. Government Printing Office, Washington, D.C.

Vickerman, R.W., 1989, "Measuring Changes in Regional Competitiveness: The Effects of International Infrastructure Investments", *Annals of Regional Science,* 23:275-286.

von Hippel, E.A., 1988, *The Sources of Innovation,* Oxford University Press, Oxford.

Wozniak, G.D., 1987, "Human Capital, Information, and the Early Adoption of New Technology", *Journal of Human Resources,* 22:101-112.

CHAPTER 15

Valuations of Environmental Externalities:
Some Recent Results

Emile Quinet

Ecole Nationale des Ponts et Chaussées, Paris

15.1 INTRODUCTION

Externalities have been thoroughly explored in economic theory; and since the mid sixties, approximately, environmental issues have become increasingly important. Nowadays every decision in the transport field places great weight upon external or environmental effects. But any real economic assessment implies a monetary valuation. To what extent is a monetary valuation meaningful, useful, and implementable as far as the environment is concerned? This is the general subject of this communication, which has four sections.

The first section, which is rather conceptual and methodological, will be devoted to the problems of definition. Different concepts of valuation will be presented and their relation to each other will be discussed. In the second section, statistics will be addressed and in the third section a survey of recent evaluations of the environmental effects of transport will be made. The fourth section will be devoted to the question of how to use these valuations in current decision-making problems. The conclusion will present some additional possible uses of the valuations and directions for further research.

15.2 METHODOLOGICAL PROBLEMS

The classical valuation of most economic goods is straightforward: the value is the market price which comes from the interaction of demand and supply. Given some current assumptions[1], it can be shown that the price is both the consumer's marginal willingness to pay as well as the marginal and the average cost of production of the good. If there are no externalities, the price is also the social value of the good.

Values are quite different for environmental goods – or more often "bads" – since there is no market for these goods and no price for them. Their value must be calculated either from the supply side, or from the demand side.

On the supply side, two methods are available:

---

[1] Essentially the convexity of producers' and consumers' space.

a) The cost of protection or abatement. For instance, the cost of a catalytic converter in order to abate air pollution.
b) The cost of damage. For instance, productivity losses or heath care costs because of air pollution.
   Two methods also exist on the demand side:
a) Willingness to pay (W.T.P.) in order to have a better environment. For example, the willingness to pay to reduce air pollution.
b) Willingness to accept (W.T.A.); i.e. the amount of money which would simply compensate for the worsening of environmental problems.
   Some comments about the measurement of these concepts follow:
- Each of them is a function of the level N of the bad: $F(N)$. It is therefore possible to define a marginal value, an average value and a total value, just in the same way as it is possible to define a marginal, average and total cost for the production of current economic goods.
- The situation is a little more complicated for environmental goods (or bads). First, sometimes the expression: "there is no 0 level; for instance the 0 level of noise" has no meaning, because the measure for noise disturbance is the logarithm of the emission power of the noise source. Second, the consequences of the bad are not limited to a single person, as is the case for current economic goods; they are often very widely spread. For instance, the emission of pollution from a car affects a lot of people near the motorway, and has the characteristics of a public good; it is necessary to take into account all the people who are affected, and to add up their W.T.P. or W.T.A.

In a somewhat similar way to the production of noise which emanates from car makers, infrastructure designers, house builders, and households, some effects are very frequently not fully perceived by those who suffer from them. For instance, air pollution may be a cause of illness, but people do not perceive the relation between their disease and the pollution; consequently their cost W.T.P. is less than the damage.

Let us mention another methodological difficulty. Some environmental phenomena are long lasting. The have inter-generational consequences. Their valuation implies adding values or costs at different points of time and therefore making use of a discount rate, as well as taking into account irreversibility effects.

For a complete discussion, see Pearce and Markandiya (1989) as well as Barde (1992), Button (1992) and Banister and Button (1992). In order to take these factors into account the value of environmental goods is often divided into:
- a user's value, representing the utility coming from the use of the good;
- an option value, which results from the fact that the consumers may want to use the good in the future, even though they are not using it now; and
- an existence value, which represents the satisfaction of an individual who does not use the good, nor intends to use the good, but is glad that it exists (for instance, he wants his children to be able to use it).

In the following, we will not deal with these concepts and we will only take the user's value into account.

In a "perfect world", where decisions are socially optimal and where economic agents have perfect information, the marginal costs of abatement and damage, and the marginal W.T.P. and W.T.A. would be equal.[2]

---

[2] Abatement costs and damage costs provide two technical ways of obtaining a given level of "bad", and should be equal at the margin. Social optimality implies equality between marginal cost and marginal W.T.P. These results are valid under the usual hypothesis of continuity and convexity.

But, as a consequence of these peculiarities, the four methods do not give the same result in the real world: in general, the marginal willingness to pay or to accept the marginal avoidance cost and the marginal damage cost are different.

The information of economic agents is far from perfect especially in regard to environmental problems. As for decisions, as many environmental goods have the characteristics of public goods, their provision cannot be optimized through market procedures. Also, the public decision-making process is far from perfect – and, to say the least, the optimality of public decisions must be checked in each specific situation.

To illustrate these considerations, let us take as an example the case of air pollution: the abatement costs result from the decisions of car makers, who are inclined to stick to the standards set by the Government. Up to now, these standards have only rarely been based on economic considerations; the damage cost is composed of health care expenses for people who suffer from the pollution – a portion of which is born by social security systems. There is no reason why those two kinds of costs should be equal in the real world (they should be equal in a perfect world). On the demand side, W.T.P. and W.T.A. may be different due to psychological biases (when no responsibility is involved, nobody is eager to pay, but everybody is willing to receive). Furthermore, there is no automatic adjustment between costs (whether abatement or damage) and W.T.P., especially when people are not aware of the health disturbances caused by air pollution.

On the contrary, in a perfect world, with optimal decisions, the following equalities would stand: marginal abatement cost = marginal damage cost = marginal W.T.P. = marginal W.T.A.

And the corresponding figure would be equal to the marginal social value of the environmental good (or "bad").

15.3   HOW TO CALCULATE THE VALUATIONS

According to Button (1992), the methods for deriving numerical values of environmental goods can be classified into different categories:

- Precedent. For instance, the compensation awarded by jurisdiction for injuries or death. This method leads to rather precise figures, but they may be very far from the real economic value. This corresponds to a kind of collective W.T.P.
- Averting behavior. The value of the environmental good – or more precisely, bad – is equated either to the cost of avoiding it (this method gives indications about the abatement term $A(N)$) or to the cost of repairing the damages (it then gives indications about $D(N)$); both measures can be different, and also different from the willingness to pay.
- Hedonic prices. With these, the value of the environment is deduced from the changes in the price of a marketable good, whose quality depends on the environment. For instance, the value of houses depends on their exposure to noise. These hedonic prices lead to W.T.P or W.T.A.
- Travel-cost method. This method is somewhat akin to the previous one: the value of a leisure park is deduced from the behavior of people visiting it and especially from the travel cost that they incure to visit it. This method also gives W.T.P. or W.T.A.
- Stated preferences. In this method, people are asked how much they are ready to pay in order to enjoy the environmental good, or to avoid the nuisance. The questionnaire technique is very precise and sophisticated. However, in this method, there are a lot of possible biases, and large discrepancies in the results. This method gives W.T.P. or W.T.A.

These methods involve a lot of difficulties. Let us dwell a little upon the problems of measuring W.T.P. or W.T.A.: the most natural way to get figures for W.T.P. or W.T.A.

is to ask people how much they would be willing to pay (or to get) for a decrease (or an increase) of the "bad". But such questionnaires are technically difficult to design and their results are very uncertain. There are several possible biases in the answers (Pearce and Markandiya, 1989): a strategic bias, due to the fact that people are inclined to declare a high W.T.P. as they are not responsible; an informational bias, because of the process of choice which is indicated, and which is quite different from the real process of choice; an operational bias, due to the fact that the knowledge of the situation is only a conceptual one, not a real one. Moreover there are very large discrepancies between W.T.P. and W.T.A. Psychological biases lead to the result that W.T.A. appears to be substantially higher than W.T.P. Theoretically it can be shown that W.T.A. is generally higher than W.T.P., but the difference should, in fact, be rather small.

Another way to get figures for W.T.P. or W.T.A. is to make use of hedonic prices. For instance, the value of noise has often been calculated as the loss of value of housing due to noise exposure. The method is simple: the price of housing depends on a large number of intrinsic variables, such as surface area and construction quality, but also on extrinsic variables, such as proximity to shops and leisure facilities, or noise exposure. Statistical analysis can determine the value of noise, i.e. the variation in housing values when noise exposure varies by 1 dB. A cash figure can then be put on the loss in value of a dwelling due to its real exposure to noise in relation to an exposure level regarded as acceptable. This method is difficult to apply for several reasons, apart from the already quoted problem of the choice of the zero level: it is difficult to identify all the variables which affect the price of housing; moreover the noise exposure is frequently correlated with other explanatory variables, e.g. the accessibility to transport facilities. Furthermore, the relation obtained is not a real demand curve; noise sensitivity is lower for occupants of exposed dwellings, the value of which is thus reduced to a lesser extent than it would be if noise sensitivity were the same whatever the level of exposure.

Thus it is clear that the method of hedonic prices is difficult to implement. Similar difficulties would arise with other methods, and make clear the fact that measurement problems are very difficult to solve, and that figures comprise a lot of uncertainty.

Calculation of the cost of damage is also very difficult, because it implies a perfect knowledge of the different forms of damage caused by the nuisance or the pollution which is far from being the case! In fact, it appears that our knowledge is improving with time, and that in general we discover more and more effects. So, the damage evaluation is generally increasing: the costs reckoned now are higher than those estimated in the past.

As for the abatement or avoidance costs, several specific problems arise: The first one is due to the indivisibilities of the measures of abatement. For instance, protection against noise in old housing can be achieved simply through double glazing or double windows. If a family does not have double glazing, it does not mean that it suffers no trouble, but just that the trouble is valued less than the cost of double glazing. The second problem stems from the non-optimality of decisions concerning the environment. This non-optimality is quite clear when one considers how quickly standards and regulations are changing and becoming stricter and stricter in this field. For that reason, many authors calculate the abatement cost not on the basis of the actual behaviour of the economic agents, but on the basis of a reasonable level of abatement generally fixed in an arbitrary manner, leading automatically to an arbitrary result.

15.4   THE RESULTS OF VALUATIONS

There are many studies about the environmental effects of transport. Most of them deal with the following effects:

- noise;
- air pollution;
- safety;
- global air pollution.

They focus the attention at different levels of aggregation. Some of them give figures at a micro-economic level, and study, for instance, the cost and the efficiency of alternative technical devices. For example, there are a lot of studies about the cost and the efficiency of catalytic convertors as a measure against air pollution by cars. There are also studies about the cost and efficiency of sound proof screens and double glazing, or double windows.

Other studies deal with specific geographic situations. The case of the urban environment has been studied extensively, especially in the Central and Northern countries of the European Union as well as in Scandinavia and Switzerland, to speak only of Europe.

Other studies deal with an entire country. We will develop their results more extensively than the results of other types of studies, because they can be more readily compared with each other, because they are expressed in terms of the percentage of the G.D.P. of the country, and because they are related to the frequently used concept of social cost.

Let us review the results of the different items:

15.4.1 Accidents

In all countries, the methods used for evaluating the cost of accidents generally involve multiplying the numbers of dead and injured people and other damages by the per unit cost of these deaths, injuries and losses. The evaluation of damages is usually assumed to be equivalent to the monetary costs of the damage. As regards deaths and injuries, the estimates typically cover the direct costs (medical care, transportation costs, etc.); the indirect costs (production losses) sometimes excluding consumption eliminated as a result of the death; and occasionally, an authoritative evaluation of the worth of the life to the community. Few evaluations are based upon individuals' willingness to pay.

Most countries make some evaluation of the value of human life and the cost of accidents in their cost-benefit analysis of investments in the road system. However, these official values generally differ from estimates provided by researchers. Table 15.1 illustrates the official estimates of the value of human life used in cost-benefit analyses in several OECD countries, and Table 15.2 indicates the resulting costs of accidents based on these values, expressed as a percentage of GNP.[3] Table 15.1 shows a fairly wide scatter from one country to another. This scatter is primarily due to the use of different methods:

- evaluation based on "willingness to pay" are the highest;
- evaluations based on "gross losses" are, of course, higher than those based on "net losses".

However, the differences also seem to be related to the difference in per capita incomes in the various countries – a result which is not entirely illogical. The data in Table 15.2 show the predominant contribution of road transport in the social cost of accidents.

Table 15.3 shows evaluations of the research into the cost of accidents, in terms of GNP, based on figures for the value of human life which have not been officially sanctioned. As noted earlier, these figures are appreciably higher than those used in government reports.

---

3   These percentages naturally also include the cost of material losses and injuries.

Table 15.1 "Official" figures for the value of human life (*)

Country	Cost in 1.000 ECU (1989)	... of which market cost	Method	Source
Belgium	300	300	Gross production costs and losses	Hansson and Marckham (1992)
Denmark	600	200	"	"
Germany	630	630	"	"
Finland	1 600	540	Willingness to pay	"
France	255	–	Life expectancy	"
U.K.	890	265	Willingness to pay	"
Luxembourg	330	330	Gross production costs and losses	"
Netherlands	85	85	Net production costs and losses	"
Norway	340	340	Gross production costs and losses	"
Austria	545	545	"	"
Portugal	12.5	12.5	"	"
Sweden	1 070	130	Willingness to pay	"
Switzerland	1 665	560	Social willingness to pay	"
Spain	145	97	Willingness to pay	"
U.S.	2 350	495	"	
U.S.	441	441	Gross production costs and losses	Le Net (1992)
France	344	315	"	"
Australia	407	407	"	"
New Zealand	155 to 451	122 to 181	"	"

(*) These percentages naturally also include the cost of material losses and injuries.

15.4.2 Noise

The effects of transport noise are not well understood. There is no fully satisfactory measurement of noise and the nuisance it causes. The most common unit – the dbA – is a relative measurement, since according to certain authors, there is a difference of 5 dbA between railway noise and road noise producing the same nuisance. The duration, frequency and regularity of noise all make contributions to the noise problem that are difficult to evaluate, and even more difficult to measure *in situ*.

Neither is the monetary evaluation of these effects very far advanced. The most common methods of evaluation are:

- *Assessing the effects on the market value of buildings.* Unfortunately, these methods tend to disregard the effects of the noise on premises other than dwellings; they also imply that the economic agents are fully aware of the effects of noise, which is not entirely true.
- *Evaluation of actions which would have to be taken to eliminate or attenuate the noise.* Compared with the "market value" method mentioned above, this approach does, in fact, incorporate the poorly perceived effects of noise, but setting the standard to be achieved is a highly uncertain and arbitrary business.

• *Evaluating the damage caused by noise and the cost of corrective action.* This consists essentially of damage to health, which is itself difficult to assess.

Table 15.2 Cost of accidents as a proportion of GNP, based on "official" values of human life

Country	Cost of accidents in million ECU		GNP in million ECU	% of GNP	Year	Source
	Road	Rail				
Belgium	2 335	8	146 200	1.60	1989	Hansson and Marckham (1992)
Denmark	635	5	97 800	0.65	"	"
Germany	14 033	132	1 080 900	1.31	"	"
Finland	1 649	60	89 000	1.92	"	"
France	7 423	51	748 900	1.00	"	"
U.K.	11 879	86	760 000	1.57	"	"
Luxembourg	60	1	6 600	0.92	"	"
Netherlands	1 130	5	204 500	0.56	"	"
Norway	359	5	78 000	0.47	"	"
Austria	1 973	34	115 100	1.74	"	"
Portugal	152	2	40 000	0.39	"	"
Sweden	2 020	21	165 000	1.24	"	"
Switzerland	2 137	99	153 800	1.45	"	"
Spain	4 426	10	350 800	1.26	"	"
Mean of above countries	1.24%	0.01%		1.25	"	"
U.S.				1.24		Deakin (OECD), quoted by Bouladon (1991)
Switzerland	780 (1)	31 (1)	142 000	0.57	1988	Jeanrenaud et al. (1993)
Switzerland	2 814 (2)	50 (2)	142 000	2.00	"	"

(1) *External* costs.
(2) *Social* costs, including both *external* costs and *expenditures* made by users.

Of course, valuing the effects of noise across a country in monetary terms will depend upon the degree of urbanisation and the geographical structure of the country. These considerations underlie the dispersion of the current evaluations shown in Table 15.4.

Table 15.3 Alternative assessments of the social cost of accidents

Country	% of GNP	Year	Source
Australia	3		Quoted by Hansson and Marckham (1992)
Austria	1.9		"
Belgium	2.5	1983	CCFE (1991)
France	2.6	1979	Quoted by Quinet (1989)
Germany	2.4	1977	"
Germany	2.54	1982	"
U.K.	1.1		"
Italy	1.5		CCFE (1991)
Luxembourg	1.85	1978	"
Luxembourg	2.5		Quoted by Quinet (1990)
Netherlands	1.67	1987	CCFE (1991)
Sweden	2.2		Quinet (1990)
U.K.	1.5	1986	CCFE (1991)
U.K.	1.45	1986	Quoted by Quinet (1990)
U.S.	2.0	1975	"
U.S.	2.4	1975	Kanafani (1983)

According to Weinberger (1992), the breakdown of costs in Germany between the different modes is as follows (willingness to pay, plus health expenditure):

Road:	70%
Rail:	27%
Air:	3%
Total:	100%

According to Merlin (1992), the breakdown in France is (in billion francs):

Road:	76%
Rail:	6%
Air:	18%
Total:	100%

According to Diekmann (1990), the distribution of noise is:

Road:	64%
Rail:	10%
Air:	26%
Total:	100%

The Green Book of the Commission of the European Communities (1992) quotes the following breakdown of the social costs of noise (from the Karlsruhe Fraunhofer Institute):

Road:	64%
Rail:	10%
Air:	26%
Total:	100%

Table 15.4 Evaluating the cost of noise

Country	Source	Year	% of GNP	Comments
Norway[1]	Ringheim	1983	0.06	Fall in property values
France[1]	Lambert	1986	0.08	"
Netherlands[1]	Opschoor	1986	0.02	"
Former FRG[1]	Wicke	1987	2	Fall in property values and losses of productivity
France	Bouladon (1991)		0.24	
U.K.	"		0.50	
Norway	Nielsen et Solberg (1988)	1987	0.3	
Germany	Weinberger (1992)	1992	1.4	Willingness to pay, plus health damage
France[1]	OECD	1990	0.2-0.6	Desirable expenditure
	Merlin (1992)	1989	1.5	Covers all modes
Finland	Himanen et al.(1992)	1989	0.3	Cost of protection
	Ministry estimate (1992)	1992	0.42	
U.S.A.	Mackenzie et al. (1992)	1992	0.2	
U.S.A.	Bouladon (1991)	1990	0.10	
Australia	NRTC (1992a)	1992	0.15	
Austria	Hansson et Marckham (1992)	-	0.1	
Sweden	"	1992	0.4	Fall in property values
Switzerland	"	-	0.1	
Germany	Diekmann (1990)		0.2	Cost of protection
Germany	PLANCO (1990)	1985	0.15	Cost of protecting to 55 dbA
			0.9	Cost of protection at 45 dbA
Switzerland	Jeanrenaud et al. (1993)	1988	0.3	Decline in property values, of which 0.26% was for road, and 0.04% was for rail; estimates based on cost of protection yield similar results

1. Data quoted in Quinet (1990)
-: No indication of the year

15.4.3 Local Pollution

Local pollution is expressed in terms of several components: sulphides, nitric oxides, and particulate matter (neglecting pollution by CO_2, which is global in nature, and which is discussed below). The methods of evaluation used here are primarily of the indirect type, involving first of all a technical estimate of the damage done, and then an evaluation of the "cost of repairs or protection". Substitution market methods are less common here than for noise. As for contingent valuation methods, these are occasionally used, but they tend to produce very different results, and much higher than the others.

Damage refers to human health, material damage and effects on plant life. These have been separated out in a number of studies (see Table 15.5). They are summarised in Kågeson (1992a), from which most of the information is drawn. It should be noted that, as for noise, the estimates based on willingness to pay are generally much higher than those based on damage. For example, the PLANCO study indicates pollution costs higher by a factor of 1.5 to 2.

15.4.4 Global Pollution

Here, the main focus in on the greenhouse effect caused by atmospheric warming due to the increase in CO_2 concentrations. Neither the physical extent nor the economic effects of the greenhouse effect are yet very well understood.

Several scenarios have been proposed as to future trends in the average temperature of the planet if no emission abatement action is taken. Estimates of the heating effect range from 0.1 to 0.5 degrees per ten-year period. The consequences of this warming are difficult to quantify and include such things as: certain species disappearing and others developing; harmful effects on agriculture; increased exposure to sunlight; a rise in sea level; and possible feedbacks from the ecosystem, tending to accelerate the temperature rise even further.

Table 15.5 Costs of local pollution

Study	Country	Year	Cost of pollution as % of GNP			
			Health	Material damage	Vegeta-tion	Total
Grupp[2]	Germany	1986	0.11-0.42	0.05-0.06	0.03-0.15	0.19-0.63
PLANCO[2]	"	1990	0.07-0.18	0.05-0.09	0.13-0.21	0.25-0.48
UPI[2]	"	1991	0.59	0.07	0.26-0.41	0.92-1.05
Marburger[2]	"	1986	0.06-0.14			
Henz&Klassen-Mielke[2]	"	1990	0.05-0.25			
Iseeke[2]		1990		0.05-0.08		
Henz[2]		1986		0.06		
Ewers[2]		1986			0.13-0.21	
Pillet[2]	Switzerland	1988	0.02-0.06	0.21	0.18-0.41	0.41-0.68
Infras[2]	"	1992	0.01-0.03	0.07-0.16	0.16-0.45	0.24-0.64
EcoPlan (1992a)	Berne	1992	0.14	0.13	0.15	0.42
Gunnarson & Leeksell[2]	Sweden	1986	0.02-0.06	0.00-0.03	0.00-0.02	0.03-0.11
Hassund et al.[2]	"	1990			0.06-0.2	
VROM[3]	Netherlands	1985	0.16-0.29	0.08-0.13	0.14-0.18	0.38-0.6
NAPAP[3]	U.S.A.	1991			0.01-0.02	
Merlin (1992)	France	1989				
N.R.T.C. (1992a)	Australia	1992				
FINNRA (1992)	Finland	1992				0.4
Mackenzie et al (1992)	U.S.A.	1992	0.22			
Himanen et al. (1992)	Finland	1989				0.23-0.7
Bouladon (1991)	U.K.	1991				0.15-0.35
Deakin[1]	U.S.A.	1990				0.48

1. Quoted by Bouladon (1991)
2. Quoted by Kågeson (1992a)
3. Quoted by Quinet (1992)

The OECD (1988) has calculated that transport is responsible for 21 per cent of CO_2 omissions in the OECD member countries. In general, there has been no direct assessment of the cost of the greenhouse effect[4], but estimates have been made of the rates of energy – or carbon – taxes which would have to be imposed to generate different levels of reduction of CO_2 emissions to, and concentrations in, the atmosphere. Assessments of the potential economic consequences of this taxation have also been made. These procedures would involve laying down targets for CO_2 concentrations, working out the tax which would allow these targets to be achieved, and measuring their economic consequences. The Academie des Sciences de France (1990) devised Figure 15.1, which indicates a range of sea level increases, depending on various CO_2 emission scenarios.

According to the different research, the reductions in CO_2 emissions which would either stabilise global warming, or hold it as an acceptable level are:

- An immediate reduction of 60 per cent according to Swedish researchers (quoted by Kågeson, 1992a) for immediate temperature stabilisation. This is clearly unrealistic.
- In order to stabilise CO_2 emissions at their present level by the year 2000 (i.e. the actual objective contained in the Framework Convention on Climate Change), the European Commission considers that the target should be a reduction of 12 per cent relative to the baseline, which would require (among other things) a tax of $10 per barrel of oil.[5]
- Barrett (see OECD, 1991a) reviews the taxes needed to reduce emissions by 20 per cent, using various assumptions as to the elasticity in energy consumption and price; these taxes range from 19 to 140 ECU per tonne of carbon.
- The OECD GREEN Model (quoted in Kågeson, 1992a) indicates that in order to reduce emissions by 20 per cent by the year 2010, the tax would have to be 5 ECU per tonne of carbon, increasing to 12 ECU by 2000 and 120 ECU by 2010.

The consequences of a carbon tax have been reviewed using different models, summarised by Hoeller et al. (1991), from which Table 15.6 has been obtained. It should be noted that carbon taxes (see Appendix 1) would also have secondary effects on local pollution. Alfsen and Glomsrød (1992) found that the stabilising CO_2 emissions by means of an international tax would lead to a reduction in the social costs caused by local pollution, virtually equivalent to the direct reduction in GNP (2.4 million NOK 1990, compared with 3.1 million NOK 1990 for reducing pollution).

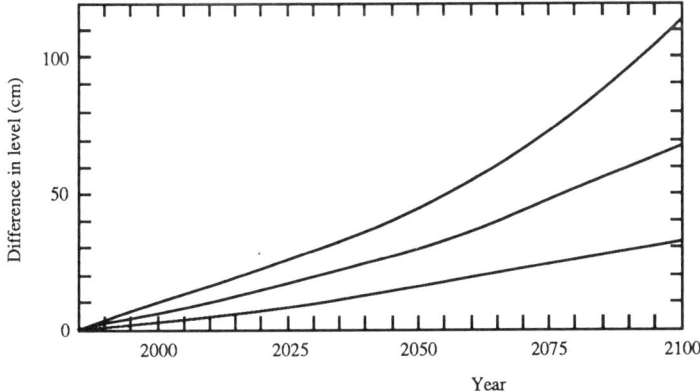

Figure 15.1 Difference in sea level according to various CO2 emission scenarios

---

4   Cline (1992) is one of the exceptions to this rule.
5   Recall that 1 metric tonne of carbon = 7.6 barrels of petrol = 1.55 m^3 of gasoline.

Table 15.6 Effect of a reduction in CO_2 emissions on growth: results by country

	(1) Reduction in emissions compared with their reference levels in the final year of the period considered	(2) Changes in the growth rate of GDP	(3) Percentage difference from reference level of GDP in final year	(4) Carbon tax (dollars per tonne of carbon) Maximum value	Final year
Manne/Richels (1990, U.S.A.)					
Pessimistic technical scenario	-88 (2100)	-0.1	-4.0	600 (2020)	250 (2100)
Intermediate technical scenario	-77 (2100)	-0.0	-2.5	–	–
Optimistic technical scenario	-50 (2100)	-0.0	-0.8	–	–
CBO (1990, USA); DRI model	-16 (2000)	-0.2	-2.0	100	100
DGEM	-36 (2000)	-0.1	-0.6	100	100
Jorgenson/Wilcoxen (1990, USA)	-20 (2060)	-0.0	-0.5	17 (2020)	15 (2060)
	-36 (2060)	-0.0	-1.1	46 (2020)	42 (2060)
Blitzer et al. (1990, Egypt)					
Scenario 1	-15[2] (2002)	-0.1	-2.7	–	–
Scenario 3	-35[2] (2002)	-1.0	-15.0	–	–
Scenario 5	-40[2] (2002)	-1.5	-19.0	–	–
Glomsrød et al. (1990, Norway)[2]	-26 (2010)	-0.4	-2.7	–	–
SIMEN (1989, Norway)[3]	-16 (2000)	-0.1 to -0.2	-1 to -2	–	–
NEPP (1989, Netherlands)[2]					
Scenario including national measures	-25 (2010)	-0.2	-4.2	–	–
Scenario including worldwide measures	-25 (2010)	0.0	0.6	–	–
Bergman (1988, Sweden)	-51 (2000)	-0.4	-5.6	–	–
Dixon et al. (1989, Australia)	-47[3] (2005)	-0.1	-2.4	–	–

1. The last year of the period is 2012, the reductions then reach -30 per cent, -35 per cent and -55 per cent.
2. The reductions of other pollutants is also taken into consideration.
3. The reductions apply to the sectors of electricity and road transport.

15.4.5 Overall Assessment

These figures are widely spread. There are several reasons to explain this:
- The many differences between the countries. Some of them suffer more severely from environmental damage than others. The share of urban traffic is not the same. The total traffic differs from one country to another. Technologies are different.
- The various measures of the value (cost of damage, or abatement, or W.T.P.) do not have the same value due to the imperfection of decisions.
- The procedures for the calculations of each of these concepts are not well established and not similar in very country.

Keeping in mind these reservations, the following mean values can be given for the different social costs, expressed as a percentage of GNP:

Accidents: 1.5 to 2%
Noise: about 0.3%
Local pollution: about 0.4%

It is clear that these figures are too uncertain to be able to determine whether they are based on marginal or averages values.

Some authors have collected data expressed in monetary value per unit of traffic (passenger-km or tonne-km). If they are taken at a wide level, for instance on a country wide basis, these figures may be misleading, because they represent an average of very widely dispensed values, which depend on a lot of parameters: share of urban traffic-density of the population, average load of car or trucks (or trains, or planes), and sensitivity of people to the environment. Moreover, some environmental effects are quite local (noise, air pollution by CO, CO_2, C_xH_y): if there is nobody or nothing valuable around the source, the effect is near zero; other environmental effects are more widely spread (air pollution by N_xO_y or S_xO_y, global warming).

Given these very importance reservations, we quote data about social costs per unit of traffic in Table 15.7.

15.5 HOW TO USE THE VALUATIONS IN DECISION MAKING PROCESSES

To valuate the environmental effects of transport is not a purely theoretical preoccupation, but it is necessary for a very practical and matter-of-fact reason : it is the only means by which it is possible to take logical and coherent decisions. Valuation is a compulsory step in each of the three principal categories of decisions :
- regulation, because one needs to balance the costs of the measure with the benefits they may apport ;
- investment, because among the costs or benefits of the investment, environmental considerations take an increasing place;
- pricing, because prices will have an impact on the environment, through the choices of the users.

Let us consider the functional relation which links valuation to the different parameters which can influence it, in the same way as the cost function links the production cost to the amount of production of the various products of the firm, or as the utility or surplus function links the utility or surplus to the amount of goods which are consumed.

But environmental goods are special; they are not "goods", but more precisely "bads". So, it is necessary to transpose the classical economic presentation. Let us do it in a rather crude manner, in order to relate some key concepts; and for that purpose, let us consider an example:

Table 15.7 Social costs in 0.01 ECU per traffic unit (passenger-km or tonne-km)

Source	Comments	Passengers				Goods		
		Car	Bus	Train	Plane	Truck	Train	Water-way
Tefra (1991)	France					0.8 to 1.0 motorway 0.3 to 0.4 highway		
Sweden 1987	Stockholm	14.3 to 27						
(Report quoted by Hansson & Marckham (1992))	Rural area	2.8						
Darbeira (1992)	Paris	3.5	0.15					
Auzannet & Bellaloun (1992)	Paris and region, without accident cost	1.6 to 4.3	0.15	0.15 to 0.30				
PLANCO (1990)	Germany	3.48	0.50	0.57		2.58	0.37	0.18
CCFE (1991)	Netherlands	1.66		0.2		1.66	0.2	
Replies to a questionnaire	Belgium	1.56				1.56		
(Assumption:	Denmark	1.51				1.51		
1 passenger = 1 tonne)	Switzerland	3.0		0.8		3.0	0.8	
	Austria	3.3		0.25		3.3	0.25	
	Sweden	5.0		0.7		5.0	0.7	
	Finland	3.1 to 4.3				3.1 to 4.3		
	Norway	2.1				2.1		
	Germany			0.006			0.006	
Directions (1992)	Canada	0.38 to 0.43	0.14 to 0.20	0.18 to 0.45				

- N ; the level of noise.
- D(N) : the total cost of noise incurred by the society at the level N. D(N) is an increasing function of N. It is the cost of damage which, under the assumption of perfect information, is equal to the sum of the W.T.P. of people who suffer from the noise.
- A(N) : the total cost which should have to be incurred by the society in order to reduce the level of noise from the present level to N. A(N) is a decreasing function of N, being maximal when N = 0 and equal to zero for N = N_m (N_m is the natural level of noise).

Let us consider the quantity :
  T(N) = D(N) + A(N).

This quantity has the interesting property of being minimal when :

$$\frac{dD}{dN} = -\frac{dA}{dN}$$

(marginal abatement cost = marginal damage cost = W.T.P.). That is, when the social optimum is fulfilled.

Furthermore, as is shown in Figure 15.2, the term T(N) has strong connections with the classical Dupuit surplus. In a way, it may be considered as the complement of the Dupuit surplus and it is a good candidate for a definition of social cost (Quinet, 1992).

How can we use these concepts for the decision-making process ?

Let us first assume that we are in the situation of a "perfect" world, where decisions are socially optimal and information is perfect. In that case, the concept to be used will differ according to the nature of the problem.

Let us suppose that we are trying to solve a first best pricing problem. In that case, the relevant concept is the marginal value, in the same manner as marginal cost is used for usual goods.

Let us now assume that we have to find the environmental impacts of a new investment, for instance its effects on noise levels. We then have to estimate the value of T(N) with the investment and without the investment. Let us name the first one T_1 and the second one T_0. Then the surplus term concerning noise to be introduced in the COBA will be: $(T_0 - T_1)$.

The same type of calculation would hold for the assessment of standard regulations.

As is usual in normative economics, things are increasingly more complicated when the assumption of a "perfect" world is cancelled; thus, the solution to the decision-making process depends upon the kind of imperfection which occurs; it also depends upon equity objectives and distributive considerations as is usual in second best problems.

In these cases there is a strong argument for introducing tutelar values in COBA ; these tutelar values are defined by a political body. They shape a collective valuation of the environmental good; and embody, often in a crude manner, both efficiency and distribution considerations. Of course, these tutelar values must be determined around the figures given by the economic and statistical analysis for abatement cost, damage cost, W.T.P. or W.T.A.

The case for a tutelar value is strengthened by the uncertainty of the statistical determinations of valuations.

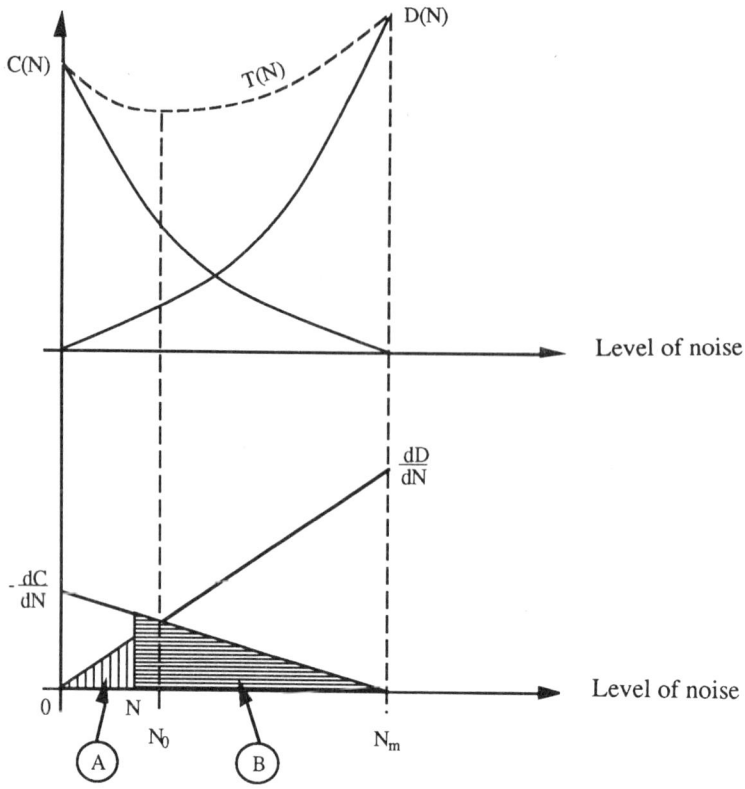

Figure 15.2 Valuations of the level of noise

15.6   CONCLUSION: POSSIBLE USES OF VALUATIONS AND FURTHER RESEARCH

These considerations and calculations are perhaps appealing from a theoretical point of view. But do they have any possible use? Can they help the decision-making process?

At first glance, the very large dispersion of the results may lead us to be inclined to answer "no". But the case deserves a more precise analysis. Let us distinguish between different kinds of decisions:

a) The strategic decisions on a nationwide basis: what mode of transport must be given priority, what level of environmental protection must be chosen? It could seem reasonable to think that for such decisions, calculations of the social cost of the environment would be useful. In fact, it is not quite the case; they are not totally unuseful. But they have several serious draw-backs:
• The present calculations give a point, not the whole function $T(N)$ (or $A(N)$, or $D(N)$); and it is difficult to derive an optimum from this single piece of information.
• Such problems always give place to numerous qualitative considerations and quantification, especially in terms of price, is not fully relevant (quantification in terms of quantities is less rare).

Nevertheless, the indications about the social costs of noise, pollution and safety do of course provide an indication about how much effort must be put into each of these items.

b) At a lower level, there are strategic decisions on a regionwide basis, for instance decisions to allocate a given budget between various regions or cities. For that kind of purpose, it seems sensible to use the quantitative tools of social costs, providing that the calculation is made on the same basis for each region or each city. There may be considerable uncertainty about each figure, but it can be presumed that the uncertainty tends towards the same direction for each region (or each city).

c) For the choice of investment, especially infrastructure investment, is it wise to include valuations of the environment in the classical Cost-Benefit Analysis? In our opinion, the answer is "yes". Whatever the uncertainty of the figures quoted in the previous section, they show that there are large discrepancies between modes. A more precise analysis would have shown possible classifications within each mode (for instance urban highways, urban motorways at ground level, urban tunnel motorways), and in each class the social cost becomes more even. Then it would be possible to assess the data about the social cost for different kinds of infrastructure, and to use the data for comparisons through COBA.

d) For pricing the use of infrastructure. Nowadays, the pricing of infrastructure is achieved without taking into account the social cost to the environment, except in a very few countries (for example, Sweden and the Netherlands). This amounts to assuming that these costs are zero. Our knowledge of these costs is not very good of course, but it is sufficient enough to ascertain that they are not zero; and that, indeed, there are large differences between modes, or within a mode and between rural and urban transport. So, it is certainly an improvement in terms of the present situation to include them in the price of infrastructure.

e) Decisions about regulations can also possibly be made on the basis of environmental valuations. However, our knowledge of social costs is too imprecise to allow us to determine that the best regulation is the one which minimizes the social cost to the environment.

In conclusion, it appears that it is already a good thing to use calculations of social costs in decision-making processes, whether it concerns the choice of investments or pricing. Of course, these calculations must be used with caution, and a lot of work needs to be done in order to improve our knowledge of social costs.

For that purpose, several directions are suggested:
- First: to set up a code of measurement. There are various types of valuations of the environment, as we have seen in the previous section. Unfortunately, the methods are very different from each other, so it is very difficult to compare the results.
- Second point: we should have a better knowledge of the physical laws which connect transport activities to various kinds of environmental damage.
- Third point: among the applications of valuations of the environment, the most obvious one is the pricing of infrastructure use. Efforts should be made to improve our knowledge on this subject.
- Fourth point: the use of social cost in regional comparisons should be encouraged as it can provide precious information about the comparative situations in different regions of a country.

Finally, a word of caution: interest in the environment has increased in recent years. We must be aware of this fact and recognize that it will probably continue to grow in the future. This means that environmental valuations will become increasingly important, as will their use in decision-making.

APPENDIX 1

Carbon taxes and energy taxes have been suggested by various researchers. The taxes being considered by the Commission of the European Union combine the two as follows :

Tax in ECU	Energy term	CO_2 term	(Tonne of carbon as toe)	Total
Heavy oil/t	19.7	26.5	(1.12)	46.2
LNG/t	30.0	30.0	(0.83)	60.0
Liquid gas/t	35.0	31.5	(0.75)	66.5
Nuclear power/kWh	8.29		(0.00)	8.29

REFERENCES

Abay, G. and C. Zehnder, 1992, "Road pricing für der Agglomeration Bern", National City and Transport Research Programme, Zurich.

Academie des Sciences, 1990, "L'effet de serre et ses conséquences climatiques", Paris.

Alfsen, K. and S. Glomsrød, 1992a, "Valuation of Environmental Benefits in Norway", Central Bureau of Statistics, Oslo.

Alfsen, K. and S. Glomsrød, 1992b, "Secondary Benefits of Climate Policies: Some Tentative Calculations", Internal Note, Central Bureau of Statistics, Oslo.

Ansen, F., 1990, "Example City of Visby", Paper to the Conference on Ecology and Transport, Gothenburg.

Auzannet, P. and A. Bellaloun, 1992, "Le coût des transports pour les collectivités", Internal Note, Paris Regional Transport Board (RATP), Paris.

Banister, D. and K. Button (eds.), 1992, *Transport, the Environment and Sustainable Development*, E. and F. Spon, London.

Barde, J.P., 1992, *Economie et politique de l'environnement*, PUF, Paris.

Barde, J.P. and K. Button (eds.), 1992, *Transport Policy and Environment*, Earthscan Publications, London.

Barde, J.P. and D. Pearce (eds.), 1991, *Valuing the Environment*, Earthscan Publications, London.

Bergman, L., 1988, "Energy Policy Modelling: A Survey of General Equilibrium Approaches", *Journal of Policy Modelling*, Vol. 10, 3:377-399.

Blitzer, C., R.S. Eckaus, S. Lahiri and A. Meeraus, 1990, "A General Equilibrium Analysis of the Effects of Carbon Emission Restrictions on Economic Growth in a Developing Country", (January).

Bouladon, G., 1979, "Coût et avantage des véhicules à moteur", OECD report, Paris.

Bouladon, G., 1991, "La mobilité en zone urbaine: apprendre l'économie des transports", OECD report, Paris.

Brandberg, A. and R. Anders, 1990, "Fuel for Cars, Trucks and Buses", Paper to the Conference on Ecology and Transport, Gothenburg, Sweden.

Button, K., 1992, "Market and Government Failure in Environmental Management", OECD report, Paris.

Cerwenka, P., G. Motz, H. Kufeld and U. Kunert, 1989, "Kosten and Umvuelteffekte", Verkehrs-politiken, *Verkehr und Technik*, No. 12.

Cline, R., 1992, "Global Warming: The Benefits of Emission Abatement", OECD report, Paris.

Commission of the European Communities, 1992, "Green Book on the Impact of Transport on the Environment", Brussels.

Communauté des Chemins de Fer en Europe (CCFE), 1991, "Les externalitis de transports en Europe", Bruxelles.

Cotton, E., 1990, "Vehicles for the Future for Southern California", Paper to the Conference on Ecology and Transport, Gothenburg.

Darbeira, R., 1992, "Le coût total de la V.P. et des T.C. dans une grande agglomération: le cas de Paris", Duplicated note, L'Oeil, Créteil.

Deistler, F., 1990, "Example City of Lubeck", Paper to the Conference on Ecology and Transport, Gothenburg.

Delsey, J. and G. Dobias, 1991, "Road Transport and the Greenhouse Effect", *Recherche Transport Sécurité*, No. 8, Paris.

Diekmann, A., 1990, "Nutzen und Kosten des Automobils", *Internationales Verkehrswesen,* November-December.

DIRECTIONS, 1992, Report of the Royal Canada Transport Commission, Ottawa.

Dixon, P.B., D.T. Johnson, R.E. Marks, P. McLennan, R. Schodde and P.L. Swan, 1989, "The Feasibility and Implication for Australia of the Adoption of the Toronto Proposal for Carbon Dioxide Emissions", CRA Report, Sydney.

Dogs, E., G. Ellwanger and H. Platz, 1991, "Externe Kosten des Verkehrs", *Die Bundesbahn*, No. 1.

ECMT, 1991, "Goods Transport and the Environment", Paris.

ECMT, 1992a, "Questioning Transport Growth", Proceedings of the Twelfth International Lisbon Symposium, Paris. (Reports by R. Befahy, J. Short, F. Crowley, K.H. Lenz and J.P. Baumgartner)

ECMT, 1992b, "International Conference on Reducing the Impact of Transport on Global Warming", Paris. (Reports by: A. Aranguena, A.N. Bleijenberg, K. Gwilliam, U. Höpfner, L. Michaelis, J.P. Orfcuil, S. Rommerskirchen, Z. Samaras, P. Tanja, J.M. Viegas and M. Walsh)

ECMT and OECD, 1990, "Transport Policy and the Environment", Paris.

ECOPLAN, 1991, "Les coûts sociaux des accidents de transport an Suisse", Report for the Transport Research Department, Berne.

ECOPLAN, 1992a, "Externe Kosten im Agglomerationsverkehr in Bern", National City and Transport Research Programme, Zurich.

ECOPLAN, 1992b, "Damage Costs of Air Pollution", Study for T. and E., Brussels.

European Railways Community, 1992, "Les externalités du transport en Europe", Brussels.

Finnish National Road Administration (FINNRA), 1992, "Pricing of Traffic Noise and Exhaust Gases in Road Planning", Report No. 15, Helsinki.

French National Audit and Budget Commission, 1992, "Croissance et environnement", Ministry of Finance, Paris.

Frey, R. and P. Langloh (eds.), 1992a, "The Use of Economic Instruments in Urban Travel Management", WWZ Report, Bâle.

Frey, R. and P. Langloh (eds.), 1992b, "Internalisierung externer Kosten im Allgomerations Verkehr", NWZ Studie, Bâle.

Glomsrød, S., T. Johnsen and H. Vennemo, 1990, "Stabilisation of Emissions of CO_2: A Computable General Equilibrium Assessment", Report no. 48, Central Bureau of Statistics, Oslo.

Grupp, H., 1986, "Die Sozialen Kosten des Verkehrs", *Verkehr und Technick*, Nos 9 and 10.

Hansson, L., 1991, "Air Pollution Fees and Taxes in Sweden", *Transportation Research Board*, 70th Annual meeting, Washington D.C.

Hansson, L. and J. Marckham, 1992, "Internalization of External Effects in Transportation", IRU, Paris.

Himanen, V., K. Maketla, K. Alppiivuori, P. Aaltonen and J. Louhelainen, 1992, "The Monetary Value of Road Traffic's Environmental Hazards", Technical Research Center of Finland, Espoo.

Hoeller, P., A. Dean and J. Nicolaisen, 1991, "Incidences macroéconomiques de la réduction des émissions de gaz à effet de serre", *OECD Economic Review*, No. 16.

Hoppe, K., 1990, "Example City of Berne", Paper to the Conference on Ecology and Transport, Gothenburg.

Hourcade, J.C., 1991, "Politique énergétique et effet de serre", CIRED Report, Paris.

Jeanrenaud, D., P. Grosclaude, N. Schwab, N. Sogueln and M.A. Stritt, 1993, "Le coût social des transports en Suisse", IRER, Université de Neuchatel.

Intergovernmental Panel on Climate Change (IPCC), 1990, *Climate Change: The Scientific Assessment*, Cambridge University Press, Cambridge.

IRU, 1987, "Tarification de l'usage des infrastructures à imputer aux exploitants des transports terrestres", Paris.

Kågeson P., 1992a, "External Cost of Air Pollution. The Case of European Transport", T. and E., Brussels.

Kågeson P., 1992b, "Marginal and Average Costs of Reducing Nitrogen Oxides and Sulfur Dioxide Emissions in Europe", T. and E., Brussels.

Kågeson P., 1992c, "Internalising Social Cost of Transport", T. and E., Brussels.

Kågeson P., 1992d, "Making Fuel Go Further", T. and E., Brussels.

Kågeson P., 1992e, "External Cost of Air Pollution", T. and E., Brussels.

Kanafani, A., 1983, "The Social Cost of Road Transport", OECD Report, Paris.

Lamure, C., 1991, "Les mesures applicables au secteur des transports pour améliorer leur bilan vis-à-vis de l'effet de serre", Internal INRETS Report, Lyon.

Lamure, C. and J. Lambert, 1993, "Impact des transports terrestres sur l'environnement", INRETS Research Report, Paris.

Le Net, M., 1992, "Le prix de la vie humaine", Report for the General Commission for the Plan, Paris.

Mackenzie, J., R. Dower and D. Chen, 1992, "The Going Rate : What it Really Costs to Drive", World Resource Institute, Washington D.C.

Maibach, M., R. Iten and S. Mauch, 1992, "Internalisieren der externen kosten des verkehrs Zurich", National City and Transport Research Programme, Zurich.

Manne, A.S. and R.G. Richels, 1990, "CO_2 Emission Reductions: An Economic Cost Analysis for the USA", *The Energy Journal*, Vol. 11.

Marchand, L., 1984, "Du bon usage de l'espace de voirie dans les centres urbains", Internal RATP Note.

Martin, Y., 1990, "Rapport du groupe interministériel de l'effet de serre", Internal Note.

Matsuzawa, T., 1989, "A Method of Estimating Congestion Loss in Urban Area", TSU Ref. 472, Oxford.

Merlin, P., 1992, "Choix de transport et environnement", Paper to the WCTR Conference, Lyon.

Monzon de Caceres, A., 1992, "Analisis de Metodologias y dieño de un balance social del transporte publico en Madrid", University of Madrid.

Monzon de Caceres, A., and R. Hamilton (eds.), 1992, Proceedings of the 4th International Symposium on Highway Pollution, Madrid.

National Road Transport Commission, 1992a, "Discussion Paper on Charges for Heavy Vehicles", Melbourne.

National Road Transport Commission, 1992b, "Issues and Objectives Paper", Melbourne.

Newman, P., 1992, "Policies to Influence Urban Travel Demand", OECD Report, Paris.

Nielsen G. and S. Solberg, 1988, "Costs and Effects of Traffic Noise Abatement Measures: Basis for a National Programme", *Applied Acoustics*, No. 25.

Nilsson, E., 1990, "The Swedish View of the Los Angeles Environment", Paper to the Conference on Ecology and Transport, Gothenburg.

OECD, 1988, "Transport and the Environment", Paris.

OECD, 1989, "Economic Instruments for Environmental Protection", Paris.

OECD, 1991a, "Environmental Policy: How to Apply Economic Instruments".

OECD, 1991b," Fighting Noise Pollution in the 1990s", Report, Paris.

OECD, 1991c, "Environmental Indicators", Paris.

OECD, 1992, "Road Transport Research Programme", Environmental Impact Assessment of Roads, (Contributions from Australia, Sweden, Finland, Austria, United States, United Kingdom and Japan.)

Ohm, A., 1990, "Future Transport Demands and Effects of Measures to Reduce Environmental Problems", Paper to the Conference on Ecology and Transport, Gothenburg.

Orfeuil, J.P. (1990). "Transport, énergie, environnement: le scénario Prométhée", *Futuribles*, November, Paris.

Pearce, D. and A. Markandiya, 1989, "L'évaluation monétaire des avantages des politiques de l'environnement", OECD Report, Paris.

Perez M., 1992, "Coûts externes du transport de marchandises", LET Lyon.

PLANCO, 1990, "Externe Kosten des Verkehrs: Schierre, Strasse, Binnenschiffart", Essen.

Prud'homme, R.,1993, "Analyse économique de l'effet de serre", Analyses de la SEDEIS, Paris, January.

Quinet, E., 1990, "Le coût social des transports terrestres", OECD Monograph, Paris.

Quinet, E., 1992, "Pour une définition de la notion de coût social de l'environnement", *Economie Appliquée*, Paris.

Quinet, E., 1993, "Propositions pour la tarification des infrastructures routières, ferroviaires et aériennes", Report for the Ministry of Transport, Paris.

RATP, 1992a, "Le bruit des transports en Ile-de-France", Paris.

RATP, 1992b, "La pollution liée aux transports de voyageurs en Ile-de-France", Paris.

Rigby, J., 1990, "The York Approach", Paper to the Conference on Ecology and Transport, Gothenburg.

Rothengatter, W., 1989, "Aspects économiques", Report to the ECMT Committee of Deputies, Paris.

Samuelson, H., 1992, "Fuel Efficient Vehicles", Paper to the XXIII* IRU World Congress, Barcelona.

SOFRETU-CETUR, 1992, "Le coût de la consommation d'espace", Internal Note, Paris.

STP-RATP, 1990, "Compte transport de voyageurs pour la région d'Ile-de-France", Internal Note, Paris.

Sviden, O., 1991, "Clean Fuel and Engine Systems for 21st Century Road Vehicles", Stencilled Note from ESF/NECTAR.

Tefra, M., 1991, "Evaluation des coûts externes créés par les transports routiers et ferroviaires de marchandises", Study for the ECC, Brussels.

ten Have, H.B.G., 1992, "Passenger Transport: Energy Use and Air Polluting Emissions", National Aerospace Laboratory, Department of Civil Aviation, The Hague.

Texas Transport Institute, 1987a, "Roadway Congestion in Major Urban Areas (1982-1987)".

Texas Transport Institute, 1987b, "Roadway Congestion. Estimates and Trends".

University of Neufchatel ,1990, "Proceedings of the Conference on the Social Cost of Transport", IRER, Neufchatel.

UPI, 1991, "Okologroche und soziale Kosten der Umweltbelastung in der Bundesrepublik Deutschland", Heidelberg.

U.S.D.O.T., 1992a, "Transportation and Air Quality", Searching for Solutions, Washington D.C.

U.S.D.O.T., 1992b, "Exploring the Role of Pricing as a Congestion Management Tool", Washington D.C.

U.S.D.O.T., 1992c, "Examining Congestion Pricing: Implementation Issues", Washington D.C.

Walsh, M., 1992, "Motor Vehicle Trends and their Implication for Global Warming", Report to the ECMT Committee of Deputies, Paris.

Weinberger, M., 1992, "Gesamt wirtschaftliche Kosten des Larms", *Zeitschirft für Lärmebekämpfung*, No. 39.

Willeke, R., 1990, "Coûts socio-économiques des accidents de la route", EEC Report, Brussels.

AUTHOR INDEX

LIST OF CONTRIBUTORS

David Batten
The Temaplan Group
P.O. Box 3026
Dendy Brighton 3186
AUSTRALIA

Edward M. Bergman
Institute for Economic Development
CB # 3140, New East Building
University of North Carolina
Chapel Hill, NC 27599-3140
U.S.A.

Susan J. Binder
Industry and Economic Analysis Branch
Room 3324, HPP-11
U.S. Department of Transportation
Federal Highway Administration
400 Seventh St., S.W.
Washington, D.C. 20590
U.S.A.

Frank Bruinsma
Department of Economics
Free University
P.O. Box 7161
1007 MC Amsterdam
THE NETHERLANDS

Kenneth Button
Department of Economics
Loughborough University
Loughborough, Leicestershire
LE11 3TU
ENGLAND

Jonathan Gifford
The Institute of Public Policy
George Mason University
4400 University Drive
Fairfax, Virginia 22030-4444
U.S.A.

Jacco R. Hakfoort
SBV/University of Amsterdam
Roeterstraat 11
1018 WB Amsterdam
THE NETHERLANDS

Andrew F. Haughwout
Woodrow Wilson School of Public and
    International Affairs
Princeton University
Robertson Hall
Princeton, NJ 08544-1013
U.S.A.

Frannie Humplick
The World Bank
1818 H Street N.W.
Washington, D.C. 20433
U.S.A.

Börje Johansson
Jönköping International Business School
Jönköping University
P.O. Box 1026
551 11 Jönköping
SWEDEN

Christine Kessides
The World Bank
1818 H Street N.W.
Washington, D.C. 20433
U.S.A.

Juliet Musso
Department of Economics
University of California
Berkeley, California 94720
U.S.A.

Gerard Pepping
Department of Economics
Free University
P.O. Box 7161
1007 MC Amsterdam
THE NETHERLANDS

Rémy Prud'homme
OEIL-IUP
Université de Paris XII
61, av Général-de-Gaulle
94010 Créteil Cedex
FRANCE

John M. Quigley
Department of Economics
University of California
Berkeley, CA 94720
U.S.A.

Emile Quinet
CERAS
Ecole Nationale des Ponts & Chaussées
28, rue des Saint-Pères
75343 Paris Cedex 07
FRANCE

Piet Rietveld
Department of Economics
Free University
P.O. Box 7161
1007 MC Amsterdam
THE NETHERLANDS

Theresa M. Smith
Industry and Economic Analysis Branch
Room 3324, HPP-11
U.S. Department of Transportation
Federal Highway Administration
400 Seventh St., S.W.
Washington, D.C. 20590
U.S.A.

Luis Suarez-Villa
School of Social Ecology
University of California
Irvine, California 92727-5150
U.S.A.

Daoshan Sun
Deptartment of City and Regional
    Planning
University of North Carolina
CP # 3140, New East Building
Chapel Hill, NC 27599-3140
U.S.A.

Rune Wigren
Institute for Housing Research
University of Uppsala
P.O. Box 785
801 29 Uppsala
SWEDEN

Springer-Verlag, P. O. Box 31 13 40, D-10643 Berlin, Germany.   IMCA.3501/MNT/SF

Advances in
Spatial and Network Economics

B. Johansson, C. Karlsson, L. Westin (Eds.)

Patterns of a Network Economy

1994. VIII, 314 pp. 33 figs., 44 tabs. Hardcover DM 148,-
ISBN 3-540-57824-2

A.E. Andersson, D.F. Batten, K. Kobayashi, K. Yoshikawa (Eds.)

The Cosmo-Creative Society

Logistical Networks in a Dynamic Economy

1993. VIII, 296 pp. 67 figs., 31 tabs. Hardcover DM 148,-
ISBN 3-540-57158-2

A. J. Reynolds-Feighan

The Effects of Deregulation on U.S. Air Neworks

1992. XIV, 131 pp. 15 figs., 30 tabs. Hardcover DM 88,-
ISBN 3-540-54758-4

M. J. Beckmann, T. Puu

Spatial Structures

1990. IX, 139 pp. 40 figs.
Hardcover DM 68,-
ISBN 3-540-51957-2

B.M. Roehner

Theory of Markets

Trade and Space-time Patterns of Price Fluctuations. A Study in Analytical Economics

1995. XVIII, 405 pp. 149 figs.
Hardcover DM 175,- ISBN 3-540-58815-9

The purpose of the book is to investigate the foundations of international and interregional trade at the microeconomic level of spatially separated commodity markets. At this level, price arbitrage and local disparities in production and demand functions are the main determinants. The model, referred to as the Enke-Samuelson model, is developed step by step.

A. Sen, T.E. Smith

Gravity Models of Spatial Interaction Behavior

1995. XVI, 572 pp. 13 figs., 28 tabs.
Hardcover DM 178,- ISBN 3-540-60026-4

This book presents an up-to-date, consistent and unified approach to the theory, methods and applications of the gravity model – which spans from the axiomatic foundations of such models all the way to practical hints for their use. "I have found no better general method for use in applied research dealing with spatial interaction... It is against this background that the present book by Sen and Smith is most welcomed."

Walter Isard

Springer

Tm.BA95.03.23